Teachers' Professional Development in Global Contexts

Teachers' Professional Development in Global Contexts

Insights from Teacher Education

Edited by

Juanjo Mena, Ana García-Valcárel
and Francisco García Peñalvo

BRILL
SENSE

LEIDEN | BOSTON

Cover illustration: Worldmap poster set at the ISATT Biennial Conference, 2017, held in Salamanca, Spain. Attendees pinned their names on it. Photograph by Rubén Ramos Fernández.

All chapters in this book have undergone peer review.

The Library of Congress Cataloging-in-Publication Data is available online at http://catalog.loc.gov

Typeface for the Latin, Greek, and Cyrillic scripts: "Brill". See and download: brill.com/brill-typeface.

ISBN 978-90-04-40535-6 (paperback)
ISBN 978-90-04-40534-9 (hardback)
ISBN 978-90-04-40536-3 (e-book)

Copyright 2019 by Koninklijke Brill NV, Leiden, The Netherlands.
Koninklijke Brill NV incorporates the imprints Brill, Brill Hes & De Graaf, Brill Nijhoff, Brill Rodopi, Brill Sense, Hotei Publishing, mentis Verlag, Verlag Ferdinand Schöningh and Wilhelm Fink Verlag.
All rights reserved. No part of this publication may be reproduced, translated, stored in a retrieval system, or transmitted in any form or by any means, electronic, mechanical, photocopying, recording or otherwise, without prior written permission from the publisher.
Authorization to photocopy items for internal or personal use is granted by Koninklijke Brill NV provided that the appropriate fees are paid directly to The Copyright Clearance Center, 222 Rosewood Drive, Suite 910, Danvers, MA 01923, USA. Fees are subject to change.

This book is printed on acid-free paper and produced in a sustainable manner.

Contents

List of Figures and Tables IX
Notes on Contributors XII
Introduction XXI
    Juanjo Mena, Ana García-Valcárel and Francisco García Peñalvo

PART 1
Teacher Professional Learning and Knowledge

1. Opening Possibilities for Research in Teacher Educators' Learning 3
    Jukka Husu and D. Jean Clandinin

2. Investigating EFL Elementary Student Teachers' Development in a Professional Learning Practicum 23
    Chiou-hui Chou

3. Becoming and Being a Teacher in Adverse Times: Iberian Perspectives 42
    Maria Assunção Flores

4. The Mediate(zati)on of Philosophy Subject Matter: A Comparative Case Study 63
    Laura Sara Agrati

5. Preservice Teachers' Reflection for the Acquisition of Practical Knowledge During the Practicum 84
    Raquel Gómez, Juanjo Mena, María-Luisa García-Rodríguez and Franciso García Peñalvo

PART 2
Teacher Beliefs and Reflective Thinking

6. The Struggle Is Real: Metacognitive Conceptualizations, Actions, and Beliefs of Pre-Service and In-Service Teachers 105
    Heather Braund and Eleftherios Soleas

7 Uncovering Preservice Teachers' Positioning of Themselves and English Learners (ELs) during Field Experiences   125
    Stefinee Pinnegar, Celina Lay, Linda Turner, Jenna Granados and Sarah Witt

8 Influence of Learning Attitudes and Task-Based Interactive Approach on Student Satisfaction and Perceived Learning Outcomes in a Content and Language Integrated Learning (CLIL) University Course in China   140
    Leah Li Echiverri and Keith Lane

9 Helping the Learning of Science in Whichever Language: The Attention to Proficiency in the LOLT, Polysemy and Context That Counts Best during Science Teaching   160
    Samuel Ouma Oyoo and Nkopodi Nkopodi

10 Emancipatory Teaching Practices in the Understandings of Social Sciences Teachers on a Diploma of Education Programme   179
    Stephen Geofroy, Benignus Bitu, Dyann Barras, Samuel Lochan, Lennox McLeod, Lystra Stephens-James and Antoinette Valentine-Lewis

11 Pedagogical Confrontations as a Lens for Reflective Practice in Teacher Education   199
    Wendy Moran, Robyn Brandenburg and Sharon M. McDonough

12 Beyond the Observed in Cross-Cultural Mentoring Conversations   219
    Lily Orland-Barak and Ella Mazor

PART 3
Innovative Teaching Procedures

13 Responsive Teachers in Inclusive Practices   243
    Hafdís Guðjónsdóttir, Edda Óskarsdóttir and Jóhanna Karlsdóttir

14 The Use of Video during Professional Experience for Initial Teacher Education   263
    Michael Cavanagh

15 Storytelling and Living Praxis in the Pre-Service Teacher Classroom   282
    Brian Mundy

16 Pedagogy Students' Attitudes towards Collaborative Learning with Video Games: Considering Demographic Information and the Variety of Digital Resources 304
Marta Martín-del-Pozo, Verónica Basilotta Gómez-Pablos and Ana García-Valcárcel

Index 325

Figures and Tables

Figures

2.1	The design of this study.	31
3.1	My journey at ISATT – ISATT conferences 1997–2017.	43
3.2	Issues wanting attention in the future (adapted from Kompft & Rust, 2013).	44
4.1	School mediation process (adapted from Damiano, 2013, p. 76).	65
4.2	The exploratory case-study design (from Stake, 1995).	70
4.3	Explanatory maps in the school textbook.	75
4.4	Visual representations used by teacher A during the lesson.	76
5.1	The mentor (teacher) roles in dialogues model (Hennissen et al., 2008).	87
5.2	The amount of positive and negative critical incidents in the lessons.	91
5.3	The relationships of the critical incidents in the reflection sessions. CR = content relationship; DR = didactic relationship; LR = learning relationship; PR = pedagogical relationship.	91
5.4	The most frequently used words in the sessions of the practicum. The more frequently used words are represented in a bigger size than the less frequently used words.	92
5.5	The types of practical knowledge that were extracted from the three types of reflections (individual, with a peer, and with a mentor).	94
5.6	The types of practical knowledge that were extracted in interactions with each mentoring role.	96
8.1	Learning attitudes description.	147
9.1	Distribution of score on 'Sensitive'.	171
9.2	Distribution of score on 'Retard'.	172
9.3	Distribution of score on 'Contract'.	174
11.1	The role of PCs in teacher educators' work.	202
14.1	Screenshot showing an annotated video.	270
15.1	What makes a good lecturer (from Mundy, 2014)?	283
15.2	A praxis model of education at Victoria University.	285
15.3	The value of learning circles.	288
15.4	Living praxis and the learning circle process (from Mundy, 2015).	289
15.5	The process of living theory development during a class.	291
15.6	Living praxis in a narrated complex classroom.	296
15.7	Visualising living praxis and the narrative.	298

Tables

4.1 Five kinds of knowledge structures (adapted from Mayer, 2005, p. 69).   68
4.2 Basic criteria of visual representations' classification (adapted from Mayer, 2005).   72
4.3 Principles for multimedia presentations (adapted from Mayer, 2005).   73
4.4 Synthetic analysis for the triangulation of data (Silverman, 2009).   74
4.5 Occurrences of Mayer's criteria for document analysis (Mayer, 2005).   77
5.1 The most frequent themes that emerged in the three reflections.   93
5.2 Roles of mentors and peers.   95
6.1 Demographic breakdown of pre-service participants for Phase 2.   110
6.2 Demographic breakdown of in-service participants for Phase 2.   110
6.3 Thematic coding breakdown of the interviews.   112
6.4 Integration of metacognition.   114
6.5 Teacher strategies for integrating metacognition.   114
6.6 Pre-service and in-service teachers report struggling.   115
6.7 What resources would be helpful?   116
6.8 Importance of building executive function.   118
8.1 Descriptive statistics of students' perceptions on task-based approach on the reinforcement of English learning in CLIL.   149
8.2 Descriptive statistics of students' satisfaction on their learning experiences.   150
8.3 Descriptive statistics of students' perceived accomplishments in their learning experiences.   151
8.4 Bivariate correlation of all variables.   152
8.5 Coefficient of determination (R^2) model results.   153
9.1 Non-technical words presented in science context in the questionnaire.   168
9.2 Respective response selections and percentage scores on the very difficult words test items.   170
11.1 Brief descriptions of the pedagogical confrontations.   206
14.1 Four levels of reflection and examples.   268
14.2 Participants' annotations coded according to the four levels of reflection   271
15.1 Student evaluation results.   294
15.2 The Praxis Inquiry Protocol and questions for its use as a teaching instrument (adapted from Mundy, 2018, p. 46).   301
16.1 Descriptive statistics for 'Attitude towards collaborative learning with video games'.   313
16.2 Analysis of statistical differences in attitude towards collaborative learning with video games according to gender.   314
16.3 Analysis of statistical differences in attitude towards collaborative learning with video games according to students' age.   314

16.4　Analysis of statistical differences in attitude towards collaborative learning with video games according to the variety of digital resources students have at home.　315
16.5　Attitudes towards collaborative learning through videogames according to the availability (yes/no) and use of digital resources at home.　316
16.6　Analysis of statistical differences in attitudes towards collaborative learning with video games according to the variety of digital resources used to play video games at home.　317
16.7　Attitudes towards collaborative learning through videogames according to the availability (yes/no) of digital resources at home.　317
16.8　Attitude towards collaborative learning with video games according to the frequency of playing video games as entertainment.　318
16.9　Post-hoc comparisons among groups generated by the frequency of play.　318

Notes on Contributors

Laura Sara Agrati
is a PhD, Associate Professor in 'Didactics and Educational Technologies', 'Special Education' and President of the degree course in 'Sciences of Education', at the 'Giustino Fortunato' University of Benevento, Italy. Her main research interests are didactic mediation and mediatization of learning content and professional development of teachers. She published monographs on teacher training and didactic mediation and scientific articles in national and international journals.

Dyann Barras
is employed at the School of Education, The University of West Indies, St Augustine, Trinidad and Tobago and is assistant lecturer in the Teaching of Social Sciences with emphasis in the teaching of Business studies.

Verónica Basilotta Gómez-Pablos
is a Professor of Madrid Open University, in Spain. She has a PhD in Education by the University of Salamanca, Spain. She holds a Degree in Psychopedagogy and a Master's Degree in ICT in Education. She is a member of the GITE-USAL research group. Her work focuses on ICT integration, the use of active methodologies in education, digital competences assessment and educational innovation.

Benignus Bitu
is employed at the School of Education, The University of West Indies, St Augustine, Trinidad and Tobago and is assistant lecturer in the Teaching of Social Sciences with emphasis in the teaching of History and Social Studies.

Robyn Brandenburg
is an associate professor and teacher educator-researcher at Federation University, Australia. Her research focuses on teacher education, mathematics education and the impact of reflection and feedback on learning and teaching. She has published widely and presented at national and international conferences. Robyn is the President of the Australian Teacher Education Association.

Heather Braund
is a PhD candidate at Queen's University Faculty of Education, specializing in cognition and assessment. She holds her Bachelor of Education from

Queen's and is OCT certified to teach Primary and Junior students. She holds an Honours Bachelor of Science Degree from Trent University with joint majors in Psychology and Biology. She has published in education journals (e.g. *Australian Educational Researcher* and *Comparative and International Education*) and medical journals (e.g. *Annals of Emergency Medicine* and *Journal of Cancer Education*). Her doctoral research is focused on bridging Kindergarten teachers' classroom assessment practices with students' self-regulation and metacognitive behaviours.

Michael Cavanagh

is Associate Professor and the Program Director for Secondary Initial Teacher Education in the Department of Educational Studies at Macquarie University in Sydney, Australia. He also lectures in mathematics education. His research interests focus on learning community models for professional experience and the development of pre-service teachers' reflective practice.

Chiou-hui Chou

is an associate professor at the department of English Instruction, College of Education, National Tsing Hua University, Taiwan. Her research areas are in teacher professional development, lesson study, English reading instruction, TEYL (Teaching English to Young Learners) and CLIL (Content and Language Integrated Learning).

D. Jean Clandinin

is Professor Emerita and Founding Director of Centre for Research for Teacher Education and Development at the University of Alberta. A former teacher, counsellor, and psychologist, she is author/co-author of 17 books and many articles and book chapters. Her last book with Michael Connelly, *Narrative Inquiry*, was published in 2000. She edited the *Handbook of Narrative Inquiry: Mapping a methodology* (Sage, 2007) and co-edited with Jukka Husu the *Handbook of Research on Teacher Education* (Sage, 2017). She published three books with Routledge: *Engaging in Narrative Inquiry* (2013), *Engaging in Narrative Inquiry with Children and Youth* (2016) and *Relational Ethics in Narrative Inquiry* (2018).

Leah Li Echiverri

is a holder of a Doctorate Degree in Curriculum and Instruction and a Master's Degree in Educational Administration and Supervision. Her research interest leans toward enhancing lifelong learning skills in teaching and learning taking into consideration the dynamics of evolving environments in the 21st century and learners' diversity. Her research studies have been presented in international conferences and internationally published in books.

She is a research professor at Wenzhou-Kean University teaching the course Research Methodology and Technology besides, Transition to Kean University. Her mission in life is making a difference in the lives of people!

Maria Assunção Flores
is an associate professor with qualification at the University of Minho, Portugal. She received her PhD at the University of Nottingham, UK. She was a visiting scholar at the University of Cambridge and at the University of Glasgow. Her research interests include teacher professionalism and identity, teacher education and professional development, teacher appraisal, leadership, and higher education. She has published extensively both nationally and internationally. She is currently the Chair of the International Study Association on Teachers and Teaching (ISATT). She is executive editor of the journal *Teachers and Teaching Theory and Practice* and co-editor of the *European Journal of Teacher Education*.

Francisco García Peñalvo
is Full Professor in the department of Computer Engineering at the University of Salamanca. He received his bachelor's degree in computing from the University of Valladolid (Spain), and his PhD degree from the University of Salamanca, where he is currently the Head of the Research Group in Interaction and e-Learning (GRIAL). His main research interests focus on eLearning, computers and education and digital ecosystems. He is the Editor in Chief of the *journal Education in the Knowledge Society* and the *Journal of Information Technology Research*. He coordinates the Doctoral Program in Education in the Knowledge Society.

María-Luisa García-Rodríguez
is tenured professor in the Department of Education at the University of Salamanca (USAL, Spain). She obtained her PhD in Education. Her specialty is early childhood education and her research interest include teacher development, mentoring and written language. She is an active member of the editorial board of a number of journals. She was a school teacher in Madrid and Salamanca.

Ana García-Valcárcel
is Professor of Educational Technology at the University of Salamanca and Director of the Master in ICT in Education. Director of the GITE-USAL Research Group. Coordinator of REUNI + D (University Network for Educational Research and Innovation), Member of RUTE (University Network of Educational Technology) and EDUTEC (Association of Educational Technology). Director

of different projects of innovation and research on the processes of digital technologies integration, teacher training in digital skills, evaluation of digital skills of teachers and students and the use of video games for educational purposes.

Stephen Geofroy
is employed at the School of Education, The University of West Indies, St Augustine, Trinidad and Tobago and is lecturer in Educational Foundations and in the Teaching of Social Sciences with emphasis in the teaching of Social Studies.

Raquel Gómez
is a school teacher for the Government of Castilla y León, Spain. She is doing a PhD at the University of Salamanca on preservice teachers' practical knowledge acquisition during the practicum.

Jenna Granados
is a recent graduate from Brigham Young University. She studied Elementary Education, and nurtured a passion for equitable education, especially among language learners. She has studied the Spanish language since 2007, and enjoys learning other world languages. Jenna is currently teaching preschool in Beaverton, Oregon, where she resides with her husband and daughter.

Hafdís Guðjónsdóttir
is a professor at University of Iceland, School of Education. Her interests are in the area of inclusive education, pedagogy and educational practices, teacher professionalism and teacher education. Hafdís has collaborated with colleagues from Europe, Australia and Northern America on research and professional projects focusing on topics considering her interest area. Her research methodology is mainly qualitative, practitioner research, and self-study of teacher education practices. She was one of three editors of the book *Taking a Fresh Look at Education: Framing Professional Learning in Education through Self-Study* (Sense Publishers, 2017). Since 2010 she has published 25 articles and 20 book chapters.

Jukka Husu
(PhD) is Professor of Education and the Dean of the Faculty of Educational Sciences, University of Turku, Finland. His research focuses on teachers' pedagogical knowledge, reflection, and ethical judgment in teaching. He has published extensively in internationally refereed journals and edited books. Professor Husu is a member of the Editorial Board of *Teaching and Teacher*

Education, and an Associate Editor in *Teachers and Teaching: Theory and Practice*. He co-edited with D. Jean Clandinin *The Sage Handbook of Research on Teacher Education* (Sage, 2017).

Jóhanna Karlsdóttir

is an assistant professor at the University of Iceland, School of Education. She completed her MEd at the University of Iceland 2001. Her research focuses on inclusive pedagogy and education, diverse learners, and teacher stories about innovative inclusive practices. Jóhanna has participated in many national and international projects focussing on these issues, such as TE4I with the European Agency for Special Needs and Inclusive Education. Her teaching focuses on inclusive pedagogy where she builds on her extensive experience working for many years as a teacher in compulsory school and a district based teaching consultant.

Keith Lane

(MEd) is a career tertiary TESL professor who specializes in classroom methodology in English as Medium of Instruction (EMI) and Content and Language Integrated Learning (CLIL) contexts. His research is especially interested in the role of motivation, and curricular and instructional approaches to facilitate it and exploit it positively. Academic integrity and instructional efficacy are important to him, as it student welfare and progress.

Celina Lay

is a PhD student at Brigham Young University. She has a Master's degree of Education with an emphasis in literacy from the University of Utah. From the time she was an undergraduate she has been involved in teacher education research and interested in the preparation and development of educators. Her first research experience was a narrative self-study, exploring the experiences of student teachers of English moving into their roles as teachers (Undergraduate Honors Thesis at BYU). Currently she is engaged in a self-study project of the teacher identity of teachers who prepared, taught, and left teaching.

Samuel Lochan

is a retired lecturer from the School of Education, UWI, St Augustine who has continued to work on a part time basis. He was formerly a teacher educator specializing in the teaching of Business and Social Studies.

Marta Martín-del-Pozo

is an Adjunct Professor in the Department of Education at the University of Salamanca (USAL, Spain). She holds a PhD in videogames and education from the University of Salamanca (Doctoral Dissertation: 'Videogames in teacher training: design, implementation and assessment of an educational proposal'). Furthermore, she holds a Degree in Pedagogy and a Master's Degree in ICT in Education. She is an active member of the GITE-USAL Research Group. Her research lines cover ICT in education, teacher education, videogames as learning resources, serious games, and game-based learning.

Ella Mazor
is senior lecturer at Gordon Academic College of Education. Her academic and professional interests lie in the areas of mentoring and mentored learning, with a focus on cross-cultural teacher education. Her research adopts socio-cultural perspectives to the study of professional teacher learning.

Sharon M. McDonough
is a researcher in initial teacher education and teacher development in the School of Education at Federation University, Australia. Sharon draws on socio-cultural theories of teacher emotion and resilience that she brings to aims of (i) how to best prepare and support teachers for entry into the profession; and (ii) how to support teacher, and teacher educator, professional learning across the lifespan of their careers. She has published in journals and edited books and she holds a role on the executive of the Australian Teacher Education Association.

Lennox McLeod
is employed part-time at the School of Education, The University of West Indies, St Augustine, Trinidad and Tobago and is lecturer in the Teaching of Social Sciences with emphasis in the teaching of History and Social Studies.

Juanjo Mena
(PhD) is Associate Professor at the department of Education in the University of Salamanca (Spain). He is a member of the GRIAL research group. He is currently an affiliate professor at the Center for the Study of Teacher Education at the University of British Columbia (Canada) and research collaborator at Kazan Federal University (Russia). He is the Treasurer of the International Study Association on Teachers and Teaching (ISATT). His research interests are focused on the analysis of the teaching practice, mentoring and the practicum, Teacher Education and ICT.

Wendy Moran
has been a researcher for more than 20 years in teacher education. She has published research concerning professional experience models in initial teacher preparation, the role of reflective practice in teachers' work, and

the nature of caring teachers. Dr. Moran recently began working at Excelsia College, a Christian higher education college in Sydney, teaching post-graduate studies in education. Currently, she is undertaking research that explores the impact of global changes in education on the moral motivations of teachers and school leaders.

Brian Mundy

is an academic working at Victoria University in Melbourne. He completed his PhD 'The Millennial School: A Theoretical Basis for Curriculum Design in a Time of Educational Transgression' at Melbourne University in 2013. This was a school based narrative study of curriculum and pedagogy change. After 31 years working as a secondary teacher he has worked for the last 9 years teaching and supporting pre-service teachers. In 2014 he was awarded an Australian Office of Learning and Teaching citation "For the development of integrated and engaging curriculum and teaching practices by an early career teacher in support of student learning in teacher education placements".

Nkopodi Nkopodi

is an associate professor of science education and Chair of the Department of Science and Technology Education, School of Teacher Education at the College of Education, University of South Africa (UNISA). He has extensive experience in teaching science in second language settings at tertiary level and has conducted numerous workshops for science and mathematics teachers in South Africa. His research interests are in Language in Science as well as Indigenous Knowledge Systems.

Lily Orland-Barak

is Professor of Education and present Dean of Graduate Studies and at the University of Haifa. Her research focuses on professional learning, mentoring and curriculum development in teacher education. She has published extensively in these areas and serves on national and international academic committees and editorial boards of leading journals in her field. Her book *Learning to Mentor-as-Praxis: Foundations for a Curriculum in Teacher Education* (Springer, 2010) was awarded 'Exemplary Research in Teaching and Teacher Education Award' at the American Educational Research Association (AERA), Vancouver, 2012.

Edda Óskarsdóttir

(EdD) is a project officer at the European Agency for Special Needs and Inclusive Education. She also holds a part time position as an adjunct at University of Iceland, School of Education. She completed her EdD in 2017 and the research was a self-study action research on constructing support as inclusive practice.

Edda has a background as a classroom teacher, special needs teacher and coordinator for support services at the compulsory school level in Iceland. She has been involved in a number of international and national projects on subjects connected to creating an inclusive education system.

Samuel Ouma Oyoo

is an associate professor of science education at the University of the Witwatersrand, Johannesburg, South Africa and a Visiting Professor of Science Education at Egerton University, Njoro, Kenya. He researches and publishes in science education and science teacher education, with a current focus on the impact of language as words and language as knowledge, on school physics and school chemistry teachers' effective classroom practice.

Stefinee Pinnegar

is a graduate of the Uof A, and associate professor of teacher education at BYU. Her research interests focus on teacher thinking, teacher development, and self-study. In examining the development of teacher thinking, she has particular interest in the development of practical memory for teaching particularly in regards to supporting English Learners (ELs). In terms of self-study, she is interested in the Methodology of self-study and in improvement of her practice as a teacher educator. She is editor of the *Advances in Research on Teaching Series* (Emerald Publishing) and specialty editor of Frontiers teacher education strand.

Eleftherios Soleas

is a PhD Candidate and Educational Consultant at Queen's University where he researches motivational processes and evidence-based practices of aspiring innovators and professionals using mixed methods approaches. His past work has incorporated educational psychology, curriculum theory, and special education as a means of understanding the motivations of interdisciplinary samples of professionals including teachers across their learning lifespan.

Lystra Stephens-James

is employed at the School of Education, The University of West Indies, St Augustine, Trinidad and Tobago and is an instructor in the Teaching of Social Sciences with emphasis in the teaching of Business studies.

Linda T. Turner

worked with student teachers pursuing a TESOL K-12 at the McKay School of Education at Brigham Young University. She retired from Wasatch County School District in Heber City, Utah, after 32 years. Her positions there included district director of alternative language services, counselor and lead teacher at the district's alternative high school, and middle and high school English and Spanish teacher. She also provided professional development to teachers in literacy instruction, strategies for working with English learners, and dual language immersion. She is passionate about teachers meeting the needs of all learners.

Antoinette Valentine-Lewis
is employed at the School of Education, The University of West Indies, St Augustine, Trinidad and Tobago, and is a part-time lecturer in the Teaching of Social Sciences with emphasis in the teaching of Geography and Social Studies.

Sarah Witt
has a bachelor's degree in Elementary Education with a minor in TESOL K-12 from Brigham Young University in Provo, Utah. During her undergraduate time she worked closely with and assisted research of teachers and their work with English language learners in the school system. She presented work at local and international research conferences: NRMERA, UCUR, I-TESOL and ISATT. After teaching for a year, she moved to Ann Arbor, Michigan, and is raising her daughter while substitute teaching.

Introduction

Juanjo Mena, Ana García-Valcárel and Francisco García Peñalvo

The book you have in your hands is a compilation of international teacher education research studies aiming at describing current teaching practices with a lens on understanding teacher training and learning processes, the importance of critical reflection, and the use of new teaching procedures. A total of 13 countries are represented in this volume: Australia, Canada, China, Finland, Iceland, Israel, Italy, Portugal, Spain, South-Africa, Taiwan, Trinidad & Tobago, and the United States. From such diverse contexts of practice the text draws upon a variety of educational perspectives that can be of interest to graduate students, teachers, teacher educators and researchers.

The book comprises sixteen selected research papers that were originally presented at the 18th International Study Association on Teachers and Teaching (ISATT) Biennial Conference that took place in Salamanca, Spain, from July 3rd to July 7th, 2017. A double-blind review process and a scoring system indicated the editors the papers that were most eligible for a post-proceeding publication. Three of them are the extended version of the key-note speeches.

The works revolve around three major themes that shape the parts of the book: (1) Teachers' professional learning and knowledge (Chapters 1 to 5); (2) Teacher beliefs and reflective thinking (Chapters 6 to 12); and (3) Innovative teaching procedures – e.g., video-games (Chapters 13 to 16). Most of them were conducted by applying qualitative research methods, using case studies, narrative inquiry and exploratory research to get a closer picture of how preservice and in-service teachers learn from their contexts of practice.

Part 1: Teacher Professional Learning and Knowledge

Teacher learning is often understood as the process of gaining expertise in the profession (Evans, 2000). In Chapter 1, Jean Clandinin and Jukka Husu address the learning of teacher educators as well as the ways teachers learn from diverse teacher educators. Up to date, they state that there is no clear knowledge base for accomplish professional learning and, thus, the scholarship of disruption could be a solution. Most of the professional learning that is referred to in their contribution comes during the practicum experience, and as such, it is considered essential requirement for preservice teacher training. In Chapter 2, Chiou-hui Chou offers an alternative view of the connections between university courses and field experiences in an attempt to bridge different learning sites and connect social spaces for EFL elementary student teachers. Chapter 3 takes a close look at teaching and teacher education conditions for learning and development in adverse times (e.g., economic crisis). Maria Flores reflects upon the concerns, specificities and challenges for teachers in the Iberian context (Portugal and Spain) knowing that these issues may apply to other contexts and regions.

In Chapter 4, Laura Sara Agrati addresses the integration of school subject matter knowledge, with the use of mediation devices. The 'collaborative' approach using multiple-case study design of two philosophy teachers give us a glance of visual representations and teacher's competence. Similarly, Raquel Gómez et al. (Chapter 5) analyze the types of practical pedagogical knowledge that preservice teachers acquire during the practicum. The teaching support they get from student teacher peers and school mentors is considered crucial in the process of learning to teach.

Part 2: Teacher Beliefs and Reflective Thinking

Teachers beliefs and conceptions play a crucial role in understanding teacher's work. Heather Braund and Eleftherios Soleas (Chapter 6) point out to the struggle between actions and beliefs, both in Preservice Teachers and in-service teachers, and highlight how the use of cognitive and metacognitive skills (e.g., self-regulation) facilitates teachers' decision making processes to make sense of their practice.

In a similar vein, Chapter 7 describes case studies from 60 preservice teachers whose beliefs let position themselves – position theory – in relationship to English learners (ELs) from 3rd to 5th elementary school grades. Stefinee Pinnegar et al. determined three clear plotlines from the teachers' positioning: Positive, pleasant and progressive that had implications to the students' social and cultural conditions.

Leah Li Echiverri and Keith Lane in Chapter 8 conducted a survey to non-native English speaking graduate students regarding their attitudes to learning both English and content in a research methodology course. Findings revealed that attitudes had a strong and positive effect to ESL student satisfaction and perceived learning.

In Chapter 9, Samuel Ouma Oyoo and Nkopodi Nkopodi present an exploratory study about linguistic understanding of scientific terms for South African High School learners. Main results show that they experienced difficulties with meaning of everyday words presented in science context.

In a more integrated vision, teacher beliefs – along with thoughts, procedures and actions – are considered as part of reflective thinking, a substantial metacognitive skill that leads to understand and change practices. The concept of emancipatory teaching practices comes to the front in postcolonial contexts of teacher development in Chapter 10. Stephen Geofroy et al. delve into the idea that critical reflection encourages teachers' thinking about their practice and about understanding their profession. Teachers must take an active role in their own professional growth, both in expanding their knowledge, interrogating theory and practice, and in the ability to feel part of a demanding community of educators to enhance their practice.

Chapter 11 further describes the complexity of teachers' reflections by analyzing pedagogical confrontations (PC): events or interactions of teaching which invite to critically examine practice. Based on participants' descriptions and responses Wendy Moran, Robyn Brandenburg and Sharon M. McDonough highlight the importance of professional roles, relationships and the changing nature of universities and teacher education. PC might be considered as a lens to new understanding of teacher educators' work.

Finally, reflection may be guided by the supervising role of mentor teachers. Lily Orland-Barak and Ella Mazor portray in Chapter 12 the encounter between two cultures (Arab and Jewish) through mentoring conversations and interviews. Combining divergent social values in teacher training strategies allow to glimpse latent and unknown conceptions both for preservice teachers and educational researchers.

Part 3: Innovative Teaching Procedures

The third theme brings together a series of works that promote the use of innovative teaching procedures and active methodologies in classroom. It is relevant in nowadays Teacher Education to count on examples of good innovative practices capable of promoting inclusive pedagogies. Through data collection techniques such as note taking, photography, videos, reflective discussion and focus group, Hafdís Guðjónsdóttir, Edda Óskarsdóttir and Jóhanna Karlsdóttir present a research study in Chapter 13 that illustrates how teachers might organize their subjects to address diversity in classroom. On the other hand, Michael Cavanagh in Chapter 14 used smartphones technology to video-record five-minute excerpts of preservice teachers' lessons and gave the opportunity to comment them and upload to a website. From the site, supervising teachers and university advisors could engage in meaningful interactions by reading, adding and reacting to comments. The research assumes a collaborative perspective involving Preservice Teachers, supervising teachers of schools and university tutors. incorporating annotations from different perspectives to stimulate reflection, provides good results.

In Brian Mundy's work (Chapter 15) a praxis innovative model of education is developed. The educators and the preservice teachers build upon initial conceptions, evaluate their progress, and immerse in an ongoing process of reflection through storytelling. The relationship between stories and living praxis are explored and suggest a process of narrative inquiry that can be used in tertiary education.

Chapter 16 explores pedagogy undergraduate students' attitudes towards collaborative learning by using videogames. Martín-del-Pozo Verónica Basilotta Gómez-Pablos and Ana García-Valcárcel argue that the use of video games in educational settings nowadays is heavily dependent on teachers' attitudes towards them. Major findings from this study indicate that they are likely to implement innovative practices using video games in the future.

Overall, the research results and conclusions contained in this book shed light on alternative ways to (re)think Teacher Education. The collaborative networks between universities and schools, the training programs in the practicum, the multiple teachers' identities, and the reflective and supervisory processes involved, let us to devise – and better comprehend – the complexities of educational situations in nowadays teaching.

Acknowledgements

The editors would like to thank the anonymous reviewers for their valuable comments and suggestions to improve the quality of the book.

PART 1
Teacher Professional Learning and Knowledge

CHAPTER 1

Opening Possibilities for Research in Teacher Educators' Learning

Jukka Husu and D. Jean Clandinin

Abstract

Based on our editorial work on the *Sage Handbook of Research on Teacher Education* (2017), this chapter reviews current research that allows us to extend the scope of teacher educators and their learning. We developed a distinction between two kinds of scholarship, *integration* and *disruption*. A scholarship of integration allows us to bring ideas together while a scholarship of disruption allows us to both to contemplate Dewey's (1929) idea of uncertainty and to take an inquiry stance. We use these two kinds of scholarship to discern different interpretations that guide understandings of teacher educator learning. By stretching the boundaries of teacher education outside of schools of education and classrooms, we review relevant research literature to offer insights that can help develop new ways of engaging in teacher education. We conclude that research on teacher education is not about clear answers, solutions, or theories but about understanding the complexities of how we are thinking about, and engaging in, the practices and policies of teacher education.

Keywords

scholarship of disruption – scholarship of integration – teacher educator learning – places of learning

Introduction

This chapter emerges from our editorial work together on the 2017 *Sage Handbook of Research on Teacher Education* (Clandinin & Husu, 2017). In editing the Handbook we worked with other scholars to review the wide ranging research in, and on, teacher education. As we looked across the chapters that reviewed the research literature in teacher education, we particularly noted interwoven ideas around who teacher educators were, the places where they were situated, and their learning. In this chapter, we take up those interwoven questions and address the identities and places of teacher educators in order to explore teacher educator learning.

The idea of stretching boundaries around who should be named as teacher educators is evident in earlier literature, such as Goodlad, Soder, and Sirotnik's (1990) call to consider not only those who work in faculties and colleges of education as teacher educators but also those who work in faculties of arts and sciences. Questions around the places where teacher educators are situated are also not new; they endure and have been taken up in diverse ways in the research literature (e.g. Ben-Peretz, 2001; Ducharme, 1996; Goodwin et al., 2014; Hadar & Brody, 2017; Loughran, Korthagen, & Russell, 2008). Stretching the boundaries around places of teacher education was visible in Schön's (1987) work as he outlined the move of teacher education from apprenticeships in practice to the university with some opportunities to practice in schools and classrooms. However, the puzzles around place, and about who are teacher educators, have become more complex from those noted in the 1990s. Questions of who are the teacher educators are necessarily intertwined with questions of place and of temporality. We cannot separate the 'who' of teacher educators from the 'where' of teacher education (Clandinin & Husu, 2017).

We begin with a brief account of the learning of teacher educators as well as the ways teachers learn from diverse teacher educators. In so doing, we seek new understandings about how to educate teachers, and how research on teacher education can help us to see, and develop, new ways of engaging in teacher education. In their extensive review of teacher educators' professional learning, Ping, Schellings, and Beijaard (2018) show that research on teacher educators' professional learning is a growing field of interest but one fragmented in focus. Their review indicates there is no clear essential knowledge base for teacher educators' work. Teacher educators undertake different activities from which to learn and generally experience the need to learn to do their work better. Besides learning through academic engagement (conducting and reading academic research, or conducting practitioner research focusing on the improvement of their practices), teacher educators learn through their collaborative activities by discussing or exchanging ideas with colleagues, student teachers, mentors, and teachers at school. With this expansive view of the learning of teacher educators in mind, we turn first to our organizing structure for our review of the literature.

Reviewing the Research Literature: Scholarships of Integration and Disruption

As we reviewed research, some of which is included in the various chapters in the Handbook, we developed the possibility of seeing two kinds of scholarship at work in the field. One kind of scholarship was *integration* (Boyer, 1990), characterized as involving "doing research at the boundaries where fields converge ... [It] also means interpretation, fitting research into larger intellectual patterns" (p. 19). The scholarship of integration involves asking, "What do the findings mean?" (p. 19) in relation to other research as well as to fields of practice. Boyer's work drew our attention to the importance of attending, not only to lines or programs of research in teacher education, but also to the boundaries where the many fields that attend, even peripherally to teacher education, meet. Thinking with this kind of scholarship drew our attention to the importance of trying to create, or discern, larger intellectual patterns at work in research in teacher education. Scholarships of integration offer us a kind of dual focus on attending to boundaries as well as on creating larger intellectual patterns.

Not long into the process of studying the research reviewed in the Handbook chapters, we began to see a need to break away from those increasingly bigger and more inclusive pictures. We sensed the need to create a rupture (or a crack) in taken-for-granted ways of seeing teacher education and the research on it. We conceptualized a second kind of scholarship that we call a scholarship of *disruption*. Working with the idea of disruption, that is, of creating a rupture, crack or break, was inspired, in part, by Leonard Cohen's song Anthem and his words "There is a crack in everything. That's how the light gets in". We used the idea of a scholarship of disruption in the Handbook with the hope that we, and others, could discern, or possibly create, cracks in research patterns, traditions, and ways of seeing teacher education. We began to imagine disruption as a way to allow us to create a scholarship through which we undid previously unquestioned frames in order to attend to enduring puzzles in new ways, with previously unheard voices, and from contexts that could not be understood without new framings. We saw the importance of developing new concepts to disrupt those 'bigger pictures' dominating our thinking and ways of seeing and doing teacher education.

Following the *Oxford Dictionary* definition of disruption, we use the concept to 'interrupt' or 'break the flow or continuity' of doing research in, and on, teacher education. While a disruption can be thought of as a negative experience, an experience of not fitting into expectations, and of being disturbed (Gans, 2016), we see it as having unexpected consequences in that it creates a disjuncture that allows us to imagine what Maxine Greene (1995) called "otherwise", what is not yet known. Through deliberate reflection and inquiry within a scholarship of disruption, we may see possibilities for change and new understandings. Disruptions are, as we are using the concept, places of tensions, places that ask us to stop and inquire, to engage in wondering about what it means to engage in research on teacher education. As we attend to the boundaries where fields converge in scholarships of integration, tensions become inevitable. Rather than smooth them over, we see the importance of identifying tensions and using them as ways to disrupt the taken-for-granted, to see them as cracks or breaks that let us think and try anew.

We use these two kinds of scholarships, integration and disruption, developed for the Handbook, as the way to structure this chapter. While integration allows us to bring ideas together, an experience of disruption allows us to contemplate Dewey's idea of uncertainty (1929), and allows us to take an inquiry stance. What does it mean to be disrupted, recognizing that new things may be happening at research edges? What new understandings, decisions, and actions are made possible in the experienced and anticipated disruptions?

Sources Indicating a Need for Scholarships of Disruption

As we worked with what we might learn through both scholarships of disruption and integration for this chapter, we became attentive to the sources of disruption. Often, disruption becomes visible when choices that once were successful are no longer successful (Gans, 2016). Put simply, sometimes it is important to disrupt something when you are doing the same things, in your own box, for too long. As we reviewed the research literature in teacher education, we saw much had changed in understandings of learning, of organizations, of knowledge. We saw that a different knowledge landscape (Clandinin & Connelly, 1996) was evolving, a landscape shaped by social media, technology and an increasingly global world shaped by dominant narratives of capitalism, development, and achievement. We saw the tensions created by these shifts and changes (Morris, 2016). We recognized that now may be a time for more attention to scholarships of disruption. After many successful years, research in teacher education may not meet current or future demands. Particularly we noted that research in teacher education needed to be more inclusive of other voices, ones outside our research and publishing boxes. We saw how crucial dialogue is.

The need for a scholarship of disruption does not mean that what we are now doing is a failure; rather it may signal that we have been satisfied with current research practices and inquiring into relatively stable research topics into what might have been effective in other times and places (Gant, 2016). For some time researchers in teacher education have continued a focus on using familiar methodologies, hearing familiar voices, framing research on familiar topics. A scholarship of disruption allows us to open new possibilities to better respond to changing circumstances and to changing research, policy, and practice communities as well as the changing knowledge landscapes in which children, families, teachers, and we all live.

The need for a scholarship of disruption also arises from inside sources in ways that we, together with our organizations, are not able to respond to situations and events that become visible. As children and families experience changing knowledge landscapes and, as technology and social media radically shift learning and living contexts, researchers can no longer proceed in what have been seen as normal or usual patterns. Small changes do not make the necessary change.

These sources for the importance of scholarships of disruption shape the need to attend to different people in different places as teacher educators and to see the interconnections among them. No one could build e.g. "constructivist-based teacher education", or "care-based teacher education" alone. Multiple people working together are necessary. To do so, every teacher educator, within and outside organizations, are required to learn new knowledge and skills. We can no longer assume that teacher educators are teachers and faculty members positioned in universities. In a scholarship of disruption we open questions around who the teacher educators are and where they work in order to disrupt the taken for granted.

When we open the questions of who are teacher educators and where do they work, we see a landscape that might be best thought of as a kind of interconnected web. Educators never operate independently. At some point, knowledge and skills must be generated in ways that establish how individual skills and competencies are linked and how they work together. Teacher education requires shared knowledge and skills (Melasalmi & Husu, 2016, 2018) that conveys how pieces in systems fit together. It may be that these connective tissues, these warps and wefts of complex weavings, are not visible and perhaps not developed in any way.

In summary then, in this chapter we take up a scholarship of integration as well as open up the possibilities for scholarships of disruption, scholarship that allows us to think about intellectual patterns that cut across a range of research as well as opening questions around which fields edge the field of research on, and for, teacher education. Working with two kinds of scholarship, integration and disruption, allows the possibility for making visible gaps, silences, omissions, and tensions. In this way perhaps we discern new ways forward for research in teacher education.

Scholarships of Integration and Disruption around Who Teacher Educators Are and Where They Work

Linor Hadar and David Broady (2017) highlight teacher educators' role in preparing the next generation of teachers as they "hold much responsibility for the success and quality of teacher education programs, and thus to the quality of teaching" (p. 1049). This has also increased research interest in teacher educators and on the processes of becoming a teacher educator, their role and educational practices, and their professional development.

While Hadar and Broady point out the importance of teacher educators, they mainly focus on teacher educators in teacher education institutions. However, as Murray (2017) noted, "teacher educators are not always a well defined or widely recognised group", something that is "particularly evident when working transnationally" (p. 1017). Murray pointed out that the lack of a definition of teacher educators as "a stable, homogeneous and clearly demarcated occupational group" has "persisted over time and national contexts" (ibid.). Ronnie Davey (2013) noted "the problems of identification and delimitation with respect to who is, and is not, a teacher educator have persisted to the present" (p. 21) with this 'vagueness' around definition increasing "in the last two decades because of moves to make in-school mentors more responsible for the preparation of future teachers in some jurisdictions, and an increasing reliance on casualised staff" (p. 20) to provide parts of teacher education programs.

Within a scholarship of integration teacher educators are most often seen as university teachers working in faculties of education and teachers and other people working in schools. In addition, and more recently, research has also focused on teacher educators as including communities of practice such as cooperating and mentor teachers, and school administrators. Some research also includes other student teachers as teacher educators (Korhonen, Heikkinen, Kiviniemi, & Tynjälä, 2017; Lamb, 2015). Considerations within a scholarship of disruption of who teacher educators are stretch far beyond those in faculties of education and faculties of arts and sciences as well as beyond those in schools and classrooms. We do not intend to say that anyone or everyone is a teacher educator. While we want to consider those who are teacher educators in universities (faculties of education as well as those in faculties of arts and sciences) and teachers and those who work in schools, including mentor teachers, other student teachers, and administrators, we also want to disrupt the boundaries around who are teacher educators.

While the boundaries around who are the teacher educators have begun to be more inclusive, questions of the learning of teacher educators are more often now being asked. Stefinee Pinnegar (2017) pointed out that "attention to the preparation and learning of teacher educators is a fairly recent topic" (p. 1011) in research in teacher education, noting that "just as teachers often assert they taught themselves to teach, most teacher educators would argue that they taught themselves to be teacher educators (see Arizona Group, 1995). While questions of preparation and learning of teacher educators are relatively new, scholarships of disruption are emerging with researchers opening up questions that disrupt these commonly accepted notions of who teacher educators are, and further complicate considerations of the preparation and learning of teacher educators.

Katharine Payne and Kevin Zeichner (2017) highlight the need for research in teacher education to be conducted with families and community members and in community places. For them, families, community members, and community places are also teacher educators. Zeichner, an advocate for a kind of third space in teacher education, noted that *Teacher Education 3.0* is teacher education where the relational voices of families and community members are included both in the practices and policy discussions of teacher education (Zeichner, Bowman, Guillen, & Napolitan, 2016). More than just naming families and community members as stakeholders in teacher education, Paine and Zeichner (2017) argue that

> teacher education needs to draw on the knowledge and assets of the communities and families that teacher education is preparing teachers to serve. Ignoring this knowledge denies access to beginning teachers of the contextual and cultural knowledge that is necessary for them to be successful in supporting student learning and development. (p. 1106)

Further they argue that *Teacher Education 3.0*

> necessitates the weaving together of knowledge from universities, schools, and communities. ... maintaining separate spheres of knowledge risks the continued dominance of university knowledge over school and community knowledge ... [and] ignores the need to come together around the common problem of educational equity and develop solutions that

are mutually beneficial to children, teacher candidates, and the multiple institutions involved in teacher education. (p. 1107)

In their view, there is an intense need to engage in research to come to know more about the kinds of knowledge that lives in communities, families, and places. It is clear that they see families, communities, and other places, and the knowledge that lives in those people and places, as teacher educators. Payne and Zeichner (2017) and others (e.g. Ellis & McNicholl, 2015; Zygmunt & Clark, 2016) draw attention to the knowledge that lives in communities, families and places that needs to be brought into the learning of teacher educators, those in the universities, schools, and communities.

Beatrice Avalos (2017) also draws attention "to the opening of the traditional teacher education space to communities and indigenous groups not as participants to be referred to, or described, but as co-constructors in the preparation of teachers, the teacher education processes and their enactment" (p. 1084). Cook-Sather and Baker-Doyle (2017) speak about "invitations to the co-construction of work" (p. 359). While their focus is on positioning students as teacher educators, along with Avalos, they are suggesting the need to disrupt the pervasive framings of who are teacher educators.

Madden and Glanfield (2017) suggest additional ways to disrupt the taken for granted framing of the places and people who are teacher educators. They open questions of indigenizing teacher education. In outlining a new pedagogical pathway, they draw on research

> situated within Indigenous communities and defined by the educative priorities of communities. Such a pathway could be named Indigenous community-driven (Eisinger & Senturia, 2001) teacher education ... We imagine that there could be many new possibilities for researchers working with Indigenous communities to position themselves and their collaborative research within the field of teacher education. (p. 1160)

The move to decolonize teacher education through shifting the people seen as teacher educators and places of teacher education is consistent with larger international moves to decolonize many institutional and social practices, including research practices. These moves are occurring around the world and with increasing forcefulness (e.g. Connell, 2013; Pillay, 2017; Smith, 2013).

Hoekstra, Brekelmans, Beijaard, Korthagen, and Imant (2009) and others (e.g. Jurasaite-Harbison & Rex, 2010; Kyndt, Gijbels, Grosemans, & Donche, 2016) also open possibilities of who teacher educators are and the places of teacher education in their research on informal learning over the span of a teacher's career. For many years they highlighted the importance of informal learning as learning that is not organized and does not have set objectives or formal intentions on the learner's part: learning occurs at home, at work, in the community, via social media and so on. A wide range of people, places, and things can be seen as teacher educators. As we widen our attention to take in what lives on the periphery of what we see as formal learning, we again see the disruption of smooth boundaries around questions of who are the teacher educators.

Michael Connelly and Jean Clandinin (Connelly & Clandinin, 1988), Freema Elbaz-Luwisch (2013), and Cheryl Craig (2009) also attended to ways teacher educators are educated by events and people in our lives over time, some of them in formal schooling situations but many of them in other educative but non-schooling or non-formal settings. As we broaden the boundaries around who teacher educators are, we also draw attention to the ways our autobiographical narratives of experience educate us as teacher educators (Lindsay et al., 2016) and shape our learning. By attending to prior and present professional and personal knowledge landscapes (Clandinin, Schaefer, & Downey, 2014) in which teachers, prospective teachers, and teacher educators live, the range of people, places, and things named as teacher educators is highlighted. Attending to familial and early learning also highlights the ways intergenerational social, institutional, and cultural narratives shape the learning of teacher educators.

While current research does not expressly note the importance of understanding students, children, and youth as teacher educators, we see that by stretching the boundaries around who counts as teacher educators, there is an important research gap around including people positioned as students, children, and youth who need to also be considered as teacher educators (see e. g. McDonald, Bowman, & Brayko, 2013; Rudduck & McIntyre, 2007; Thiessen & Cook-Sather, 2007).

In line with this, Kelchtermans and Vanassche (2017) emphasize constant negotiation between teacher educators, student teachers, and students with whom they work. They underscore that learning to teach

> requires value-laden choices, ethical judgement, personal commitment, and care from the part of the teachers or educators. It is about doing justice to the educational needs of the children and youth that have been confined to their care and for whom they feel responsible. (p. 441)

However, teachers differ in their views and commitments of the best interests of their students (Tirri & Husu, 2002), and thus educational practices involve issues of influence, power and negotiation.

Learning of Teacher Educators in Multiple Places

As we considered the possibilities for scholarships of disruption that were beginning to be visible in our review (Clandinin & Husu, 2017) of research in teacher education, we saw the importance of attending to the ways teacher educators learned wise practices, and learned to create spaces for those learning to be teacher educators to study research, to engage in autobiographical reflective and reflexive work, and to try out ideas of what might be possible. We saw the importance of more intentionally including the knowledge of communities, children, and youth in teacher education by inviting others to see themselves as teacher educators, not in order to assimilate other knowledge in a scholarship of integration but to start to change teacher education in significant ways.

By including others, and other communities, as teacher educators we begin to make the complexities of knowledge visible, to open it to inquiries that lead us to question what we know, how we know, and what kind of spaces are necessary in order to sustain ourselves in teacher education. However, this is not work that can be undertaken lightly, easily, or quickly. It is difficult work that asks each of us to attend carefully to questions of who are teacher educators, and how do they work with, and engage with, those learning to teach as well as to consider their own learning as teacher educators.

Place is inextricably intertwined with consideration of questions around those who teacher educators are. In our review of research in the Handbook, we most commonly saw the place of teacher education as in university classrooms, and schools and school classrooms. Research highlighted that teacher educators worked, sometimes collaboratively, sometimes less collaboratively, in the university and in the schools.

However, there is also an emerging scholarship of disruption around place. Sometimes what we see as a scholarship of disruption around place is connected to the calls made by Payne and Zeichner (2017) and others around who teacher educators are. Craig Deed (2017) draws on a metaphor of 'schoollessness' that "broadly references learning environments that are representative of the affordances of digital spaces, including openness and the individualization of learning" (p. 1087). Deed reviews research that shows the ways that "digital technology fragments and intensifies the contextual milieu of teacher preparation and expands the scope and reach of teacher educator work and identity into different learning environments beyond the formal structured campus experience" (pp. 1087–1088). By including virtual learning places, Deed opens up other questions around places in research in teacher education, ones that increasingly shape practices in teacher education.

In opening up questions around the places of teacher education, Sean Lessard (2014) engaged in research focussed on the lives of Indigenous youth. By attending to the youth and their families' lives, he showed that shifts in places of teaching, from urban centers to reservation places, and including families and communities and places as teacher educators, that more educative spaces for Indigenous youth are created. In doing so, teacher educators found ways to both acknowledge and honour the youths' experiences within their communities and to make visible the importance of place as an educative agent in teacher education.

Claire Desrochers (2017) also highlighted the importance of place in considerations of the learning of teacher educators. She worked with preservice teachers in afterschool places as preservice teachers took courses at university. Each different place (with the youth in after school programs and in university courses) "created a learning space that had contextual, relational, and temporal qualities that combined to create an educative experience" (p. 75). Desrochers described the pre-service teachers' experiences in the after school program as "dispositioning contexts", "qualitatively different from traditional field placements" (ibid.). She noted that the "youth club setting was also unique in that it provided an opportunity to engage with children in a context that was neither like home, nor like school … Situated somewhere in between what education students typically experience as theory-driven teacher education classrooms and practice-driven practicum settings, the youth club provided a learning space where [the student teachers] could engage with children from diverse backgrounds as children, and not as students" (p. 77).

What Lessard and Desrochers show fits with what Oyler, Morvay, and Sullivan (2017) report, that is

> how teacher educators move teacher education from inside the walls of universities and classrooms to teacher education that is in the world – and not just in the world, but designed to act upon the world and leave it changed by enacting pedagogies of teacher social actions. (p. 232)

These shifts in place also occur as teacher educators move outside school and university places in experiential learning sites and to work with pre-service and practicing teachers in art galleries, museums, community settings, and outdoor locations. What is remarkable is the ways that shifting the place of teacher education outside schools or university settings opens up other ways to compose relationships among people and to open new possible questions about social relations and the learning of teacher educators. Different places also work in agentic ways, that is, as active participants in teacher education. Anne Edwards (2017) argues that

> if agency is understood in terms of the part it plays in student teachers' learning, we might clear up some of the misconceptions that inhibit the development of the teacher education needed for the twenty-first century. The argument will centre on the learning dialectic between person and practice or culture, where individual and collective shape each other and where the professional knowledge and values embedded in practices are important. (p. 269)

While we still engage in teacher education in schools and in universities, the places where teacher education occurs are shifting if we are attentive to a scholarship of disruption. The importance of being able to imagine otherwise will, of necessity, ask us to be ready to find ways to engage spaces in the middle, spaces where light makes visible what was unseen or as yet unknown or unknowable.

Spaces of Learning in Teacher Education

In the Handbook, we wanted to keep our focus on teacher educator learning as well as on how they worked with teachers to create situations for them to learn professional knowledge and skills during the formal years of teacher education, and to develop their professional competencies during their careers. Using different theoretical frames as connective tissues we aimed to come to grips with how a particular theoretical frame drives research tasks, positions research in different contexts, and brings a different set of interpretations to understand and develop those areas of learning in teacher education. As we reviewed chapters, we were reminded that keeping our research focus only, and too closely, on the learning of children in classrooms keeps hidden the central importance concerning the learning of teachers and teacher educators. We saw that too close a focus on K-12 classrooms as the major sites of learning and students as the only learners was problematic.

Grossman and McDonald (2008) highlighted the importance of considerations of what counts as the field of research in teaching, and what counts as the field of research on teacher education, as well as how the two research fields are positioned in relation to each other. Often research (just) explores the factors (outside teacher education) and how those factors may influence teacher learning in teacher education rather than researching what constitutes teacher learning during teacher education. As Russ, Sherin, and Sherin (2016) argue, perhaps we should concentrate more on researching "entities that change with learning and the processes that result in those changes" (p. 392). Would that help us see how "different entities and processes [in teacher education] are involved in [teacher] learning and [how] those entities and processes interact with each other in complex ways [in teacher education]" (ibid.)? We became convinced of the need for clarity around what is research on teacher education.

While we intended to keep what counts as research on teaching and research on teacher education separate, we wondered if it is important to consider other fields of research, which also converge at the boundaries with research on teacher education. What becomes visible if we loosen the tight coupling between research on teaching and research on teacher education, and begin to consider other fields of importance in research on teacher education?

A scholarship of Disruption in Understanding Teacher Educators' Learning

As Auli Toom, a Handbook Section Editor noted, while it is now broadly accepted that teachers are the most important influence on students' learning (e.g., Hattie, 2012; Sanders & Horn, 1998), and that teacher quality is a key determinant to successful student learning, it is surprising that there does not exist more research focusing on the learning or the assessment of the learning of core competencies – in a wider sense – during teacher education (Struyven & De Meyst, 2010; Toom, 2017). Without close attention to teachers as learners across the continua of teacher education we may fail to recognize the importance of creating schools and classrooms as sites for teachers' continuous learning.

Student teachers, in part, learn in the context of the teacher education programmes in which they are involved. The ways in which teacher education is organized and the pedagogies and assessment practices (Shavelson, 2013) that are used in the programme influence the capabilities with which student teachers enter the teaching profession (Toom, 2017). This implies that we must pay close attention not only to teacher education curriculum but also to pedagogies of teacher education.

Juanjo Mena (2017) noted that how learning to teach and educate is best accomplished and supported, is, in part, a question of pedagogies used in pre- and in-service teacher education. He underlines the task of pedagogies of teacher education to "organize knowledge, skills and experiences in order to understand practice" (p. 509) and to take up challenges in learning teaching in teacher education.

We know many researchers are working to engage in a scholarship of disruption. However, as we completed the Handbook, we were somewhat surprised that, while many authors espouse a more critical edge, there appear to be few examples of living critical edges in teacher education practices. This can be described as 'talking the talk' (Cochran-Smith, 2004), that is, we more often 'talk' about conceptual ideas and beliefs being disseminated, rather than 'walk' with those ideas.

However, it is clear that there is a developing scholarship of disruption emerging in which teacher educators, in multiple places, work together with student teachers and students to make a difference in their learning (see e.g. Ishimaru & Takahashi, 2017; Ma, 2016; Morris, 2016). For example, Oyler, Morvay, and Sullivan (2017) draw attention to studies where teacher education is undertaken for social action. They explore how students, teachers, teacher educators, and nonprofit leaders – all moved by their own critical consciousness – forge unique relationships that exceed the typical school-university partnerships. It is teacher education that works toward building critical consciousness that enables teachers to integrate activism into their work and identities as teachers.

Payne and Zeichner (2017) show ways that communities can be part of teacher education by together seeking solutions to social justice problems affecting students, teacher candidates, schools and communities. They advocate 'third spaces' where unofficial spaces in interaction with official spaces and discourses are included and supported. They note barriers that make this move a difficult one, but also show ways in which co-working towards a more relevant teacher education can take place. Many researchers encourage us to move towards broader understandings of teacher learning over time, and in and out of formal learning places.

In this emerging scholarship of disruption, the fixed settings of 'Who are the key learners in teacher education' and 'Where and how are learners learning' are being recalibrated. Researchers are demonstrating the importance of studying teacher learning during teacher education and, in so doing, search for new pedagogical tools and methods to support this broader attentiveness to learning. There are searches for new directions that can help us attend in multi perspectival ways in which children, youth, teachers, and teacher educators are all understood as learning simultaneously, albeit with different contents, different learning goals, and different future-oriented trajectories. In this way, perhaps we can make connections between the multiple ways in which learning is occurring and the multiple people who are learning in teacher education research.

As we completed the Handbook we acknowledged that research in teacher education will not be able to offer explanatory and predictive theories. Teacher education is a web of highly complex social phenomena and it cannot be studied within a conventional meaning of the word 'science'. Research in teacher education is not done in order to build and develop theories, but to contribute shared understandings that will help "in clarifying where we are, where we want to go, and what is desirable according to diverse sets of values and interests" in our societies (Flyvbjerg, 2001, p. 167). This requires constant re-examination of our basic premises in, and for, teacher education.

We take up Flyvbjerg's point, as we understand that what we are trying to do in research on, and for, teacher education is not to arrive at clear answers, solutions, or theories but to understand the complexities of how we are thinking about, and engaging in, the practices and policies of teacher education. It is research, understood as searching again, through these complex phenomena that allow us to come to new insights and, perhaps, to wiser practices.

Gathering Thoughts

There is a rich field of research in teacher education that becomes visible when questions around who counts as teacher educators, and where are the places of teacher education, are opened. More inclusive boundaries disrupt how teacher education has been conceptualized. "There is a crack in everything. That's how the light gets in" wrote Leonard Cohen. As we thought about cracks that allow light in, we were drawn to the importance of questions such as "I wonder why", "I wonder how", and "I wonder what if". Wonders draw forward imagination and curiosity more than evidence and certainty. These wonders turn our minds to those inquiry edges, to what happens when "the light gets in" through an emerging scholarship of disruption.

When we discern larger patterns in what we know so far, we see the importance of a scholarship of integration. But perhaps wondering will turn us more to a scholarship of disruption, to the 'what ifs', the whys and the possibilities of imagining otherwise. Wonders that cause us to evoke our imaginations leave open the necessary troubling questions in teacher education that emerge in a scholarship of disruption. This is not an easy thing, this openness to otherwise. And yet it is this that will move us forward, will help us see what moves us to new possibilities, will help us learn more about what we do not yet know about research in teacher education.

References

Arizona Group. Guilfoyle, K., Hamilton, M. L., Pinnegaar, S., & Placier, M. (1995). Becoming teachers of teachers: The path of four beginners. In T. Russel & F. Korthagen (Eds.), *Teachers who teach teachers: Reflections on teacher education* (pp. 35–55). London: Falmer Press.

Avalos, B. (2017). Section introduction: The evolving social and political contexts of teacher education. In D. J. Clandinin & J. Husu (Eds.), *The Sage handbook of research in teacher education* (pp. 1081–1084). London: Sage Publications.

Ben-Peretz, M. (2001). The impossible role of teacher education in a changing world. *Journal of Teacher Education, 52*(1), 48–56.

Boyer, E. L. (1990). *Scholarship reconsidered: Priorities of the professoriate.* New York, NY: Carnegie Foundation for the Advancement of Teaching.

Clandinin, D. J., & Connelly, F. M. (1996). Teachers' professional knowledge landscapes: Teacher stories-stories of teachers-school stories-stories of school. *Educational Researcher, 25*(3), 24–30.

Clandinin, D. J., & Husu, J. (Eds.). (2017). *The Sage handbook of research on teacher education.* London: Sage Publications.

Cochran-Smith, M. (2004). The problem of teacher education. *Journal of Teacher Education, 55*(4), 295–299.

Connelly, F. M., & Clandinin, D. J. (1988). *Teachers as curriculum planners: Narratives of experience.* New York, NY: Teachers College Press.

Connell, R. (2014). Using southern theory: Decolonizing social thought in theory, research and application. *Planning Theory, 13*(2), 210–223.

Cook-Sather, A., & Baker-Doyle, K. (2017). Developing teachers' capacity for moral reasoning and imagination in teacher education. In D. J. Clandinin & J. Husu (Eds.), *The Sage handbook of research on teacher education* (pp. 354–368). London: Sage Publications.

Craig, C. (2009). Flights from the field and the plight of teacher education: A personal perspective. *Journal of Curriculum Studies, 41*(5), 605–624.

Davey, R. (2013). *The professional identity of teacher educators. Career on the cusp?* London: Routledge.

Deed, C. (2017). Adapting to the virtual campus and transitions in 'scholl-less' teacher education. In D. J. Clandinin & J. Husu (Eds.), *The Sage handbook of research on teacher education* (pp. 1085–1100). London: Sage Publications.

Desrochers, C. (2017). Shaping service-learning spaces for preservice teachers to experience and learn to teach for diversity. In K. L. Heider (Ed.), *Service learning as pedagogy in early childhood education: Theory, research, and practice* (pp. 59–80). New York, NY: Springer.

Dewey, J. (1929). *The quest for certainty: A study of the relation between knowledge and action.* New York, NY: Minton, Balch & Company.

Ducharme, M. (1996). A study of teacher educators: Research from the USA. *Journal of Education for Teaching: International Research and Pedagogy, 22*(1), 57–70.

Edwards, A. (2017). The dialectic of person and practice: How cultural-historical accounts of agency can inform teacher education. In D. J. Clandinin & J. Husu (Eds.), *The Sage handbook of research on teacher education* (pp. 269–285). London: Sage Publications.

Eisinger, A., & Senturia, K. (2001). Doing community driven research: A description of Seattle partners for healthy communities. *Journal of Urban Health: Bulletin of the New York Academy of Medicine, 78*(3), 519–534.

Elbaz-Luwisch, F. (2013). *Auto/biography & pedagogy: Memory & presence in teaching.* New York, NY: Peter Lang.

Ellis, V., & McNicoll, J. (2015). *Transforming teacher education: Reconfiguring the academic work.* London: Bloomsbury Publishing.

Flyvbjerg, B. (2001). *Making social science matter: Why social inquiry fails and how it can succeed again.* Cambridge: Cambridge University Press.

Gans, J. (2016). *The disruption dilemma.* Cambridge, MA: MIT Press.

Goodwin, A. L., Smith, L., Souto-Manning, M., Cheruvu, R., Tan, M. Y., Reed, R., & Taveras, L. (2014). What should teacher educators know and be able to do? Perspectives from practicing teacher educators. *Journal of Teacher Education, 65*(4), 284–302.

Goodlad, J. I., Soder, R., & Sirotnit, K. A. (1990). *Places where teachers are taught.* San Francisco, CA: Jossey-Bass.

Grossman, P., & McDonald, M. (2008). Back to the future: Directions for research in teaching and teacher education. *American Educational Research Journal, 45*(1), 184–205.

Hadar, L., & Brody, D. (2017). Professional learning and development of teacher educators. In D. J. Clandinin & J. Husu (Eds.), *The Sage handbook of research on teacher education* (pp. 1049–1064). London: Sage Publications.

Hattie, J. (2012). *Visible learning for teachers: Maximizing impact on learning.* London: Routledge.

Hoekstra, A., Korthagen, F., Brekelmans, M., Beijaard, D., & Imants, J. (2009). Experienced teachers' informal workplace learning and perceptions of workplace conditions. *Journal of Workplace Learning, 21*(4), 276–298.

Ishimaru, A. M., & Takahashi, S. (2017). Disrupting racialized institutional scripts: Toward parent–teacher transformative agency for educational justice. *Peabody Journal of Education, 92*(3), 291–293.

Jurasaite-Harbison, E., & Rex, L. A. (2010). School cultures as contexts for informal teacher learning. *Teaching and Teacher Education, 26*(2), 2010, 267–277.

Kelchtermans, G., & Vanassche, E. (2017). Micropolitics in the education of teachers: Power, negotiation, and professional development. In D. J. Clandinin & J. Husu (Eds.), *The Sage handbook of research on teacher education* (pp. 441–456). London: Sage Publications.

Korhonen, H., Heikkinen, H. L. T., Ulla Kiviniemi, U., & Tynjälä, P. (2017). Student teachers' experiences of participating in mixed peer mentoring groups of in-service and pre-service teachers in Finland. *Teaching and Teacher Education, 61*, 153–163.

Kyndt, E., Gijbels, D, Grosemans, I., & Donche, V. (2016). Teachers' everyday professional development: Mapping informal learning activities, antecedents, and learning outcomes. *Review of Educational Research, 86*(4), 1111–1150.

Lamb, P. (2015). Peer-learning between pre-service teachers: Embracing Lesson Study. *International Journal for Lesson and Learning Studies, 4*(4), 343–361.

Lessard, S. (2014). *Red worn runners: A narrative inquiry into the stories of Aboriginal youth and families in urban settings* (Unpublished doctoral dissertation). University of Alberta, Edmonton, Canada.

Lindsay, G. M., Schwind, J. K., Papaconstantinoua, E., Smyea, V., & Crossc, N. (2016). Autobiographical reflections on what it means to experience disruption. *Reflective Practice, 17*(5), 583–591.

Loughran, J., Korthagen, F., & Russell, T. (2008). *Teacher education that makes a difference: Developing foundational principles of practice*. In C. J. Craig & L. F. Deretchin (Eds.), *Imagining a renaissance in teacher education* (pp. 405–421). Lanham, MD: Rowan & Littlefield Education.

Ma, J. Y. (2016). Designing disruptions for productive hybridity: The case of walking scale geometry. *Journal of the Learning Sciences, 25*(3), 335–371.

McDonald, M. A., Bowman, M., & Brayko, K. (2013). Learning to see students: Opportunities to develop relational practices of teaching through community-based placements in teacher education. *Teachers College Record, 115*(4), 1–35.

Melasalmi, A., & Husu, J. (2016). The content and implementation of shared professional knowledge in early childhood education. *Early Years, 36*(4), 426–439.

Melasalmi, A., & Husu, J. (2018). A narrative examination of early childhood teachers' shared identities in teamwork. *Journal of Early Childhood Teacher Education, 39*(2), 90–113.

Mena, J. (2017). Learning through pedagogies in teacher education. In D. J. Clandinin & J. Husu (Eds.), *The Sage handbook of research on teacher education* (pp. 509–512). London: Sage Publications.

Morris, L. V. (2016). Disruption in economies, industries, and political affairs: Can postsecondary education be far behind? *Innovative Higher Education, 42*, 1–2.

Murray, J. (2017). Defining teacher educators: International perspectives and contexts. In D. J. Clandinin & J. Husu (Eds.), *The Sage handbook of research on teacher education* (pp. 1017–1032). London: Sage Publications.

Payne, K., & Zeichner, K. (2017). Multiple voices and participants in teacher education. In D. J. Clandinin & J. Husu (Eds.), *The Sage handbook of research on teacher education* (pp. 1101–1116). London: Sage Publications.

Ping, C., Schellings, G., & Beijaard, D. (2018). Teacher educators' professional learning: A literature review. *Teaching and Teacher Education, 75*, 93–105.

Pinnegaar, S. (2017). Section Introduction: The education and learning of teacher educators. In D. J. Clandinin & J. Husu (Eds.), *The Sage handbook of research in teacher education* (pp. 1011–1015). London: Sage Publications.

Oyler, C., Morvay, J., & Sullivan, F. R. (2017). Developing an activist teacher identity through teacher education. In J. D. Clandinin & J. Husu (Eds.), *The Sage handbook of research on teacher education* (pp. 228–246). London: Sage Publications.

Pillay, S. R. (2017). Cracking the fortress: Can we really decolonize psychology? *South African Journal of Psychology, 47*(2), 135–140.

Rudduck, J., & McIntyre, D. (2007). *Improving learning through consulting pupils*. London: Routledge.

Russ, R. S., Sherin, B. L., & Sherin, M. G. (2016). What constitutes teacher learning? In D. H. Gitomer & C. A. Bell (Eds.), *Handbook of research on teaching* (5th ed., pp. 391–438). Washington, DC: The American Educational Research Association.

Sanders, W. L., & Horn, S. P. (1998). Research findings from the Tennessee Value-Added Assessment System (TVAAS) database: Implications for educational evaluation and research. *Journal of Personnel Evaluation in Education, 12*(3), 247–256.

Schaefer, L., Downey, C. A., & Clandinin, D. J. (2014). Shifting from stories to live by to stories to leave by: Early Career teacher attrition. *Teacher Education Quarterly, 41*(1), 9–27.

Schön, D. (1987). *Educating the reflective practitioner*. San Francisco, CA: Jossey-Bass.

Shavelson, R. J. (2013). On an approach to testing and modeling competence. *Educational Psychologist, 48*(2), 73–86.

Smith, K. (2003). So, what about the professional development of teacher educators? *European Journal of Teacher Education, 26*(2), 201–215.

Smith, L. T. (2012). *Decolonizing methodologies: Research and indigenous peoples*. London: Zed Books.

Struyven, K., & De Meyst, M. (2010). Competence-based teacher education: Illusion or reality? An assessment of the implementation status in Flanders from teachers' and students' points of view. *Teaching and Teacher Education, 26*, 1495–1510.

Thiessen, D., & Cook-Sather, A. (Eds.). (2007). *International handbook of student experience in elementary and secondary school*. Dordrecht: Springer.

Tirri, K., & Husu, J. (2002). Care and responsibility in 'the best interest of the child': Relational voices of ethical dilemmas in teaching. *Teachers and Teaching: Theory and Practice, 8*(1), 65–80.

Toom, A. (2017). Teachers' professional and pedagogical comptetencies: A complex devide between teacher work, teacher knowledge and teacher education. In D. J. Clandinin & J. Husu (Eds.), *The Sage handbook of research on teacher education* (pp. 803–819). London: Sage Publications.

Zeichner, K., Bowman, M., Guillen, L., & Napolitan, K. (2016). Engaging and working in solidarity with local communities in preparing the teachers of their children. *Journal of Teacher Education, 67*(4), 277–290.

Zygmunt, E., & Clark, P. (2016). *Transforming teacher education for social justice.* New York, NY: Teachers College Press.

CHAPTER 2

Investigating EFL Elementary Student Teachers' Development in a Professional Learning Practicum

Chiou-hui Chou

Abstract

The preparation of teachers through practicum is a central component of teacher education programs all around the world. Over the years, teacher educators have been arguing for a rethinking of the connections between campus courses and field experiences, on the grounds that more closely connecting these social spaces might enhance the learning of student teachers and better prepare them to be successful in the classrooms. How can teacher educators bridge the different learning sites and enhance prospective teachers' learning? The researcher, implementing the concept of professional learning community, investigated EFL elementary student teachers' development in their practicum in Taiwan. A qualitative case study approach was applied. Data were collected from discussions during each meeting, the student teachers' reflective journal writing, semi-structured interviews, and the researcher's classroom observations. The study found a carefully structured teaching practicum helped student teachers to analyze teaching practices critically and reflectively. It is suggested that university programs, teacher educators, and elementary schools can work together to make the teaching practicum a professional development opportunity for both student teachers and mentoring teachers.

Keywords

EFL – practicum – professional learning community – student teaching

Introduction

Preparing teachers through practicum is a central component of teacher education programs all around the world. Over the years, the practicum experience as an important component in the process of learning to teach has never been challenged. According to Zeichner (2010), the practicum plays a significant role in initial teacher education programs, providing authentic opportunities for teacher candidates to gain understandings of the professional practice of teaching in today's diverse classrooms. It should be regarded as an ongoing process of teacher development. In a review of practice-based teacher preparation, Mattson, Eilertsen, and Rorrison (2011) report evidence demonstrating how practicum experiences are used to support prospective teachers' professional knowledge, skills and dispositions. Rozelle and Wilson (2012) find new teachers often cite student teaching or field experience as the most beneficial, authentic, or practical aspect of teacher education. Moreover, Ibrahim (2013) indicates practicum experiences can lead to student teachers' personal and professional development and ease their induction to the profession. To sum up, empirical studies have shown that student teachers view their practicum experiences as extremely important and essential for their induction into professional life.

Although the practicum is considered important in the process of teaching and learning, a number of criticisms are attached to it. For example, Qazi, Rawat, and Thomas (2012) indicate that primary teacher certification programs neither provide the general education necessary to foster effective communication skills, critical thinking and creative instructional leadership nor promote in-depth content knowledge. In addition, much of the criticism is on the method the practicum operates. Zeichner (2010) states that for many years the obstacles to student teacher learning are associated with the loosely planned model of field experiences. Thus, Zeichner (2010) has argued for a rethinking of the connections between "campus courses" and "field experiences", on the grounds that more closely connecting these social spaces might enhance the learning of student teachers and "better prepare them to be successful" in 21st-century classrooms (p. 89). Indeed, educators all around the world have advocated that teacher education programs must be improved if they are to prepare competent teachers to meet the challenges of the 21st century (Darling-Hammond, 2010; Hökkä & Eteläpelto, 2014; Hollins, 2011; Korthagen, 2010; Wetzel, Hoffman, Roach, & Russell, 2018).

How can teacher educators bridge the different learning sites and enhance prospective teachers' learning? Earlier, Zeichner and Hutchinson (2008), in their description of characteristics of exemplary teacher education programs, have cited field experiences that can contribute to a program's success, including the need to closely connect supervision during student teaching to content of courses so that faculty and curriculum experiences reflect one vision of teaching and learning. Recently, Gelfuso, Parker, and Dennis (2015) indicate high-quality teacher education programs must create a space to support the simultaneous construction and understanding of theory and practice and their intricate intertwining. How can this happen? Recent research into student teaching has started to examine supervisors as key players in the teacher education process (Bates & Burbank, 2008; Bates, Drits, & Ramirez, 2011; Gelfuso et al., 2015; Soslau, 2015). For example, Bates et al. (2011) focus on the concept of supervisor stance (a supervisor's professional knowledge, perspective, and conceptualization about how student teachers learn to teach) and how it influences supervisory practice. They argue that the supervisor's stance could have a clear impact on student teachers' learning opportunities and could result in substantive improvements to the process and experience of student teaching. Therefore, exploring the role of the university supervisor in the practicum can contribute to the understanding of enacting innovative education reforms.

According to sociocultural theory, professional learning is socially and culturally situated in contexts of everyday living and work (Lave & Wenger, 1991). Based on sociocultural theories, researchers suggest that student teachers should be members of communities where they actively, critically, and collaboratively examine their teaching practices (Gelfuso et al., 2015; Korhonen, Heikkinen, Kiviniemi, & Tynjala, 2017; Rigelman & Ruben, 2012; Soslau, 2015). Over the years, implementing the concept of professional learning community (PLC) into a teaching practicum has been advocated in the prestigious journals. Hollins (2011) indicates that the benefits of participating in a professional community are enhanced by a strong professional identity and the ability to engage in self-directed professional growth and development and to work collaboratively with colleagues to improve learning outcomes for students. Moreover, teacher education should provide opportunities for student teachers to experience the reality of teaching that is inquiry-oriented, collaborative and student-oriented (Sachs, 2016).

This chapter was guided by the leading education researchers' advice of improving teacher education and improving the role of the practicum within teacher education. To understand how teacher educators can better support elementary student teachers' learning during their practicum, this researcher investigated the impacts of a professional learning community on EFL (English as a Foreign Language) student teachers' professional knowledge development in Taiwan. The purpose of this chapter is to explore how a professional learning community in conjunction with teaching practicum can help student teachers' development. Situating student teachers in a theory-based learning community contributes to our understanding of the effects of PLCs. The guiding research questions are: (a) How does participating in a professional learning community facilitate English student teachers' professional development? (b) How do the mentors play the role in the professional learning community? (c) How does the university supervisor play the role in the professional learning community?

In the following sections, the researcher presented the background for the study and provided some relevant information about the Taiwanese teacher education context. Relevant literature on professional learning communities and previous attempts to implement them was reviewed. Then the methodological considerations were presented. Research results and discussion were concluded with possible implications and suggestions for future research.

Literature Review

Professional Development

The task of educating teachers for the complex work of teaching in the 21st century constitutes a significant challenge for teacher education (Bjuland & Mosvold, 2015). In order to professionally conduct the work of teaching, teachers need compound professional knowledge that includes subject matter knowledge, pedagogical knowledge, curricular knowledge, pedagogical content knowledge (Shulman, 1986) as well as the cognitive dimensions of interactive decision-making in the classroom (Burns, Freeman, & Edwards, 2015; Konig, Tachtsoglou, Lammerding, Straub, Nold, & Rohde, 2017). Avalos (2011) points out that the professional development of teachers is presented in the literature in many different ways; the core of such endeavors is the understanding that "professional development is about teachers learning, learning how to learn, and transforming their knowledge into practice for the benefit of their students' growth" (p. 10). Zeichner (2012) states "teaching rather than teachers" makes an important contribution to the improvement of classroom instruction by developing a sharper focus in initial and continuing teacher education on learning to enact core instructional practices (p. 376). It is part of a growing literature on making teaching practice the central element of teacher education, an approach that has been referred to as practice-based, teacher education (Zeichner, 2012). Advocate of implementing practice-based teacher education to eliminate the disconnection between course work and practicum has been discussed over the years (e.g., Gelfuso et al. 2015; Wetzel et al., 2018). As Douglas and Ellis (2011) point out, school-based training is intended to emphasize the teaching skills and thereby, highlights the relevance in student teacher education courses the task of teaching in schools.

Research suggests that professional development targeting a specific practice is more effective than general professional development as teachers need substantial opportunities to learn a particular practice (e.g., Stanulis, Little, & Wibbens, 2012). Moreover, many researchers perceive that in order to be properly prepared, teacher candidates need considerable experience with whole-class and solo teaching since they will ultimately be alone in their future classrooms. Just as Ball and Forzani (2010) argue, time in the field alone is not sufficient for teacher learning; rather, disciplined inquiry about practice can support that learning. This is confirmed by Johnson (2010), who concluded that it was "carefully supervised apprenticeship experiences whereby students and master teachers engage in reflective dialogue that made the difference, not necessarily the number of hours of coursework or field experiences" (p. 28). Stanulis et al. (2012) also advocate that mentoring programs need to "provide professional development that targets a clear, high-leverage practice linked with instructional quality" (p. 33). Targeted professional development happens when teachers receive substantive preparation over time with a focus on deep and challenging content, facilitated by university representatives who have studied this same targeted content (Bausmith & Barry, 2011).

As indicated, practicum can provide student teachers opportunities to connect theory with practice under the guidance of their supervisors (Gelfuso et al. 2015; Wetzel et al., 2018; Zeichner, 2010) and good mentors who have teaching experience and a commitment to professional learning (Clarke, Triggs, & Nielsen, 2014; Hudson, 2016). From the above perspectives, educative supervision might be an effective supervision approach to educate reflective teachers, who strive to grow continuously.

Professional Learning Community

Hiebert and Morris (2012) and others have argued that working directly to improve teaching as part of a professional community provides the most authentic and rewarding intellectual challenge that can keep teachers engaged in the profession (e.g., Lampert & Graziani, 2009; Rigelman & Ruben, 2012; Soslau, 2015). Soslau (2015) indicates that teachers are expected to transform what they experienced in a professional learning community so that they are able to pose problems, identify discrepancies between theories and practices, and challenge common routines. There have been some attempts to implement a PLC in practicum. Some reported on possible challenges and constraints and some on stories of success. It can also be observed that the researchers often had a double role in the studies. They not only investigated the implementation of a professional learning community, but they also served as teacher educators in the program in which the community was implemented. For example, Rigelman and Ruben (2012) investigated the topic of utilizing professional learning communities to support student teachers' learning and their visions of teaching. They examined collaborative professional learning communities within a teacher education program. They believed it was this group that had the potential to ultimately shift the culture of schools toward more collaboration in order to better meet the needs of all learners. Their study examined the impact of multiple layers of professional collaboration intentionally integrated into a one-year preservice teacher education program working with two elementary schools. Their professional learning approach centered on attending to student learning through collaboration. They proposed a shift in teacher education toward collaborative inquiry about teaching and learning within school/university partnerships.

Over the years, university professors have begun responding to the need to support student teachers in reflection on their practice, recognizing that mere imitation of teaching strategies is not sufficient in the new context for teacher preparation (e.g., Gelfuso et al., 2015; Soslau, 2015). Under educative supervision, prospective teachers need to reflect on instructional decisions and plan for their future instruction.

In conclusion, the above empirical studies on student teachers' learning during practicum have employed the concept of professional learning community and focused on structured and guided systems of practicum. They have found student teachers benefited from participating in this type of learning community. Therefore, it is on the above premises that this chapter emphasizes that student teachers need an opportunity to practice and examine their teaching practice in the practicum, not just immerged in a classroom with a mentoring teacher.

Methodology

Context of the Study

In Taiwan, in order to qualify as an elementary school teacher, students first need to attend a four-year bachelor program in universities which provide elementary teacher education programs. After graduation, student teachers need to practice teaching practicum for a semester to fulfill the teacher preparation credits. During the practicum, student teachers are arranged with a university supervisor from their university. The practicum school will assign a mentor, offering his or her class for student teachers to practice teaching and serving the mentoring work. Mentors are invited by their school principals or directors and so far most of them are not required to receive supervision from teacher education programs.

Participants

Five female student teachers, fulfilling their practicum in an elementary school near the researcher's university, were invited to participate in this study. They were graduates from the researcher's department, in ages from 21 to 22 years old. They will be prospective elementary school teachers with an additional certificate of teaching the subject English. Pseudonyms were used throughout the chapter to protect anonymity of all the participants. They were Cindy, Hazel, Patty, Sandy, and Tracy. According to the university and the elementary school's collaboration contract, each student teacher was assigned to a classroom with a homeroom teacher, serving as the mentor. In this study, the researcher invited another two English teachers from the student teachers' practicum school to serve as the English-subject mentor. They were Sue and Emma. Sue and Emma only taught the English subject at their school. Both have an average of five years of teaching experience. They were at their 30s.

Ethics approval for conducting this study was obtained from the institution responsible for reviewing the proposal. The classroom teachers, the student teachers, and the mentors were all given informed, written consent to participate in this study. The use of pseudonyms for participants was applied in this study to preserve anonymity and confidentiality.

Data Collection

A qualitative case study was applied in this study. Merriam (1998) describes a case study as having the following characteristics: "particularistic, descriptive, and heuristic (p. 29). This study design is generally used to uncover the interaction of significant factors and characteristics of a phenomenon. It thus suits this present study for the researcher to explore English student teachers' professional development in a professional learning community.

In September, the professional learning community was formed, where student teachers, mentors, and the researcher met twice a month. At the first meeting, the researcher, serving as the university supervisor, clarified what she hoped for the student teachers and the mentors to do during the study. In particular, the researcher and the mentor examined how to help the student teachers develop specific knowledge, skills and dispositions by examining their own practice. During the second meeting, student teachers and the researcher engaged in a lesson planning task – working toward for their first teaching demonstration in October. Each month, the student teachers worked together to plan a lesson and taught a lesson.

In the practicum semester, the student teachers were arranged to teach a grade 2, a grade 3, and a grade 4 class individually. Their lesson plans and teaching ideas were discussed before they went to teach a grade level. Following a lesson study model (Fernandez, 2010), all the student teachers and the researcher designed the lessons, implemented the lessons, observed the lessons, and discussed the practiced lessons as well as the students' learning results. While one student teacher was teaching the lesson, the others and the researcher as well as the mentors were observing the lesson. After each teaching demonstration, the participants had a post-lesson conference, feedbacks were shared and modifications were made for the next lesson. In this professional learning community, everyone could publicly disclose the questions and dilemmas in supporting everyone's learning.

At the end of the practicum, the researcher conducted semi-structured interviews with each participant, regarding their perspectives on participation in this learning community. Each interview lasted about thirty minutes. All the interview data were transcribed verbatim for analysis. Data also included the researcher's field notes, classroom observations, post-lesson conference data with participants, student teachers' lesson plans, and student teacher's reflective journal writing after each teaching.

To maximum the student teachers' professional development, the researcher designed an inquiry-oriented teaching practicum, supported with quality mentoring and supervision, presented in Figure 2.1, which depicted the design of the study and the purpose for exploring this research topic.

Data Analysis

Drawing on sociocultural theories (Lave & Wenger, 1991), this study examined student teachers' learning in a professional learning community, where they could actively, critically, and collaboratively examine their teaching practices (Gelfuso et al., 2015; Korhonen et al., 2017; Shulman & Shulman, 2004; Soslau, 2015). Analysis of the data included reading and rereading interview transcripts, field notes, lesson plans, post-lesson discussion data and the participants' reflective journal writing (Creswell & Plano-Clark, 2007). A constant comparative analysis (Miles & Huberman, 1994) method was applied to generate categories and themes, which were then used as evidence to document the aspects of participating in a professional learning community that the student teachers expressed during their practicum regarding planning lessons, teaching practice, student learning, and professional growth. Mentors' expressions of their experiences in this study were added into the new categories.

As Merriam (1998) suggests, strategies for establishing internal validity, which include triangulation, member checks, and long-term observations. In this study, different sources of data were collected to achieve triangulation.

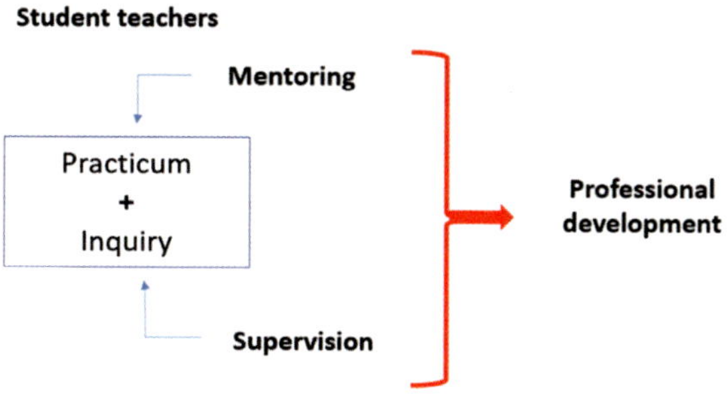

Student teachers

```
           Mentoring
    ┌─────────────────┐
    ↓                 │
┌─────────┐           ├──→  Professional
│Practicum│           │     development
│    +    │           │
│ Inquiry │           │
└─────────┘           │
    ↑                 │
    │                 │
    └─ Supervision ───┘
```

FIGURE 2.1
The design of this study

In addition, a broad and in-depth literature review in the topic also achieve expert knowledge to support the validity of the interpretation of the result. Moreover, data triangulation can help enhance reliability (Merrian, 1998). Thus the use of multiple sources of data as described above contributes to the trustworthiness of the data and to the methodological rigor of this study.

Results and Siscussion

The Role of the Mentor

What are the roles of an English mentor in this project? First, this study found that the mentors were like the student teachers' peers – providing feedbacks, guiding them to reflect on teaching events, and providing experiences of monitoring students' learning in the classroom. Basically, the above characteristics are all about how to teach more professionally. One possible reason might be that these mentors were new in the profession with an average of five years. Their learning experiences in a university and in the process of becoming an English teacher were much the same as these student teachers'.

> As the mentor [Sue] just became the classroom teacher these years – she has just gone through the recruitment process – she knew how to prepare for the teaching demonstration during recruitment. She would offer suggestions for our preparation and give us directions for improvement. (Cindy's interview)

Both mentors hoped student teachers could care more about students' learning results. Student teachers expressed, "Sue observed our teaching practice with more details regarding the learning and teaching in the classroom. She would remind us to balance the strategies guiding students to learn in the real teaching contexts with the theory learned in coursework" (Cindy's interview).

> For me, the most valuable help both mentors offered is, after each teaching practice, they offered us suggestions regarding students' learning … They have their real teaching experiences different from ours so they paid attention to the real learning situation in relation to theories. During teaching practice, they focused on whether we paid attention to individual students' learning. And this indeed is what we should take into consideration. After all we will enter the teaching context and we will have to face the situation. (Sandy's interview)

Overall, the mentors focused on how to present a successful lesson during recruitment contest, how to balance the gap between the university coursework and the real teaching context, and how to pay attention to students' learning. In this study mentors provided emotional support, served as a peer in the professional relationship, collaborated, and provided feedback – which is similar to the findings of Korhonen et al. (2017). In this study, the researcher did not find mentoring as a contested practice (Kemmis, Heikkinen, Fransson, Aspfors, & Edwards-Groves, 2014), in which mentors and mentees hold strong points of any assertion. Kim and Danforth (2012) indicate that when a more traditional, hierarchical mentor–mentee relationship is maintained, student teachers' voices are constrained and unheard. This study did not follow such a framework.

Next, Langdon (2014) indicates that numerous studies have addressed the critical role that mentoring plays for prospective teachers' professional development and many of them are about how mentoring matters to the mentee. For example, effective mentoring is a critical component of early career development and the development of quality teachers (Feiman-Nemser, 2001). However, less has been revealed about what classroom teachers learn about mentoring when undertaking this role and little is understood about how the mentor-mentee relationship contributes to the mentors' growth and development. The results of this study filled the gap. Mentor Sue mentioned in the interview, saying "these student teachers demonstrated excellent teaching performance and I actually learned with them" (Sue's interview data). Mentor Emma talked about how she could contribute different perspectives to the student teachers' development in this community – not the same as the student teachers' and the researcher's opinions. In particular, she found student teachers mainly focused on their teaching performance and paid little attention to some individual students' learning. She said,

> If the student teachers could pay more attention to monitoring individual students' learning, they might then know why some of their activities

or teaching flow did not work that smoothly with some students. And I myself actually learned about this aspect during the past few years' teaching experiences. (Emma's interview)

Indeed, teachers' knowledge development takes time. As Langdon (2014) writes, in the literature there is no universal definition of mentoring. While some think mentoring as a type of coaching, others see the exact reverse (Mullen, 2012). In this study, the researcher and the mentors did not see mentoring as a coaching. And this makes the researcher think more critically about how teacher education programs and teacher educators should include mentors in a practicum. Findings from this study show that teacher education programs first need to select mentors who are now or already practicing the reforms of recent education innovations in order to achieve the educational goals. Over the years, research in Taiwan as well as worldwide has shown that a lot of mentors did not receive good preparation work for playing the mentor role (e.g., Clarke et al., 2014). In addition, research indicates that experience and expertise as a classroom teacher are necessary for mentors but not sufficient for effectively mentoring student teachers. According to Trubowitz (2004), mentoring in a profession relies on at least three elements: (1) the mentor's own depth of knowledge, skills, and experiences in the profession, (2) the mentor's ability to identify accurately the potential in a mentee, and (3) the mentor's ability to enable a mentee to achieve his or her potential. In this study, the researcher finds when a classroom teacher serves as a TESOL (Teaching English to Speakers of Other Languages) mentor, the role requires a foundation of craft skill and experience, pedagogical content knowledge, assessment for learning, and the knowledge about contemporary educational policies and reforms so that they can live up to the standards of experts with TESOL professional knowledge (Burns et al., 2015; Konig et al., 2017). In other words, there is a specialized set of knowledge and skills for mentoring. In conclusion, experience as a classroom teacher is not likely to be adequate of itself to serve effectively as a mentor. More attention should be paid to preparing appropriate quality mentors to keep up with the educational policies and reforms.

The Role of the University Supervisor

Just as the literature indicates, student teaching is one of the most crucial moments of preservice teacher learning. Supervision thus is crucial. In this study, the researcher played the first role as a supervisor, facilitating student teachers' professional knowledge development. In response to Zeichner's (2010) as well as other educators' advocacy of closely connecting the campus courses with field experiences (e.g., Gelfuso et al., 2015; Soslau, 2015), the researcher, responsible for the supervision of student teaching in the practicum, is positioned to help student teachers to bridge the university-based content of their preparation programs and the practical knowledge of teaching emerging during practicum.

Next, as the instructor of some courses in the participants' university, the researcher tended to support student teachers' implementation of recent educational reforms as well as theories they learned in the university coursework and to offer opportunities for them to reflect critically during their teaching. This study followed the concept of educative supervisor's stance, in which a supervisor's professional knowledge and perspective can have a clear impact on student teachers' learning opportunities and result in improvements of student teaching (Bates et al., 2011). It was this type of educative supervision that motivated student teachers to link theory with practice. In this study, Cindy said,

> After teaching practice, during the discussion, you would notice what we needed to improve for future instruction and you would ask questions for us to reflect on the teaching events and instructional activities ... For example, during the lesson planning sessions, while we were planning teaching activities, you would bring about questions for us to think what would work best for different levels of students. (Cindy's interview data)

Similarly, Tracy talked about the same impressions that she had on the supervisor. She said,

> You would usually leave some space for us to reflect on the lesson planning and to work out solutions on our own. You asked: What are the objectives in a lesson? How can you support students' leaning process? What are the purposes of the learning activities? How to successfully deliver the activities. (Tracy's interview data)

Sandy detailed about her reflection. She said while she was planning a lesson, during each step, she would ask herself questions, such as: How will the activity be effective for students' learning? How to monitor students' learning results? Are the activities meaningful for English learning? After this study, Sandy said she learned how to refine her teaching strategies for future teaching contexts. Without systematically monitoring their own participation within a community, student teachers would "lack the capacity for learning from experience" (Shulman & Shulman, 2004, p. 264). In this study, targeted professional development happened when student teachers received substantive preparation with a focus on deep and challenging content, facilitated by the university supervisor who have studied this same targeted content (Bausmith & Barry, 2011).

The Benefits of Participating in a Professional Learning Community
In this professional learning community, everyone learned with one another. Everyone gains different sources of expert knowledge and grows together. Firstly, student teachers knew how to look to the university professor and the classroom instructors as sources of the information that they need to be effective professional teachers. In this study, three different levels of classes were arranged for each student teacher to practicing teaching, which led these student teachers to focus on adapting to the classroom contexts. Thus, looking to mentors as experts to resolve classroom dilemmas was common in this study. For example, in post-lesson discussions, student teachers generally proposed questions in related to classroom management disciplines. In the meanwhile, during observations, the mentors usually gave feedbacks on managing classroom disciplines. Thus, student teachers expressed they learned a lot from the mentors regarding the aspect of classroom management strategies.

Secondly, in this study, mentors acknowledged that they learned from the student teachers about how to design a variety of language learning activities to engage students in learning. During one observation in a grade four classroom, Mentor Sue found a boy paid great attention to a student teacher's instruction and actively participated in that period's language activities – which she had never in her class found this type of learning attitude. This made her reflect on her teaching styles and strategies. She thought about using different types of activities to engage students with different learning styles in learning.

> Frankly speaking, as I have different levels of classes to teach, I usually do not design a variety of activities to engage students to learn and I don't have the passion that the student teachers have. About observing the grade-four lesson they taught, I found the activities interesting and attracted students' attention. I saw they learned with a lot of fun. (Sue's interview)

Just as Hudson (2016) indicates, forming positive and productive relationships requires student teachers to exhibit desirable attributes and practices and both parties need to be aware of the personal–professional actions that can aid in forming a successful mentoring relationship.

Thirdly, from the university supervisor's perspective, the teaching practicum is the final stage that teacher educators can see how prospective teachers are well prepared. Thus, in this study, the researcher's main focus was on how to facilitate the development of student teachers' competencies in constructing professional practice in real classrooms (Soslau, 2015; Wetzel et al., 2018; Zeichner, 2010). Questions and reflection guidelines from the researcher regarding practicing TESOL principles usually posed student teachers an ongoing challenge.

> For example, while we were designing lessons, although we have learned about it in the university and we knew what we wanted to do, we still had some hesitations about teaching techniques and how to present the content. But how? And no concrete activities came out. You would point out and remind us, saying since you had set up the aim of the lesson, think about activities that could help you achieve the goal. Then we had to think deeper. (Tracy's interview)

In this professional reflective practicum, the student teachers were engaged in ongoing reflection on their own teaching and carefully examining how they connected their teaching practice with related university coursework. They had implemented different teaching pedagogies in their lessons. They demonstrated successful strategists to engage students in learning English meaningfully.

> The activities we designed in this lesson were engaging. In addition to the board games, we used real objects to present a real-life learning context. During oral practice, we presented a basket of fruits and foods and walked to students to give them the chance to have the interaction with us. They expressed their own ideas. I saw students showing enthusiastic attitudes towards learning in this class. I deeply felt that the more relevant the context to students' life and experiences, the more the activity could arouse students' learning motivation! (Sandy's reflective journal writing: #3)

Critical events happened in the real classrooms during the research period. They thus offered a significant area of inquiry for the development of the teachers as well as the university supervisor. For example, while teaching a grade 3 class, Tracy did not manage the time well for each activity. Unexpected situations happened – students responded with no color pens for the activity and then not enough time for them to finish coloring, following the teacher's directions and steps. The third graders actually needed more time to finish the coloring activity than she planned. This then led to insufficient time for the wrap up activity – finishing a writing worksheet. When the bell rang, she hastily ended the lesson. This type of situation offered the student teachers opportunities to deal with students issues. Thus, the discussions in post-lessons were contextual and dynamic because the teaching content, the teaching level, and critical incidents were different. From a sociocultural perspective, knowledge about teaching is socially constructed (Lave & Wenger, 1991). This view of knowledge suggests student teachers should be involved in a discourse community to analyze teaching practices critically and reflectively (Gelfuso et al., 2015). Soslau (2015) indicates that teachers are expected to transform the knowledge and experience that they acquired in a professional learning community so that they are able to pose problems, identify discrepancies between theories and practices, and challenge common routines. The discussion sessions in this practicum project provided a context to help student teachers learn how to engage in these types of activities towards the goal of transforming their participation and becoming contributors to professional learning communities. All the members in this learning community acknowledged their personal benefits of the participation in this study. Tracy said,

> I valued the opportunities we five had to talk about lesson planning. This is better than I alone thinking about teaching ideas. We [in the practicum] are still at the learning stage. We as peers encourage each other and offer suggestions. And we can refine our knowledge. (Tracy's interview)

Furthermore, learning smoothly in a professional learning community requires the mentors, student teachers, and the university supervisor worked well together. As the student teachers were new to the practicum elementary school, the job of bridging the parties in this community and school is important for the university supervisor. Building the university connection with the practicum school before student teachers' entering thus is necessary. Lastly, as a university supervisor, the researcher was actively involved in the community. The researcher, the student teachers, and the mentors knew how the three parties could examine the teaching events more critically with each one's professional knowledge and experience.

Conclusion

The researcher has initiated a small-scale study, demonstrating how the mentor, the university supervisor, and the student teachers can all engaged in a professional learning community to develop their professional knowledge.

Situating all the participants in a learning community, they develop together. It was in this study that the researcher witnessed how everyone learned with one another and gained different sources of practical knowledge. Professional development is "about teachers learning, learning how to learn, and transforming their knowledge into practice for the benefit of their students' growth" (Avalos, 2011, p. 10). In this learning community everyone developed professionally. The university supervisor learned how to guide the preserve teachers to teach different graders. She found the strategies to guide preservice teachers to teach lower graders should be different from the strategies teaching higher graders. The mentors learned from these student teachers about how to implement innovative English theories of instruction. The student teachers learned about classroom management strategies from the mentors. In particular, this study found good mentor-mentee relationship could not only contribute to the student teachers' growth, but also the mentor's development. The mutual benefits thus contributed to the development of more quality teachers and mentors. Little is known about how the mentor-mentee relationship contributes to the mentors' growth and development. The study contributed to fill the gap.

Implications

Recently, practice-based teacher preparation programs, which highlight the relevance in student teacher education course content to the task of teaching in schools, has been strongly recommended (e.g., Gelfuso et al., 2015; Wetzel et al., 2018). This study highly recommend early filed-teaching crucial for preserve teachers so that collaborative problem solving, planning, and peer observations can be a regular part of student teachers' professional growth across the span of their career.

Although the 2011 National Council on Teacher Quality report on student teaching made several recommendations about mentoring teacher selection, it remains silent on the issue of training (Greenberg, Walsh, & McKee, 2015). A recent review on mentors by Clarke et al. (2014) reveals mentors lack specific preparation to enable high quality and developmentally appropriate support for student teachers, indicating that they tend to be under-prepared for their work as mentors. Still, universities rely on classroom teachers serving as mentors yet do not prepare them for that role.

Over the years, the educational policies of teaching English to young learners (TEYL) have been implemented in EFL Asian contexts as well as many parts of the word. However, little has been discussed about TEYL mentoring to keep up with the new policy. This study suggests that training teachers for playing the role as TEYL mentors is imperative. Establishing a model of mentoring may be strengthened by university educators' further research projects – such as beginning a project with their partnership elementary schools. More empirical research results can help educators provide a better TEYL teacher education all around the world.

References

Avalos, B. (2011). Teacher professional development in teaching and teacher education over ten years. *Teaching and Teacher Education, 27,* 10–20.

Ball, D. L., & Forzani, F. M. (2010). What does it take to make a teacher? *Phi Delta Kappan, 92*(2), 8–12.

Bates, A., & Burbank, M. (2008). Effective student teacher supervision in the era of no child left behind. *The Professional Educator, 32*(2), 1–11.

Bates, A., Drits, D., & Ramirez, L. (2011). Self-awareness and enactment of supervisory stance: Influences on responsiveness toward student teacher learning. *Teacher Education Quarterly, 38*(3), 69–87.

Bausmith, J. M., & Barry, C. (2011). Revisiting professional learning communities to increase college readiness: The importance of pedagogical content knowledge. *Educational Researcher, 40*(4), 175–178.

Bjuland, R., & Mosvold, R. (2015). Lesson study in teacher education: Learning from a challenging case. *Teaching and Teacher Education, 52,* 83–90.

Burns, A., Freeman, D., & Edwards, E. (2015). Theorizing and studying the language-teaching mind: Mapping research on language teacher cognition. *The Modern Language Journal, 99*(3), 585–601.

Clarke, A., Triggs, V., & Nielsen, W. (2014). Cooperating teacher participation in teacher education: A review of the literature. *Review of Educational Research, 84,* 163–202.

Creswell, J. W., & Plano-Clark, V. L. (2007). *Designing and conducting mixed methods research.* Thousand Oaks, CA: Sage Publications.

Darling-Hammond, L. (2010). *The flat world and education: How America's commitment to equity will determine our future.* New York, NY: Teachers College Press.

Douglas, A. S., & Ellis, V. (2011). Connecting does not necessarily mean learning: Course handbooks as mediating tools in school-university partnerships. *Journal of Teacher Education, 62*(5), 465–476.

Feiman-Nemser, S. (2001). From preparation to practice: Designing a continuum to strengthen and sustain teaching. *Teachers College Record, 103*(6), 1013–1055.

Fernandez, M. L. (2010). Investigating how and what prospective teachers learn through microteaching lesson study. *Teaching and Teacher Education, 26*(2), 351–362.

Gelfuso, A., Parker, A., & Dennis, D. V. (2015). Turning teacher education upside down: Enacting the inversion of teacher preparation through the symbiotic relationship of theory and practice. *The Professional Educator, 39*(2). Retrieved from http://wp.auburn.edu/educate/wp-content/uploads/2015/11/gelfuso-fall_15.pdf

Hiebert, J., & Morris, A. M. (2012). Extending ideas on improving teaching: Response to Lampert, Lewis, Perry, Friedkin, and Roth, and Zeichner. *Journal of Teacher Education, 63*(5), 383–385.

Hökkä, P., & Eteläpelto, A. (2014). Seeking new perspectives on the development of teacher education: A study of the Finnish context. *Journal of Teacher Education, 65*(1), 39–52.

Hollins, E. R. (2011). Teacher preparation for quality teaching. *Journal of Teacher Education, 62*(4), 395–407.

Hudson, P. (2016). Forming the mentor-mentee relationship. *Mentoring & Tutoring: Partnership in Learning, 24*(1), 30–43.

Ibrahim, A. S. (2013). Approaches to supervision of student teachers in one UAE teacher education program. *Teaching and Teacher Education, 34*, 38–45.

Johnson, D. (2010). Learning to teach: The influence of a university-school project on pre-service elementary teachers' efficacy for literacy instruction. *Reading Horizons, 50*(1), 23–48.

Kemmis, S., Heikkinen, H. L. T., Fransson, G., Aspfors, J., & Edwards-Groves, C. (2014). Mentoring of new teachers as a contested practice: Supervision, support and collaborative self-development. *Teaching and Teacher Education, 43*, 154–164.

Kim, T., & Danforth, S. (2012). Non-authoritative approach to supervision of student teachers: Cooperating teachers' conceptual metaphors. *Journal of Education for Teaching, 38*(1), 67–82.

Konig, J., Tachtsoglou, S., Lammerding, S., Straub, S., Nold, G., & Rohde, A. (2017). The role of opportunities to learn in teacher preparation for EFL teachers' pedagogical content knowledge. *The Modern Language Journal, 101*(1), 109–127.

Korhonen, H., Heikkinen, H. L. T., Kiviniemi, U., & Tynjala, P. (2017). Student teachers' experiences of participating in mixed peer mentoring groups of in-service and pre-service teachers in Finland. *Teaching and Teacher Education, 61*, 153–63.

Korthagen, F. A. J. (2010). Situated learning theory and the pedagogy of teacher education. *Teaching and Teacher Education, 26*, 98–106.

Lampert, M., & Graziani, F. (2009). Instructional activities as a tool for teachers' and teacher educators' learning. *Elementary School Journal, 109*, 491–509.

Langdon, F. J. (2014). Evidence of mentor learning and development: An analysis of New Zealand mentor/mentee professional conversations. *Professional Development in Education, 40*(1), 36–55.

Lave, J., & Wenger, E. (1991). *Situated learning: Legitimate peripheral participation.* Cambridge: Cambridge University Press.

Lewis, C. C., Perry, R. R., Friedkin, S., & Roth, J. R. (2012). Improving teaching does improve teachers: Evidence from lesson study. *Journal of Teacher Education, 63*(5), 368–375.

Mattsson, M., Eilertsen, T. V., & Rorrison, D. (Eds.). (2011). *A practicum turn in teacher education.* Rotterdam, The Netherlands: Sense Publishers.

Merriam, S. B. (1998). *Qualitative research and case study applications in education.* San Francisco, CA: Jossey-Bass.

Miles, M. B., & Huberman, A. M. (1994). *Qualitative data analysis: An expanded sourcebook* (2nd ed.). Thousand Oaks, CA: Sage Publications.

Mullen, C. A. (2012). Mentoring: An overview. In S. J. Fletcher & C. A. Mullen (Eds.), *The Sage handbook of mentoring and coaching in education* (pp. 7–23). London: Sage Publications.

Qazi, W., Rawat, K. J., & Thomas, M. (2012). The role of practicum in enhancing student teachers' teaching skills. *American Journal of Scientific Research, 44,* 44–57.

Rigelman, N. M., & Ruben, B. (2012). Creating foundations for collaboration in schools: Utilizing professional learning communities to support teacher candidate learning and visions of teaching. *Teaching and Teacher Education, 28,* 979–989.

Rozelle, J. J., & Wilson, S. M. (2012). Opening the Black box of field experiences: How cooperating teachers' beliefs and practices shape student teachers' beliefs and practices. *Teaching and Teacher Education, 28*(8), 1196–1205.

Sachs, J. (2016). Teacher professionalism: Why are we still talking about it? *Teachers and Teaching, 22*(4), 413–425.

Shulman, L. S. (1986). Those who understand: Knowledge growth in teaching. *Educational Researcher, 15*(2), 4–14.

Shulman, L. S., & Shulman, J. (2004). How and what teachers learn: A shifting perspective. *Journal of Curriculum Studies, 36,* 257–271.

Soslau, E. G. (2015). *Exploring intersubjectivity between student teachers and field instructors in student teaching conferences.* Retrieved from https://www.cogentoa.com/article/10.1080/2331186X.2015.1045219.pdf

Stanulis, R. N., Little, S., & Wibbens, E. (2012). Intensive mentoring that contributes to change in beginning elementary teachers' learning to lead classroom discussions. *Teaching and Teacher Education, 28,* 32–43.

Trubowitz, S. (2004). The why, how, and what of mentoring. *Phi Delta Kappan, 86,* 59–62.

Wetzel, M. M., Hoffman, J. V., Roach, A. K., & Russell, K. (2018). Practical knowledge and teacher reflection from a practice-based literacy teacher education program in the first years: A longitudinal study. *Teacher Education Quarterly, 45*(1), 87–111.

Zeichner, K. (2010). Rethinking the connections between campus courses and field experiences in college- and university-based teacher education. *Journal of Teacher Education, 61*(1–2), 89–99.

Zeichner, K. (2012). The turn once again toward practice-based teacher education. *Journal of Teacher Education, 63*(5), 376–382.

Zeichner, K., & Hutchinson, E. (2008). The development of alternative certification policies and programs in the U.S. In P. Grossman & S. Loeb (Eds.), *Alternative routes to teaching* (pp. 15–29). Cambridge, MA: Harvard Education Press.

CHAPTER 3

Becoming and Being a Teacher in Adverse Times: Iberian Perspectives

Maria Assunção Flores

Abstract

In this chapter I look at major trends in becoming and being a teacher in Portugal and Spain in adverse times. Even though I take into consideration existing international literature, I will focus on some of the key aspects that characterise the teaching profession and teacher education in Iberia by drawing upon empirical work carried out in both countries. The intention is not to do an exhaustive literature review nor to undertake a state of the art. Rather, my aim is to look at major trends characterising teaching and teachers' work as well as teacher education in terms of current challenges in order to identify possible directions. Contradictory trends may be identified in the ways in which teacher professionalism has been defined as well as in real conditions of teachers' work in schools and classrooms with implications for teacher education.

Keywords

being a teacher – Iberian perspectives – teacher education – professionalism – teachers

Introduction: My Journey at ISATT

I would like to start this chapter with a personal note. It has to do with my personal journey at the International Study Association on Teachers and Teaching (ISATT). I joined ISATT in 1997, when I was completing my Master's degree dissertation. My first ISATT conference was in Kiel, in Germany, in 1997, and I have not missed an ISATT conference since then (see Figure 3.1). My participation in such an engaging and friendly international research community was, and still is, an inspiration for me both as a teacher educator and as a researcher.

FIGURE 3.1   My journey at ISATT – ISATT conferences 1997–2017

Reviewing the last 20 years, I found that the themes travelled from one conference to the other and how important the discussions and reflections were in these events to enhance knowledge about teachers and teacher education. Issues such as teachers' practice, challenges for the profession, professionalism, relevance of the research on teachers and teaching, identities and cultures, legacies and changes in policy, practice and research, the excellence of the teachers and the future of teaching, etc., were at the forefront of many of the conference themes. Some of the issues discussed over the last two decades remain key concerns for us as researchers and teacher educators in many parts of the world, while changes at the social, cultural, economic and political level make them even more challenging.

Twenty years later, the University of Salamanca is the gracious host of yet another inspiring ISATT international conference, this time focusing on "Teaching Search and Research", a timely and relevant topic. It takes into account the challenges related to the digital era in which we live, the issues pertaining to the knowledge economy, the political instability in many regions, the significant changes in migration patterns, the growth of refugee camps and the rise in terrorism and violence in society (Madalińska-Michalak, O'Doherty, & Flores, 2018).

In a book published to celebrate the 30th anniversary of ISATT, Kompt and Rust (2013) identified issues in need of attention in the future, such as Environment, Unemployment, Bullying, Poverty, Political, Technology, Union, Crisis, Pollution, Financial, Aging, etc. These deserve further attention in 2017 as we discuss "Teaching search and research", our conference theme. My goal is, therefore, to look at teaching and teacher education in adverse times, taking a perspective that reflects the concerns, the specificities and challenges of this part of the world – the Iberian context – knowing that these issues may apply to other contexts and regions.

My Stance and the Context: Iberian Perspectives

In this chapter I look at major trends in becoming and being a teacher in Portugal and Spain in adverse times by drawing upon empirical work carried out in both countries. The reason for my choice lies in the geographic location: we are at the Iberian Peninsula; we are in Europe, and this is my stance. In other words, even though I take into consideration existing international literature, I will focus on some of the key aspects that characterise the teaching profession and teacher education in Portugal and Spain. These two countries of the Iberian Peninsula have their own specific features in cultural, social, economic and political terms but they also share some issues resulting from a relative common history (Heitor, Horta, Dopazo, & Fueyo, 2016). Both countries joined the European Union in 1986 and both have developed a great deal since then. As Heitor et al. (2016, p. 129) assert, "In the late 20th century, both Iberian states have become democracies, joined the European Union, developed fast and recovered some of the lost ground in relation to the rest of Western Europe". They add that "After the mid-1980s, both countries managed to tackle several challenges and substantial changes occurred, mainly developing physical infrastructure and consolidating democratic values, and to a lesser extent, increasing the qualifications of the younger generations and investing more in knowledge".

FIGURE 3.2

Issues wanting attention in the future (adapted from Kompft & Rust, 2013)

However, both countries recently faced severe financial and economic crises, with implications for all sectors of society, particularly education. Austerity measures were intensified. Their impact was visible in the deterioration of the situation of families, mostly related to job losses, under-employment, higher taxes, and cuts in social transfers and public services which occurred mainly between 2008 and 2012. According to Heitor et al. (2016, p. 130), these were often "blind" cuts aimed at "reducing public deficit, to the detriment of other strategic goals that both countries were pursuing, some of them requiring stability and long-term investment in knowledge". These measures have greatly affected people's lives, in terms of unemployment, low income, high taxation, poverty and inequalities, and through their impact on social protection, health, and education. Thus, alongside the financial and economic downturn, a social crisis has also become apparent. The teaching profession has been affected by salary cuts, high rates of unemployment, high taxation, worsening career progression (Flores & Ferreira, 2016).

Both in Portugal and in Spain, there have been precarious job conditions in teaching, short-term teaching contracts, high level of unemployment and a teacher surplus unlike other countries (Flores, 2014; Sancho-Gil, Correa, Giró, & Fraga, 2014). However, teacher attrition or dropout rates are low which runs counter to the situation of other European and non-European countries (For instance, in general, unemployment reached 25% in Spain and 17% in Portugal and for young people it was 52% in Spain and 35% in Portugal during the period of financial and economic crisis). Along with these were changes at the policy level such as new mechanisms for teacher evaluation; new legal framework for Initial Teacher Education; new protocols for school governance; reduction in the school curriculum; increase of number of pupils per class; introduction of national exams, school evaluation, etc. In general, more pressure was placed on schools and teachers to increase teaching standards and student achievement (Flores, 2014).

Cuts in the budget for education and new policy initiatives have led people and teachers in particular to fight against them. There were several demonstrations and strikes in both countries. Teachers fought against austerity measures, cuts in budget for education, increase of tuition fees, teacher evaluation, worsening of working conditions, unemployment, etc. There were massive demonstrations and strikes; in Spain the biggest demonstration included 250.000 people and in Portugal 100.000. Another critical issue relates to the aging of the teaching force. According to the last official statistics, 48.4% of the teachers in Portugal are 50 years or older and only 0.4% are 30 years or younger, figures that apply to the public sector (DGEEC, 2018).

With this scenario in mind, there are a number of questions that might be asked: What kinds of teachers are to be educated for today's society? What are the key competences, attitudes, dispositions and knowledge required of a teacher? How does it feel to be a teacher today? What are the key challenges of teaching and learning in today's schools and classrooms? How do teachers understand their professionalism in such challenging times? What can be learned from past and current practice, policy and research in the face of an uncertain future? The goal of this chapter is to look at issues that characterise the teaching profession and teacher education drawing upon recent research carried out in Spain and Portugal. The intention is not to conduct an exhaustive literature review nor to undertake a state of the art on the topics due to the word limit for this chapter. Rather, my aim is to look at major trends characterising teaching and teachers' work as well as teacher education in terms of current challenges in order to identify possible directions taking an Iberian perspective.

Teaching and Teachers' Work: Plural and Contradictory Practices of Professionalism

Teachers' work and lives have been affected in different ways in many European countries and elsewhere. Quality has become the keyword and the need to raise the standards of education a priority for all governments. However, the conditions and priorities as well as the pace of reforms vary from country to country. There are issues that deserve further consideration in the 21st century: the classroom as a space for learning and the role ascribed to teachers and pupils; existing resources and characteristics of today's school contexts; disparities in education; topics such as inclusion, diversity, and equity; the digital era and its implications for teaching and learning (and to learning to teach); and the social, cultural and political changes impacting school and teachers' work. Day (2017, p. 6) identified five consequences of policy reform for teachers' work and lives: (i) an increase in the demands on teachers in terms of workload and bureaucracy associated with ever more detailed, often standardised recording and reporting procedures; (ii) the management of teachers' professional learning and development, in which participation has become less of a choice and more a formal requirement; (iii) the traditional isolation of teachers has diminished so too have acts of collaboration between teachers and between schools become more normal; (iv) increased pressures on teachers to enlarge their classroom teaching and learning approaches, becoming knowledge brokers and mediators rather than "expert" content knowledge holders; and (v) teachers' negative response to changes.

In many contexts, teachers' work became characterised by 'ruptures rather than continuities' (Carlgren, 1999, p. 44). Issues such as standard-based models, evaluation and surveillance mechanisms, testing regimes, intensification and bureaucratisation, increased forms of managerialism, and greater accountability and public scrutiny are but a few examples of the changes in the teaching profession identified in the literature (Day, 1999; Day, Flores, & Viana, 2007; Helsby, 2000; Kelchtermans, 2009; Osborn, 2006). These trends have led to a decrease in teacher motivation and job satisfaction, to feelings of powerlessness (Estrela, 2001) and to an outcome-oriented view of teaching with implications for a decrease in teacher status (Gimeno, 1991; Imbernón, 1994). In other words, teachers' sense of professionalism and their identities have been affected in different ways including teachers' experience of their daily work at school as well as the public image of teachers and the teaching profession.

New and more demanding expectations were placed upon schools and teachers even if their working conditions, their education and professional learning opportunities, and the resources allocated to them have not been congruent with their needs and increased demands placed on them (Flores, 2012, 2016). A sense of fragmentation of teachers' work (Day, 1999; Day & Sachs, 2004; Hargreaves, 2001; Klette, 2000) and the emergence of 'clear unrealistic social pressure on teachers' (Estrela, 2001), and the 'hyper-responsibility' placed upon them for the quality of teaching (Gimeno, 1991) emerged.

In a study on the construction of professional identity conducted in Spain, Sancho-Gil, Correa, Giró, and Fraga (2014) pointed to the lack of career prospects, to poor working conditions and precarious jobs in teaching, low salaries and low morale. These authors concluded that policies have led to the deprofissionalisation of teaching associated with contradictions between the rhetoric of autonomy, responsibility and accountability, on the one hand, and prescription, external and internal bureaucratic control on the other hand. Issues such as isolation and lack of opportunities to undertake collaborative work also emerged.

In another study carried out in Portugal (n=2702 teachers), Flores and colleagues (2014) found that teacher motivation has decreased (61.6%) which was associated, amongst other features, with the increase of workload (96.7%); increase of bureaucracy in teaching (95.4%); an accentuation of criticism to teachers (92.2%); greater control over teachers' work (75.6%) and an increase of teachers' public accountability (74.6%). The participating teachers agreed that the deterioration of the teaching profession has been affected by the negative image of teaching and teachers in the media (90.0%). As mentioned by two participating teachers: "It is very difficult to define what being a teacher means nowadays" and "The love for teaching comes with a price". Issues such as low morale, deterioration of the working conditions, feelings of tiredness and giving up, lack of social recognition, etc. also emerged.

When asked about the most valued dimensions of their work, teachers identified collaborating with colleagues (63.4%); supporting students (58.7%); reflecting on one's own work (51.1%); planning teaching (49.1%) and continuous professional learning (45.1%) as the most important ones. The least valued dimensions were: performing administrative tasks (7.5%); involvement within the local community (14.5%); developing teamwork (18.7%), using ICT (19.7%) and participating in decision-making process (19.7%). In other words, teachers considered the pedagogical dimension of their work within the individual and collegial dimensions of professionalism as more important in detriment to managerial dimensions. Flores, Ferreira and Parente (2014) highlighted the key themes emerging from the study which was carried out in particular adverse times, namely during the intervention programme of the implementation of the Memorandum of Understanding with the International Monetary Fund, the European Central Bank and the European Commission (known as the Troika) (2011–2014). Amongst other themes were the intensification and bureaucratisation of teachers' work; the precarious job situations and impoverishment of teaching workforce; the lowering of teachers' status and their social image; the lack of career prospects; the climate of collaboration and sharing versus competitive individualism; and the tensions between disappointment and resignation from the part of the teachers on one hand, versus energy and resilience on the other hand (Flores, Ferreira, & Parente, 2014).

In the same study the classroom emerged as a space for autonomy and professional satisfaction which, in some cases, was associated with practices of collegial, supportive and collaborative professionalism. These made a difference for the teachers who, despite the disappointment and lack of motivation due to external factors such as policy initiatives (e.g. evaluation mechanisms, the merging of schools; reduction of school curriculum and changes in school governance) were able to be resilient and maintain hope in teaching (Flores, 2018a). These made decisions and choices between what is essential and nonessential in teaching, highlighting the ethics of care as well as the moral and social purposes of teaching. These teachers were led by their commitment to pupils, to their learning and well-being. This commitment was evident as they spoke of hope and resilience which were dependent upon personal, relational and organisational conditions, beliefs and professional values.

In a similar vein, a study conducted in Spain looked at how situations of adversity were reappraised by teachers in ways that allowed them to transit from states of suffering and despair to states of restored well-being and commitment (Clarà, 2017). Findings suggest that reappraisals involve important transformations at the deepest level of the appraisal but are driven by the desire to eliminate contradictions at the intermediate level.

In such demanding policy and school contexts it is possible to identify plural and, sometimes, contradictory understandings and practices of teacher professionalism. As Ben-Peretz and Flores (2018, p. 207) assert, "The nature and dynamic of teachers' interactions, their beliefs and professional values are to be considered to fully understand the ways in which they respond to the challenging and sometimes contradictory nature of their work". The interplay of these variables are key to look at professionalism in context and the ways in which teachers make use of their professional judgment. They might be situated within constrained professionalism as their autonomy in classroom contexts might be influenced by standardisation of curriculum and national exams (Willis & Haymore Sandholtz, 2009). Looking at the opportunities and threats in teaching, amongst other features, Hargreaves and Fullan (2012, p. 43) warned that it "can turn into hyperactive professionalism as teachers are thrown into hurried meetings to devise quick-fix solutions that will lead to instantaneous gains in student achievement results". In fact, teachers' decisions, professional judgment and expertise may be influenced by contextual pressures and time demands but they may make use of their professional space even in contexts marked by growing standardisation (Oolbekkink-Marchand et al., 2017).

It is possible, therefore, to identify the tensions and conditions which point to a managerial professionalism (Day & Sachs, 2004) led by top-down initiatives within a rather constrained professionalism (Wills & Haymore Sandholtz, 2009). 2009). This view suggests that teachers' autonomy is constrained by contextual factors such as intensification, standardisation of curriculum and national exams. It may also be associated with the identification of a set of skills and competencies that focus on what teachers must be capable of doing (overlooking dimensions such as on how they think) leading to a "performative professionalism" (Evans, 2011, p. 861) within a reductionist view of the role of the teacher aligned with a narrow view of school curriculum. Yet, it is also possible to identify situations or contexts in which more interactive and collaborative professionalism (Fullan, 2017) can be found: more positive (and proactive) vision of teacher professionalism in which teachers' sense of agency and their moral purposes in improving the quality of education provided for pupils and young people are key features. In this regard teacher education plays a key role.

Initial Teacher Education: The Challenges of Innovation

Unemployment in teaching, difficulties in recruiting teacher candidates, changes in the preparation of teachers as a result of the implementation of the Bologna process are issues that have an impact upon initial teacher education (ITE). Existing international literature points to a number of convergences and divergences in ITE curriculum, linked, for instance, to the place of practicum, to the role of the foundational studies, to the partnership between universities and schools and to the role of research (Flores, 2016; Al-Barwani, Flores, & Imig, 2018). Issues such as the diversity of ITE curriculum both in its content and form; different forms of government intervention; and fragmentation versus integration of different components are but a few examples identified in international literature (Flores, 2016). In a recent review of 40 years of publications in the European Journal of Teacher Education, Livingston and Flores (2017) stress:

> a language shift from teacher training to teacher education alongside philosophical and political shifts in beliefs about the role of teachers in the twenty-first century. This includes shifts in expectations about the contribution education makes to the economy and society and what contribution teachers make to improving student learning. (p. 555)

Developing a Research Culture in Settings Marked by a Technical and Individualistic Perspective

Over the last decades ITE in Portugal and Spain evolved greatly but it still needs improvement especially if one takes into account the challenges and demands of the digital era. In Portugal, the 1970's were marked by a growing focus on ITE with the creation of the so-called "new universities" aimed at educating teachers for the school system. In the following decades, the professionalisation of practicing teachers was emphasised since many teachers were recruited as a result of the expansion of the school system. In 1992 the In-service and Training of Teachers (INSET) was institutionalised and made compulsory for all teachers for improving teaching and innovation in schools and also for career progression purposes. In the late 2000's ITE was again the major focus as a result of the implementation of the Bologna process. It involved the creation of Master degrees in Teaching in accordance with the Decree-Law No. 43/2007, published after the Decree-Law 74/2006, which regulates the organisation of study cycles in higher education in general. Thus, to become a teacher in Portugal now requires a Master level (from pre-school to secondary education). Before 2007, teacher qualifications were obtained in two types of undergraduate programmes: five-year *integrated* programmes which included content knowledge training, educational training, and the practicum in the final year, and *sequential* programmes where students could engage in teacher training for one or two years, after completing three years of subject-related education. As Flores, Vieira, Silva, and Almeida (2016, p. 111) state, "National and institutional policies did not prescribe any particular approach to teacher education and supervision, and a theory-to-practice understanding of professional learning was generally assumed in the practicum".

The main structural change in ITE after the implementation of the Bologna process was, therefore, the replacement of the former four to five-year undergraduate teaching degrees by a consecutive model: a three-year undergraduate degree in a given subject (e.g., Mathematics) followed by a two-year professional master degree in teaching. This entailed substantial curricular changes, which involved discussions about the nature of teaching as a profession and the kinds of teachers that are to be educated within the context of school curricula and challenges in the Portuguese society (Flores, 2011). According to the current legal framework (Decree-Law No. 79/2014, 14 May), master programmes have 90 or 120 credits and must integrate five curricular components: subject knowledge, general education, specific didactics, initiation to professional practice, and ethical, social and cultural education. For each component except for the last one, a minimum of credits is established, and initiation to professional practice is the component with most credits.

Challenges and demands to be met during the process of designing the new master degrees curricula included tensions related to study plans and to teacher education assumptions, profiles, goals, contents, strategies and outcomes (Vieira, Flores, Silva, & Almeida, 2018). Thus, reaching consensus on the proposals to be sent for external assessment and accreditation of the programmes demanded a collective effort under time pressure, within a rather individualistic work culture (Vieira et al., 2018). In other words, there was a need to manage dilemmas and challenges in teacher education and to making the best of difficult circumstances in post-Bologna context. Different paces and ways of operating were in place in diverse institutions. At the University of Minho, the practicum model of ITE aims at linking teaching and research, theory and practice. A key challenge in restructuring ITE, for instance at the University of Minho, related to the integration of inquiry into the practicum. This was seen as an opportunity to enhance the transformative potential of ITE, but it implied "to design a model for the practicum within a tradition of practicum without a model" (Vieira et al., 2013, p. 2642). The Flores, Vieira, Silva and Almeida's study (2016), based on data collected through a survey questionnaire and focus group interviews to practicum participants, as well as on the analysis of a *corpus* of student teachers' practicum reports, shows that the emergence of an inquiry-based culture in the practicum was both innovative and controversial, including tensions and challenges to the visions of teacher education, as well as (mis)matches between curriculum rhetoric and implementation. The authors point to the need to develop a scholarship of teacher education whereby ITE programmes are investigated and improved on the basis of negotiated understandings, particularly with regard to research and teaching nexus. The reflective component of the model is oriented towards student teacher professional development under a democratic view of education. Integrating teaching and research and promoting teaching practice as a space of transformation rather than a process of adaptation or of application of theory may contribute to knowledge mobilisation and research-informed practice (Flores, 2018b). In a similar vein, Martins, Costa and Onofre's study, in Portugal (2015) argue for the role of the practicum in teacher education programmes and the importance of educating supervisors in the implementation and management of the training experience, thus contributing to student teachers' self-efficacy development.

Recently, key features of the new model of teacher education have been discussed in the literature including the need to reconsider its curriculum to respond to the increasing uncertainties and complexities of teaching in the 21st century (Flores, 2018b), especially at a time when more pressure and demands are placed schools and teachers in contexts marked by growing accountability and greater multiculturalism (Ben-Peretz & Flores, 2018). In particular, Flores (2018b) advocates for the development of a more consistent research-based programme which would be better achieved within the context of an Integrated Master degree of Teaching (i.e. a 5-year degree). This kind of model would make it possible for the development of professional knowledge in its various components, as it would articulate both subject knowledge and educational sciences as well as teaching practice in a more integrated and solid way. In her view, the consecutive model entails both structural and institutional constraints that make the gradual contact with the practice and the engagement with research in a more combined and integrated way more difficult (especially for teaching in upper and lower secondary education). She concludes that an integrated master degree model, apart from enhancing the teaching profession, would create the conditions for the development of a more solid professional identity of the student teacher.

The process of change is always complex and demands time, and change in teacher education has proven to be challenging due to all the variables, contexts and agents involved. As Vieira, Flores, Silva and Almeida (2018, p. 53) stress when reporting the restructuring process of a teacher education programme in Portugal, the process of change involves dealing with resistance, tensions and dilemmas, and outcomes are never as progressive as they might be, namely because tradition and innovation are difficult to reconcile within organisational cultures that tend to be conservative, and where divergent interests and power imbalances often undermine democratic debate and the resolution of problems.

Moving towards Professionalization within a Prescribed and Fragmented Culture

ITE has been identified as one of the key elements in driving change in education (Marcelo, 1994). It has been seen in many contexts paradoxically as essential and irrelevant at the same time (Sancho-Gil, 2014). In fact, internationally, ITE is sometimes described as the panacea to improve education, and teaching and learning in schools, but at the same time it has been subjected to criticisms which call into question its quality and effectiveness in preparing high quality teachers for the 21st century (Flores, 2016).

In a recent paper, Sancho-Gil, Sánchez-Valero, and Domingo-Coscollola (2017), drawn from two research projects carried out in Spain, identified three phases in ITE for primary education. In the last decades, according to the authors ITE in Spain has experienced a significant improvement. It went from a rather artisanal and ideological model towards a more academic and professional one during the three phases: (i) developmentalism and the last stage of Franco's dictatorship; (ii) constructing democracy; and (iii) the implementation of the European Higher Education Area. The reform implemented in each period represents for the authors a clear intention to professionalize teachers' work, to go beyond the idea of a vocational training transferring it completely to the university. However, the prescribed curricula maintain a discipline-based and a compartmentalised notion of knowledge that makes it difficult for student teachers to foresee and be prepared to face the complex challenges of education (Sancho-Gil, Sánchez-Valero, & Domingo-Coscollola, 2017).

Added to this is the idea that ITE is not enough as teachers need to continue to learn and develop throughout their professional lives (Sancho-Gil, Correa, Giró, & Fraga, 2014). In a study carried out in ITE for primary education in Spain, Sancho-Gil (2014) explored a number of issues identified by those who completed it: lack of quality; lack of adequacy of the training sessions; difficulties associated with promoting learning opportunities; lack of preparation for the profession; outdated practices. The lack of pedagogical frameworks to guide teaching practice in ITE and in schools has been also identified (Sancho-Gil, Correa, Giró, & Fraga, 2014). This study showed that new teachers find it difficult to associate pedagogical ideas learned at university and their practice with pedagogical thinking and theories. Similar results were found by Clemente and Ramírez (2008, p. 1256) in the Spanish context. They identified the distance between the language of theory and that of practice: "Knowing how to do it (procedural representations) and knowing how to say it (declarative representations) are cognitively different systems, (although they do not necessarily have to work independently)".

In a similar vein, Santiago, Guarro, and Begoña (2015), drawing upon empirical research, highlight the procedural logic of content approach in teacher education within a restricted and technical rationality. The same study show that classroom observation, analysis and collaborative reflection on the practice were the least valued activities identified by the participating teachers. Similar results were found by Trillo, Rubal, and Nieto (2015) which point to a model of training based on individual consumerism of knowledge in detriment to a collaborative and institutional logic linked to the creation of knowledge.

The need to revisit models of teacher education and the importance of fostering opportunities to reflect on learning in ITE and on learning how to teach (Sancho-Gil, Sánchez-Valero, & Domingo-Coscollola, 2017) are important features that deserve further consideration. There has been research in Spain and elsewhere on issues related to reflection in and on teacher education, for instance, through the use of portfolios and other reflexive tools (Belvis, Pineda, Armengol, & Moreno, 2013; Cáceres, Chamoso, & Azcárate, 2010; Chamoso & Cáceres, 2009; Chamoso, Cáceres, & Azcárate, 2012; Mauri, Clarà, Colomina, & Onrubia, 2017; Mena-Marcos, García-Rodríguez, & Tillema, 2013), on the process of identity formation (Correa, Martínez-Arbelaiz, & Aberasturi-Apraiz, 2015; Sancho-Gil, Correa, Giró, & Fraga, 2014) and on the role and practice of teacher educators (Wassell, Kerrigan, & Fernandez, 2018). For instance, Mauri, Clarà, Colomina, and Onrubia (2017) found that what is learned in teacher education tends to be implemented in the classroom, but it is done in an isolated manner, i.e, individually and without becoming a part of the culture of the school. The same study suggest that there is a relationship between interaction patterns of joint reflection and progress in students' individual reflection. Also, Mena-Marcos, García-Rodríguez, and Tillema (2013)'s study concluded that a relationship was found between producing high levels of knowledge and precision of reflective statements. The authors argue that while deliberate reflection can support the construction of professional knowledge, this only rarely occurs.

The above-cited research pointed to future directions but also highlighted the need for a more systemic and broader understanding of ITE, one which articulates in a more consistent and clear way policy, practice and research, universities and schools as well as teacher educators, teachers, mentors, student teachers and school principals work together. As Ling (2017, p. 562) suggests, looking at teacher education entails "an iterative process rather than a linear one and needs to be backwards, forwards, inside-out and outside-in somewhat simultaneously, because it is complex, recursive and has multiple layers". She warns that there is a need to account for the "broader issues faced within a supercomplex, twenty first century knowledge society, where the future is not only unknown but unknowable, and where the frameworks by which we make sense of our world are moving, blurring and shifting as well as being highly contested and contestable".

Final Thoughts

Teaching as a profession has been facing demanding challenges in the Iberian context, particularly over the last decade during which austerity measures and policy initiatives have greatly impacted upon schools and teachers' work. Unemployment in the education sector, precarious jobs, lack of career prospects, low socio-economic status, poor working conditions along with the prevalence of an outcome-led orientation to teaching are but a few examples of key features of being a teacher in Portugal and Spain. Along with this are the challenges in ITE. In addition, issues such as teacher surplus, difficulties for new teachers to find jobs in teaching, difficulties in recruiting student teachers as well as the challenges resulting from the implementation of the Bologna process both in terms of curriculum content and form have been identified.

Teaching is at the crossroads in the Iberian context. It has been facing a number of demands, tensions and paradoxes that entail the discussion about the old and new professionalisms (Estrela, 2014). In some cases it may represent progress, but in other cases it may mean drawbacks. Nevertheless, it is still a hot potato that needs to be addressed. Or, to put it differently, as Estrela (2014, p. 8) stresses:

> research about teacher professionality and professionalism is still in its infancy. We still know little about how teachers define their professionality and professionalism, how they live in their day-to-day situations, how their professional identity is shaped by that definition, what kinds of threats they feel that might challenge it, what kinds of ethical conflicts they live related to the different roles they perform at school, what is the role of reasoning and emotion in their perception and resolution ...

As such, teacher professionalism is a dynamic, contested, and contextualised concept that needs to be understood in context and beyond the normative view. Contradictory trends may be identified in the ways in which teacher professionalism has been defined as well as in real conditions of teachers' work in schools and classrooms. Drawing upon research findings (Flores, in press) identify a number of key issues such as the view of teachers as leaders of learning and its core dimensions, namely motivation, resilience, innovation of practice and committed professionalism.

In a paper on teacher professionalism, Sachs (2016) asks why we are still talking about it and she identifies the factors that are still influencing and shaping the teaching profession. She argues that different times require different responses and that current thinking and debates around teacher professionalism circulate around professional learning. Sachs (2016) advocates that the time for an industrial approach to the teaching profession has passed and she makes the case for systems, schools and teachers to be more research active with teachers' practices validated and supported through research. In a similar vein, Estrela (2014) warns that teaching may be seen as a risky profession, or may be a profession at risk or finding itself in the process of reprofessionalisation. There might be different answers in different contexts and different ways.

Ben-Peretz and Flores (2018) assert that a number of tensions and paradoxes have been marking teaching with implications for teacher education. They highlight the obligation to prepare teachers for diverse student populations, living in a highly varied context which creates several competing expectations of the meaning of teacher education, for instance, preparing for professional autonomy in a world of externally imposed educational policy, along with the tension between achieving immediate results and success in external exams versus the need to prepare students in an era of migration and growing multiculturalism in school contexts.

Despite the developments in this field in both countries, education, and particularly ITE, remains a hot topic that deserves further reflection. Teacher education needs to address the question of what it means to be a teacher in the digital era and on the development of teacher professional identity if it is to be seen as seriously seeking to make a difference through the lens of teachers as professionals with a view of teacher education as a space of transformation (Flores, 2016). In this section I highlight some key features that in my view are necessary to improve the education of teachers and, consequently, the education of children and young people.

– *Make teaching a more attractive and rewarding profession.* Teaching is far too important for society to ignore the necessary recognition of the professionals who invest their "best-loved self" (Craig, 2013) to educate children and young people. A clear political investment in teachers is mandatory so that to ensure and enhance their social and economic status which might

imply the definition of key priorities when it comes to make decisions about resources and budget to be allocated to the education sector;
- *Invest in more rigorous criteria and modes for selecting and recruiting teachers.* Again, teachers are far too important in society in this digital era in which their role has become even more crucial. Thus, there is a need to examine who can be a teacher or who should become a teacher. Children and young people are entitled to be taught by good teachers; this cannot be left to chance. Thus, a political initiative as well as an institutional concern related to recruiting and selecting the best candidates must be seen as a priority. We are in the enviable position with current aging of the teaching workforce. We need to focus on investing on the education and recruitment of quality teachers. As one of the teachers participating in one of my research project said, "Being a teacher is not for everyone".
- *Define clear standards or frames of reference for teacher education.* A teacher is required to possess a solid pedagogical and scientific knowledge of the subject to be taught. But this is not sufficient. The mastery of multiple literacies (e.g. digital, emotional, informational, research) is also important as it is the cultural dimension which is more and more relevant at a time when the technological revolution presents to schools and classrooms more complex challenges and demands. In addition, being a teacher also requires a strong ethical and social dimension for making the best decisions for the benefit of the children and young people. Teachers' attitudes and behaviour need to be marked by a clear ethical commitment to pupils' learning and well-being.
- *Be attentive to the educators of teachers.* If teachers are very important to society, teacher educators also play a key role. Who educates the teachers and who should educate them? In this regard it is crucial to look at issues of selection and recruitment of teacher educators and the importance of addressing their needs in terms of professional learning and development. It is also essential to focus on their professional identity and their practices of learning how to teach and how to learn how to become a teacher. In other words, besides looking at their processes and practices as teacher educators it is also necessary to focus on their beliefs, professional knowledge, professional values and ethical dimension.

The challenges and future directions to teaching and teacher education are open to debate and reflection. These must involve all the stakeholders. The learners must be put at the centre of the debate – not at a rhetoric level but a genuine concern with the children and young people. The demands are enormous and the future is uncertain. But teaching and teachers will always be needed even if within new frameworks and contexts that might be still unknown. As Ling (2017, p. 570) states,

Rather than lamenting the fact that the role of teacher education and indeed of the University in a world of supercomplexity is now radically changed, it is perhaps even more exciting to be a part of this era as it has unbounded possibilities, unknown unknowns, space for risk and experimentation, permission to be uncertain and insecure, and contains the awkward spaces in which we can find some of those unknown unknowns.

Change is a slow process, particularly in Education and in teacher education, where there has been a gap between discourse and practice. Maybe it is important to question or rethink our perspectives. Maybe we as teacher educators, researchers and academics need to talk about it in a more open and explicit, researching these topics in different manners and work with other stakeholders in more engaging and explicit ways. Challenging the status quo is a critical issue and therefore there is a need to go beyond the more apparent and taken-for-granted (and sometimes overused) assumptions. I would argue that as teacher educators and as researchers in the field of education we may need to look at teaching and teacher education from different perspectives or from different angles in order to go a step further and to see what lies underneath our practices and understandings. This may entail a process of unveiling whose voice is heard in education and in teacher education and what we can do about it. This may imply the need to deconstruct discourses and practices that have been prevalent in education, including our own.

Acknowledgements

This chapter draws on the keynote address given at the 17th Biennial Conference of the International Study Association on Teachers and Teaching (ISATT), held in Salamanca, Spain, in July 2017. For this reason the colloquial tone is kept in the text. I would like to thank the conference organisers for the invitation, particularly the chair of the conference, Juanjo Mena-Marcos.

References

Al Barwani, T., Flores, M. A., & Imig, D. (Eds.). (2018). *Leading change in teacher education. Lessons from countries and education leaders around the globe.* Milton Park: Routledge.

Belvis, E., Pineda, P., Armengol, C., & Moreno, V. (2013). Evaluation of reflective practice in teacher education. *European Journal of Teacher Education, 36*(3), 279–292.

Ben-Peretz, M., & Flores, M. A. (2018). Tensions and paradoxes in teaching: Implications for teacher education. *European Journal of Teacher Education, 41*(2), 202–213.

Cáceres, M. J., Chamoso, J. M., & Azcárate, P. (2010). Analysis of the revisions that preservice teachers of mathematics make of their own project included in their learning portfolio. *Teaching and Teacher Education, 26*, 1186–1195.

Carlgren, I. (1999). Professionalism and teachers as designers. *Journal of Curriculum Studies, 31*(1), 43–56.

Chamoso, J. M., & Cáceres, M. J. (2009). Analysis of the reflections of student-teachers of mathematics when working with learning portfolios in Spanish university classrooms. *Teaching and Teacher Education, 25*, 198–206.

Chamoso, J. M., Cáceres, M. J., & Azcárate, P. (2012). Reflection on the teaching-learning process in the initial training of teachers. Characterization of the issues on which preservice mathematics teachers reflect. *Teaching and Teacher Education, 28*, 154–164.

Clarà, M. (2017). Teacher resilience and meaning transformation: How teachers reappraise situations of adversity. *Teaching and Teacher Education, 63*, 82–91.

Clemente, M., & Ramírez, H. (2008). How teachers express their knowledge through narrative. *Teaching and Teacher Education, 24*, 1244–1258.

Correa, J. M., Martínez-Arbelaiz, A., & Aberasturi-Apraiz, E. (2015). Post-modern reality shock: Beginning teachers as sojourners in communities of practice. *Teaching and Teacher Education, 48*, 66–74.

Craig, C. (2013). Teacher education and the best-loved self. *Asia Pacific Journal of Education, 33*(3), 261–272.

Day, C. (1999). *Developing teachers. The challenges of lifelong learning.* London: Falmer Press.

Day, C., Flores, M. A., & Viana, I. (2007). Effects of national policies on teachers' sense of professionalism: Findings from an empirical study in Portugal and in England. *European Journal of Teacher Education, 30*(3), 249–266.

Day, C., & Sachs, J. (2004). Professionalism, performativity and empowerment: Discourses in the politics, policies and purposes of continuing professional development. In C. Day & J. Sachs (Eds.), *International handbook on the continuing professional development of teachers* (pp. 3–32). Maindenhead: Open University.

Direção-Geral de Estatísticas da Educação e Ciência (DGEEC). (2018). *Perfil do Docente 2016/2017.* Lisboa: DGEEC.

Estrela, M. T. (2001). Questões de Profissionalidade e Profissionalismo Docente. In M. Teixeira (Ed.), *Ser Professor no Limiar do Século XXI* (pp. 113–142). Porto: ISET.

Estrela, M. T. (2014). Velhas e novas profissionalidades, velhos e novos profissionalismos: tensões, paradoxos, progressos e retrocessos. *Investigar em Educação, IIª Série, 2*, 5–30.

Evans, L. (2011). The 'shape' of teacher professionalism in England: Professional standards, performance management, professional development and the changes proposed in the 2010 White Paper. *British Educational Research Journal, 37*(5), 851–870.

Flores, M. A. (2011). Curriculum of initial teacher education in Portugal: New contexts, old problems. *Journal of Education for Teaching, 37*(4), 461–70.

Flores, M. A. (2012). Teachers' work and lives: A European perspective. In C. Day (Ed.), *The Routledge international handbook of teacher and school development* (pp. 94–107). London: Routledge.

Flores, M. A. (Coord.). (2014). *Profissionalismo e liderança dos professores*. Santo Tirso: De Facto Editores.

Flores, M. A. (2016). Teacher education curriculum. In. J. Loughran & M. L. Hamilton (Eds.), *International handbook of teacher education* (pp. 187–230). Dordrecht: Springer Press.

Flores, M. A. (2018a). Teacher resilience in adverse contexts: Issues of professionalism and professional identity. In M. Wosnitza, F. Peixoto, S. Beltman, & C. F. Mansfield (Eds.), *Resilience in education concepts, contexts and connections* (pp. 167–184). Cham: Springer.

Flores, M. A. (2018b). Linking teaching and research in initial teacher education: Knowledge mobilisation and research-informed practice. *Journal of Education for Teaching, 44*(5), 621–636.

Flores, M. A., & Ferreira, F. I. (2016). Education and child poverty in times of austerity in Portugal: Implications for teachers and teacher education. *Journal of Education for Teaching, 42*(4), 404–416.

Flores, M. A., Ferreira, F. I., & Parente, C. (2014). Conclusões e Recomendações. In M. A. Flores (Ed.), *Profissionalismo e Liderança dos Professores* (pp. 217–236). Santo Tirso: De Facto Editores.

Flores, M. A., Vieira, F., Silva, J. L., & Almeida, J. (2016). Integrating research into the practicum: Inquiring into inquiry-based professional development in post-Bologna initial teacher education in Portugal. In M. A. Flores & T. Al-Barwani (Eds.), *Redefining teacher education for the post-2015 era: Global challenges and best practice* (pp.109–124). New York, NY: Nova Publisher.

Fullan, M. (2017, January 7–10). *The deeper meaning of deep learning*. Keynote address given at the International Congress for School Effectiveness and Improvement, Ottawa, Canada.

Gimeno, J. (1991). Consciência e Acção sobre a Prática como Libertação Profissional dos Professores. In A. Nóvoa (Ed.), *Profissão Professor* (pp. 61–92). Porto: Porto Editora.

Hargreaves, A. (2001). Teaching as a Paradoxical profession: Implications for professional development. In P. Xochellis & Z. Papanaoum (Eds.), *Continuing teacher education and school development (Symposium Proceedings)* (pp. 26–38). Thessaloniki: Department of Education, School of Philosohy AUTH.

Hargreaves, A., & Fullan, M. (2012). *Professional capital: Transforming teaching in every school*. New York, NY: Teachers College Press.

Heitor, M., Horta, H., Dopazo, C., & Fueyo, N. (2016). Iberia thirty years after Saramago's Stone Raft: Opportunities for technical change and challenges for science and technology policy under increasing uncertainty. *Technological Forecasting & Social Change, 113*, 129–145.

Helsby, G. (2000). Multiple truths and contested realities. The changing faces of teacher professionalism in England. In C. Day, A. Fernandez, T. E. Hauge, & J. Moller (Eds.), *The life and work of teachers. International perspectives in changing times* (pp. 93–108). London: Falmer Press.

Imbernón, F. (1994). *La Formación y el Desarrollo Profesional del Profesorado. Hacia una Nuvea Cultura Profesional*. Barcelona: Editorial Graó.

Kelchtermans, G. (2009). O comprometimento profissional para além do contrato: Auto-comprensão, vulnerabilidade e reflexão dos professores, In M. A. Flores & A. M. Veiga Simão (Eds.), *Aprendizagem e desenvolvimento profissional de professores: contextos e perspectivas* (pp. 61–98). Mangualde: Edições Pedago.

Klette, K. (2000). Working-time blues. How norwegian teachers experience restructuring in education. In C. Day, A. Fernandez, T. E. Hauge, & J. Moller (Eds), *The life and work of teachers. International perspectives in changing times* (pp. 146–158). London: Falmer Press.

Kompf, M., & Rust, F. O'. (2013). The International Study Association on Teachers and Teaching (ISATT): Seeing tracks and making more. In C. Craig, P. Meijer, & J. Broekemans (Eds.), *From teacher thinking to teachers and teaching: The evolution of a research community advances in research on teaching* (Vol. 19., pp. 3–37). New York, NY: Emerald Publishers.

Ling, L. M. (2017). Australian teacher education: Inside-out, outside-in, backwards and forwards? *European Journal of Teacher Education, 40*(5), 561–571.

Livingston, K., & Flores, M. A. (2017). Editorial. Trends in teacher education: A review of papers published in the European journal of teacher education over 40 years. *European Journal of Teacher Education, 40*(5), 551–560.

Madalińska-Michalak, J., O'Doherty, T., & Flores, M. A. (2018). Editorial. Teachers and teacher education in uncertain times. *European Journal of Teacher Education, 41*(5), 567–571.

Marcelo, C. (1994). *Formación del profesorado para el cambio educativo*. Barcelona: PPU.

Martins, M., Costa, J., & Onofre, M. (2015). Practicum experiences as sources of preservice teachers' self-efficacy. *European Journal of Teacher Education, 38*(29), 263–279.

Mauri, T., Clarà, M., Colomina, R., & Onrubia, J. (2017). Patterns of interaction in the processes of joint reflection by student teachers. *Journal of Education for Teaching, 43*(4), 427–443.

Mena-Marcos, J., García-Rodríguez, M.-L., & Tillema, H. (2013). Student teacher reflective writing: What does it reveal? *European Journal of Teacher Education, 36*(2), 147–163.

Oolbekkink-Marchand, H. W., Hadar, L.L., Smith, K., & Helleve, I. (2017). Teachers' perceived professional space and their agency. *Teaching and Teacher Education, 62*, 37–46.

Osborn, M. (2006). Changing the context of teachers' work and professional development: A European perspective. *International Journal of Educational Research, 45*, 242–253.

Sachs, J. (2016). Teacher professionalism: Why are we still talking about it? *Teachers and Teaching Theory and Practice, 22*(4), 413–425.

Sancho-Gil, J., Sánchez-Valero, J.-A., & Domingo-Coscollola, M. (2017). Research-based insights on initial teacher education in Spain. *European Journal of Teacher Education, 40*(3), 310–325.

Sancho-Gil, J. (2014). Fundamental e irrelevante: Las paradojas de la formación inicial del professorado. In M. A. Flores & C. Coutinho (Eds.), *Formação e Trabalho Docente: Diversidade e Convergências* (pp. 17–34). Santo Tirso: De Facto Editores.

Sancho-Gil, J. M., Correa, J. M., Giró, X., & Fraga, L. (Coord.). (2014). *Aprender a ser docente en un mundo en cambio. Simposio internacional.* Barcelona: Dipòsit Digital de la Universitat de Barcelona. http://hdl.handle.net/2445/50680

Santiago, J., Guarro, A., & Begoña, M. (2015). Descripción, análisis y valoración de las políticas de formación del profesorado en la Comunidad Autónoma de Canarias. In M. A. Flores & F. I. Ferreira (Eds.), *Formação e trabalho docente. Projetos, políticas e práticas* (pp). Santo Tirso: De Facto Editores.

Trillo, F., Rubal, X., & Nieto, J. M. (2015). La formación docente continuada en Galicia: políticas y perspectivas del profesorado de educación obligatoria. In M. A. Flores & F. I. Ferreira (Eds.), *Formação e trabalho docente. Projetos, políticas e práticas* (pp). Santo Tirso: De Facto Editores.

Vieira, F., Flores, M. A., Silva, J. L., & Almeida, J. (2018). Understanding and enhancing change in post-Bologna pre-service teacher education: Lessons from experience and research in Portugal. In T. Al Barwani, M. A. Flores, & D. Imig (Eds.), *Leading change in teacher education. Lessons from countries and education leaders around the globe* (pp.41–57). Milton Park: Routledge.

Vieira, F., Silva, J. L., Vilaça, T., Parente, C., Vieira, F., Almeida, M. J., Pereira, I., Solé, G., Varela, P., Gomes, A., & Silva, A. (2013). O papel da investigação na prática pedagógica dos mestrados em ensino. In B. Silva et al. (Eds.), *Atas do XII Congresso Internacional Galego-Português de Psicopedagogia* (pp. 2641–2655). Braga: Universidade do Minho.

Wassell, B. A., Kerrigan, M. R., & Fernández Hawrylak, M. (2018). Teacher educators in a changing Spain: Examining beliefs about diversity in teacher preparation. *Teaching and Teacher Education, 69*, 223–233.

Wills, J. S., & Haymore Sandholtz, J. (2009). Constrained professionalism: Dilemmas of teaching in the face of test based accountability. *Teachers College Record, 111*(4), 1065–1114.

CHAPTER 4

The Mediate(zati)on of Philosophy Subject Matter: A Comparative Case Study

Laura Sara Agrati

Abstract

In order to improve student learning, the teacher's mediation function works as 'integration' of subject matter. Referring to the theoretical model of 'pedagogical (and technological) content knowledge' and the construction of 'mediation', the study addresses the process of integration and transformation that undergoes the school subject matter through the mediation devices used by the teacher.

The contribution presents the research design and first results of an exploratory study accomplished at University of Bari 'Aldo Moro' in a High school. The research is inspired by the 'collaborative' approach and uses a multiple-cases design through an in-depth study on mediation procedures of two philosophy teachers about same content knowledge – G. B. Vico's difference between philology and philosophy.

The analysis refers to specific levels of the teacher practice: the integration of the school books and worksheet with other resources (personal notes, digital repository etc.) using the document analysis; the choice of mediators (active, iconic, symbolic, real or virtual) using the video observation and in-depth interview.

First findings are highlighting aspects concerning the dynamic of visual representation as support of students' learning and the epistemic function of the teacher's meta-representative competence: as, for example, the use of the criterion of *completeness* (not of *simplicity*) in the elaboration of explanatory images to be used in class.

These findings will be useful to the operational definition of the unit of analysis in subsequent study to be conducted on a broader investigation basis and on different learning contents.

Keywords

didactic mediation – PCK – case-study – semiotic

Introduction: The Didactic Mediati(zati)on Process

'Mediation' is a trans-disciplinary concept that refers the primary disposition of person toward the world (Damiano, 2007, p. 25). According the evolutionary science, mediation would be inherent the human being because of his immaturity and incompleteness (Bolk, 1926). On the metaphysical level, the philosopher C.S. Peirce considers 'mediation' as the only authentic way in which the subject comes into contact with reality.

From an educational point of view, mediation takes on two meanings: (a) the indirect relationship (Vygotsky, 1934) that the child has with the things of life and that starting the conceptual elaborations (Laurillard, 1993); (b) the process of socialization that takes place first in the family (Levi-Strauss, 1949) then at school (Petitat, 1982) and provide the child with cultural tools and social rules in order to live.

From the point of view of the teaching sciences, in the socio-constructivist perspective (Altet, 1997; Latour, 1989), the mediation process is understood as the set of all strategies that the teacher uses to promote student learning (Damiano, 2013, p. 25; Xipas, Fabre, & Hétier, 2011), not only at the communicative and relational level (Feuerstein, 1999) but also cognitive – as 'integration' (Cochran, 1997) of the subject matter.

From this perspective, the *teacher* (T) realizes the mediation process when he/she provides *students* (St) with a system of *devices* (Md) that fosters their learning and interaction with *cultural objects* (Co) (Figure 4.1).

The whole process of mediation is characterized by mutual relations (Figure 4.1): each item (teacher, student, mediation devices, cultural objects) affects the others and would be in turn influenced, in a dynamic system. The double directional arrows meant that teacher and student modify mediator devices but also that themselves are modified by the use of mediator devices.

Analyzing more in depth:
- the teaching intervention is influenced by the characteristics of the student, the cultural object and the type of mediation device (Md);
- the student in learning is influenced by the action of teaching, by the cultural object and by the chosen mediation device;
- the cultural object (as a 'learning object') is transformed by the teacher and the student, as well as by the mediation device in use;
- finally, the mediation devices are chosen based on the characteristics of the teacher, the student and the cultural object to mediate.

This process, already sophisticated and multiple (Houssaye, 1988), becomes even more complex at the level of "mediatization" (Rézoul, 2002, 2004), understood as the mediation through the use of technologies.

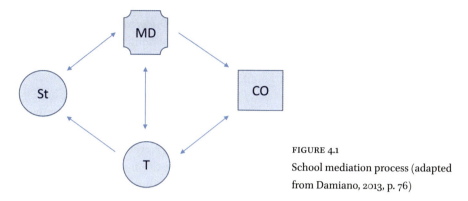

FIGURE 4.1
School mediation process (adapted from Damiano, 2013, p. 76)

The term "mediation", in general, refers to all the changes that the communication process undergoes when it occurs through technological mediation (Lundby, 2009; Hepp & Krotz, 2014).

Specifically, in didactic research (Rézoul, 2002) it refers to the descriptive model of teaching-learning processes through technological means and digital resources.

As Damiano explains, "the first result of this 'complexification' is the attribution of more or less autonomous tasks to didactic artifacts, which come to exercise the function of true teachers" (Damiano, 2013, p. 160). Even more explicitly, Hepp (2012) talks about the "molding force" of technological mediators with respect to teaching: they are not limited to clarifying the teaching contents but reinventing them.

Theoretical Framework

The study aims to deepen the mediation process activated by the secondary-school philosophy teachers, specifically the dynamic (Figure 4.1) between teacher (T), mediation devices (Md) and cultural objects (Oc). It is mainly inspired by Shulman's theoretical model of Pedagogical Content Knowledge (PCK) (Shulman, 1986; 1987) – extended by the Technological Pedagogical Content Knowledge (TPCK) of P. Mishra and M.J. Koehler's (2006, 2007; Koehler & Mishra, 2008) – and the two concept of 'integration' (Cochran, 1997) and 'meta-representation' (Eiliam, 2012; Eiliam & Gilberti, 2014; Mayer, 2001, 2005).

In this background, are asked questions as: 'which types of diagrams are appropriate for what teaching goals? (…) How use of diagrams can facilitate education in all subjects (and in philosophy, specifically)? When and how and to what extent should we use diagrams in a textbook or a classroom presentation?' (Blackwell & Engelhardt, 2002, p. 58).

Pedagogical (and Technological) Content Knowledge

The Pedagogical Content Knowledge (PCK) model of Shulman (1986) is useful as a reading/analysis tool of the mediation process because it clarifies the concept of 'content knowledge'[2] and, in it, distinguishes among:

1. *Subject matter content knowledge*: different structures of content knowledge that refers to concepts and specific domains (as Schwab's 'discipline', 1978);
2. *Pedagogical content knowledge*: subject matter content knowledge *for teaching*[3], such as 'the forms of representation of ideas, the most powerful analogies, illustrations, examples, explanations (...) the way of representing and formulating the subject that make it comprehensible to others' (Shulman, 1986, p. 9);
3. *Curricular knowledge*: 'the full range of programs for teaching of particular subject and topics at a given level' (p. 10) – as 'materia'.

The PCK has been defined as a 'type of knowledge that is unique to teachers, and is based on the manner in which the teachers relate their pedagogical knowledge (what they know about teaching) to their subject matter knowledge (what they know about what they teach)' (Cochran, 1997, p. 13): the 'integration' of teachers' pedagogical knowledge and their subject matter knowledge that comprises pedagogical content knowledge. Cochran (1997) highlights the 'personal representation' inherent the construct of 'pedagogical content knowledge' that – citing Gudmunsdottir (1987) – differentiate the teacher from the scholar: 'pedagogical content knowledge is a form of knowledge that makes science teachers teachers (...). Teachers differ from scientists, not necessarily in the quality or quantity of their subject matter knowledge, but in how that knowledge is organized and used' (Cochran, 1997, p. 78; Cochran, Druiter, King, 1993).

The Technological Pedagogical Content Knowledge (TPCK) is a conceptual model that describes the knowledge and the skills held by the teachers and to which they resort in practice when they use technological mediators. TPCK as an extension of PCK, was the first interpretation offered in the literature (Voogt et al., 2012), based on the conceptual distinction between the specific knowledge of the teacher (personal knowledge), the knowledge of the disciplinary area (content knowledge) and the knowledge regarding how to translate into an educative form the disciplinary contents (pedagogical content knowledge). The TPCK's base components (De Rossi & Trevisan, 2018) are:

- *Technological Knowledge* (TK), knowledge of technologies and the skills required to operate with them;
- *Pedagogical Knowledge* (PK), teaching/learning processes and practices, methods and approaches;

- *Content Knowledge* (CK), teachers' understanding of a discipline's organization (Starkey, 2010).

These are overlapped in three areas of knowledge:

- *Technological Pedagogical Knowledge* (TPK), pedagogical awareness about technology's affordances and constraints (Terpstra, 2015);
- *Pedagogical Content Knowledge* (PCK), ability to teach a content from the learners' perspective (Ben-Peretz, 2011);
- *Technological Content Knowledge* (TCK), understanding the most effective technologies for learning a content and how this, in turn, are modeled (Mishra & Koehler, 2006).

As suggested by Koehler & Mishra (2009), 'the TPACK framework for teacher knowledge is described in detail, as a complex interaction among three bodies of knowledge: content, pedagogy, and technology. The interaction of these bodies of knowledge, both theoretically and in practice, produces the types of flexible knowledge needed to successfully integrate technology use into teaching' (p. 65).

But how works the technological and pedagogical knowledge of the discipline in practice? The meta-representation construct could clarify this aspect.

Meta-Representational Competence of Teachers

Described for the first time as an aspect of the spatial intelligence of a person (Di Sessa, 2004) the meta-representational competence (Eilam & Gilbert, 2014; Eilam, 2015) refers to the 'ability to choose the optimal external representation for a task (or) invent new representations as necessary' (Hegarty, 2010, p. 273).

Referring to the definition of PCT's Shulman as 'the most useful forms of representations', Eilam (2012) underlines the need for the teacher's visual literacy, i.e. the ability to represent disciplinary knowledge for student learnings, a skill needed for successful instruction, learning and disseminating the knowledge' (Eilam, 2012, p. 97).

The reflections on the meta-representative competence (Di Sessa, 2004; Eilam, 2015) shifts the focus on the teacher's relationship with the signs (image, graphic, map etc.) used to communicate and to give meaning to the learning contents.

Regarding this aspect Eilam also clarifies that in order to develop the meta-representational competence teachers should be trained to a semiotic analysis of the means of representation of knowledge to be learned[4] and better know some of the main taxonomies (Mayer, 2001) in order to verify the relevance (Elia, Gagatsis, & Demetriou, 2007) of textbook illustrations and the function (Ainsworth, 2014) of the multimedia.

TABLE 4.1   Five kinds of knowledge structures (adapted from Mayer, 2005, p. 69)

Type of structure	Description	Representation	Example
Process	Explain a cause-and-effect chain	Flow chart	Explanation of how the human ear work
Comparison	Compare and contrast two or more elements along several dimension	Matrix	Comparison of two theories of learning with respect to the learner, teacher, and instructional methods
Generalization	Describe main idea and supporting details	Branching tree	Presentation of thesis of the major causes of the American Civil War along with evidence
Enumeration	Present list of item	List	List of the names of twelve multimedia design
Classification	Analyze a domain into set and subsets	Hierarchy	Description of a biological classification system for sea animals

As the studies onf the visual learnings and the visual thinking suggest (Tversky, 2015), the mediation function of images refers to their ability to show a 'schema' of reality, that represent and explain it. In the didactic activities for enhancing student learnings (i.e., learning complex concepts; learning difficulties,[5] through the explanatory images the learners observe how information are connected and organized (*first* level of knowledge) and how new concepts are related to the information given (*second* level of knowledge).

Methodology

The exploratory study (Stake, 1995) focuses on how teachers relate their 'pedagogical content knowledge' and their 'subject matter content knowledge' (Shulman, 1986, 1987); in particular, considers the way in which the teachers represent and formulate the content to promote students' understanding, or – in other words – how they organize and use their subject matter knowledge (Cochran, 1997).

Multiple case-study design (Yin, 2003) proceeded through in-depth analysis of the mediation devices used by two high school philosophy teachers (Teacher A, Teacher B) on the same content knowledge (CK), the Italian philosopher G. B. Vico (see Figure 4.2).

Two types of mediation devices have been examined: the lesson with interactive whiteboard (Md1) and all the tools used by teachers to clarify the lesson and to integrate the information of the school books (Md2) – such as personal notes and diagrams, digital tools, etc., shared with students on school e-learning environment.

The empirical inquiry aimed to investigate both teacher' beliefs and real practices using a 'mixed-method approach' (Creswell & Plano, 2011; Cresswell, 2014) in three phases. The data collection (Seltman, 2015) has been carried out through specific tools based on the type of mediation devices examined: observation of participants during the lesson (Waxman & Huang, 1999); in-depth interviews after the lesson (Md1 – Boyce & Neale, 2006); document analysis (Bowen, 2009) of the mediation tools (Md2).

The analysis of the data has been performed through the triangulation (Denzin, 2006) of verbal / non-verbal, semiotic and textual elements. In order to ensure the verification and validity of different types of data (Silverman, 2009), the triangulation of data has been conducted following the main procedures as: the refutational analysis, the constant data comparison, the comprehensive data use, the inclusion of the deviant case and the use of tables (Silverman, 2009, p. 472). As data has been extracted from the original sources, the analysts verified their accuracy in terms of form and context with constant comparison, either alone or with peers (a form of triangulation).

Analysis of the Data
In accordance with the 'collaborative' method (Day & Townsend, 2009; Perla, 2015) and in order to support the co-construction of practical knowledge, the first elaboration of the three collections of data (observation, in-depth interview, document analysis) has been done by the involved teachers and the researchers, after sharing the research procedures and same semiotic and meta-representation categories (Eilam, 2012; Waldrip & Prain, 2013; Damiano, 2013).

The literature offers a numerous series of criteria for the classification of visual representations in the context of scholastic teaching (Tversky, 2015; Blackwell & Engelhardt, 2002; Bonaiuti, 2011; Damiano, 2013), a real meta-taxonomy system. The analysis followed the criteria suggested by Blackwell and Engelhardt (2002), integrated by the typology and the characteristics of visual representation (Mayer, 2001; Eilam, 2012)[6]:

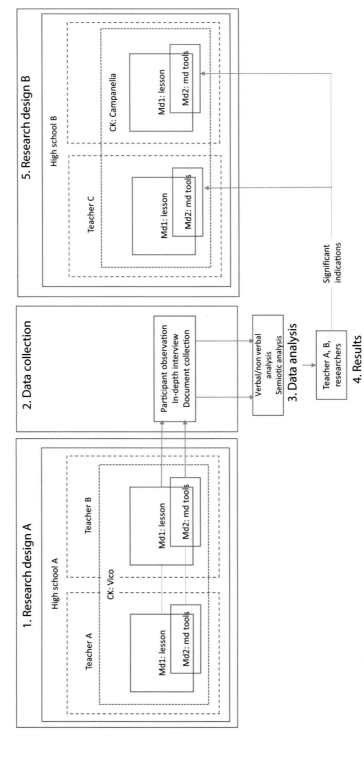

FIGURE 4.2   The exploratory case-study design (from Stake, 1995)

1. *Basic graphic vocabulary*: use of point, line, area or color, size, shape etc.;
2. *Conventional elements*: use of words, shapes and pictures;
3. *Pictorial abstraction*: depiction of physical objects or scenes – realistic, schematic or abstract etc.;
4. *Graphic structure*, or 'configuration': how the signs are combined into a diagram (linear sequence, two-axis-chart, table, tree structure etc., see Table 4.1);
5. *Mode of correspondence*: meaning of representation related the communicative context;
6. *Represented information*: classifications of information domains (space, time, etc.) and/or relational properties (nominal, ordinal, quantitative, etc.);
7. *Task and interaction*: activity of a person interacting with a diagram (drawing, sketching, transcribing, restructuring etc.);
8. *Cognitive processes*: perceptual characteristics and support for cognitive function of users (image-like mental representations or propositional representations), related to perception, interpretation and problem solving, as well as individual differences in ability, expertise or strategy;
9. *Social context*: refers the information present in the diagram or coming from other sources and relating the cultural/discourse context that support the right interpretation of user.

Mayer distinguished five main kinds of internal knowledge structures (see Table 4.2) and offers useful criteria to classify – 'arbitrarily' (Eilam, 2012, p. 141) – the visual representation in:

Mayer also offered, at first, seven principles for multimedia learnings (2001), then integrated by other more extensive. Mayer presents (2005, p. 266, Table 4.3) twelve principles that shape the design and organization of multimedia presentations in order to enhance the learnings (see Table 4.3).

The first level of analysis has highlighted aspects dealing with the personal strategies that the teacher uses in order to explaining the subject of lesson and integrating the school-books information. In this chapter it is useful focusing on the specific visual resources by which teacher promotes students' learnings, without considering the dynamic of communicative interaction during the lesson (use of words, gestures aimed at the involvement of students etc.).

The early data analysis showed that teachers tend to avoid the representational tools (cognitive maps, figures, tables etc.) available on the school books. See Table 4.1 used in the synthesis of triangulation analysis.

These 'traces' – the avoiding of the maps offered by school books and the use of personal diagrams for information synthesis – directed the analysis on

TABLE 4.2 Basic criteria of visual representations' classification (adapted from Mayer, 2005)

Static	Dynamic
Text and writing	Films, videos
Photographs and pictures	animations
Diagrams and charts	
Maps	
Graphs and numerical tables	

the personal materials used by the two teachers (i.e. personal notes and digital resources) and on the comparison of these with the 'visual representations' on the school texts.

Document Analysis

For exemplum purposes only, is reported below the analysis procedure conducted on a document – concept maps used by Teacher A during the interactive lesson and shared in the school repository.

The maps organize the information concerning the work of the philosopher G. B. Vico 'New Science', in particular:
- the distinction between the *philology* (make known the 'certain', the real history of the human beings) and the *philosophy* (explain the 'true', the intrinsic laws of events),
- the explanation of the forms of government that characterized three historical periods.

The explanatory maps of this subject, found in the school book, are given in Figure 4.3).

The explanatory maps of the same subject, used in class by the Teacher A during the interactive lesson, are given in Figure 4.4.[7]

Referring to the Mayer's criteria adapted to the visual static representations (Mayer, 2005, Table 4.3), several differences between the documents can be immediately noticed: the first are 'maps', the latter are 'text', 'diagrams' and 'photo'. The latter respond to the principles (Mayer, 2005) of:
- signaling (2) – cues that highlight the organization of the essential meanings (the use of bold, color and two different types of quotes);
- redundancy (3) – the explanatory box with the original quote that reinforces the concept expressed before[8] (Figure 4.4);
- pre-training (7) – the introductory sentence 'as said previously' ('come detto in precedenza' – Figure 4.3);

TABLE 4.3 Principles for multimedia presentations (adapted from Mayer, 2005)

Cognitive function	Principles	Definition
Reducing extraneous processing	Coherence	when 'extraneous words, pictures and sounds are excluded rather than included'
	Signaling	when 'cues that highlight the organization of the essential material are added'
	Redundancy	there are 'graphics and narration than from graphics, narration and on-screen text'
	Spatial contiguity	when 'corresponding words and pictures are presented near rather than far from each other on the page or screen'
	Temporal contiguity	when 'corresponding words and pictures are presented simultaneously rather than successively'
Managing essential processing	Segmenting	when a multimedia lesson is presented in user-paced segments rather than as a continuous unit
	Pre-training	in a multimedia lesson, when the names and characteristics of the main concepts are known
	Modality	from graphics and narrations than from animation and on-screen text
Fostering generative processing	Multimedia	from words and pictures than from words alone
	personalization	in a multimedia lessons, when words are in conversational style rather than formal style
	Voice	when the narration in multimedia lessons is spoken in a friendly human voice rather than a machine voice
	Image	not necessarily from a multimedia lesson when the speaker's image is added to the screen

– spatial/temporal contiguity (4/5) and multimedia (9) – the simultaneous use of words and pictures, not words alone;
– personalization (10) – the use of a conversational style of words, not formal.
There are others substantial aspects to be emphasized, which will be commented later:
a   in Figure 4.4 teacher A used both the image of the original edition of the text of Vico and the original quotation in the box: referring to the original

TABLE 4.4 Synthetic analysis for the triangulation of data (Silverman, 2009)

Teacher A		Teacher B	
Md1: Lesson	Md2: Mediation tools	Md1: Lesson	Md2: Mediation tools
Observation	Documentation	Observation	Documentation
teacher draws personal schemes (maps), on whiteboard	personal schemes ans image (different from schoolbook's)	teacher provides students with personal schemes (maps and tables) on copies	personal synthesis (tables and maps)
In-deep interview		In-deep interview	
Motivation: they are more effective *Criterion*: completeness *Consequence*: common reference		*Motivation*: they are more effective *Criterion*: comprehensiveness *Consequence*: common reference	

sources, the teacher wanted to favor a direct relationship between the students and the philosopher, almost a sort of 'invitation' to address the original source of knowledge, without 'mediation';

b   the relation linking the three concepts of 'age' (of gods, heroes and men) in Figure 4.3 is disjoined, in Figure 4.4 is recursive: this is a really new 'form of knowledge' (Shulman, 1987), different from that found usually in the school textbooks.

Using the criteria of Mayer for the analysis of static visual representations (Mayer, 2005) and through the procedure just described, a synthetic table of the 22 analyzed documents has been elaborated (Silverman, 2009) (12 of Teachers A, 10 of Teachers B).

As can easily be inferred, the 22 documents analyzed almost completely respect Mayer's multimedia criteria. The pre-training, spatial and temporal continuity criteria have been evident in the totality of the documents; the multimedia criterion in the minor number. Furthermore, the documents of the teacher A correspond to the criteria identified, rather than the documents of the teacher B.

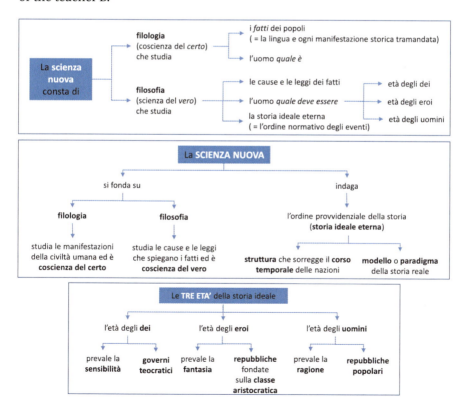

FIGURE 4.3   Explanatory maps in the school textbook

La «scienza nuova»: la storia

Come detto in precedenza, l'uomo conosce ciò che fa, dunque la **storia**, opera eminentemente umana, è l'oggetto privilegiato della conoscenza: di essa si ha «**vera scienza**»

Nell'intreccio dei «**fatti**» storici, accertati mediante la «filologia» (che indaga mediante testi, "resti", monumenti ecc.), possiamo riconoscere la **verità** di un ordine razionale, mediante la «filosofia»

«La **filosofia** contempla la ragione, onde viene la **scienza del vero**; la **filologia** osserva l'autorità dell'umano arbitrio, onde viene la **coscienza del certo**» (Degnità X)

Le età della storia, i corsi e i ricorsi

Vico è consapevole che la «fragilità» e il limite dell'uomo può condurlo al disordine e alla corruzione e la stessa **filosofia decade in** interminabili e sofistici dibattiti, in uno «**scetticismo**» permanente, sicché la «provvidenza» interviene e porta le nazioni nuovamente alla condizione primitiva e alla dispersione primordiale: la storia ricomincia il suo ciclo, i «**corsi e ricorsi**»

FIGURE 4.4   Visual representations used by teacher A during the lesson

In-Depth Interview

The analysis of the in-depth interviews follows the 'traces', found in the document analysis and it allows to better understand the relationship that the teachers establish with school textbooks.

They consider the schoolbooks as 'sufficient resources' to explain the general subject matter knowledge (as the philosopher G. B. Vico) but somewhat 'improper' to explain some specific subject matter (as the difference philology/philosophy in 'Scienza nuova') and, for this, unsuitable to support the processes of learning. About this, Teacher A says:

> I've always used my schemes at lesson. I think they're more effective than the maps that I find on the schoolbooks (...) they help me to better explain what I mean.

The teachers prefer to use personal schemes and develop them preferring completeness rather than simplification. About the criterion of schemes' composition, Teacher B says:

> My notes don't need to simplify the concepts and the contents of the schoolbooks, but to connect them in a more useful way to students' learning. I find sometimes the schoolbooks' synthesis very basic, my notes instead are more comprehensive.

The teachers are also able to share with students and spread in the school context an original 'structure' of subject matter (Shulman, 1997; Cochran, 1997), sometimes different from the configuration in the textbooks but more useful for students' learning (as difference between Figures 4.3 and 4.4). About this 'original structure' of the subject matter, Teacher A clarifies:

TABLE 4.5 Occurrences of Mayer's criteria for document analysis (Mayer, 2005)

Criteria	Teachers A	Teachers B	Tot.
Signaling	12	8	20
Redundancy	11	9	20
Spatial contiguity	12	10	22
Temporal contiguity	12	10	22
Pre-training	12	10	22
Multimedia	11	8	19
Personalization	12	9	21

Number of documents

> I often need to find a useful mode to representing the philosopher's true thought, even if it is difficult to understand; the problem, in fact, is not to simplify the concepts but to find an effective way to communicate them to the students.

This 'new' structure, made by the teacher, works at the same time as a *landmark* that unifies different representations of the subject matter (school text book, free resources online etc.) and also as a *scaffold* for the students' learning processes.

Teachers produce these personal schemes in different ways: hand-made on block notes, drawn on the blackboard, visualized on the whiteboard, digitized and shared through the school e-learning environment. About this, Teacher B says:

> Students know that (schemes) are made by me; so they pay more attention and use them for studying. Also they find the same pattern in shared on-line materials and they can share a single common reference.

Results

The teacher's personal artefacts, as the iconic mediation tools (i.e. schemes, tables, mind maps, examples images), analyzed in this study, works not only as cognitive structures that support the students learning processes but also as *landmarks* that unify the different representations of a specific subject matter. In this way, the teacher's mediation function works not only at the communicative and relational level but also at *epistemic*, as 'integration' of subject matter (Cochran, 1997).

Moreover, that subject matter mediated by teachers assume a specific identity, certainly different from that of school textbooks, not simplified.

As emerged, teachers would follow the criterion of *completeness*, not *simplicity*, for elaborating the representation of knowledge. It would be useful to further how teachers develop personal mediation tools in order to understand the teachers' meta-representation competence, in other words, 'the ability to generate new knowledge (Eilam & Gilbert, 2015).

> The meta-representational work of teachers springs up, at first, as a need of communication (to communicate effectively to the students) but assumes, then, a cognitive and epistemic value (Mayer, 2001). The new configuration that teacher A uses in order to explain the relationship between the 'ages' (see Figures 4.3 and 4.4) is not just a communicative need, but a *novelty*, in other words, a *revolution*, in terms of episteme of the discipline.

These findings will be used in a further studies as significant indications to the unit of analysis' operational definition (Stake, 1995). The forthcoming studies will be conducted at different levels: a) with same teachers but on other philosophical subject matter; b) in other high school on the same subject matter. This will detect if this results (features of personal schemes, different ways of use) are connected to specific subject matter, personal strategies of teachers or characteristics of learning environment.

Implications and Discussion

As stated by Eilam (2012), the teachers' meta-representative competence is so powerful from the communicative, cognitive and epistemic point of view; the teacher should be aware of it not just in order to answer to communicative and cognitive questions[9] but above all to pose epistemic issues – is the content knowledge of school-books really useful?; respects the philosopher's thought?; or is it a mere ideological and partisan reading? – as made by Bloom in the question of the 'western canon' in literature studies (1994). But this would require a radical change in the training paths of teachers and the same curriculum of teacher's education.

Furthermore, as suggested by Blackwell and Engelhardt (2000, p. 61), this type of issues require different research methods, even different academic disciplines. 'An interdisciplinary science of thinking with diagrams cannot afford to concentrate only on formal analyses without context'. Nowadays, a unique and common meta-taxonomic framework that describes the characters of visual representations is not there yet: this is the limit of the study of such a complex object but also the sign of the vitality of today's investigations on the multimedia means of communication of learning contents.

Conclusions

At the time, it is possible to confirm, as Hennessy (2011), the central role of teacher's artefacts in supporting the students learning process. This applies not only to Mathematics but also Philosophy subject matter.

The study of teachers' mediation devices and the analysis of representational tools used in the teaching-learning process allow to understand the PCK model, from a specific perspective: how teachers relate their pedagogical knowledge to their subject matter knowledge – as Cochran's 'integration' suggests.

Shulman's definition of PCK is once again apt to describe teaching-learning processes although it should be extended by Cochran's concept of 'integration', as this helps to better understand the personal component of the teacher's work of representation – "the way in which (disciplinary) knowledge is organized and used" (Cochran, 1997, p 78).

Although from the theoretical point of view the relation between pedagogical and subject matter knowledge is described, nevertheless on the practical and procedural levels even today it needs to be explained.

All this implies a change of perspective, the assumption, therefore, of new paradigms of reference, oriented at the same time towards an education *of* media and *to the* media.

The use of visual representations as the teaching mediation devices – also digital – is an opportunity for the teacher to become aware of the often unconscious mediation processes. A systematic study on the functions of visual representations in didactic practice could favor, in general, the rethinking on the canonically accepted relationship between the teacher (T), the learner (St) and the contents (Co); in the teacher, the reflecting on the personal relationship with the 'knowledge to teach'.

Notes

1 For example, a math teacher (T) teaches integrals, a content of the syllabus of Mathematics (Co), in a High School V class (St) through a lesson based on a textbook or an interactive whiteboard lesson (Md).
2 'The amount and organization of knowledge itself in the mind of the teacher' (Shulman, 1986, p. 7).
3 As Shulman (1986), it refers to *teachability* but not to other elements as classroom organization and management, even though 'terribly important' (p. 14).
4 See the distinction between 'content' (the elements of thoughts or concepts that must be transformed into systems of signs) and 'form' (the means chosen to represent such contents, which are found in a given system and are governed by rules belonging to this system); (Eilam, 2012, p. 125; see also Mayer, 2005, Table 4.1); between dyadic (*signifier – signified*, as F. de Saussure) and triadic (*representamen – interpretant – object*, as C.S. Peirce) models of sign; between monosemic and polysemic sign systems (Bertin, 1983).
5 We do not use the Eilam MRCMs construct – 'curriculum materials rich with visual representation' (2012) – as this refers to already existing tools, specially as textbooks sources, not created by the same teacher.
6 As suggest Blackwell and Engelhardt (2002), 'any visual representation that is not purely textual or purely pictorial can usefully be analyzed to discover its diagrammatic content, whether or not it should formally be defined as a *diagram*' (Blackwell & Engelhardt, 2002, p. 56).
7 The analysis is in the original Italian language. Although implies difficulty of comprehension in the reader, however this does not affect the level of analysis that is representative and not interpretative. It is not our intention, in fact, to enter into the merit of the translation of specific terms but to highlight precisely the 'representative' work carried out by the teachers involved in the study.
8 See Figure 4.3: philology as 'consciousness' and philosophy as 'science'; philology and philosophy as 'study'; philology as a study of the 'manifestations of human civilization' (expression not used before); philosophy as a study of the causes and laws that explain the facts (a term that is first used to define philology instead). Such incorrect redundancy could confuse and not encourage the student learning process.
9 'Which types of diagrams are appropriate for what teaching goals? (…) How use of diagrams can facilitate education in all subjects (and in philosophy, specifically)? When and how and to what extent should we use diagrams in a textbook or a classroom presentation?' (Blackwell & Engelhardt, 2002, p. 61).

References

Ainsworth, S. (2014). The multiple representation principle in multimedia learning. In R. E. Mayer (Ed.), *Cambridge handbooks in psychology. The Cambridge handbook of multimedia learning* (pp. 464–486). New York, NY: Cambridge University Press.
ALTET, M. (1997). *Les pédagogies de l'apprentissage*. Paris: PUF.
Ben-Peretz, M. (2011). Teacher knowledge: What is it? How do we uncover it? What are its implications for schooling? *Teaching and Teacher Education, 27*(1), 3–9.
Blackwell, A. F., & Engelhardt, Y. (2002). A metataxonomy for diagram research. In M. Anderson, B. Meyer, & P. Olivier (Eds.), *Diagrammatic representation and reasoning* (pp. 47–64). London: Springer.
Bloom, H. (1994). *The western canon. The books of the ages*. New York, NY: Harcourt & Brace.
Bogdan, R. C., & Biklen, S. K. (2006). *Qualitative research in education: An introduction to theory and methods*. Boston, MA: Allyn & Bacon.
Bolk, J. (1926). *Das Problem der Menschwerdung*. Jena: Gustav Fischer.
Bonaiuti, G. (2011). Organizzatori grafici e apprendimento. In A. Calvani (a cura di), *Principi di comunicazione visiva e multimediale. Fare didattica con le immagini* (pp. 75–128). Roma: Carocci.
Bowen, G. A. (2009). Document Analysis as a qualitative research method. *Qualitative Research Journal, 9*(2), 27–40.
Cochran, K. (1997). Pedagogical content knowledge: Teachers' integration of subject matter, pedagogy, students, and learning environments. *Research Matters to the Science Teacher, 9702*.
Cochran, K. F., Deruiter, J. A., & King, R. A. (1993). Pedagogical content knowing: An integrative model for teacher preparation. *Journal of Teacher Education, 44*, 263–272.
Creswell, J. W. (2014). *Research design. Qualitative, quantitative and mixed methods approaches*. Thousand Oaks, CA: Sage Publications.
Creswell, J. W., & Plano, V. L. (2011). *Designing and conducting mixed methods research*. London: Sage Publications.
Damiano, E. (2007). *Il sapere dell'insegnante*. Milano: FrancoAngeli.
Damiano, E. (2013). *La mediazione didattica. Per una teoria dell'insegnamento*. Milano: FrancoAngeli.
Darling-Hammond, L. (1990). Teacher professionalism, why and how. In A. Lieberman (Ed.), *Schools as collaborative cultures: Creating the future now*. London: Falmer Press.
Day, C., & Townsend, A. (2009). Networked action research. In B. Somekh & S. Nofke (Eds.), *The Sage handbook of educational action research*. London: Sage Publications.
Denzin, N. (2006). *Sociological methods: A sourcebook*. Chicago, IL: Aldine Transaction.

De Rossi, M., & Trevisan, O. (2018). Technological pedagogical content knowledge in the literature: How TPCK is defined and implemented in initial teacher education. *Italian Journal of Educational Technology, 26*(1), 7–23.

Di Sessa, A. A. (2004). Meta representation: Native competence and targets for *instruction*. *Cognition and Instruction, 22*(3), 293–331.

Eilam, B. (2012). *Teaching, learning and visual literacy. The dual role of visual representation*. New York, NY: Cambridge University Press.

Eilam, B. (2015). Promoting preservice teachers' meta-representational (visual) competencies: The need for a new pedagogy. In C. J. Craig & L. Orland-Barak (Ed.), *International teacher education: Promising pedagogies (Part C) (Advances in research on teaching, Volume 22C)* (pp. 65–68). Bingley: Emerald Group Publishing Limited.

Eilam, B., & Gilbert, J. K. (2014). *Science teachers' use of visual representations*. Dordrecht: Springer.

Elia, I., Gagatsis, A., & Demetriou, A. (2007). The effects of different modes of representation on the solution of one-step additive problems. *Learning and Instruction, 17*(6), 658–672.

Gudmundsdottir, S. (1987). *Pedagogical content knowledge: Teachers' ways of knowing*. Paper presented at the Annual Meeting of the American Educational Research Association, Washington, DC.

Hegarty, M. (2010). Components of spatial intelligence. In B. H. Ross (Ed.), *The psychology of learning and motivation: The psychology of learning and motivation: Advances in research and theory* (Vol. 52., pp. 265–297). San Diego, CA: Elsevier Academic Press.

Hepp, A. (2012). Mediatization and 'molding force' of media. *Communication, 37*(1), 1–28.

Hepp, A., & Krotz, F. (2014). *Mediatized worlds. Culture and society in a media age*. London: Palgrave Macmillan.

Hjarvard, S. (2013). *The mediatization of culture and society*. London: Routledge.

Houssaye, J. (1986). *Théorie et pratiques de l'éducation*. Berne: Peter Lang.

Koehler, M. J., & Mishra, P. (2008). Introducing TPCK. In AACTE Committee on Innovation and Technology (Ed.), *The handbook of Technological Pedagogical Content Knowledge (TPCK) for educators* (pp. 3–29). Mahwah, NJ: Lawrence Erlbaum Associates.

Koehler, M. J., & Mishra, P. (2009). What is technological pedagogical content knowledge? *Contemporary Issues in Technology and Teacher Education, 9*(1), 60–70.

Laurillard, D. (1993). *Rethinking university teaching, a framework for the effective use of educational technology*. London & New York, NY: Routledge.

Lundby, K. (Ed.). (2009). *Mediatization: Concept, changes, consequences*. New York, NY: Peter Lang.

Mayer, R. E. (2002). Multimedia learning. *Psychology of Learning and Motivation, 41*, 85–139.

Mayer, R. E. (Ed.). (2005). *The Cambridge handbook of multimedia learning.* Cambridge: Cambridge University Press.

Mishra, P., & Koehler, M. J. (2006). Technological pedagogical content knowledge: A framework for integrating technology in teacher knowledge. *Teachers College Record, 108*(6), 1017–1054.

Mishra, P., & Koehler, M. (2007). Technological Pedagogical Content Knowledge (TPCK): Confronting the wicked problems of teaching with technology. In C. Crawford et al. (Eds.), *Proceedings of society for information technology and teacher education international conference 2007* (pp. 2214–2226). Chesapeake, VA: Association for the Advancement of Computing in Education.

Perla, L. (2015). Il rapporto Università-Scuola: una quaestio 'semplessa'. In G. Elia (Ed.), *La complessità del sapere pedagogico fra tradizione e innovazione.* Milano: FrancoAngeli.

Rabardel, J. (1995). *Les hommes et les technologies, Approche cognitive des instruments contemporains.* Paris: Armand Colin.

Rawolle, S., & Lingard, B. (2014). Mediatization of the knowledge economy discourse. In K. Lundby (Ed.), *The handbook on mediatization.* Berlin & Boston, MA: Mouton de Gruyter.

Shulman, L. S. (1986). Those who understand: Knowledge growth in teaching. *Educational Researcher, 15*(2), 4–14.

Shulman, L. S. (1987). Knowledge and teaching: Foundations of the new reform. *Harvard Educational Review, 57*(1), 1–22.

Silverman, D. (2009). *Doing qualitative research* (3rd ed.). London: Sage Publications.

Stake, R. E. (1995). *The art of case study research: Perspective in practice.* London: Sage Publications.

Starkey, L. (2010). Teachers' pedagogical reasoning and action in the digital age. *Teachers and Teaching, 16*(2), 233–244.

Terpstra, M. (2015). TPACKtivity: An activity – Theory lens for examining TPACK development. In C. Angeli & N. Valanides (Eds.), *Technological pedagogical content knowledge. Exploring, developing, and assessing TPCK* (pp. 63–88). New York, NY: Springer.

Tversky, B. (2015). The cognitive design of tools of thought. *Review of Philosophy & Psychology, 6*, 99–116.

Tversky, B., & Suwa, M. (2009). Thinking with sketches. In A. B. Markman & K. L. Wood (Eds.), *Tools for innovation* (pp. 182–199). Oxford: Oxford University Press.

Vygotsky, L. S. (1934). *Thought and language.* Boston, MA: MIT Press.

Waxman, H. C., & Huang, S. J. L. (1999). Classroom observation research and the improvement of teaching. In H. C. Waxman & H. J. Walberg (Ed.), *New directions for teaching practice and research.* Berkeley, CA: McCutchan.

Yin, R. K. (2003). *Case study design and research: Design and methods* (3rd ed.). Thousand Oaks, CA: Sage Publications.

CHAPTER 5

Preservice Teachers' Reflection for the Acquisition of Practical Knowledge during the Practicum

Raquel Gómez, Juanjo Mena, María-Luisa García-Rodríguez and Franciso García Peñalvo

Abstract

In this chapter we describe teachers' professional practice by scrutinizing the type of practical knowledge that preservice teachers acquire during the practicum period as well as by assessing the type of support they receive from their mentors and peers. We conducted the study with preservice students from the Primary Education degree at the University of Salamanca, Spain. They were recorded a teaching a lesson and also reflecting on it afterwards: first individually, then with a peer preservice teacher and, finally, with a mentor.

The data analysis followed three stages. We first identify critical incidents (positive and negative) according to three major themes: the teacher, the student and the content. Secondly, we conducted a propositional analysis to classify the contet of the preservice teachers' reflections according to four types of practical knowledge. Thirdly, we analyze the mentoring support according to the MERID model (Hennissen et al., 2008).

The results show that reflecting with the help of another person (either a peer or a mentor) is more beneficial than acomplishing reflection individually since they elicit more inferential and sophisticated knowledge than individual reflections do. In addition, our data suggest that the assistance of mentors leads to more generalizable knowledge that preservice teachers can use in future school experiences.

Keywords

primary education – practicum – teaching practices – practical knowledge – mentoring

Introduction

It is generally accepted that one of the problems in education is the lack of quality performance by teachers. According to the philosopher José Antonio Marina, "Our teachers are discredited, they live isolated and they have lost their passion for their work" (SanMartin, 2015, p. 1). Teachers have these experiences because the education system fails in assigning syllabi that are more adapted to current social needs in the teacher training programs.

Consequently, the education system needs reflective educators to improve teaching–learning processes. To do this, preservice teachers need quality training that involves critical reflection and mentors who help them to learn relevant teaching knowledge for their future professional practices (Ripamonti, Galuppo, Bruno, Ivaldi, & Scaratti, 2018; Ryan & Murphy, 2018).

The practicum as the professional experience period during the teaching career plays a fundamental role in teacher training because it allows preservice teachers to apply the knowledge that they acquired during their studies; that is, preservice teachers relate the theories that they learned at university to the knowledge that they obtain during their school practice (Liesa & Vived, 2010). Providing preservice teachers with the opportunity to apply theoretical frameworks in their school practice helps turn their experiences into practical knowledge (Carl & Strydom, 2017).

Portfolios are used as typical methodological resources to reflect on the practicum experience. Barragán (2005) defines portfolios as "… techniques of compilation, collection of evidence and repertoires of professional competencies that leads to satisfactory professional development" (p. 122). Portfolios are commonly used individually; therefore, mentors are needed to help preservice teachers develop their skills and collaborate (Bejar, 2018; Sánchez, 2013). Mentoring is a process of guidance by which cooperating teachers help in the process of learning to teach (Valverde, Ruiz, García, & Romero, 2004). Malderez and Bodóczky (1999) expand upon this definition and refer to mentoring as a form of "learning to teach – how to help each individual learner to become the best teacher" (p. 67). Orland-Barak (2003) further explains it as "an intellectual, cultural and contextualized activity" (p. 98).

Thus, individual reflection (through portfolios) and mentoring interactions are fundamental for quality teacher education training. This study aims to (a) describe significant critical incidents (both motivating and challenging) that occur during teaching lessons in schools; (b) identify what preservice teachers learn about their experiences through reflective situations (individual, with a partner, and with a mentor); and (c) assess what type of mentor assistance better facilitates teaching learning in practice.

Theoretical Framework

Teacher training at all educational levels should not only address quality instructional processes but also explore ways to connect theory to practice (reflections on actions) (Onrubia, Colomina, Mauri, & Clarà, 2014; Universidad Internacional de Valencia, 2015). For this to occur, teacher educators need to train preservice teachers in critical and reflective practices so that they can acquire practical knowledge that can be used in future classroom situations (Carl & Strydom, 2017; Cuevas, 2013).

The practicum is an important phase of the teacher training, as it provides undergraduate students with the opportunity to develop professional skills (Delors, 1999). According to Zabalza (2016), the practicum involves periods of training outside the university that allow future teachers to understand the school reality. For this experience to be of quality, preservice teachers should incorporate reflection on action (Shön, 1983) as a fundamental metacognitive skill (Onrubia et al., 2014) while their mentors guide them and help them improve their teaching practice (Font, Rubio, Giménez, & Planas, 2009). This type of reflection is called guided reflection (Johns, 2002; Toom & Husu, 2016), a process of learning in practice in which a mentor guides a preservice teacher through critical reflection. In this process, preservice teachers are expected to think of the motivations and challenges that they experience in the practicum by identifying meaningful events that represent a turning point in the development of the lesson (Monereo, 2010). These critical incidents revolve around three main categories (teacher, class student, and subject content) that are present in the teaching episodes (Johnson, 1995; Patrikainen, 2012; Toom, 2006). Guided reflection is a procedure that helps preservice teachers to acquire greater knowledge, techniques, and resources to improve their teaching practice.

As such, a reflective practicum allows preservice teachers to elicit practical knowledge (Mena et al., 2016) and improve their teaching performance by relating theory and practice (Matos, 2006). The practical knowledge that they acquire through reflection can be divided into two main types: narrative knowledge – descriptions (recalls or appraisals) of an event of practice – and inferential knowledge – explications (rules or artifacts) given to any event of practice (Mena et al., 2016). Following Mena and Clarke (2015), we consider

- recalls as images that are remembered from the lesson,
- appraisals as value judgments (positive and negative) of action,
- rules as methodological strategies that are extracted from the practice, and
- artifacts as instruments that teachers extract from what they have experienced.

Practical knowledge can be also facilitated through mentoring assistance. Hennissen, Crasborn, Brouwer, Korthagen, and Bergen (2008) classify mentoring assitance into directive or non-directive according to the *Mentor (teacher) Roles In Dialogues* (MERID) model. Mentors in the directive category provide advice, opinions, or information, whereas mentors in the non-directive category listen, ask, or summarize the information of the lesson (Hennissen et al., 2008). Furthermore, the mentors can adopt active (bringing in topics into the conversation) or reactive (responding to the turns introduced by the preservice teachers) stances.

By combining these two dimensions (active/reactive and directive/non-directive), mentors position their work into four roles: imperator, advisor, initiator, and encourager (Figure 5.1); the first two types use mentoring skills, and the last two types do not use mentoring skills (Hennissen et al., 2008).

As shown in Figure 5.1, the initiator introduces the topic of conversation and encourages the preservice teacher to talk more about the topic, while the encourager reacts to the topic that the preservice teacher introduces in practice and leads him o her to reflect on his o her performance. Furthermore, the imperator introduces the topic and uses directive mentoring supervisory skills, whereas the advisor reacts to what the preservice teacher says and provides advice about what he or she should do.

Mentors with supervisory roles can improve the acquisition of practical knowledge, as they improve the connections between theory and practice, (Crasborn, Hennissen, Brouwer, & Bergen, 2011; Kuswandono, 2017). The aim of this study is to analyse what preservice teachers learn about their practice

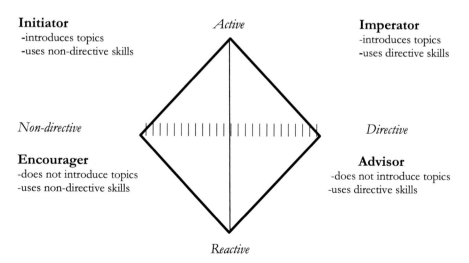

FIGURE 5.1   The mentor (teacher) roles in dialogues model (Hennissen et al., 2008)

during the practicum. More specifically, we will focus on (a) describing the critical incidents that preservice teachers highlighted in their reflections about their practice; (b) identifying the types of knowledge that develop during the three types of reflection; and (c) describing the mentoring skills and roles that mentors and peers adopted while reflecting with preservice teachers.

Methodology

In this study, forty-three preservice teachers studying for a primary education degree at the University of Salamanca taught lessons to students aged 6 to 12 years in primary schools in Spain. These preservice teachers voluntarily participated in the European Project ACTTEA (2012–2015), reference number 526318-LLP-1-2012-1-EE-COMENIUS-CMP. Preservice teachers were video recorded while teaching. They explained a lesson that was previously planned with their mentors. Two days after the lessons were recorded, the preservice teachers critically reflected individually on their experiences, identifying the critical incidents (either motivating or challenging) that they considered significant. In their reflections, the preservice teachers focused on their actions and answered questions such as "What happened during the lesson?", "What were the most significant incidents for you?", "Why do you think this incident occurred?", and "How are you going to put these ideas into practice in your future teaching?" Later, they watched the recorded lessons again with a peer student teacher (a preservice teacher partner) and reflected on the aspects that could be improved. Finally, the preservice teachers reflected with their mentors, observing the recorded lessons again. To conduct the analysis, the necessary permissions for data protection were requested to meet ethical standards.

Out of the total sample, thirty-two preservice teachers performed the three types of reflection (individual reflection, peer reflection, and mentor reflection), seven preservice teachers only conducted individual and peer reflection, two preservice teachers reflected with only one peer, and two recorded their lessons but did not reflect on them. To compare the three types of reflection, in this chapter, we consider the thirty-two preservice teachers who completed the three reflections. All the videos were literally transcribed for analysis at two different levels (general and specific). Mixed methodology was used by following a QUAN-QUAL analysis (Creswell, 2008). We started with a qualitative analysis to describe the facts observed during the lessons and interpret them in a global context. We also performed a quantitative analysis to transform these observed facts into quantifiable measures and verify the relationships between the variables.

We analysed the critical incidents – the motivators and challenges that preservice teachers experienced in their school practice – and the most frequently discussed topics of the lessons using NVivo 10 software. To identify the types of knowledge from the three types of reflections, we conducted a propositional analysis, whereas we analysed the mentoring skills and roles using the MERID model. We also conducted a quantitative analysis in which we used the SPSS v12 software to perform statistical tests.

The critical incidents were split into units of thought, that is, semantic units related to the motivations or challenges that preservice teachers considered significant. The units were thematically ordered, gathering the most frequently discussed topics in the sessions and classifying them into three main categories: preservice teachers, students in the classroom, and content. We used these three categories because the models of Johnson (1995), Toom (2006), and Patrikainen (2012) mention that teaching practice revolves around these three elements. We divided each of these categories into subcategories so that we could classify the topics more specifically. We derived these subcategories from the transcripts of the lessons and established them as follows.

1. Preservice teachers
    1.1. Intruction (techinique)
        1.1.1. Planning
        1.1.2. Development
        1.1.3. Evaluation
    1.2. Professional identity
        1.2.1. Experience
        1.2.2. Cultural background
    1.3. Practicum
        1.3.1. Institutional program
        1.3.2. Investigation project
2. Classroom students
    2.1. Behaviour of the students in the session
        2.1.1. Attention
        2.1.2. Metacognition (reflection)
        2.1.3. Discipline (control of the classroom)
    2.2. Diversity (attention)
        2.2.1. Students' characteristics and needs
        2.2.2. Individual differences
3. Content
    3.1. Knowledge domain
        3.1.1. Conceptual knowledge
        3.1.2. Competencies and procedures
        3.1.3. Cross elements (values)

3.2. Activities
   3.2.1. Knowledge consolidation
   3.2.2. Summary and recapitulation

Finally, the relationships between the three major topics were analysed: pedagogical relationship (PR: relationship between the preservice teachers and the classroom students); content relationship (CR: relationship between the preservice teachers and the content of the lessons); learning relationship (LR: relationship between the preservice teacher and the students' learning); and didactic relationship (DR: relationship between the preservice teachers, the content of the lessons and the classroom students).

In the second phase, we divided the individual reflections and dialogues (peer and mentor) into basic ideas or propositions and analysed them according to the propositional discourse analysis (PDA) model (Mena & Clarke, 2015), classifying the propositions into four types of professional knowledge (recalls, appraisals, rules, and artifacts).

Finally, in the third phase, we analysed the types of mentoring support based on the MERID model (Hennissen et al., 2008). This model describes mentoring skills according to the directivity, differentiating between directive (providing advice, opinions, or information) and non-directive (listening, asking, or summarizing the lesson) mentoring. In addition, we characterized the roles of the mentors (the partners and mentors) by determining which of them helped preservice teachers to improve their practical knowledge. We classified these roles as imperator, advisor, initiator, and encourager.

Results

Critical Incidents that Preservice Teachers Found in Their Lessons

We analysed the positive (motivations) and negative (challenges) critical incidents that preservice teachers identified in their teaching lessons and considered significant. We analysed 103 units of thought, obtaining a total of 1,491 critical incidents. Out of them, 903 were positive incidents (60.56%) and 588 were negative incidents (39.43%).

Figure 5.2 shows critical incidents (both positive and negative) of the three types of reflections (individual, with a peer, and with a mentor). Peer reflection produced the most positive incidents (n = 414; e.g., "activation of prior knowledge", "structure of the organized class", "good control of the class", etc.). Reflections with the help of mentors produced more negative incidents (n = 198; e.g., "little movement in the classroom when [the teacher explains the content]",

ACQUISITION OF PRACTICAL KNOWLEDGE

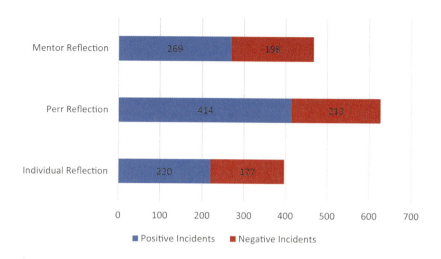

FIGURE 5.2   The amount of positive and negative critical incidents in the lessons

"use of fillers", "disorder and noise in the classroom", etc.) compared to the other types of reflection.

In addition, we classified these critical incidents according to the relationships between the three major categories that led the analysis: preservice teachers, classroom students, and subject content. Figure 5.3 shows that most

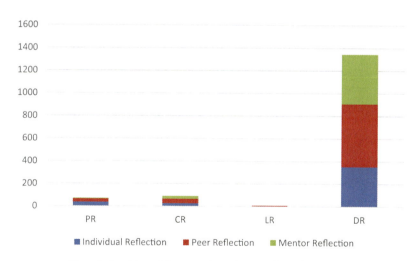

FIGURE 5.3   The relationships of the critical incidents in the reflection sessions. CR = content relationship; DR = didactic relationship; LR = learning relationship; PR = pedagogical relationship

of the incidents were related to the DR (88.90%). In contrast, incidents representing the PR, CR, and LR, represent only 4.62%, 5.94%, and 0.52%, respectively. This may be due to the fact that the preservice teachers of this study found it difficult to relate these critical incidents to only one of the categories mentioned, that is, the teacher, the content, or student. Therefore, these data are similarly distributed in the three types of reflections.

In the next step, we completed a word count of all reflections using the NVivo 10 program to determine the prevalence of the four aforementioned relationships: CR, DR, LR, and PR.

Figure 5.4 shows that the most frequently used words were "mentor" (n = 364), "class" (n = 224), "students" (n = 134), "activity" (n = 110), "time" (n = 108), "blackboard" (n = 85), "session" (n = 86), "knowledge" (n = 42), "explanation" (n = 50), and "theme" (n = 79). On the other hand, 64.65% of the words were related to the preservice teacher topic, 25.09% to the classroom students topic, and 10.25% to the subject content topic.

We then developed the corresponding subcategories (Table 5.1).

Table 5.1 shows that the most frequently discussed topic (in 47.7% of reflections; e.g., "Through your previous knowledge you start to connect ideas") in the reflections was the development of the session; the second most frequently discussed topic was planning (in 13.5% of reflections; e.g., "You have specified the stage objectives, cycle objectives, and level objectives for the area of mathematics"). Both topics belong to Category 1, preservice teachers, and Subcategory 1.1, instruction. The least frequently discussed topics were experience (in 0.24% of reflections; e.g., "I teach in a music school") and cultural background (in 0.48% of reflections; e.g., "It is important to know a little about general culture"); these topics also belong to Category 1, preservice teachers, but are within Subcategory 1.2, professional identity.

FIGURE 5.4   The most frequently used words in the sessions of the practicum. The more frequently used words are represented in a bigger size than the less frequently used words

Types of Practical Knowledge that Emerged in the Three Conditions of Reflection

In the second phase, we conducted a propositional analysis by following the PDA model (Mena & Clarke, 2015), which allowed us to determine what kind of practical knowledge emerged in the three types of reflections: individual reflection, peer reflection, and mentor reflection (Figure 5.5).

TABLE 5.1 The most frequent themes that emerged in the three reflections

Themes	Frequency
1. Preservice teachers	
1.1. Instructions	517
1.1.1. Planning	112
1.1.2. Development	396
1.1.3. Evaluation	9
1.2. Professional identity	6
1.2.1. Experience	2
1.2.2. Cultural background	4
1.3. Practicum	13
1.3.1. Institutional program	5
1.3.2. Investigation project	8
2. Classroom students	
2.1. Behaviour of the students in the session	182
2.1.1. Attention	83
2.1.2. Metacognition	27
2.1.3. Discipline	72
2.2. Diversity	26
2.2.1. Students' characteristics and needs	13
2.2.2. Individual differences	13
3. Content	
3.1. Knowledge domain	20
3.1.1 Conceptual knowledge	10
3.1.2. Competencies and procedures	5
3.1.3. Cross elements	5
2. Activities	65
3.2.1 Knowledge consolidation	32
3.2.2. Summary and recapitulation	33

Figure 5.5 shows that peer reflection and mentor reflection generated most of the practical knowledge, whereas individual reflection elicited fewer propositions. Regarding the type of knowledge, we found that positive appraisals were dominant in the three reflections: accounting for 6.32% in individual reflections, 17.24% in peer reflections, and 16.24% in mentoring reflections. Conversely, artifacts were less referred to: 0.21% in individual reflections, 0.02% in peer reflections, and 0.03% in mentor reflections. Rules, or teaching principles, were elicited most often in reflections with mentors, constituting 9.82% of the content. In conclusion, preservice teachers had more opportunities to learn from practice when they reflected with the help of another person, either a peer preservice teacher or a mentor.

Type of Support Offered by the Teacher Mentors

We used the MERID model (Hennissen et al., 2008) to analyse the mentoring skills that were used in the conversations. We identified 5,135 utterances that revealed mentoring skills to encourage preservice teachers' professional learning. Of the mentoring skills, 96.75% were directive whereas 3.25% were nondirective. Giving opinions (e.g., "I liked the session") was the most commonly

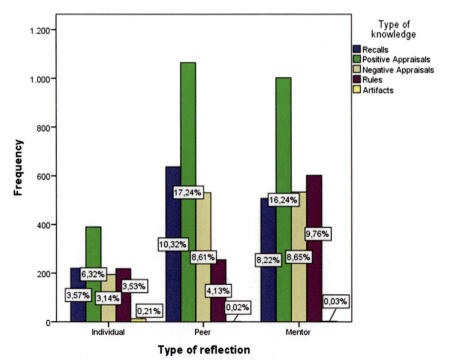

FIGURE 5.5   The types of practical knowledge that were extracted from the three types of reflections (individual, with a peer, and with a mentor)

used mentoring skill (73.13% in peer and mentor reflections), followed by giving advice (e.g., "Next time you should tell [the child] …") used in 19.68% of the peer and mentor reflections. On the other hand, giving information (e.g., "Family situation is not good"), listening (e.g., "hmm"), asking (e.g., "How did you feel in the session?"), and summarizing (e.g., "You conducted activities of all kinds") were used in 3.94%, 0.10%, 1.48%, and 1.68% of the contents of the dialogues, respectively. Therefore, based on the displayed mentoring skills, peers and mentors basically fell into the imperator role. In other words, they showed a greater degree of influence in directing the course of the dialogue.

In all cases, giving opinions was the most utilized skill; it was used in 30.55% of all scrutinized data (5.135 mentoring skills) and 42.58% of the mentoring reflections. However, we must emphasize that the mentors gave more advice (in 16.68% of the mentor reflections) than the peers did (in 3% of the peer reflections). The use rate for non-directive skills (listening, asking, and summarizing) was low in peer and mentor reflections. The preservice teachers' peers barely used listening (0.03% of the conversations), asking (0.39%), or summarizing (1%). The teacher mentors used listening (0.06% of the conversations), asking (1.10%), and summarizing (0.68%).

The use of mentoring skills (e.g., giving opinions, advice, or information; listening; asking; or summarizing) combined with the mentors' active/reactive stance gave rise to four possible mentor roles: imperator, advisor, initiator, and encourager (Hennissen et al., 2008).

TABLE 5.2   Roles of mentors and peers

Role	Number of times the role was used	%
Imperator	1,394	45.0
Advisor	1,610	51.9
Initiator	49	1.6
Encourager	47	1.5
Total	3,100	100

Table 5.2 shows that the mentors or peers most frequently adopted the advisor (51.9%) and imperator roles (45%) and that they barely fell into the initiator (1.6%) and encourager (1.5%) roles. This means that the peers and mentors adopted more directive stances (the imperator and advisor roles) when reflecting with the preservice teachers, and they rarely used a non-directive role (initiator or encourager).

Figure 5.6 shows which mentoring role helped preservice teachers the most to elicit more practical knowledge. The propositions in the imperator role accounted for 1,192 (85.5% of the narrative knowledge) and the propositions of the advisor role constituted 72.9% of the narrative knowledge (1,174 propositions). In the initiator role, 100% of the knowledge was narrative (49 of 49 propositions), and in the encourager role, 93.6% (44 of 47 propositions) of the knowledge was narrative. It is interesting to note that 27.1% of inferential knowledge (436 of 1,612 propositions) was extracted in interactions with the advisor role; 14.5% of inferential knowledge (202 of 1,394 propositions) was elicited in interactions with a predominately imperator role, 6.4% was extracted in interactions with the encourager role (3 of 47 propositions), and no inferential knowledge was extracted in interactions with the initiator role.

Regarding the type of knowledge obtained in the peer and mentoring interactions within each role, we found the following:
- The imperator role produced recalls in 12.5% of these reflections, positive appraisals in 55.6%, negative appraisals in 17.4%, rules in 14.4%, and artifacts in 0.1%.
- The advisor role produced recalls in 16.8% of these reflections, positive appraisals in 38.3%, negative appraisals in 17.8%, rules in 27%, and artifacts in 0.1%.
- The initiator role produced recalls in 51% of these reflections, positive appraisals in 28.6%, negative appraisals in 20.4%, and no rules or artifacts.

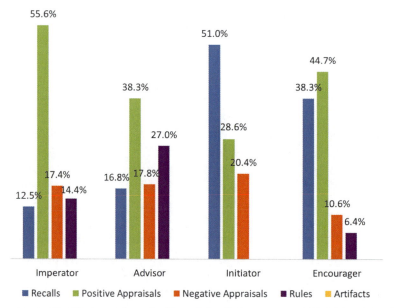

FIGURE 5.6   The types of practical knowledge that were extracted in interactions with each mentoring role

– The encourager role produced recalls in 38.3% of these reflections, positive appraisals in 44.7%, negative appraisals in 10.6%, rules in 6.4%, and no artifacts.

Thus, the pattern of practical knowledge found in peer and mentor reflections was of a descriptive nature: e.g., based on positive appraisals, recalls and negative appraisals. The exception was found in the advisor role where more rules were elicited than in the rest of the roles.

Finally, mentor teachers helped preservice teachers to elicit more knowledge about the practice (51.5% of the knowledge) than peers (48.5% of the knowledge). Furthermore, they helped preservice teachers to gain more sophisticated knowledge than the peers did, producing more rules (22.7% vs. 10.2%) and artifacts (0.1% vs. 0.0%). Conversely, peer reflection favoured narrative knowledge (recalls and appraisals): It produced 637 recalls (25.65%), 1,064 positive appraisals (42.8%), and 531 negative appraisals (21.3%), whereas mentor reflection generated 507 recalls (19.2%), 1,002 positive appraisals (37.9%), and 534 negative appraisals (20.2%).

Implications

This study focused on the importance of preservice teachers' reflections (individual, peer-assisted, and mentor-assisted) in practice during the practicum. We conducted a triple analysis of the critical incidents, practical knowledge gained, and mentoring support.

Regarding the critical incidents, the preservice teachers considered it easier to reflect on what they had done well (motivations) than on what had gone wrong (challenges). We also observed that more incidents were identified in the mentor and peer reflections than in the individual reflections. These results are in line with those of Alsina and Batllori (2015), who concluded that support given during the practicum allows preservice teachers to build democratic, reflective, and critical models about what motivates or challenges them to improve their practice.

We found that most of the critical incidents (88.90%) were related to three elements: the student teachers, classroom students, and subject content. We demonstrated a great imbalance among the other relationships. This imbalance occurred because all three elements are usually involved in teaching practice, which is a necessary aspect of learning. Elmore's (2004) research shows that increases in learning occur when the levels of the content, the teacher's knowledge and skills, and the students' commitment improve; that is, a relationship exists between all elements involved in the teaching–learning process.

Additionally, we thematically classified the critical incidents to determine which themes arose in the reflections on the teaching practice. Thanks to this identification, organization, and detailed analysis of the topics, we can infer results that can help us to better understand the concerns of our students during the practicum (Braun & Clarke, 2006). In the reflections, the most frequently discussed topic (in 47.7% of the reflections) was the development of the session, followed by the activation of previous knowledge, loss of time in the explanation, clear or wrong explanations, and so on.

Our analysis of the acquired practical knowledge using the PDA model showed that the practical knowledge was mostly of narrative nature (82.31% of the knowledge), whereas 17.69% was inferential (rules and artifacts). This data distribution might indicate that preservice teachers found it easier to evaluate what they did during their lesson (e.g., recalls and appraisals) than to extract knowledge to be used in other situations because inferential knowledge entails reflection on a more abstract level.

It is important to note that reflections with another person (either a preservice teacher partner or a mentor teacher) generated more knowledge than individual reflections did. However, the preservice teachers acquired more inferential knowledge with mentors than with peers. Therefore, compared to reflections with peers, reflections with mentors produced knowledge that was more complex and generalizable due to the mentors' greater experience.

Finally, our analysis of the mentoring support according to the MERID model (Hennissen et al., 2008) helped us to understand that most of the mentors (peers and mentors) used a directive mentoring style (giving opinions or advice) in which the preservice teachers contributed less to the conversation. Hawkey (1998) and Hennissen et al. (2008) suggest that using non-directive skills helps teachers to acquire higher levels of knowledge. Therefore, mentors should be able to use non-directive skills to increase the quality of the students teachers' knowledge. As for the mentors' roles, the results showed that the imperator and advisor roles were the most predominant, proving that the mentors used directive roles when they wanted the preservice teachers to learn quickly (i.e., in a period of time such as that of the practicum; Crasborn, Hennissen, Brouwer, Korthagen, & Bergen, 2010; Orland-Barak, 2005).

In another investigation (Mena, Hennissen, & Loughran, 2017) regarding mentors' roles, the imperator and initiator roles stood out in three of the mentors. However, one of the mentors adopted the encourager role in 43.4% of his mentoring interactions; conversely, he adopted the imperator role in 22.1% of his mentoring interactions, the initiator role in 11.5%, and the advisor role in only 4.7%.

Narrative knowledge (e.g., recalls and appraisals) was the most frequently obtained type of knowledge, and inferential knowledge was the least frequently obtained. For example, in the advisor role, 27.1% of knowledge obtained was inferential (rules and artifacts). Therefore, we can verify that the advisor role – that is, the role of partners or mentors who react to what the teachers say in practice and give advice on what they should do by using managerial skills (giving advice, opinions, or information) – is the professional role that most helps preservice teachers to improve their practical knowledge (both narrative and inferential). These results are not in line with those of other studies (Orland-Barak, 2005; Mena et al., 2016) that show that the encourager role – that is, the role of mentors who summarize, ask questions, and encourage the teachers in training to use their theoretical knowledge and the ideas from their practice and reflect on them – is the most appropriate for helping teachers to acquire inferential knowledge. In addition, the data show that reflecting with a mentor helps teachers to acquire more sophisticated knowledge, and reflecting with a partner increases teachers' narrative knowledge.

Conclusions

The results of this study suggest that, to generate quality learning, teachers in training should reflect on their practice with another person, preferably a mentor because the knowledge acquired in reflections with mentors is more abstract than that from reflections with a partner. In addition, it is important to know what kind of knowledge is transmitted with each mentoring skill and what mentoring role produces inferential knowledge so that teachers in training can learn from their practice and use this knowledge in their future teaching experiences.

Therefore, to improve the quality of education for aspiring teachers, they should not only use portfolios or logs to individually conduct critical reflections on their experiences but also conduct critical reflections with others (e.g., peers and mentors) to acquire all the skills that they need to be effective teachers. As Paulo Freire (1997) stated, "Teaching is not transferring knowledge but creating the possibilities for its own construction" (p. 47).

References

Alsina, A., y Batllori, R. (2015). Hacia una formación del profesorado basada en la integración entre la práctica y la teoría: una experiencia en el Practicum desde el modeo realista. *Revista de Investigación en la Escuela, 85*, 5–18.

Barragán, R. (2005). El Portafolio, metodología de evaluación y aprendizaje de cara al nuevo Espacio Europeo de Educación Superior. Una experiencia práctica en la Universidad de Sevilla. *Revista Latinoamericana de Tecnología Educvativa, 4*, 121-140.

Bejar, L. H. (2018). La tutoría como instrumento esencial para desarrollo personal, comunitario, social y el aprendizaje intelectual de los/as estudiantes de nivel superior, de manera integrada e integradora a la vida. *Universidad y Sociedad, 10*(1), 52-58. Recuperado de http://rus.ucf.edu.cu/index.php/rus

Braun, V., & Clarke, V. (2006). Using thematic analysis in psychology. *Qualitative Research in Psychology, 3*(2), 77-101. doi:10.1191/1478088706qp063oa

Cuevas, M. S. (2013). La docencia universitaria a través del conocimiento profesional práctico: pistas para la formación. *Sinéctica, 41*.

Carl, A., & Strydom, S. (2017). E-Portfolio as reflection tool during teaching practices: The interplay between contextual and dispositional variables. *South African Journal of Education, 37*(1).

Crasborn, F. J. A. J., & Hennissen, P. (2010). *The skilled mentor. Mentor teachers' use and acquisition of supervisory skills.* Eindhoven: Eindhoven School of Education.

Crasborn, F., Hennissen, P., Brouwer, N., Korthagen, F., & Bergen, T. (2011). Exploring a two-dimensional model of mentor teacher roles in mentoring dialogues. *Teaching and Teacher Education, 27*(2), 320-331.

Delors, J. (1999). *La educación encierra un tesoro. Informe a la UNESCO de la Comisión Internacional sobre la Educación para el Siglo XXI.* París: UNESCO.

Domingo, A. (2013). Práctica reflexiva para docentes, 397.

Elmore, R. (2004). The instructional core. *City, R. Elmore, S. Fidman, & L. Teite, Instructional Rounds in Education. A network.*

Freire, P. (1997). *Pedagogía de la Autonomía.* México DF: Siglo XXI (Trabajo original publicado en 1996).

Font, V., Rubio, N., Giménez, J., y Planas, N. (2009). Competencias profesionales en el Máster de Profesorado de Secundaria. *UNO, 51*, 9-18.

Hawkey, K. (1998). Mentor pedagogy and student teacher professional development: A study of two mentoring relationships. *Teaching and Teacher Education, 14*, 657-670.

Hennissen, P., Crasborn, F., Brouwer, N., Korthagen, F., & Bergen, T. (2008). Mapping mentor teachers' roles in mentoring dialogues. *Educational Research Review, 3*(2), 168-186. Retrieved from https://doi.org/10.1016/j.edurev.2008.01.001

Johns, Ch. (2002). *Guided reflection.* Oxford: Blackwell Publishers.

Kuswandono, P. (2017). Mentor teachers' voices on pre-service English teachers' professional learning. *Indonesian Journal of Applied Linguistics, 6*(2), 213-221.

Liesa, M., & Vived, E. (2010). El nuevo practicum del grado de magisterio. Aportaciones de alumnos y profesores. *Estudios sobre educación, 18*, 201-228.

Malderez, A., & Bodóczky, C. (1999). *Mentor courses*. Cambridge: Cambridge University Press.

Matos, R. (2006). La práctica de la reflexión durante el aprendizaje de un instrumento musical. *Revista de investigación, 59*, 65–88.

Mena, J., & Clarke, A. (2015). Eliciting teachers' practical knowledge through mentoring conversations in practicum settings: A Propositional Discourse Analysis (PDA). In H. Tillema, G. J. Westhuizen, & K. Smith (Eds.), *Mentoring for Learning: Climbing the Mountain* (pp. 47–78). Retrieved from https://doi.org/10.1007/978-94-6300-058-1_3

Mena, J. García, M. L., Clarke, A., & Barkatsas, A. (2016). An analysis of three different approaches to student teacher mentoring and their impact on knowledge generation in practicum settings. *European Journal of Teacher Education, 39*(1), 53–76.

Mena, J., Hennissen, P., & Loughran, J. (2017). Developing pre-service teachers' professional knowledge of teaching: The influence of mentoring. *Teaching and Teacher Education, 66*, 47–59. Retrieved from https://doi.org/10.1016/j.tate.2017.03.024

Monereo, C. (2010). La formación del profesorado: una pauta para el análisis e intervención a través de incidentes críticos. *Revista Iberoamericana de educación, 52*, 149–178.

Onrubia, J., Colomina, R., Mauri, T., y Clarà, M. (2014). Apoyando procesos de reflexión sobre la prácticas docente en el practicum de maestro, 1–14.

Orland-Barak, L. (2003). In between worlds: The tensions of in-service mentoring in Israel. In F. K. Kochan & J. T. Pascarelli (Eds.), *Global perspectives on mentoring: Transforming contexts, communities, and cultures* (pp. 191–210). Greenwich, CT: Information Age.

Orland -Barak, L., & Klein, S. (2005). The expressed and the realized: Mentors' representations of a mentoring conversation and its realization in practice. *Teaching and Teacher Education, 21*(4), 379e402.

Patrikainen, S. (2012). *Luokanopettajan pedagoginen ajattelu ja toiminta matematiikan opetuksessa* [Class teachers' pedagogical thinking and action in mathematics education]. University of Helsinki: Research report 342. (Diss.)

Ripamonti, S., Galuppo, L., Bruno, A., Ivaldi, S., & Scaratti, G. (2018). Reconstructing the internship program as a critical reflexive practice: The role of tutorship. *Teaching in Higher Education, 23*(6), 751–768.

Ryan, A., & Murphy, C. (2018). Reflexive practice and transformative learning. *Reflexivity and Critical Pedagogy, 67*.

SanMartín, O. (2015, 3 de noviembre de). Los cinco grandes problemas del profesorado español. *El Mundo*. Retrieved from http://www.elmundo.es/sociedad/2015/11/03/5637c9dc268e3e02488b456c.html

Schön, D. A. (1983). *The reflective practitioner: How professionals think in action*. London: Temple Smith.

Toom, A. (2006). *Tacit pedagogical knowing: At the core of teacher's professionality* (Research Reports 276). Finland: University of Helsinki, Department of Applied Sciences of Education.

Toom, A., & Husu, J. (2016). Finnish teachers as 'makers of the many'. In *Miracle of education* (pp. 41–55). Rotterdam, The Netherlands: Sense Publishers.

Universidad Internacional de Valencia. (2015). La formación del profesorado: un elemento clave para el éxito educativo. *Universidad Internacional de Valencia*. Retrieved from https://www.universidadviu.es/la-formacion-del-profesorado-un-elemento-clave-para-el-exito-educativo/

Valverde Macías, A., Ruiz de Miguel, C., García Jiménez, E., & Romero Rodríguez, S. (2004). Innovación en la orientación universitaria: la mentoría como respuesta. *Contextos Educativos, 6–7*, 87–112. Retrieved from http://dialnet.unirioja.es/descarga/articulo/1049470.pdf

Vicuña, J., Etxaburu, J., Hernández, M., Xabier Iturbe Gabikagojeaskoa, Jon López Armendáriz, Lourdes Ormaza Larrocea, Kepa Portillo Sanz, Ismael Redondo Rojo, Jokin Rodríguez de la Fuente y Lurdes Uriarte. (2013). *Mejora de la práctica docente. Una experiencia de autoevaluación*. San Sebastián: Servicio Central de Publicaciones del Gobierno Varcos.

Zabalza, M. A. (2016). El practicum y las prácticas externas en la formación universitaria. *Revista Prácticum, 1,1*.

PART 2

Teacher Beliefs and Reflective Thinking

CHAPTER 6

The Struggle Is Real: Metacognitive Conceptualizations, Actions, and Beliefs of Pre-Service and In-Service Teachers

Heather Braund and Eleftherios Soleas

Abstract

Metacognition has recently re-emerged as a central focus of educational initiatives. Developing students' metacognition can improve academic performance by increasing their self-regulation across learning domains. Research has consistently shown that explicit instruction about metacognitive processes is necessary for developing metacognitive thinking. However, teacher readiness and understandings to do so, have not been studied extensively leaving a significant gap in our understanding of teachers' knowledge of metacognition and beliefs. This sequential explanatory mixed methods study compared pre-service ($n = 43$) and in-service ($n = 45$) teachers' metacognitive beliefs and reported teaching practices. Data were collected through a questionnaire that informed subsequent semi-structured interviews. Non-parametric statistical tests elucidated differences across teaching samples, while qualitative data were thematically analyzed. Both in-service and pre-service teachers reported struggling to implement metacognition. In-service teachers demonstrated practical, concrete knowledge, as well as creative classroom integration of metacognition while pre-service conceptualizations lacked coherence pointing to specific areas where additional support is needed.

Keywords

in-service teachers – metacognition – metacognitive support – mixed methods – pre-service teachers

Introduction

"Hardly anyone questions the reality or importance of metacognition" (Schraw & Moshman, 1995, p. 351). Despite understanding the importance of metacognition, where consensus is sparse and definitions vary (Baker & Cerro, 2000; Veenman, Van Hout-Wolters, & Afflerbach, 2006) metacognition can be understood as the awareness and control that an individual has over their thinking (Baker, 2010). Simply put, metacognition is 'thinking about thinking' as pioneered by John Flavell (1979). However, the construct has proven to be difficult to define (Balcikanli, 2011). Hacker (1998, p. 11) expanded, "metacognition includes both knowledge of one's knowledge, processes, cognitive and affective states, and the ability to consciously and deliberately monitor and regulate one's knowledge, process, and cognitive and affective states". This definition is more all-encompassing and incorporates the affective processes.

Further, before metacognition research can move forward, the construct must be defined more clearly and discussed using a universally accepted framework (Braund, 2017). One issue that may contribute to the range of definitions surrounding metacognition is that the construct is frequently studied alongside other factors and constructs (Dinsmore, Alexander, & Loughlin, 2008). For example, a recent study focused on the relationship between metacognition, achievement goals, and self-efficacy in university students with no demonstrated relationship between students' metacognitive thinking and their achievement goals (Li & Wong, 2017). Another study conducted by Baas and colleagues (2015) examined the relationship among elementary students' (grades 4–6) metacognitive and cognitive strategy use and assessment for learning. Findings demonstrated that monitoring activities predicted students' use of planning. Activities that helped to scaffold student learning also related positively to surface and deep-level learning strategies. Increased use of scaffolding activities led to students using more surface and deep-level learning strategies while also resulting in increased evaluation of their learning following completion of a task.

Research findings posit that teachers' beliefs directly inform their teaching practices (Calderhead, 1991; Pajares, 1992; Woolfolk Hoy et al., 2006). Yet, teachers' beliefs and teaching practices aimed at developing students' metacognitive thinking are understudied (Zohar & Barzilai, 2013). Therefore, it is important to gain an appreciation of the struggle to integrate metacognition and identify crucial supports for teachers, as the lack of research hinders ability to design more effective teacher education in pre-service and in-service settings.

An important direction for metacognitive researchers to explore is to focus on more effective strategies to be implemented in classrooms to promote metacognitive skills. This would involve fostering students with strong metacognitive skills who can effectively problem-solve, strategize, and regulate their learning while becoming increasingly independent thinkers who can tackle the challenges that they will inevitably encounter throughout their learning (Efklides, 2009; Pilling-Cormick & Garrison, 2007; Zimmerman, 2002). Understanding the differences in metacognition conceptualization would inform the way that teacher education programs develop metacognitively aligned teacher pedagogy. Furthermore, the current study provides unique insight into how pre-service and in-service teacher populations understand metacognition as a construct and their practices necessary for developing students' metacognition. The following manuscript will provide readers with an overview of metacognition as a construct followed by the methodology used for the study, and results organized according to the research questions. The manuscript will end with a discussion section outlining the findings in relation to other literature, implications of the findings, and limitations of the current study.

Conceptualization of Metacognition

Metacognition can be conceptualized as having three dynamic and interrelated components: metacognitive knowledge, metacognitive regulation, and metacognitive experiences (Efklides, 2006; Flavell, 1979). The first component, *metacognitive knowledge* refers to the thoughts and beliefs that an individual has about their cognitive capabilities. These thoughts can be in relation to one's self, the task, or strategies. The knowledge can be declarative ("knowing that"), procedural ("knowing how"), or conditional ("knowing when") (Flavell, 1979). The second component, *metacognitive regulation* refers to an individual's capacity to monitor and control their learning. This component can be broken down further into three stages: planning, monitoring, and evaluating (Flavell, 1979). Lastly, *metacognitive experiences* are the judgements and feelings that an individual has about their learning and thinking, such as: feelings of confidence, or difficulty (Ben-David & Orion, 2013; Efklides, 2006). A balanced instructional approach to teaching metacognition includes both the affective and cognitive components (Braund, 2017). Further, it is imperative that students learn and practice developing all three metacognition components. Hence, teachers must be comfortable with all three components of metacognition.

Importance of Metacognition

Generally, students with well-developed metacognition are successful in their academic endeavors (Sternberg, 1998). Students with developed metacognition are aware and able to regulate their cognitive processes (Griffith & Ruan, 2005)and are successful learners because they understand how to learn rather than just focusing on the content (Wilson & Bai, 2010). Metacognition is a key component of self-regulated learning (SRL). Self-regulated learning relates to the capacity to control one's learning and develop knowledge about the learning environment (Pintrich, 2000). Self-regulation is often demonstrated through the ability to: (a) set goals, (b) determine and use appropriate strategies to help meet goals, and (c) monitor learning progress (Schunk, 1996). Students demonstrate self-regulated behaviors when they are able to control and monitor their learning through metacognitive regulation (Zimmerman, 2008). Metacognition is also a crucial part of critical thinking (Choy & Cheah, 2009). For students to think critically about the content that they are learning, they must use metacognitive skills, such as, monitoring their learning and evaluating their progress (Halpern, 1998). The development of these skills leads to more efficient and productive learners. The fostering of these skills in schools, begins with ensuring that teachers have the foundational knowledge, strategies, and confidence to propel the development of their students' metacognition. To better support new teachers entering the field we need to identify areas of concern to inform the development of teacher education programs.

It is crucial that the next generation of teachers have a strong understanding of what metacognition is, and how best to support metacognitive skills in their classrooms. Teachers' beliefs and practices are related (e.g., Hoy et al., 2005; Lombaerts et al., 2009; Pajares, 1992). If teachers are uncomfortable with metacognition or have a lack of understanding, then they would be less likely to effectively integrate it into their classrooms. By increasing our understanding of pre- and in-service teachers' beliefs about students' abilities to be metacognitive and their understanding of the concept, we can adapt professional development opportunities to the needs of both teaching populations (Ben-David & Orion, 2013; Spruce & Bol, 2015; Wilson & Bai, 2010; Zohar, 2006).

Wilson and Bai (2010) identified a relationship between teachers' metacognitive knowledge and pedagogical understandings through their survey of 105 American M.Ed. students. Rich awareness of metacognition was essential for developing students' metacognition. Participants discussed the active development of metacognitive thinking and identified explicit instruction and opportunities for practice as crucial practices to promote metacognition. Wilson and Bai highlighted the need for investigating what instructional strategies and resources teachers utilize in their classrooms as a means of more effective provision for which strategies must be taught in teacher education.

Previous investigations have pointed to the need to contrast the knowledge of pre- and in-service teachers as a means to establish what knowledges or capacities should be better developed through teacher education

(Metallidou, 2009; Soleas, 2015; Zohar & Barzilai, 2013). Metallidou (2009) showed that in-service teachers' strategies were often supported by the literature while pre-service teachers' choice of strategies were less likely to be supported by research, making it important to investigate concrete supports for their development. A first step in doing so involves investigating what teachers know and do in their early practice, as a means of identifying what is to come and what is needed.

In order to determine the current state of knowledge and illustrate the differences between two teaching groups, we investigated pre- and in-service teachers' metacognitive beliefs and their teaching practices directed at developing students' metacognition through the following research questions:
1. To what extent does teaching experience change teachers' comfort with integrating metacognition in their teaching?
2. To what extent is metacognition conceptualized differently between pre-service and in-service teachers in their teaching practices?

Methodology

This study used diverse samples of pre-service and in-service teachers to examine conceptualizations and integration of metacognition in their teaching practice through a sequential explanatory mixed methods design (Ivankova, Creswell, & Stick, 2006).

Participants

Participants were recruited via email invitations, listservs, and social media. For the pre-service population the recruitment notice was emailed out through a teacher education program listserv. The in-service teacher recruitment message was posted in teaching network groups of varying grades and subjects while also being circulated through a newsletter through the Science Teachers' Association of Ontario. 43 pre-service and 45 in-service teachers from a variety of teaching subjects participated in Phase 1 of the research which consisted of an online questionnaire. Of the 45 in-service teachers, only 41 completed the Likert responses. The demographic breakdown of the respondents from the statistically analyzed data was: 31 females, 9 males, 1 other, 31% of the participants had science backgrounds with a mean number of years of experience being 7.34 and their experience ranged from 0.5 to 25 years. The pre-service sample fairly represented both genders, with 22 females and 21 males, 42% had science backgrounds, and all had completed at least one teaching practicum. Participants were purposively selected from Phase 1 and invited to participate in semi-structured interviews for Phase 2 of the study. Participants selected for interviews were those that indicated their willingness to participate and had interesting conceptualizations of metacognition. Please refer to Tables 6.1 and 6.2 for a demographic breakdown of participants from Phase 2. Participants were assigned pseudonyms to protect their identities.

Data Collection

The questionnaires featured Likert-items and open-ended questions aimed to capture the broader view of metacognition in pre-service and in-service populations. The questionnaire administered to in-service teachers had 37 items including four demographic items, 26 Likert-type items (19 novel, but with 7 questions modified from other sources; $\alpha = 0.88$), and seven open-ended questions. The 7 modified questions came from two scales: 5 from the 'Teacher's Metacognitive Scale' (Wilson & Bai, 2010) and 2 from the 'Self-Regulated

TABLE 6.1 Demographic breakdown of pre-service participants for Phase 2

Participant	Gender	Age	Education	Teachable subjects	Teacher education
Thomas	Male	28	B.A., B.Ed.	Geography, Mathematics	Consecutive
Lyanna	Female	24	B.Sc., B.Ed.	Physics, Mathematics	Concurrent
Don	Male	24	B.A., B.Ed.	Dramatic Arts, History	Concurrent
Hussein	Male	25	B.A., B.Ed.	History, Geography	Concurrent
Marigold	Female	24	B.A., B.Ed.	Dramatic Arts, English	Concurrent
Olga	Female	24	B.Sc., B.Ed.	Biology, Chemistry	Consecutive

TABLE 6.2 Demographic breakdown of in-service participants for Phase 2

Participant	Gender	Years of experience	Education	Current assigned grade
Amanda	Female	24	B.A., B.Ed.	5
David	Male	15	B.Sc., B.Ed., M.Ed.	7/8
Jacob	Male	3	B.Sc., B.Ed., M.Ed.	1/2, 6 (French Immersion)
Ben	Male	18	M.Ed.	Kindergarten
Anna	Female	12	B.Sc.	7

Teacher Belief Scale' (Lombaerts, De Backer, Engels, Van Braak, & Athanasou, 2009). The questionnaire given to pre-service teachers contained 19 questions including four demographics questions, 10 Likert-items (α = 0.89), and five open-ended questions to expand on teacher perceptions and provide examples of their integration. Despite the use of different surveys for the two samples, it is important to note that for analyses we only compared the same questions across the two surveys.

Phase 2 was conducted with respondents who indicated willingness to be interviewed, six pre-service and five in-service teachers were purposively chosen for follow-up. Interviews focussed on how the participant integrated, conceptualized, and supported metacognition in their classroom. Interviews ranged from one to three hours and were audio-recorded.

Analyses

The quantitative responses were analysed using non-parametric tests including Fisher's exact tests, chi-square, and Mann-Whitney U tests in SPSS (v24). The analyses were completed separately for both teaching samples. This was complemented by thematic coding of the open-ended questions (Patton, 2015). Additionally, open-ended responses were quantitized, transforming qualitative data into numerical data (Sandelowski, Volis, & Knafl, 2009). For example, both teaching samples listed their desired supports; these supports were counted and compared across groups. The interviews were transcribed verbatim and were thematically analysed (see Table 6.3) using open coding using ATLAS.TI (v8). The two researchers coded all interviews and open-ended questionnaire items together to achieve 100% inter-coder reliability. Disagreements in coding were resolved through discussion and consultation with the literature.

Results

The results below are organized according to the research questions with qualitative and quantitative data represented. The term "respondents" refer to participants who completed the questionnaire only, whereas the term interviewees is used for those participants that completed the questionnaire and semi-structured interviews. A 'P' represent a pre-service participant whereas an 'I' represents an in-service participant.

> RQ1. To What extent does teaching experience change teachers' comfort with integrating metacognition in their teaching?

TABLE 6.3 Thematic coding breakdown of the interviews

Theme	Code family	Code (hyphens indicate categorizations)	Pre-service occurrence	In-service occurrence	Frequency across interviews
Pre-service and in-service teachers expressed discomfort when integrating metacognition	Developing teaching practice	Skepticism	83%	20%	17
		Supports	33%	40%	6
		Collaboration among teacher colleagues	50%	60%	11
		Lack of comfort	33%	80%	7
		Engagement- Related to understanding	33%	100%	15
		Teaching approach- Student choice	33%	80%	6
	Student engagement	Getting students engaged	100%	100%	47
	logistical challenges	Logistical challenges	33%	100%	23
Both pre-service and in-service teachers valued developing metacognitive thinking	Metacognitive awareness	Checking in	17%	100%	18
		Collaborative learning		100%	16
		Individual learning- Getting to know learners	67%	80%	16
		Individual learning- Learning preferences	67%	100%	26

(cont.)

TABLE 6.3 Thematic coding breakdown of the interviews (*cont.*)

Theme	Code family	Code (hyphens indicate categorizations)	Pre-service occurrence	In-service occurrence	Frequency across interviews
Pre-service and in-service teachers conceptualized metacognition differently	Developing metacognition	Activating knowledge	67%	80%	12
		Articulating thinking	0%	100%	14
		Beliefs- Providing students with skills	0%	100%	19
		Class culture	33%	100%	28
		Defining success	67%	100%	16
		Explicit modeling- Discussion of learning strategies	17%	100%	17
		General strategy- Developing an inclusive class culture	100%	80%	16
		Making connections	17%	100%	25
		Monitoring	33%	100%	10
		Motivating metacognition	17%	80%	10
		Resources-Specific resources	0%	100%	21
		Scaffolding	50%	100%	14
		Teaching approach	100%	100%	94
		Teaching approach- Self-directed learning	0%	100%	13
		Tech use	83%	80%	12
		Developing metacognition	17%	100%	18
		Feedback	33%	100%	16
		Prompting students-Reflective thinking	50%	100%	22
		Strategies	100%	100%	28
		Student thinking-Range	33%	100%	50
		Teacher reflection-Informing practice	100%	80%	19

Three main subthemes emerged relating to the first research question. Teachers emphasized the importance of applying practical strategies yet readily discussed challenges that they had experienced when trying to promote the development of metacognitive thinking. Lastly, teachers discussed some resources that they would find helpful.

The Importance of Practical Strategies

Both pre-service and in-service teachers understood the importance of metacognition. However, a difference occurred in the explicit integration of metacognition as in-service teachers reported integrating metacognition more often than pre-service when usage was analysed using a Fisher's exact test (see Table 6.4; p = 0.006).

In-service teachers demonstrated significantly more concrete strategies to develop students' metacognition such as: explicit instruction, articulating thinking, think aloud protocols, and getting students engaged through actively participating in the learning process (see Table 6.5). There was a significant difference elucidated using a chi-square test that showed that the implemented strategy type was different between groups (χ^2 = <0.0006). Specifically, in-service teachers were more likely to prioritize explicit instruction rather than more theoretical pedagogies.

TABLE 6.4   Integration of metacognition

	In-service		Pre-service	
Yes	40	88.90%	28	65.10%
No	5	11.10%	15	34.90%
			sig	0.006

TABLE 6.5   Teacher strategies for integrating metacognition

	In-service	Pre-service
Teaching for metacognition	13	5
Metacognitive regulation/strategies	15	7
Student centred	8	17
Assessment focussed	6	13
χ^2		<0.0006

Pre-service (P) students typically stated idealistic goals about their lessons as opposed to concrete strategies. For example, Don (P) discussed the importance of meeting students where they are at", without detailing what specific strategy he would utilize. In-service interviewees, however, would often focus on the practical strategies they would use in their lessons. For example, Ben (I) described the importance of not being in charge of his students' learning; "I'm there to help you, to get you materials and to point out when you are wrong". In-service teachers often gave practical strategies, whereas pre-service teachers underscored the importance of strategies without providing a specific strategy that they would use.

Challenges and the Struggle to Integrate Metacognition

Both pre-service and in-service teachers discussed various challenges with implementing teaching practices aimed at developing students' metacognition. Indeed, there was no significant difference between the proportions reporting struggling (see Table 6.6; χ^2 = 0.30). Lyanna (P) discussed how "genuine confidence only comes from applying those theories to a specific experience". In-service teachers echoed these frustrations. David (I) explained that "you can't just jump from A to Z and expect that the kids will figure out all the stuff in between".

What Resources Would Be Helpful?

Pre-service and in-service teachers differed in their preferred resources (see Table 6.7). A Fisher's exact test compared the identified resources that pre-service and in-service teachers would find helpful and found that the desired resources of each sample was significantly different (p = 0.009).

Pre-service teachers preferred "professional development courses" and "workshops" rather than more concrete resources. In-service teachers overwhelmingly preferred concrete resources like "books", "sharing activities", and "course profiles", all supplemented by "a supportive administration".

TABLE 6.6　Pre-service and in-service teachers report struggling

	In-service		Pre-service	
Yes	16	35.60%	20	46.50%
No	29	64.40%	23	53.50%
			χ^2	0.30

TABLE 6.7   What resources would be helpful?

	In-service		Pre-service	
Classroom resources	11	39.00%	8	30.77%
Policy and admin support	11	39.00%	6	23.08%
Teacher development	6	22.00%	12	46.15%
			sig	0.009

> RQ2. To What extent is metacognition conceptualized differently between pre-service and in-service teachers in their teaching practices?

Three main subthemes emerged in relation to the second research question. Teachers' conceptualizations of metacognition differed and in-service teachers better understood the need to develop a class culture that encouraged students to think metacognitively. Lastly, teachers discussed practices and strategies used to promote metacognitive development in their classrooms.

Pre-Service and In-Service Teachers Conceptualized Metacognition Differently

Pre-service teachers generally knew the literal translation for metacognition, "thinking about thinking" (Don, P). The most advanced understanding of metacognition from a pre-service teacher was "Yes, it's thinking about your own thoughts and being aware of your own thought processes", (Marigold, P). In contrast, in-service teachers had deeper conceptualizations of metacognition, linking the concept to other higher-order thinking processes, such as, critical thinking. Ben (I) described the perceived value of metacognition as "it's the heart of critical thinking. The heart of learning. If we don't have that then we're not learning how to learn". In-service teachers also reported that metacognitive strategies were transferable across domains, as Anna (I) described "well the self-assessment and peer-assessment and modeling. I think that's even the critical thinking. I think that's seen in every subject". In-service teachers additionally conceptualized metacognition differently regarding the domain specificity of metacognitive strategies with in-service teachers reporting the use of metacognitive strategies across subject domains. Amanda (I) describes these strategies' versatility, "I think my strategies still for metacognition were very similar to how I approached my other subjects". In contrast, pre-service teachers did not elaborate on whether or not they used strategies across contexts. When describing instances of their practices aimed at developing students' metacognition, pre-service teachers discussed them solely in a domain-specific manner.

The Intersectionality of Metacognition and Class Culture

In-service teachers better understood the intersectionality of metacognition and class culture and often articulated how they were inter-dependent. An in-service teacher, David, described what he thought a metacognitive aligned classroom looked like: "When big learning is happening, and the kids are engaged, my classroom is productive and busy. Not loud, not super loud". He clarified that he would be floating around the class "trying to keep track of what people are doing the best I can". To set a class culture, David thought "the one thing that you have to do, you've got to set the tone in advance". This sentiment of a classroom culture being the product of teacher planning was echoed frequently by in-service teachers who often simultaneously described how they planned for opportunities to be metacognitive. For example: Indeed, in their description of the importance of metacognition, a majority of in-service teachers stated that metacognition was important for its own sake, while only a minority of pre-service teachers reported feeling the same way, choosing instead to describe metacognition as a stepping stone to greater skills.

Although it was far more common for in-service teachers to link the two concepts of class culture and metacognition, pre-service teachers occasionally connected the establishment of a class culture with the establishment of metacognition as routine. In response to the question of how have you seen metacognition practiced in the classroom, Olga offered, "I had one student who never really participated, they mostly just sat there. We had this one lesson where everyone was working with a partner, and it just clicked". "You saw him start to work, share, and have a vested interest in the progress of his learning". When prompted, Olga hypothesized that "The point was that he felt a sense of trust, care, and respect in the class, which was brought about by him feeling safe in the class environment".

Teaching Practices and Tools to Enhance Metacognition

Pre-service and in-service teachers understood the importance of defining success as demonstrated through co-construction of success criteria, although there was a significant difference between the relative importance placed on success criteria by in-service and pre-service teachers as elucidated by a Mann-Whitney U Test (see Table 6.8, sig <0.0001). Thomas (P) described his

TABLE 6.8   Importance of building executive function

	In-service		Pre-service	
Strongly Agree	29	64.40%	4	9.30%
Agree	13	28.90%	19	44.20%
Neither Agree nor Disagree	3	6.70%	17	39.50%
Disagree	0	0%	3	7%
Strongly Disagree	0	0%	0	0%
	Mann-Whitney U		**Sig**	<0.0001

most common strategy "with metacognition is construct[ing] success criteria". Jacob (I) described how he displayed his success criteria: "I'll have prompts around. For example, one of the prompts I'm trying to out up now is a visual, what do you call it? Success criteria". Similarly, David (I) describes the importance of success criteria. "It's allowing them to know where we're starting, what we're kind of going to be doing and where we're going". Both pre-service and in-service teachers reported success criteria as a tool to enhance students' metacognition.

All in-service teachers and a couple of pre-service teachers understood the importance of prompting students' reflective thinking. Hussein (P) discussed the importance of reflective thinking, "just having them write down and reflect what we just did, what are the next steps". Similarly, Jacob (I) had come to understand reflective thinking's importance, despite its over-emphasis during his Bachelor of Education training. "So that's pretty much all we talked about. Reflection at teacher's college and we kind of got fed up with it but I know why … reflection is the cement that solidifies your learning".

Both teaching samples also described how students learn from each other when they collaborate. Thomas (P) discussed how collaborative learning promotes metacognition, "so, one of the biggest things is collaboration". He explained that students were "learning from working together, that they have to work together for everyone to learn". Ben (I) elaborated on the importance of learning through dialogue in his Kindergarten classroom, "And to understand that our learning is connected. It's influenced by dialogue. Dialogue is an important tool. When I've figured out that they've learned something from a peer, I'll point it out". Dialogue was seen as a beneficial tool alongside collaborative learning across elementary and secondary grade levels.

Discussion

> RQ1. To what extent does teaching experience change teachers' comfort with integrating metacognition in their teaching?

In-service teachers were able to name, explain, and articulate more concrete strategies than pre-service teachers. We, like Metallidou (2009) attributed this to experience in the classroom, as pre-service teachers do not have as much practical classroom experience as their in-service colleagues. In this study, the in-service teachers sought simple, applicable, and easily implemented ways of integrating metacognition that fit within their existing teaching routines. They wanted tools that fit the way that they teach and would have a positive impact on their students, while making minimal changes. While pre-service teachers were keen to make their inclusive classrooms informed by metacognition research, they often stated they would do so through less direct means like differentiated learning surveys. Harfitt (2015) points to choices like this, that sound like effective practice, but lack practicality in the classroom as contributing to the burnout of new teachers. Attempting to implement metacognitively-aligned practices without practical resources may contribute to frustrations and consume their available time. Bryce and Whitebread (2012) described the difficulties in assessing metacognition in five and seven-year-olds as being exacerbated by metacognition's latent nature, hence, teachers have trouble seeing metacognition itself and rely on proxies to gauge progress (Schellings, Van Hout-Wolters, Veenman, & Meijer, 2013).

> RQ2. To what extent is metacognition conceptualized differently between pre-service and in-service teachers in their teaching practices?

Pre-service and in-service teachers differed in their preferred resources and identified different aids as being potentially helpful. This finding is congruent with previous teacher professional development research that revealed that in-service teachers seek practical tools, rather than additional training (Avalos, 2011; McCormack, Gore, & Thomas, 2006). Teachers had different levels of understanding when discussing metacognition. Pre-service teachers knew the literal translation of metacognition, "thinking about thinking" (Flavell, 1979), and tended to have surface level understandings of metacognition. Whereas, in-service teachers had deeper conceptualizations, as they could better understand different facets of metacognition. These differences may be attributed to in-service teachers working to integrate metacognition more frequently and having a greater awareness of metacognition's complexities. These results are promising, when comparing it with the work of Ben-David and Orion's (2013), who found that 40 out of 45 in-service teachers were unfamiliar with metacognition prior to participating in their study. In addition, the few pre-service teachers that did demonstrate understandings of metacognition were more surface level when compared to the in-service participants from the current study pointing to a need for deep and richer explanation in teacher education.

In the present study, both pre- and in-service educators discussed common strategies for enhancing students' metacognition including: success criteria and collaborative learning. Pre-service teachers reported infrequent use of these strategies, whereas in-service teachers prioritized these more practical strategies over theoretical ones. Black and Wiliam (2003) emphasized the use of success criteria as a key strategy for formative assessment. When success criteria are constructed by students and shared with their teachers, it encourages students to be more responsible for their learning. Defining success through success criteria provides students with the opportunity to assess their progress in relation to the success criteria, encouraging independent learning (Black & Wiliam, 2009). Whitebread, Bingham, Grau, Pasternak, and Sangster (2007) provided evidence that children aged 3–5 demonstrated more instances of metacognitive monitoring and control when they were learning in groups. This supports the current study's findings as pre-service and in-service teachers discussed the importance of having students learn collaboratively.

Limitations

The over-reliance on self-report measures when examining metacognition must be acknowledged. However, these self-report measures are necessary first steps to ascertain teachers' perspectives. Future studies can benefit from these first steps as they aim to utilize additional methods such as think aloud protocols and classroom observations. We recognize the difficulty with generalizing results from a small sample size, but we believe that our findings demonstrate initial understandings of how these two populations differ in their understanding of metacognition and integration of metacognition. Additional research should be conducted to examine the extent to which other teaching populations' conceptualizations of metacognition differ to those examined in the current study.

Conclusions

This study illustrates the differences between pre-service and in-service teachers regarding their conceptualizations and integration of metacognition.

In-service teacher participants were much more likely to point out that metacognitive development and class culture were entangled events that were often symbiotic goals. In-service teachers frequently articulated their belief that a classroom that is conducive to inclusion is much more likely to foster metacognition, while also suggesting that a classroom that asks students to articulate their thinking is frequently inclusive. Goh and Taid (2006) showed that the process of think aloud protocols, a frequent demonstration of verbally articulating one's thoughts, facilitated learning in second language learners while also developing their confidence and making them feel welcome. Further, as articulated by Pintrich (2002), students who have the ability to demonstrate their thinking are more likely to participate and contribute in collaborative and class environments. In-service teachers echoed these understandings to a far greater extent than pre-service teachers, calling into question what might support pre-service teachers in reaching this critical understanding.

Pre-service and in-service teachers both appreciated that metacognition was important however, their knowledge and preferred resources differed, pointing to a need for revisiting how teacher education programs develop pre-service teachers' ability to make practical decisions that contribute to student metacognitive development. Both teaching samples readily reported logistical challenges in their practice; one notable example was "the struggle is real" when it came to integrating metacognition. In-service teachers were as likely to report struggling to integrate metacognition as were pre-service teachers. Quite simply, the struggle remained real long after a teacher gained experience. One common challenge was that metacognitive development improves with age, however, it must start somewhere. A way in which we can better support pre-service teachers is to further incorporate metacognition into teacher education programs. Further, specific strategies that promote metacognitive thinking should be introduced, discussed, and practiced by pre-service teachers.

References

Avalos, B. (2011). Teacher professional development in teaching and teacher education over ten years. *Teaching and Teacher Education, 27*(1), 10–20. Retrieved from http://doi.org/10.1016/j.tate.2010.08.007

Baas, D., Castelijns, J., Vermeulen, M., & Martens, R. (2015). The relation between assessment for learning and elementary students' cognitive and metacognitive strategy use. *British Journal of Educational Psychology, 85*, 33–46. Retrieved from http://doi.org/10.1111/bjep.12058

Baker, L. (2010). Metacognition. In P. Peterson, E. Baker, & B. McGaw (Eds.), *International encyclopedia of education* (3rd ed., pp. 204–210). Oxford: Elsevier.

Baker, L., & Cerro, L. (2000). Assessing metacognition in children and adults. In G. Schraw & J. C. Impara (Eds.), *Issues in the measurement of metacognition* (pp. 99–145). Lincoln, NE: Buros Institute of Mental Measurments.

Balcikanli, C. (2011). Metacognitive Awareness Inventory for Teachers (MAIT). *Electronic Journal of Research in Educational Psychology, 9*, 1309–1332.

Ben-David, A., & Orion, N. (2013). Teachers' voices on integrating metacognition into science education. *International Journal of Science Education, 35*(18), 3161–3193. Retrieved from http://doi.org/10.1080/09500693.2012.697208

Black, P., & Wiliam, D. (2003). "In praise of educational research": Formative assessment. *British Educational Research Journal, 29*(5), 623–637. Retrieved from http://doi.org/10.1080/0141192032000133721

Black, P., & Wiliam, D. (2009). Developing the theory of formative assessment. *Educational Assessment, Evaluation and Accountability, 21*(1), 5–31. Retrieved from http://doi.org/10.1007/s11092-008-9068-5

Braund, H. (March, 2017). Exploring the dynamic relationship between metacognition and the curriculum: suggestions for integration and implementation. *Graduate Student Symposium, Selected Papers, 11*.

Bryce, D., & Whitebread, D. (2012). The development of metacognitive skills: Evidence from observational analysis of young children's behavior during problem-solving. *Metacognition and Learning, 7*(3), 197–217. Retrieved from http://doi.org/10.1007/s11409-012-9091-2

Calderhead, J. (1991). The nature and growth of knowledge in student teaching. *Teachers and Teacher Education, 7*, 531–535.

Choy, S. C., & Cheah, P. K. (2009). Teacher perceptions of critical thinking among students and its influence on higher education. *International Journal of Teaching and Learning in Higher Education, 20*(2), 198–206.

Dinsmore, D. L., Alexander, P. A., & Loughlin, S. M. (2008). Focusing the conceptual lens on metacognition, self-regulation, and self-regulated learning. *Educational Psychology Review, 20*(4), 391–409. Retrieved from http://doi.org/10.1007/s10648-008-9083-6

Efklides, A. (2006). Metacognition and affect: What can metacognitive experiences tell us about the learning process? *Educational Research Review, 1*, 3–14.

Efklides, A., & Sideridis, G. D. (2009). Assessing cognitive failures. *European Journal of Psychological Assessment, 25*(2), 69–72.

Flavell, J. H. (1979). Metacognition and cognitive monitoring: A new area of cognitive—developmental inquiry. *American Psychologist, 34*(10), 906–911.

Goh, C., & Taib, Y. (2006). Metacognitive instruction in listening for young learners. *ELT Journal, 60*, 222–232. Retrieved from http://doi.org/10.1093/elt/ccl002

Griffith, P. L., & Ruan, J. (2005). What is metacognition and what should be its role in literacy instruction? In S. Isreal, C. Block, K. Bauserman, & K. Kinnucan-Welsch (Eds.), *Metacognition in literacy learning: Theory, assessment, instruction, and professional development* (pp. 3–18). Mahwah, NJ: Lawrence Erlbaum Associates.

Hacker, D. J., Dunlosky, J., & Graesser, A. C. (Eds.). (1998). *Metacognition in educational theory and practice*. Mahwah, NJ: Lawrence Erlbaum Associates.

Halpern, D. F. (1998). Teaching critical thinking for transfer across domains: Disposition, skills, structure training, and metacognitive monitoring. *American Psychologist, 53*(4), 449.

Harfitt, G. J. (2015). From attrition to retention: A narrative inquiry of why beginning teachers leave and then rejoin the profession. *Asia-Pacific Journal of Teacher Education, 43*(1), 22–35. Retrieved from http://doi.org/10.1080/1359866X.2014.932333

Hoy, A. W., & Spero, R. B. (2005). Changes in teacher efficacy during the early years of teaching: A comparison of four measures. *Teaching and Teacher Education, 21*(4), 343–356. Retrieved from http://doi.org/10.1016/j.tate.2005.01.007

Ivankova, N. V., Creswell, J. W., & Stick, S. L. (2006). Using mixed-methods sequential explanatory design: From theory to practice. *Field Methods, 18*(1), 3–20. Retrieved from http://doi.org/10.1177/1525822X05282260

Li, K. C., & Wong, B. T. M. (2017). Ways to enhance metacognition through the factors of learning processes, achievement goals and self-efficacy. *International Journal of Innovation and Learning, 21*(4), 435–448.

Lombaerts, K., De Backer, F., Engels, N., Van Braak, J., & Athanasou, J. (2009). Development of the self-regulated learning teacher belief scale. *European Journal of Psychology of Education, 24*(1), 79–96. Retrieved from http://doi.org/10.1007/BF03173476

McCormack, A., Gore, J., & Thomas, K. (2006). Early career teacher professional learning. *Asia-Pacific Journal of Teacher Education, 34*, 95–113. Retrieved from http://doi.org/10.1080/13598660500480282

Metallidou, P. (2009). Pre-service and in-service teachers' metacognitive knowledge about problem-solving strategies. *Teaching and Teacher Education, 25*(1), 76–82. Retrieved from http://doi.org/10.1016/j.tate.2008.07.002

Pajares, M. F. (1992). Teachers' beliefs and educational research: Cleaning up a messy construct. *Review of educational research, 62*(3), 307–332.

Patton, M. Q. (2015). *Qualitative research & evaluation methods* (4th ed.). Saint Paul, MN: Sage Publications.

Pilling-Cormick, J., & Garrison, D. R. (2007). Self-directed and self-regulated learning: Conceptual links. *Canadian Journal of University Continuing Education, 33*(2), 13–33. Retrieved from http://doi.org/10.21225/D5S01M

Pintrich, P. R. (2000). The role of goal orientation in self-regulated learning. In M. Boekaerts, P. R. Pintrich, & M. Zeidner (Eds.), *Handbook of self-regulation* (pp. 451–502). Burlington, MA: Academic Press. Retrieved from http://doi.org/10.1016/B978-012109890-2/50043-3

Pintrich, P. R. (2002). The role of metacognitive knowledge in learning, teaching, and assessing. *Theory into Practice, 41*(4), 219–225.

Sandelowski, M., Volis, C. I., & Knafl, G. (2009). On quantitizing. *Journal of Mixed Methods Research, 3*(3), 208–222.

Schellings, G. L. M., Van Hout-Wolters, B. H. A. M., Veenman, M. V. J., & Meijer, J. (2013). Assessing metacognitive activities: The in-depth comparison of a task-specific questionnaire with think-aloud protocols. *European Journal of Psychology of Education, 28*(3), 963–990. Retrieved from http://doi.org/10.1007/s10212-012-0149-y

Schraw, G., & Moshman, D. (1995). Metacognitive theories. *Educational Psychology Review, 7*(4), 351–371. Retrieved from http://doi.org/10.1007/BF02212307

Schunk, D. H. (1996). *Learning theories*. Englewood Cliffs, NJ: Prentice Hall.

Soleas, E. K. (2016). New teacher perceptions of inclusive practices: An examination of contemporary teacher education programs. *Alberta Journal of Educational Research, 61*(3), 294–313.

Spruce, R., & Bol, L. (2015). Teacher beliefs, knowledge, and practice of self-regulated learning. *Metacognition and Learning, 10*(2), 245–277.

Sternberg, R. J. (1998). Metacognition, abilities, and developing expertise: What makes an expert student? *Instructional Science, 26,* 127–140.

Veenman, M. V. J., Van Hout-Wolters, B. H. A. M., & Afflerbach, P. (2006). Metacognition and learning: Conceptual and methodological considerations. *Metacognition and Learning, 1*(1), 3–14. Retrieved from http://doi.org/10.1007/s11409-006-6893-0

Whitebread, D., Bingham, S., Grau, V., Pino Pasternak, D., & Sangster, C. (2007). Development of metacognition and self-regulated learning in young children: Role of collaborative and peer-assisted learning. *Journal of Cognitive Education and Psychology, 6*(3), 433–455.

Wilson, N. S., & Bai, H. (2010). The relationships and impact of teachers' metacognitive knowledge and pedagogical understandings of metacognition. *Metacognition and Learning, 5*(3), 269–288. Retrieved from http://doi.org/10.1007/s11409-010-9062-4

Woolfolk Hoy, A., Davis, H., & Pape, S. (2006). Teacher knowledge and beliefs. In P. A. Alexander & P. H. Winne (Eds.), *Handbook of educational psychology* (pp. 717–737). Mahwah, NJ: Erlbaum.

Zimmerman, B. J. (2002). Becoming a self-regulated learner: An overview. *Theory into Practice, 41*(2), 64–70.

Zimmerman, B. J. (2008). Investigating self-regulation and motivation: Historical background, methodological developments, and future prospects. *American Educational Research Journal, 45*(1), 166–183.

Zohar, A. (2006). The nature and development of teachers' metastrategic knowledge in the context of teaching higher order thinking. *Journal of Learning Sciences, 15,* 331–377.

Zohar, A., & Barzilai, S. (2013). A review of research on metacognition in science education: Current and future directions. *Studies in Science Education, 49*(2), 121–169. Retrieved from http://doi.org/10.1080/03057267.2013.847261 A

CHAPTER 7

Uncovering Preservice Teachers' Positioning of Themselves and English Learners (ELs) during Field Experiences

Stefinee Pinnegar, Celina Lay, Linda Turner, Jenna Granados and Sarah Witt

Abstract

Because of refugees and immigrants, teachers face the challenge of educating the children of these populations to become literate and academically successful. Yet, most teacher education programs do not provide extensive education for preservice teachers to meet the needs of these students. Just as importantly, Goldenberg (2008) argues that even when teachers are educated about teaching children a second language they are often not willing to enact those practices. This study examined case studies of English learners (ELs) created by preservice teachers during student teaching and explored how preservice teachers positioned themselves in relationship to ELs. The researchers used positioning theory to examine case studies from 60 preservice teachers. The cases were of 3rd to 5th grade students in schools that had at least a 10% EL population. We identified three plotlines from the cases. Common across the plotlines was the positioning of ELs as positive, pleasant and progressing based on the preservice teachers work with them. There are implications for both teacher education and research.

Keywords

second language learners – preservice teachers – teacher/student relationships – positioning theory

Introduction

Across the world societies are currently confronted with a range of economic and physical disasters causing increases in global mobility. The impact of earthquakes, tsunamis, hurricanes, drought and other natural disasters cause populations to migrate, seeking refuge, food and shelter. War, political unrest and upheaval, tyrannical or unstable governments, and waves of terrorism make many families' cities and countries unsafe. Indeed, these issues lead to increased immigration, both voluntary and forced, resulting in millions moving across national boundaries seeking safety and economic hope. Since this immigrant population includes large numbers of families with school age children, there are educational implications for this migration. Many children now need to gain academic prowess in a new language. We begin here by reviewing the increasing need for all teachers to be able to work with second language learners and the challenges in doing so. Then we explain the power of positioning theory to provide teacher educators with insight into preservice teachers' thinking and potential action as second language teachers.

Increased Need and Challenge of Educating Second Language Teachers

International migrants worldwide increased from 22 million in 2010 to 24.4 million in 2015. The U.S. population of ELs in K-12 schools also continues to grow (Counts, 2009; NCES, 2016; Pandya, Batalova, & McHugh, 2011; Payan & Nettles, 2008). In the U.S., the average number of ELs for all states is 9.6% (OELA, 2017). Across the state of Utah where our teacher education program exists, the average English learner population is 6%. When a school's enrollment is higher than 10% ELs, it is considered highly impacted. Many schools in Utah have as many as 50% of the students in a school needing to become proficient in English. Often in U.S. statistics the number of school aged children included within the statistic is masked because the refugee data includes the number of individuals but does not often include their ages. Currently, in Utah the refugee population numbers include the total number of refugees, ignoring the fact that about half of that refugee population are school-age children (see http://health.utah.gov/epi/healthypeople/refugee/datastatistics/2015/annual%20Arrivals%202015.pdf). Thus, the challenges of providing an appropriate educational response to these refugees includes the resources needed to educate their children. Education for refugee children – particularly in helping them acquire academic language – is central since in most cases these refugees will remain in the United States. We need these children to meet their intellectual and economic potential if they are to be fully contributing citizens. Often overlooked as well is the need for educating not only the children but the teachers who will teach them. The challenges are often seen as professional development rather than an issue for teacher education and the education of preservice teachers. These preservice teachers need to know how to teach ELs in their general education classrooms as well as being willing to enact the practices most likely to result in the success of all ELs.

An increasing number of second language learners are without teachers who can and will provide educational support and engage in best practices. In fact, only 12% of the universities across the U.S. prepare preservice teachers to work extensively or effectively with ELs. Most preservice teachers are not being adequately prepared to support ELs (Lucas, Villegas, & Freedson-Gonzalez, 2008; Samson & Collins, 2012). In fact, while 17 states have general requirements related to EL needs, 15 states do not (Ballantyne, Sanderman, & Levy, 2007).

While it is difficult to educate preservice teachers to enact the practices most likely to lead to student success, what may be more troubling is that many preservice teachers, like the inservice teachers who will mentor them in their early years, may be unwilling to regularly use or even try out the strategies and techniques most likely to support academic language development. Academic language development is essential for these students to succeed. Goldenberg (2008) argues that while there has been a massive professional development effort, most teachers never practice the strategies and techniques they are taught. At least in the U.S., teachers continue to hold false assumptions about second language learners (Gonzalez, 2016). To meet the educational needs of second language learners, it is essential that colleges of education prepare preservice teachers to teach these students (Daniel, 2014).

Understanding Preservice Teachers' Potential Action as Teachers Using Positioning Theory

Most often associated with Harré and van Langenhove (e.g., 1999), positioning theory explores the ways identities and the accompanying duties, obligations and responsibilities emerge as individuals position self and others. Thinking of preservice teachers' development as second language teachers through the lens of positioning theory allows teacher educators to think about how our courses position them and how they position themselves as teachers of ELs. What is particularly relevant for preservice teacher education is Harré and van Langenhove suggestion that it is not always how people are positioned but which positions they take up and how they embrace and enact the rights, responsibilities and duties entailed in one position rather than another.

Positioning theory also allows for an exploration of what plotline is implicit in the position taken up by the preservice teacher through speech or action. It allows the researcher to identify the roles beyond that of the main character (the teacher) that are available in the preservice teacher's implicit plotline. Thus, examining preservice teachers reflections on their teaching through positioning theory, allows insight into thinking and potential actions of preservice teachers in relationship to second language learners as well as track issues of power. Positioning theory can allow teacher educators to pay attention to the ways preservice teachers interact with and represent students, in given times and places.

In past research, there was a focus on how preservice teachers assumed the role of teacher and the stages they progressed through as they moved from students, to student teachers, to teachers Carter & Doyle, 1996). These earlier conceptions of teacher development suggest a single path in the learning to teach process. Further, at the same time, research on teacher identity development focused on uncovering the role teachers put on as they become teachers. This view of teachers' development seemed to suggest that there is a static thing called a teacher's role and that one puts it on (Ball & Goodson, 1985).

More recently, researchers have called into question this potentially unidimensional conception of the permanence of identity and role construction. Harré and van Langenhove (1998) argue that instead individuals position themselves and are positioned by others and that it is this moment to moment positioning that across time reveals identity and builds it. They argue further that acts of positioning reveal conceptions of self and assumptions about the world and just as importantly reveal the obligations, duties and responsibilities that underlie a particular act of positioning. As preservice teachers respond to assignments based in their field work experience they reveal their understanding of their work as teachers in relationship to the students they teach. Their assignments can reveal their knowledge, skills and dispositions for teaching second language learners particularly the obligations, responsibilities, and duties they feel toward teaching and students (particularly ELs), and the teaching plotlines they are prepared to enact.

This study examined case studies of ELs created by preservice teachers during student teaching to explore how these preservice teachers positioned themselves in relationship to second language learners.

Methodology

The data for this study were the capstone projects of preservice teachers. The projects were constructed during the preservice teachers' student teaching experience. During this time, they taught intraditional semester long placements or as the teacher of record across a year. The cases came from 60 preservice teachers' capstone projects. The cases analyzed here were from 60 teachers in 3rd to 5th grade classrooms. The preservice teachers were placed in schools with EL student populations of at least 10% in order for preservice teachers to have choices about who to study for their cases. The preservice teachers and the student who is the subject of the case study are referred to by pseudonyms throughout the document.

We worked with a team of researchers which included, one professor, two adjunct faculty who taught the courses and managed the EL student teaching and two preservice teachers who were student researchers but not the student teachers we were studying. We began with the student researchers coding five of the cases for potential emergent themes evident in the cases, explanations and details.

Next, we met as a group and reviewed the codes utilized in the student researchers analysis. We collectively reviewed the codes use focusing particularly on whether the codes identified accounted for the case as a whole. Together, we created a codebook, which included definitions and examples for each code.

Then working independently we coded ten cases, including the five originally coded by the student researchers. Once this coding was complete, we met together reviewing the independent coding collectively and worked until we reached consensus on the codes applied to the cases we used for the independent coding (Miles & Huberman, 1994). We then each analyzed additional cases using the coding categories, seeking disconfirming evidence, and ascertaining whether codes accounted for all data in each case we coded. We met again, to review the codes. We continued coding. Then met again. At this third meeting, having coded more than 75% of the data, we sought to uncover patterns in the ways in which themes came together and formed plotlines or patterns (Maxwell & Miller, 2010).

In this analytic session, we came to realize that we could use positioning theory in relationship to the coding to identify the ways preservice teachers positioned students and themselves as teachers within certain plotlines. To do this, we utilized the analytic triad. This is an analytic tool developed by Harré and van Langenhove (1998), which allowed for a targeted socio-linguistic analysis of the data. The triad utilized for analysis was an examination of the position inherent in the preservice teachers' statements, the storyline implicit in the statement, and the illocutionary force of the statement.

- The *position* refers to the parts or roles that the person assigns to the self and others.
- The *storyline* is the plot of the story implicit in the positioning.
- The *illocutionary force* is the social force behind the statement. Illocutionary force is the quality of the action inherent in what is said. For example, a declarative illocutionary force is evident when the queen says, "I knight you

Sir John". The statement itself brings into existence a knighthood. An assertive illocutionary force is evident in the statement "I am in charge here". The speaker asserts dominance or "being in charge", yet that may or may not be the resulting situation (perlocutionary force is the name of what actually happens after the statement) (Harré & van Langenhove, 1998).

Through using positioning theory, specifically the triad, we identified three plotlines and the attendant positioning of the preservice teacher in relationship to their students along these plotlines. We reviewed our earlier coding, identifying the plotline and positioning of the earlier coded cases, and then coded the uncoded cases. To further triangulate our analysis, we presented our analysis to colleagues and preservice teachers to strengthen the trustworthiness of our findings.

Results

Through the positioning analysis we uncovered plotlines in the case studies of the preservice teachers. In addition we found that the preservice teachers reported surprise in their work with the ELs they studied. This surprise seemed to suggest that in interacting with the ELs, their plotlines of teacher student interaction became more open and complex. Their surprise usually centered in developing a more holistic idea about the identity of the EL beyond merely a language deficit. Finally, preservice teachers plotlines consistently but usually subtly positioned themselves as heroes, narrating themselves as overcoming barriers or using knowledge from teacher preparation to improve the lives of the students they worked with.

Three Case Study Plotlines

We will begin by reporting the three distinct but related plotlines we uncovered in our analysis. A fundamental plotline across all cases involved the development of positive teacher student relationships. In this plotline, attractiveness and positive personality of the student was important. In all of the plotlines, the preservice teachers positioned themselves as successful and the students as pleasant, hard-working, and learning. All of this has implications for teacher education and research.

Plotline 1

The first is a plotline where the preservice teacher chose a student to work with and universally described their student in positive terms. Even when they reported difficulties like "shy" or "struggling" or "talks too much in class", these were accompanied with phrases like "very kind and caring", "social", "sweet", "eager to learn", "bright", "funny", "happy", "has leadership abilities", or "friendly". One preservice teacher, Scheel, described her EL's personality saying, "Johnny is intelligent, easy to work with, cooperative ... He has a pleasant personality, and although he is timid, he gets along well with his peers and other adults". In her reflection on working with this EL, she said:

> I enjoyed working with my EL student. He had such a sweet disposition and pleasant personality. His smile could melt an iceberg. He was most comfortable with a one-on-one or small group situations, so this was the best way to get to know him. His overall personality was timid, but he was very cooperative when he worked with me for guided reading or other projects that the teacher would ask me to specifically zone in on him and possibly one or two other children.

Notice the plotline is one in which the EL student is positive and pleasant. Implicit in the phrase "most comfortable working with a one-on-one ... situation" and the description of his personality as "timid" indicates that the EL might not have worked with others but liked her and worked for her.

Plotline 2

In the second plotline, the preservice teacher positions him/herself as the person who is most aware of the EL's needs and corrects or adjusts things the teacher or others such as aides and specialists might overlook. In describing the support the school provides (either the mentor teacher, special education teacher or ESL teacher), the student teacher judges the support as not really attending carefully enough to the EL's learning needs. This plotline occurred most frequently when the mentor teacher selected the EL that the preservice teacher did the case study on. For example, Flake is a preservice teachers who notices that her mentor teacher seems to "forget" Julie, the EL the mentor teacher assigned her. The irony here is that the mentor teacher potentially assigned Flake to work with this EL in order to give Julie additional attention and help. Flake describes how Julie was no longer receiving pull-out ESL services yet still struggled with English. She then explains how nice it was to get to know Julie one-on-one. Flake comments that her mentor teacher "didn't allow Julie to be excused from things because she was "still learning English". Flake indicates that she is very aware of Julie and knows that Julie still needs help in developing language and literacy skill even though she has moved beyond the direct language instruction provided in pull-out settings. Flake positions herself here as the one who really knows and understands what Julie needs and she, rather than the teacher, is positioned to put Julie first – she does not forget Julie. While this plotline of being the most informed about the EL is found primarily in cases where the preservice teachers was assign to work with a particular EL. However this plotline also occurred in the case studies of preservice teachers, who selected their EL. In addition, preservice teachers assigned an EL as well as some who selected the case study EL also reported the El specialists either did not really understand the language skill of the EL student or did not work carefully enough with the EL. In a few situations, the preservice teacher argued that the ELs English was strong enough they did not need special services or that the EL specialist had removed the EL from needed direct language instruction services. Again, the pattern is that the preservice teacher knew best what should or could be done for the EL.

Plotline 3

In plotline 3, the preservice teacher is an intern and the teacher of record who will work with the student across the year. Interns do their case studies at the end of the first semester rather than in the first four weeks. These preservice teachers had worked with ELs in their classroom across an entire semester. They almost always selected an EL for their case study who had made, according the intern, amazing academic learning strides. This positioned the intern as an outstanding teacher who had the capability of moving struggling students to being competent (or almost competent) readers with strongly improved language and literacy skills.

For example, one intern teacher, reporting about her case study student Karol, said that in a parent teacher conference she emphasized to Karol's parent the importance of reading 20 minutes a day and then encouraged the mother to have her daughter read even in their first language. After this meeting, the preservice teacher reports:

> After having talked to Karol's mom and made the clarification that reading in Karol's native language was okay, I began to see a lot more improvement in the reading getting done, and Karol making progress in her level of fluency and comprehension.

Notice that the intern is positioned as someone who knows little and simple tricks (reading at home in the first language) that will lead an EL to make great strides in learning a second language.

In another example, the intern talks about how her insight and action led to changes for Edgar, her case study student:

When Edgar first started school at Marsh Elementary we were unaware of his special educational needs. I noticed that he was far below any of the other students in my class, which concerned me. He seemed to really struggle with everyday class work. Once we realized that he needed special services and began to provide those services for him, his classroom behavior and classroom work has dramatically improved.

Notice the change in subject from "We" to "I" and then "we" again. The use of "we" is in contrast with her use of "I". Using "we" is a form of avoiding criticism or judgement of the teacher and the school since "we" also included the preservice teacher. In switching to "I', she asserts herself as the one who knows something everyone else is overlooking. Here, like in the earlier example of Karol, the intern notices and acts on the "simple" thing and this results in great improvement. This theme of the preservice teacher acting on knowledge that then results in great progress repeats in other case studies of preservice teachers, usually the interns, but also with the student teachers as well.

Opening the Plotline

As preservice teachers narrated or explained their case studies they often expressed surprise at how their student was different from how they had supposed them to be at first. In their initial reported conceptions of their ELs, they represented them as more unidimensional or stereotypic. For us, we named this "opening the plotline" because instead of identifying their ELs as flat characters in their plotlines they represented them more holistically and multi- rather than unidimensional. These opened plotlines were more complex. The preservice teachers reported more details about the ELs and their interactions with them. This resulted in preservice teachers articulating deeper knowledge about their ELs, resulting in their articulating individualized strategies for working with the ELs to promote their literacy and language development.

Stacy was a preservice teacher whose account exemplifies this concept of opening the plotline. Initially, Stacy was concerned about Geraldine (her EL) because she was so quiet, seemingly shy and disengaged in Stacy's general education classroom. As Stacy studied and interacted with Geraldine, she was surprised about how wrong she had been. She said:

> … when I asked her Spanish teacher about her behavior in Spanish class, I could not have been more shocked! The teacher said that Geraldine often offered to help the teacher with various tasks in the classroom, was considered a leader in the class, and stayed in from recess to interact with the teacher and other students.

Notice in the original plotline that Stacy was enacting, Geraldine was shy, withdrawn and not a particularly strong student. When Stacy explored further by communicating with the Spanish teacher, she came to see that Geraldine was more complex and more competent as a learner than she had initially supposed.

Stacy reported further, "That opened my view of Geraldine in a huge way. I began to see her as a student that emerged as a leader when she felt comfortable and appreciated, but did not feel that way in her English class". Stacy opened her view of Geraldine, and was able to conceptualize her as a more interesting and competent learner through her interaction with another teacher who worked with Geraldine. Thus we see that preservice teachers' plotlines often open in two ways. One, as they learn to collaborate with other colleagues, school staff or sometimes families new characters are added to the teacher's plotline of being a teacher for ELs. Second plotlines open as their characterizations of the ELs they are working with become more holistic.

As the plotline opened for Stacy she suddenly understood more fundamentally the value in finding out the strengths and needs of individual ELs. This realization led her to rethink her duties and responsibilities. She asked "… how a teacher would have time to complete an extensive evaluation and plan for each ELL in her class like this one". Stacy was torn. Her study of Geraldine revealed to her a more complex and competent child than she had supposed, which then led her to think in more sophisticated ways about how she was positioning Geraldine as a learner in her classroom and how others on the school landscape could provide valuable information about learners if she sought them out. Yet, she was troubled because it took lots of time to uncover this more complex view of the child – one of many she worked with – she wondered how she would be able to do this with all of her students. She asked: "Is there a way that I would be able to simplify this assignment for my future students?"

Other preservice teachers reported similar misconceptions and enlightenment about their students, which then resulted in them providing more holistic representations of their EL. For example, she got to know her EL better, Jane began describing her EL student differently, beyond her initial observation that her EL "raises her hand frequently in class". Jane become more open and aware of supports at the school that she had not thought of accessing, such as using a translator. In coming to see these support possibilities, the preservice teacher's plotline opened and she began to notice that working with a student was not a teacher's isolated responsibility but that schools offered resources and also held responsibility. In addition, if the preservice teacher sought collaboration with others such as a student's mother, a staff member, another teacher, a school translator, or even developing a closer relationship with the EL, they began to see that they could rely on others to support language learning for ELs. As preservice teachers' plotlines opened and new and more comprehensively represented characters populated the teacher's landscape, new possibilities for supporting student success emerged. Further, the preservice teachers identified new ways to meet the duties and obligations they felt toward promoting the success of ELs.

Preservice Teachers as Hero

The three plotlines we identified as underlying the case studies are reminiscent of hero stories in which the preservice teacher is successful in promoting the learning or class and school participation of ELs who the preservice teacher perceives as unlikely to succeed in general. One such example comes from Rosie. She is an intern and her hero story is more strongly articulated than most of the students. She reported:

> I believe the opportunities I have given Brittany to apply what she knows and thinks creatively have added to the success she is having in mathematics. Succeeding and having her thinking spotlighted and shared with the class has given her confidence. This confidence has taken her a long way. [Math curriculum] has given her opportunities to speak with her partner about mathematical concepts and encourages her to use the vocabulary that is built in to our learning targets. Brittany has been very successful in our lessons and is excelling above the class in math.
>
> Since the beginning of the school year how Brittany's speaking abilities have improve and I accredit much of this to the frequent opportunities I provide for her to converse with classmates. Today, she shares her ideas in our guided reading group comfortably, and will raise her hand to share in a whole group lesson, which simply did not occur when we started the school year. She also is comfortable approaching me about non-academic topics.

Notice that Rosie asserts that Brittany's English language skills have increased and the main reason this occurred was because of the way Rosie taught math and the opportunity she had provided for Brittany to develop strong vocabulary skills.Rosie identified her curriculum and her effort as the sole reason for Brittany's progress. Rosie saw her teaching practices as primarily practice in meeting her obligation to support Brittany in developing language skills.

Sharon, another preservice teacher, described her student Steven in similar ways. She chose to study him because he was a struggling language learner and because he was a pleasant student. She initially argued that he was considered a strong English speaker, but then she realized (unlike other teachers) the he had limited academic language proficiency. She also described Steven as lacking motivation. As she described her success in getting him to participate and take notes, Sharon was also experiencing for herself what it was like to be a knower and to have made a good judgement as a teacher that would fulfill student needs. She, also, described a moment when because of her knowledge and teaching practices Steven's learning is magically transformed which she reported as follows:

> Another great experience we had was with writing our narrative. When he found out that he was drawing a picture first his eyes lit up. He drew his picture and immediately started writing a story for it. He needed some scaffolding, as far as organization goes, but he had ideas in his head! It was magical. He didn't finish first but he wasn't the last! It was amazing. I will never forget that moment.

Notice how Sharon commanded the language of supporting ELs in their learning: using drawing, providing scaffolding, recognizing he had ideas. This was reminiscent of the opening of the plotline we discussed earlier, but just as relevant was the way Sharon storied herself as a hero able to transform Steven's learning.

These examples revealed two kinds of hero stories. The first was represented by Rosie providing Math instruction which led to Brittany's progress and Sharon's use of pictures with Steven which led him to be able to write which he had not done before. In addition, the preservice teachers represented themselves as heroes who had ideas and knowledge others on the landscape did not have or use in their interactions with ELs. The second plotline was more clearly represented by Wendy, who reported telling a parent whose EL child struggled to have the child read in their first language. Something according to Wendy no one else had mentioned to the mother.

These hero stories could be seen only as self-aggrandizement, but when we looked closer they could also be seen as preservice teachers relishing and being surprised by their ability to use their learning to meet their obligation to second language learners and move them forward in developing English skills.

Conclusions and Implications

One of the tensions the plotlines revealed was the preservice teachers' understanding of their duties, obligations, and responsibilities in their new identity as teachers. In their accounts they positioned themselves as knowers who acted on things they learned in teacher education which others in their schools seemed not to know. They also represented themselves as "good teachers" who constructed positive pleasant relationships with their ELs and were able to act in ways that made these students successful within their classrooms. The hero stories they constructed provided evidence they were meeting their obligations and responsibilities as teachers who made a difference in the lives of their students. They wanted to see progress in the student but may not have had a broad vision or sense of the complete context of students' lives in schools and out.

Thus their analysis is often skewed. For example Flake could not see that the mentor teacher had not forgotten Julie because the mentor teacher was the one who recommended Julie to Flake, so that Flake could provide that needed attention and extra education. The preservice teachers are required to interpret available data on a student and make real-life determinations about curriculum based on that data. They are also required (for the first time) to administer language proficiency testing, analyze the results, and come up with real-life recommendations. We recognized that it was scary for the preservice teachers to to transition to a place where their professional knowledge were asked for and know that your decisions affect another's life. Many of the preservice teachers found comfort in getting to know a bright and cheerful EL and were often surprised at the personal (and often typical) details they learned about the ELs and their families.

In the case studies, it was clear that this was a good experience for preservice teachers to assess, work one-on-one with, and support ELs in their education. As researchers, we think that providing such experiences is important in the development of preservice teachers. We are uncertain whether this work will transfer into their regular teaching practices in the future, but we had some assurance that it might as the preservice teachers narrated these experiences as important in their identity development as good teachers.

Rather than disparaging these preservice teachers because they represented their experiences in such a positive light and themselves as good teachers, we, the researchers, wondered what the implications are. We wondered if the fact that preservice teachers here gravitated toward more pleasant personalities and represented themselves as heroes in their plotlines could result in their being more willing to work with a larger range of ELs. If their first encounters were positive ones, will they feel more confident and be more willing to enact the practices for teaching ELs they learned in their preservice teaching? We wondered if being able to represent themselves as knowers who have tips and tricks and proprietary knowledge that will promote the learning of their ELs will make them more confident. We wondered if their positive first encounters would influence their view of themselves as future teachers of ELs who are willing to invest and enact ESL strategies in their regular classrooms.

We also wondered about the propensity of preservice teachers to report on the social and affective experience of working with ELs. Most often the preservice teachers focused on the social skills and personality traits rather than ELs language or academic skills. We wondered how and whether such a focus would expand and shift, enabling teachers to focus on the academic and linguistic development of their students alongside their social development. While in the case study preservice teachers reported on the assessment results and interpretation of them, in their reflections on the experience preservice teachers seldom if ever commented on the academic skills, the ELs language or literacy development or their actions to support the students' development of language and linguistic skills.

In interpreting these case studies, the plotlines of working with pleasant children and the hero stories and opening plotlines could be characterized as evidence of preservice teachers deficit orientations, but we wondered whether their sense of being able to meet obligations they held for teaching ELs would ultimately lead to their being advocates for these students in their future teaching roles.

Future research could explore more deeply the issues of positioning of preservice teachers in their accounts so that we could understand better the variance, hesitancies, and knowing they display. It would also be interesting to ask these teachers to look again at their case after two or more years of teaching or follow them into their practice to see how willing they were to work closely with ELs.

References

Ball, S. J., & Goodson, I. (1985). Understanding teachers: Concepts and contexts. In S. J. Ball & I. F. Goodson (Eds.), *Teachers' lives and careers* (p. 6). London: Falmer Press.

Carter, K., & Doyle, W. (1996). Personal narrative and life history in learning to teach. In J. Sikula (Ed.), *Handbook of research on teacher education* (2nd ed., pp. 120–142). New York, N.Y.: Macmillan.

Counts, Q. (2009). Portrait of a population: How English language learners are putting schools to the test. *Education Week,* 28(17).

Daniel, S. M. (2014). Learning to educate English language learners in pre-service elementary practicums. *Teacher Education Quarterly,* 41(2), 5–28.

Gersten, R., Baker, S. K., Shanahan, T., Linan-Thompson, S., Collins, P., & Scarcella, R. (2007). *Effective literacy and English language instruction for English learners in the elementary grades: A practice guide* (NCEE 2007-4011). Washington, DC: National Center for Education Evaluation and Regional Assistance, Institute of Education Sciences, U.S. Department of Education. Retrieved from http://ies.ed.gov/ncee/wwc/PracticeGuide.aspx?sid=6

Goldenberg, C. (2008, Summer). Teaching English language learners what the research does – and does not – say. *American Educator*.

Goldenberg, C. (2013, Summer). Unlocking the research on English learners what we know – and don't yet know – about effective instruction. *American Educator*.

Gonzalez, A. (2016, November). 10 assumptions to rethink about English language learners. *Ed Week*. Retrieved from http://www.edweek.org/tm/articles/2016/11/01/10-assumptions-to-rethink-about-english-language-learners.html?qs=10+assumptions (Web only)

Harré, R., & van Langenhove, L. (Eds.). (1999). *Positioning theory: Moral context of international action*. Oxford: Blackwell Publishers.

Maxwell, J. A., & Miller, B. A. (2008). Categorizing and connecting strategies in qualitative data analysis. In S. N. Hesse-Biber & P. Leavy (Eds.), *Handbook of emergent methods* (pp. 461–477). New York, NY, US: The Guilford Press.

Miles, M., & Huberman, M. (1994). *Qualitative data analysis* (2nd ed.). Thousand Oaks, CA: Sage Publications.

NCES. (2016). *English language learners in public schools*. Washington, DC: U.S. Department of Education, National Center for Education Statistics. Retrieved from https://nces.ed.gov/programs/coe/pdf/coe_cgf.pdf

Pandya, C., McHugh, M., & Batalova, J. (2011). *Limited English proficient individuals in the United States: Number, share, growth, and linguistic diversity*. Washington, DC: Migration Policy Institute.

Payan, R. M., & Nettles, M. T. (2008). Current state of English-language learners in the U.S. K-12 Student Population. *ETS*.

Schramm-Possinger, M. (2016). Pre-service teachers' humanistic vs. custodial beliefs: Before and after the student teaching experience. *Journal of Education and Training Studies, 4*(1), 74–87. Retrieved from http://files.eric.ed.gov/fulltext/EJ1078434.pdf

CHAPTER 8

Influence of Learning Attitudes and Task-Based Interactive Approach on Student Satisfaction and Perceived Learning Outcomes in a Content and Language Integrated Learning (CLIL) University Course in China

Leah Li Echiverri and Keith Lane

Abstract

Non-native English speaking students studying in an English medium university program in China, and taking a research methodology course (RM), were surveyed regarding attitudes to learning both English and course content, attitudes about a task based interactive approach – an ESL active learning construct – and influence of these on student satisfaction and learning. Convenience and purposive sampling of 72 students, a response rate of 72%, enrolled in RM completed the survey of this descriptive-correlation study.

Findings revealed that the students came to RM with a tacit English learning expectation in addition to the learning of the specified course content. They responded positively to interactive activities, similar to the types common to ESL classes, which simultaneously provided classroom interaction in English in tasks related to communication about RM. Attitudes and a task-based interactive approach had a strong and positive significant correlation to ESL student satisfaction and perceived learning. It is proposed that CLIL instructors should incorporate student to student speaking interaction to learning in CLIL courses.

Keywords

task-based interactive approach – ESL – EFL – student satisfaction – content and language integration – EMI

Introduction

Attention to opportunities, ways, and means of instructing and learning curriculum through the medium of what is variously called a 'second', 'foreign', or 'other' language is expanding. To some extent, related issues have always been present, as developing countries have strived to model their educational processes after comprehensive systems from developed countries, often with other language textbooks and wholesale imported libraries. Elsewhere, heterogeneous countries have strived to grapple with educational needs for immigrants and language minority populations.

However, modern expansive demands of economic and social globalization, and the expanded role of English as a professional lingua franca, appears to have thrust language policy into the spotlight of international educational and curricular initiatives more than ever. The nations of Europe, as part of their efforts to create a more united community, have often been at the forefront of these initiatives, formally defining and launching 'Content and Language Integrated Learning' (CLIL) as an educational reform in the mid-1990s (Darn, 2006).

The effort to achieve an education in a foreign language has typically followed a somewhat different pattern in China and Far East Asia. While China has made tremendous efforts to promote English language learning, they have tended not to complicate their curricular policies, or their high stakes and centralized university examination strategy, with content and language integration. The vast majority of secondary Chinese students do not study in a CLIL environment. Instead, traditionally, they have sent record numbers of university students out into the international arena to compete with native speakers for university placements and grades. Between 1998 and 2013 there was a 25% annual increase in Chinese university students overseas (Liu, 2016, 2018) particularly in English speaking countries, and in 2017 it is reported that there were over 600 million Chinese university students studying abroad (Kennedy, 2017), mostly privately funded.

In response to this outpouring of interest in global education in English, The Chinese Ministry of Education has promoted the establishment of six operating Sino-Foreign Cooperative Universities with established foreign university partners that strive to give Chinese students an undergraduate study abroad experience within China by recruiting instructors internationally and conducting coursework almost entirely in English. This relates Chinese efforts with European CLIL efforts and establishment of English as Medium of Instruction (EMI) institutions and programs around the world.

What is not recognized by this scheme is that the study abroad experience typically occurs in a rich language learning environment in which learners must use English for transactions with classmates – who are typically not Mandarin speakers – as well as with retailers, school administrators, landlords and utilities providers. When Chinese students discuss the morning's lecture with classmates in the American university cafeteria, they are likely to be doing that in English. Instead, EMI students' opportunities for interactional English development will likely be limited to the actual classrooms. In hallways, dining halls, dormitories, university offices, and shopping malls near campus, Chinese EMI students are unlikely to find any opportunities to use English. This limited opportunity to develop an integral skill speaks to the importance of examining student attitudes to, and satisfaction with, instruction which purposely integrates opportunities to practice English discussion in the context of learning content during lessons.

Eom, Ashill, and Wen (2006) studied course structure, instructor feedback, motivation, learning style, and instructor facilitation as determinants of perceived learning and learner satisfaction. While they found a positive relationship of all variables to satisfaction, only learning style and instructor feedback showed a positive significant relationship to perceived learning, though satisfaction was a significant predictor of perceived learning. In addition, in the follow-up study of course organization and structure, student engagement, learner interaction and instructor presence and their relationships to student satisfaction and perceived learning, Gray and DiLoreto (2016) found a positive relationship for each of the variables except learner interaction. Learner interaction did not have a significant positive relationship either on perceived learning or satisfaction.

Caution should be used applying these results to the current study, however, because, firstly, both studies were investigating online course delivery, whereas the current study involves a classroom setting, and secondly, the respondents were not described as English as foreign/second language (EFL/ESL) learners, as they are in the current study.

In the current study, the researchers hypothesized that learner interaction will be considered important to students as EFL learners coincidentally while they take Research Methodology (RM) and that interaction is an aspect of the course 'structure' that students will consider important as it provides opportunities for English language improvement through elaboration, clarification, and vocabulary and fluency development. These students are enrolled in an English as medium of instruction (EMI) university in China.

Assuming that learning activities similar to ESL task-based interactive activities would be predictors of EFL student satisfaction and perceived learning outcomes in a 'content course', the overall objective of this research was to determine the existence of a relationship between variables. Student learning attitudes, perceptions on task-based interactive activities, satisfaction level and perceived learning outcomes were described and analyzed.

In this report, the term ESL will relate to educational approach, which underscores the similarity of ESL and EFL; however, EFL will relate to the EMI context and students in it, to emphasize how these effect the context of learning in EMI – a foreign language environment – in contrast to being international students in a host country.

Theoretical Framework

Learning Attitudes

Second Language Acquisition motivational research conducted by Gardner and Lambert (1959) provides some insight regarding why a social construction approach to learning language would be attractive to ESL and EFL students. Their construct characterizes language learning motivations as integrative and/or instrumental. Integrative motivation relates to learners' desires to involve themselves in a speech community and culture of 'native speakers'. Instrumental motivation implies perceived and tangible advantage obtainable as a learning outcome, such as grades or promotion. Similarly, motivation has been described as "intrinsic" and "extrinsic" (Clement, Dorynei, & Noels, 1994). Gardner and Lambert provide empirical support for an assertion that an integrative orientation in motivation is more strongly associated with language learning than instrumental motivation. Essentially, the motivational types express the degree that learning a language is integral to the conception of "self" and personal actualization, versus mere advantages that can be gained.

However, Liu (2007) found that Chinese university students had a high level of motivation to learn English, but that the instrumental motivation was stronger than the integrative, and that the instrumental motivation correlated more to success. Like the Chinese students in Liu's study, the Chinese students in the current study are not English majors. However, unlike students in the current study, those in Liu's study were not reported to have had any experience in an EMI program. It is reasonable that electing the difficulty of university study in English, a second language is an expression of strong motivation, and accordingly an integrative orientation. Reasonably, students with integrative motivation will respond positively to purposeful opportunities to practice their spoken English expression while pursuing their studies.

In the current study, students were asked how they feel about the purposes of taking courses such as RM in English, the balance of importance of learning English and research methodology, communicating in English and whether satisfaction were solely conditioned on grades. The researchers hypothesized:

H1a: Learning attitudes significantly influence student satisfaction.
H1b: Learning attitudes significantly influence learning outcomes.

Task-Based Interactive Approach

While the term 'task-based interactive approach' is terminology borrowed from the ESL instruction domain, the term as used here involves general active learning principles. As such, the motivating theories find complementation and resonance in Content-Based Instruction (CBI) or Content and Language Integrated Learning (CLIL) environments.

When students are enrolled in university courses in a second/foreign language which they have not formed what is commonly thought of as 'complete mastery', especially when they are enrolled as a group in an otherwise 'mainstream course' conceptually equivalent as one for 'native speakers', then a CBI/CLIL context tacitly exists. In contrast to this concept of 'context' are practices of CBI/CLIL as an approach. As an approach, the purpose of CBI is to provide simultaneous instruction to ESL/EFL learners in English and 'content areas' (Brinton, Snow, & Wesche, 1989). Instruction in the CBI/CLIL classroom will be informed by some degree of balance between ESL instruction and the particular content area.

ESL instruction is strongly informed by active learning theory. This practice of providing purposeful and practical social foci for language instruction is an offshoot of Communicative Language Teaching, which typically incorporates features such as learning to communicate through target language interaction, the inclusion of authentic texts, opportunities for learner reflection on learning, valuing the learners' personal experiences as contributions to classroom learning, and attempts to connect classroom learning to real life goals, needs and contexts (Nunan, 1991).

Task Based (language) Instruction involves students interacting socially to complete meaningful tasks, usually of a 'non linguistic' nature, meaning they are not focused on a grammatical form or vocabulary list (Prabhu, 1987). The implication here is that language instruction does not need to focus and restrict student attention to a set of language forms for practice, and that by establishing the conditions for meaningful interaction instructors can establish conditions for language learning.

The Interaction Hypothesis may be referred to for an explanation of why this is so. This theory suggests that language proficiency is promoted by immediate, spoken, interaction and communication (Long, 1996), especially when it is accompanied by the need to negotiate and refine communication to achieve a mutual and compatible understanding (Ellis, 1997, p. 95).

The parallels in active learning pedagogy beyond the ESL classroom are telling. According to the engagement theory of Kearsley and Shneiderman (1998), "... students must be meaningfully engaged in learning activities through interaction with others and worthwhile tasks". The theory provides for interaction with content placing special emphasis on human interaction (Miller, 2015).

In the current study, active learning pedagogy refers to the task-based interactive approaches like group discussion, peer critiquing, peer pair quiz, and peer pair presentation and takes into account the learners' needs to develop English communication skills while learning the course content. The study focuses on learner-learner interaction. The instructional structure of these learning activities requires students' active engagement with peers to accomplish task assignments/requirements in RM. The researchers hypothesized:

H2a: A task-based interactive approach will lead to a higher level of ESL student satisfaction.
H2b: A task-based interactive approach will lead to a higher level of perceived learning outcomes.

Student Satisfaction

Moore (2009) cited the Sloan Consortium definition of student satisfaction as "Students are successful in the learning experience and are pleased with their experience". Sweeney and Ingram (2001) define student satisfaction as "the perception of enjoyment and accomplishment in the learning environment". Both definitions imply a sense of success and accomplishment in the learning experiences; both imply positive feelings of pleasure and enjoyment.

Gray and Diorite (2016) cited the complex model developed by Marsh and Roche (1997) for defining students' perceptions of satisfaction in terms of: learning value, instructor enthusiasm, rapport, organization, interaction, coverage, and assessment.

In this study, ESL student satisfaction refers to the students' positive feeling of pleasure and perceived accomplishment in their learning experiences. Aspects in the learning experiences are interactive activities, English learning opportunities, course content, course textbook, assessment tools and instructor's course design.

Learning Outcomes

Learning outcomes are "statements of what a learner is expected to know, understand and/or be able to do at the end of a period of learning" (Ministry of Science, Technology and Innovation 2005, p. 29 cited in Gil-Jaurena & Softic, 2016). Research Methodology, a liberal arts course in Wenzhou Kean University, includes eight student learning outcomes (SLOs) that need to be assessed. Five content SLOs and three values SLOs namely: transdisicplinarity, critical thinking, quantitative literacy, communication literacy, and information and technology literacy for the former and active citizenship, ethical judgment and integrity and diversity for the latter (https://sites.google.com/a/kean.edu/sgsassess/).

In the current study, SLOs were measured according to students' perceived learning outcomes as follows: transciplinarity measures the ability of students to apply research skills in other courses and in the future; communication literacy measures the students' English skills ability to speak, listen and write effectively; critical thinking, quantitative literacy and information and technology literacy measures students' ability to make decisions based on shared information including numerical data during task-based interactive activities and required to deliver presentations. Diversity measures the students' ability to team work with others.

Methodology

Descriptive-correlational research was used in the study. Convenience and purposive sampling were used for the survey instrument. Of the 100 students invited to participate in the study who were enrolled in RM in spring 2017 at Wenzhou-Kean University in China, 72 completed the ESL Student Satisfaction survey online; a response rate of 72%.

Content validity of the self-constructed questionnaire was established based on extensive literature review that the researchers believed to be logically related with the variables of the study. A 5-point Likert scale was used for participants to indicate their attitudes and perceptions related to learning attitudes, task-based interactive approaches, ESL student satisfaction and perceived learning outcomes. Numbers closer to 1 represented strong disagreement (SD) and number closer to 5 represent strong agreement (SA). The "Student Learning and Satisfaction in Online Learning Environments Instrument" developed by Gray and DiLoreto (2016) was the model in developing the concepts of the research instrument.

Mean and standard deviation were used to calculate responses to the scaled questionnaires of learning attitudes, task-based interactive approach, student satisfaction and perceived learning outcomes. Bivariate Correlation Analysis, using Pearson-Product Moment was used to measure relationships between two random variables to determine the strength and direction of the linear relationship. Multiple regression analysis was used to determine correlation between criterion variables, and the best combination of predictor variables, and relative importance of each variable in the equation. The level of significance used for each test was set at 0.05.

Results and Discussion

Descriptive Analysis

Figure 8.1 shows the descriptions of the students' attitudes about the purposes of taking the courses Research Methodology and English language and the balance of importance of learning English and Research Methodology and their motivation for language learning. Based on mean ranking, findings showed that students "*agree*" on the duality of importance of students' learning needs of both Research Methodology content and English learning skills.

The prediction that students would bring language learning purposes to CLIL classes, regardless of course syllabus content, was supported by the two highest mean scores for agreement in Learning attitudes: "It is important that (RM) supports my knowledge of research and ability to conduct it" ($\bar{X}$ = 4.29), and "Developing English abilities is essential to developing my research skills" ($\bar{X}$ = 4.26).

Instead of the predicted strongly integrative motivation, the results yield considerable contradiction. They show only mild agreement that "speaking

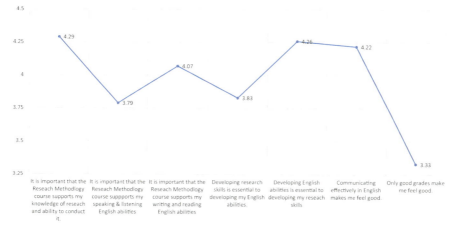

FIGURE 8.1   Learning attitudes description

and listening to English in class was *important*" ($\bar{X}$ = 3.79), though also more convincing agreement that "communicating effectively in English" provided positive feelings ($\bar{X}$ = 4.22). Perhaps "important" is a word that elicits instrumental responses, whereas "feel good" encourages an integrative response. In either case, the response is positive.

A litmus test, of sorts, was set by the item, "only good grades make me feel good". This emphatic and unequivocal statement invited students to reject the instrumental orientation, but instead the response was neutral ($\bar{X}$ = 3.33). Although this is the lowest measure of agreement for any item in the survey, because it is neutral, it neither confirms nor disconfirms the notion of a prevailing orientation and instead, when taken with the other items, suggests high motivation of both types, and that both types of motivation are catered to by collaborative speaking activities in class.

This is not inconsistent with Liu's (2007) description of Chinese English learners who were strongly motivated, but showed a stronger instrumental orientation, except that in the current study the balance of orientation was not determined. It is important to keep in mind that in both cases the students were not English majors.

Table 8.1 presents the descriptions of students' perceptions on the importance of task-based approach reinforcement to English learning in the CLIL course.

Descriptive analysis supports the assumption of learning effectiveness of a task-based interactive approach in the development of students' competence in both content and language. Students agree that "The interactive activities provide information sharing that enhances my understanding of research methods"($\bar{X}$ = 4.14); "Group discussion in English promotes more involvement and better learning compared to only listening to lectures in English" ($\bar{X}$ = 4.13); and "Group discussion in English helps me learn how to work well with others"($\bar{X}$ = 4.13).

This indicates that the task based approach goes beyond benefitting the learning of content knowledge and development of language skills. It also contributes to positive intellectual and eventual workplace attitudes and abilities that inevitably are purposeful functions of a university education. Students who can work harmoniously and candidly share and consider one another's ideas are a commendable objective.

Table 8.2 presents the descriptions of students' satisfaction with the various aspects of their learning experiences as to the following: interactive activities, English learning opportunities, course content, course textbook, assessment tools and instructor's course design.

TABLE 8.1 Descriptive statistics of students' perceptions on task-based approach on the reinforcement of English learning in CLIL

Task-based approach	Mean $\bar{X}$	SD	Scaled responses
The interactive activities provide for information sharing that enhances my understanding of research methods.	4.14	.78	Agree
The interactive activities in English help me to develop a deeper understanding of Research Methods	4.10	.78	Agree
The interactive activities develop my English expression ability.	3.99	.81	Agree
The interactive activities develop my English comprehension ability	3.94	.78	Agree
Group discussion in English helps me learn how to work well with others.	4.13	.67	Agree
Group discussion in English promotes better learning compared to only listening to lectures in English	4.13	.79	Agree
Group task activities create a comfortable and beneficial atmosphere for critical thinking.	4.11	.85	Agree
Peer Pair presentation helps me to develop analytical thinking skills.	3.89	.91	Agree
The peer pair quiz helps me to communicate different ideas.	4.00	.82	Agree
Through peer pair quiz I get to understand my relative strengths and weaknesses	4.00	.80	Agree
The peer pair quiz encourages the development of my team decision making, which is an important skill for the real world	4.04	.88	Agree
Overall mean	4.04	.80	Agree

Legend: Strongly Agree (4.51–5.00); Agree (3.51–4.5); Undecided (2.51–3.5); Disagree (1.51–2.5); Strongly Disagree (1.0–1.5)

Descriptive analysis supports that the task based approach supported satisfaction. The strongest measure of satisfaction ($\bar{X}$ = 4.14) directly supported satisfaction with interactive activities. While students were satisfied also with individualized activities ("individual activities" ($\bar{X}$ = 3.89); "textbook" ($\bar{X}$ = 3.88)),

TABLE 8.2   Descriptive statistics of students' satisfaction on their learning experiences

Students' satisfaction	Mean $\bar{X}$	SD	Scaled responses	Descriptive interpretation
I am satisfied with the learning effectiveness of interactive activities.	4.14	.72	Agree	Satisfied
I am satisfied with the learning effectiveness of individual activities.	3.89	.81	Agree	Satisfied
I am satisfied with the course research content.	3.96	.72	Agree	Satisfied
I am glad there were English discussion opportunities.	4.07	.81	Agree	Satisfied
I am glad there were English writing development opportunities.	4.00	.80	Agree	Satisfied
I am glad there were English listening opportunities.	3.90	.81	Agree	Satisfied
I am glad there were English reading opportunities.	4.03	.79	Agree	Satisfied
I am satisfied with the learning effectiveness of the course textbook.	3.88	.89	Agree	Satisfied
I am satisfied with the learning effectiveness of the assessment tools.	3.99	.78	Agree	Satisfied
I am satisfied with my instructor.	4.07	.78	Agree	Satisfied
I am satisfied by how my instructor teaches Research Methods.	4.03	.79	Agree	Satisfied
I am satisfied how my instructor supports my English development	4.06	.73	Agree	Satisfied
Overall mean	**4.0**	**.78**	**Agree**	**Satisfied**

Legend: Strongly Agree (4.51–5.00); Agree (3.51–4.5); Undecided (2.51–3.5); Disagree (1.51–2.5); Strongly Disagree (1.0–1.5)

such measures were noticeably lower. This supports the view that the interactive activities were a more favored aspect of the CLIL course.

Table 8.3 presents the descriptions of students' perceived learning outcomes in relation to their learning needs and future goals.

All scores in Table 8.3, 'perceived learning', are in the higher range of agreement. The task based interactive approach in this CLIL context significantly gave students confidence that they were learning the content, research skills ($\bar{X}$ = 4.32), and learning English ($\bar{X}$ = 4.19). Students were confident that they were developing good team work skills in interactive activities ($\bar{X}$ = 4.17). Specific task types – peer pair quiz and peer pair presentation – individually yielded positive scores for "decision making" and "analytical thinking".

Bivariate Correlational Analysis
To establish relationships of independent and dependent variables, researchers used Bivariate Correlational analysis as shown in Table 8.4. Findings showed that learning attitudes and task-based interactive approaches significantly influenced both ESL student satisfaction and perceived learning outcomes. All independent variables were positively and strongly correlated with dependent variables.

Contrary to previous research (Gray and DiLoreto, 2016; Eom, Ashill and Wen, 2006), the study found strong and positive relationships for learning attitudes and student interaction, as actualized within task-based interactive approaches, on both satisfaction and perceived learning.

TABLE 8.3   Descriptive statistics of students' perceived accomplishments in their learning experiences

Perceived learning outcomes	Mean $\bar{X}$	SD	Scaled responses
I am learning research skills that I can use in other courses and in the future.	4.32	.67	Agree
I am learning team working skills in interactive activities.	4.17	.71	Agree
I am learning decision making skills in peer pair quiz activities.	4.14	.72	Agree
I am learning analytical thinking skills in peer pair presentation.	4.01	.74	Agree
I am improving my English, which will support my continued learning and future goals.	4.19	.66	Agree
Overall mean	4.17	.70	Agree

Legend: Strongly Agree (4.51–5.00); Agree (3.51–4.5); Undecided (2.51–3.5); Disagree (1.51–2.5); Strongly Disagree (1.0–1.5)

TABLE 8.4 Bivariate correlation of all variables

	ESL student satisfaction	Perceived learning outcome
	R	R
Learning attitudes	.731[a]	.717[a]
Task-based interactive approaches		
– Interactive activities	.752[a]	.767[a]
– Group discussion	.535[a]	.571[a]
– Peer pair presentation/peer pair quiz	.416[a]	.479[a]
Overall task-based interactive approaches	.679[a]	.726[a]
ESL Student satisfaction	1	.766[a]

a Correlation is significant at the 0.05 level

These findings supported researchers 'hypotheses that learning attitudes and task-based interactive approach have statistically significant influence on ESL student satisfaction and perceived learning outcomes.

Surprisingly, the two dependent variables, ESL student satisfaction and perceived learning outcomes showed the strongest relationships of the variables of this study (r = .77) at the .05 level of significance.

Considering a strong and positive correlation between independent and dependent variables was established, multiple regression analysis (MRA) was conducted

Multiple Regression Analysis

The study examined factors that influence both student satisfaction and perceived learning outcomes of ESL learners' studying in a CLIL/EMI context. The research model was tested using multiple regressions on the survey data as both independent variables showed statistically significant strong and positive relationship to the dependent variables.

The multiple regression model was used to determine the strength of effects of independent variables on dependent variables, and to forecast how changes among independent variables will impact dependent variables.

Using the adjusted R^2, the theoretical implication of the MRA explains that 60.4 percent of the variation in ESL student satisfaction and 63.1 percent of the variation in perceived learning outcomes can be accounted for from the combined changes in learning attitudes and task-based interactive approaches (see Table 8.5).

The strong positive correlation suggests that students' learning attitudes significantly influence student satisfaction. This outcome was predicted given the nature of the duality of learning agenda in CLIL – language and content – and the presumption of an integrative orientation for language learning. Although that dominant integrative orientation was not confirmed, the significantly high score of $\bar{X}$ = 4.22 for the statement that communicating effectively in English made the students feel good is sufficient evidence that the integrative motivation was very high, whether or not it was dominant, and reflection informs us that a strong instrumental motivation might also support the incorporation of in-class spoken interaction

Also, the strong positive correlation suggests that students' learning attitudes significantly influence learning outcomes. Thus, students' level of motivation has an effect on students' learning outcomes as revealed by the three highest score "I am learning research skills that I can use in other courses and in the future" ($\bar{X}$ = 4.32), and "I am improving my English, which will support my continued learning and future goals" ($\bar{X}$ = 4.19). "I am learning team working skills in interactive activities" ($\bar{X}$ = 4.17).

Likewise, the strong positive correlation suggests that the task-based interactive approach will lead to a higher level of EFL student satisfaction and learning. Thus, when content specialist instructors support students' English development in a CLIL environment by providing task-based interactive

TABLE 8.5 Coefficient of determination (R^2) model results

	Adjusted R^2	Coefficients	P-value
Influence on ESL-student satisfaction	.604[a]		
R^2 = .615[a]			
Learning attitudes		+.525	1.59437E-06
Task-based interactive approaches		+.406	0.000305825
Influence on perceived learning	.631[a]		
Outcomes R^2 = .641[a]			
Learning attitudes		+.423	1.45E-05
Task-based interactive approaches		+.476	5.52E-06

a Correlation is significant at the 0.05 level

activities, students are highly satisfied with their course content and English development.

Practical Implications

The students expected this course, RM, to cater to dual needs to learn English and about the specific content of the course, and were satisfied when the methods provided focused and purposeful opportunities for spoken English practice and development. The internal logic of CLIL and EMI programs also speaks to this purpose. While the syllabus of a particular course, such as RM, may not explicitly establish English language development as a grading criterion, the purposes of students, and the establishment of such programs in the first place, imply English development as a curricular necessity.

The task-based interactive approach (TBIA), a social constructivist pedagogy, has established that, by focusing on content rather than language per se, a CLIL content specialist instructor can establish conditions for language development without jeopardizing progress in terms of content. Content specialist instructors do not specifically need ESL teaching experience to accomplish English learning support, though such expertise could be useful and exposure to ESL classroom processes, either as observer or instructor participant, is suggested for development of professional practice development. These findings are applicable to similar students in similar programs – ones that integrate language development with content instruction – and inform instructors to take an active learning, social constructivist, approach. The forgoing suggests that instructors in CLIL or EMI contexts should consider active learning principles in general, and discussion based instruction pedagogy in particular, for at least some portion of the class time.

Consequently, content specialist instructors are encouraged to consciously include discussion based instruction pedagogy that directs students to actively discuss course content, such as those employed in this study: group discussion, group task activities, peer presentation and peer pair quiz. In this study and others, interactive learning activities promote students' deeper understanding of course content through information sharing. When students are involved in group discussion, their English expression, comprehension ability and critical thinking are better developed compared to only listening to lectures. Furthermore, students attest that the approach supports their learning how to work well with others, too. Hence, task-based interactive activities as an 'instructional approach' will lead to high level of student satisfaction and perceived learning outcomes in CLIL contexts.

Students enjoyed interactive learning and felt it was efficacious compared to individualized activities. In this study, students rated their success learning content and language highly and were satisfied, and the content teacher was appreciated for including speaking tasks that improved student ability to communicate and understand the content, and additionally develop English.

As a result, content specialist instructors are encouraged to include opportunities for spoken English practice and development similar to those designed by ESL instructors in designing their own lessons. As shown in this study, TBIA, as an instructional approach, can contribute to high student satisfaction, and high self-evaluations for learning, in terms of learning content and English. However, we recognize that these statements may depend somewhat on the specific content. While some disciplines may not be as amenable to the TBIA approach as RM, we suggest that instructors should give some attention to providing opportunities for students in CLIL and EMI programs to communicatively work with content in the target language in classwork.

While Gray and DiLoreto (2016) did not find that learner interaction contributed to student satisfaction and perceived learning, those results are contradicted by this study for clearly discernible reasons. Gray and DiLoreto were exploring a course delivered online, which may render attempts to create a 'community' through interaction a superficial distraction. In contrast, students enrolled in face-to-face courses might hold very different attitudes and do not have to mediate through electronic devices.

In fact, ESL practitioners expend a great deal of effort in developing learning environments with a great deal of rapport, believing is it important to support spoken interaction. This involves the other difference in the study; Gray and DiLorento's subjects were not reportedly ESL students enrolled in an EMI program who would depend on such interaction to fulfill primary learning goals. While it would be interesting to determine whether there are attitudinal differences among students according to disciplines in EMI, we believe our findings are generally applicable to any courses in an EMI program and EFL students who share a classroom together.

The researchers presumed that EFL students would display these preferences because students would show a high level of integrative motivation and not differentiate greatly their approaches to learning EFL and their CLIL course. Liu (2007) described Chinese university students as instrumentally motivated, but the certainty and the importance of this finding is questionable. In fact, we found that the motivations of the students were complex, but that both an integrative and instrumental orientation were served by the task-based speaking approach. In other words, we surmise that the nature of the ESL and Content division is one of placement on a continuum rather than representing a strict dichotomy from the student viewpoint, and that the nature of their motivational orientation – integrative vs. instrumental – is also a matter of degree.

While the study results support the movement of instruction in an EMI/CLIL context toward active learning and discussion based pedagogy, it does not argue necessarily for the abandonment of any and all other methodologies. Effective methodology in one curricular domain may, on balance, be different from effective methodology in another. Furthermore, effective teaching is based on rehearsal, practice, and reflection. However, for instructors who are accustomed to relying on lecturing, a gradual but deliberate and certain process of supplementing classroom routines with active learning opportunities is endorsed.

As an example of this principle, the traditional 10–15 minute Q&A at the conclusion of a lecture can be exchanged with several five minute focused question tasks sequenced after key parts of a lecture to be answered in pairs or small groups. This would not only improve learner focus on the content, but provide opportunity for instructors to monitor and reinforce main ideas, more so and increasingly as these procedures evolve from being novelties to being usual classroom routines. Such routines simulate the type of conditions described as TBIA used in the RM course in the current study. This research argues that active learning and discussion based pedagogy is effective, motivational, and satisfying, but not that it is incompatible with other educational processes.

The results of the study provide insight into student attitudes, perceptions and satisfaction that may be of interest to content specialist instructors interested in designing 'content' courses in a CLIL context. The implication is that such instructors can promote their students' satisfaction in content courses and their perceptions of learning by adopting active learning methods which, purposefully or incidentally, also address the learners' ESL agenda.

Interestingly, ESL student satisfaction showed a strong and positive relationship with perceived learning outcomes. This finding suggests that a high level of student satisfaction for content learning and English development leads to high levels of students' capabilities to apply their content knowledge and skills in various settings outside the parameters of a specific course content. The strong correlation suggests that cross curricular integration affords higher levels of students' continued learning that will support their academic success and future goals. The issue of satisfaction is generally important in education, but perhaps particularly so in an EMI program because students need to exert higher levels of attention to cope with the second language challenges they face on a day to day, hour to hour, basis.

Moreover, the TBIA instructional model is further encouraged for its strong influence on developing learners' life skills such as team working skills, decision making skills and analytical thinking skills. Thus, for both instructors and higher educational institutions, such models should be attractive since student satisfaction is linked to improved academic performance, student recruitment (Sinclaire, n.d.), continued learning (Sloan cited in Sinclaire), and decisions to take additional classes (Booker & Remon, 2005).

Conclusions

The task-based interactive approach as an 'instructional approach' in course planning and implementation is a strong predictor of student satisfaction and learning outcomes. A strong and positive significant correlation of student attitude and use of interactive tasks to student satisfaction and perceived learning was established for Chinese tertiary students learning in a CLIL (EMI) context. Students found meaning by using sessions and instruction as opportunities to collaboratively complete tasks, using English, in Research Methods, and they attributed purposeful discussion based methodology to motivation, satisfaction and learning.

In this study, it is manifest that such an instructional approach can be successfully applied to challenging coursework in English, in China – a context where it is a foreign language – with demonstrable success. As Chinese students seem no more likely to be receptive to such a methodology than students in another country, or another context, we argue that such approaches offer a promising successful instructional pathway in CLIL or EMI contexts generally.

Classroom instructors are advised to consider task-based interactive approach as an 'instructional approach' in course planning and implementation, even though they might feel the methods of such an approach slow rate of coverage. After all, learning does not necessary increase merely because presentation accelerates, and student satisfaction is a reasonable objective for instruction.

There is advice here also for educational administrators. In order for EMI/CLIL programs to be something other than 'poor cousins' of programs that match curricular content to first languages, EMI programs must necessarily accentuate the opportunities for developing multilingual professionals, and the theoretical frameworks of ESL – such as CBI, communicative language teaching, active learning, etc. – do not support the notion that language learning, or even content learning, is provided for through lecturing. Administrators are encouraged to take a broad language across the curriculum approach when conceiving and reforming curricula and developing, and rewarding, faculty human resources.

References

Booker, Q. E., & Redman, C. E. (2005). E-student retention: Factors affecting customer loyalty for online program success. *Issues in Information Systems, 1*(1), 183–189.

Brinton, D. M., Snow, M. A., & Escher, M. B. (1989). *Content-based second language instruction.* New York, NY: Newbury House.

Clement, R., Dornei, Z., & Noels, K. A. (1994). Motivation, self-confidence, and group cohesion in the foreign language. *Language Learning, 3,* 417–448.

Darn, S. (2006). Content and Language Integrated Learning (CLIL) A European Overview. Teacher Development Unit, School of Foreign Languages, Izmir University of Economics, Izmir, Turkey. Retrieved from ERIC database. (ED490775) April 15, 2018. https://files.eric.ed.gov/fulltext/ED490775.pdf

Ellis, R. (1984). *Classroom second language development: A study of classroom interaction and second language acquisition.* Oxford: Pergamon.

Eom, S., Ashill, N., & Wen, J. (2006). The determinants of students' perceived learning outcomes and satisfaction in university online education: An empirical investigation. *Decision Sciences Journal of Innovative Education, 4*(2), 215–235.

Gardner, R. C., & Lambert, W. E. (1959). Motivational variables in second-language acquisition. *Canadian Journal of Psychology, 13,* 266–272.

Gil-Jaurena, I., & Softic, S. K. (2016). Aligning learning outcomes and assessment methods: A web tool for e-learning courses. *International Journal of Educational Technology in Higher Education, 13,* 1–16. Retrieved from http://dx.doi.org.kean.idm.oclc.org/10.1186/s41239-016-0016-z

Gray, J., & DiLoreto, M., (2016). The effects of student engagement, student satisfaction, and perceived learning in online learning environments. *NCPEA International Journal of Educational Leadership Preparation, 11*(1), 1–20.

Kearsley, G., & Shneiderman, B. (1998). A framework for technology-based teaching and learning. *Educational Technology, 38*(5), 20–23.

Kennedy, K. (2017). China outbound student numbers at record high. *The PIE News: News and Business Analysis for Professionals in International Education* (Online). Retrieved December 30, 2018, from https://thepienews.com/news/outbound-student-numbers-increased-2017/

Liu, M. (2007). Chinese students' motivation to learn English at the tertiary level. *The Asian EFL Journal Quarterly, 9*(1), 126–146.

Liu, W. (2016). The international mobility of Chinese students: A cultural perspective. *Canadian Journal of Higher Education, 46*(4), 41–59.

Liu, X. (2018). Transnational education: Sino-Foreign cooperative universities in China. *World Education News and Reviews* (Online). Retrieved January 1, 2018, from https://wenr.wes.org/2018/08/sino-foreign-cooperative-universities

Long, M. (1996). The role of the linguistic environment in second language acquisition. In W. C. Ritchie & T. K. Bhatia (Eds.), *Handbook of second language acquisition* (pp. 413–468). San Diego, CA: Academic Press.

Miller, G. (2015). Association between learner interaction and achievement in an online course: A longitudinal study. *NACTA Journal, 59*(3), 197–201.

Moore, J. C. (2009). A synthesis of SLOAN-C effective practices. *Journal of Asynchronous Learning Networks, 13*(4), 73–97.

Moore, M. G. (1989). Three types of interaction. *The American Journal of Distance Education, 3*(2), 1–6.

Nunan, D. (1991). Communicative tasks and the language curriculum. *TESOL Quarterly, 25*(2), 279–295.

Prabhu, N. S. (1987). *Second language pedagogy*. Oxford: Oxford University Press.

Sinclaire, J. K. (n.d.). An empirical investigation of student satisfaction with college courses. *Research in Higher Education Journal, 22*, 1–21. Retrieved April 5, 2017, from http://www.aabri.com/manuscripts/131693.pdf

Sweeney, J. C., & Ingram, D. (2001). A comparison of traditional and web-based tutorials in marketing education: An exploratory study. *Journal of Marketing Education, 23*(1), 55–62.

CHAPTER 9

Helping the Learning of Science in Whichever Language: The Attention to Proficiency in the LOLT, Polysemy and Context That Counts Best during Science Teaching

Samuel Ouma Oyoo and Nkopodi Nkopodi

Abstract

This chapter draws from an exploratory study of the difficulties South African High School physical science learners encounter with everyday English words when presented in the science context. Data were obtained from participants (1107 learners and 35 respective physical science teachers/educators from 35 public secondary schools in Johannesburg area of South Africa) through a word test to participant learners followed by group interviews but one-on-one interviews with respective physical science educators. Findings have revealed that South African learners also face difficulties with meanings of everyday words presented in the science context. While the main source of difficulties encountered was learner inability to distinguish between the meanings of familiar everyday words as used in everyday parlance from the 'new' meanings of the same everyday words when used in the science context, fewer difficulties will be experienced by learners if science educators (1) take to being more precise in their talk and use of language, and/or (2) generally explain the nature and context meanings of all the words used during teaching. The findings thus suggest that focusing on precise use of language as well as contextual proficiency more than on general proficiency in the language of learning and teaching (LOLT) during teaching perhaps holds more promise for enhanced learning and achievement in science. Steps necessary to raise teacher awareness of the potential impact of attention to precise use of language, nature and context meanings of everyday words of the LOLT science are discussed.

Keywords

science classrooms – language proficiency – contextual of use – polysemy – South Africa

© KONINKLIJKE BRILL NV, LEIDEN, 2019 | DOI: 10.1163/9789004405363_009

Introduction

Language has long been recognised as a tool that facilitates communication between the teacher and the learners during learning and teaching. One of the major functions of language relevant to science educators therefore is its use in facilitating learning: for trying to put new ideas into words, for testing the learners' thinking, and for fitting together new ideas with old ones in order to bring about new understanding in the learner's mind (Hamid, Nguyen, & Baldauf Jr, 2013). In science education, the deep analysis of the purposes of language as talk (Scott 1998), used by the science teachers/educators, the knowledgeable others, during teaching episodes has made it very apparent that for learners' recognition of the words of the language of the science classrooms and science texts, a high level of learner proficiency in the language of learning and teaching (LOLT) is the key attribute. As discussed shortly in this chapter however, proficiency in the LOLT is only one of the factors of successful learning and retention of scientific concepts; if learners are to learn science easily, they, in addition to possessing adequate proficiency in the LOLT, 1) must have an attendant ability to handle the [science] concepts (Achebe, 1990) as well as 2) an understanding of the 'new' meanings of everyday words when used in the science context, i.e. the learners need to understand the meanings of all words used in the science classrooms and science texts.

Theoretical Framework

The Anatomy and Nature of the Language of Science Classrooms and Science Texts

The language of the science classroom or science texts can be divided into two broad parts namely, the technical component and the non-technical component. The *technical component* comprises of words that have meanings specific to a science subject or discipline, and which by association, seem to give identity to particular subjects and/or the science discipline; these words (of the science classroom or science texts) are those that are interchangeably often referred to as 'technical words', 'science concepts', 'science terms' or 'science terminology'. Examples include *photosynthesis, respiration* and *genes* in Biology; *pressure, capacitance* and *voltage* in Physics and *atoms, elements,* and *cations* in Chemistry (Oyoo, 2012, 2017). In essence, learning science is often the learning of the (science) meanings of these technical terms that in many instances are common everyday words deliberately used as science concepts, and which used thus, become polysemous in nature.

Non-technical component of the language of the science classroom on the other hand is made up of words that define or give identity to the particular LOLT in use in a classroom or the language of a science text. This is to the extent that we are able to tell which language is in use, whether the language is Spanish, Greek or any other. Although all words in the non-technical component of the LOLT of science are non-technical words, three categories within have been derived in research literature on LOLT in science education, namely: '*logical connectives*', '*metarepresentational terms*', and '*non-technical words used in the science context*', and are distinguishable from one another.

While '*logical connectives*' are words or phrases which serve as links between sentences or between a concept and a proposition e.g. 'since', 'because', 'conversely' and 'therefore' (Fensham, 2004; Gardner, 1977), Wilson (1999) has described '*metarepresentational terms*' as words or terms which signify *thinking*, and comprise 'metalinguistic verbs' and 'metacognitive verbs'. Metalinguistic verbs are words which take the place of the verb to *say* such as, 'define', 'suggest', 'explain', 'describe' etc. Metacognitive verbs on the other hand take the place of the verb to *think* such as 'calculate', 'observe', 'analyse', 'deduce', 'predict', 'hypothesize' etc. The functional value of metarepresentational terms is in the fact that knowledge of their meanings may enhance students' understanding of the demands of the questions presented them during assessment or in a learning situation, to accordingly, design the correct responses (Bulman, 1986). Metarepresentational terms have been referred to as "command words" (Childs, Markic, & Ryan 2015, p. 436) perhaps based on the fact that each of these words when used with learners always seem to ask of them to *think* or to *say* something. Students' understanding of the meanings of these words may therefore be expected to enhance their classroom participation or 'argumentation skills' (Murphy et al., 2018).

The category of non-technical words referred to as '*non-technical words used in the science context*' are those words which have become part of the language typical of science subjects but do have meanings in the science context that are different to their meanings in everyday use of a language. The context specific meanings that everyday words possess while presented in the science context do embody certain concepts important to the process of learning and teaching of specific science subjects (Gardner, 1971). The focus of discussions in this chapter is around learner understandings of the *non-technical words used in the science context* as a means to highlight the need for precision in talk and use of language during science learning. The difficulty of science, especially to the learners who have to learn in languages that are not their first or home languages, has generally been attributed to whether such learners have communicative competence (proficiency) in the LOLT or not. The linguistic origin of the general difficulty of science content as well as of the language characteristic of science classrooms and science texts can now be derived.

Proficiency in, and Polysemy of Science Words and the Difficulty of LOLT Science

As already mentioned in this chapter, learning science content is essentially an attempt to master the meanings of words interchangeably referred to as *science terms, science words* or *science terminology*. The universal dissatisfaction with outcomes in science globally, including in the context of the study that this chapter draws from (see Oyoo, 2017), is a clear message that students of science generally encounter difficulties with the words that comprise the technical component of the science classroom language and/or science texts. This difficulty with science is attributed here to the foreignness of the science words to the learners. As already mentioned here, the foreignness of the science words stems from the polysemy that everyday words acquire when used as science words.

The difficulty of the LOLT in addition, has been suggested by the outcome in a review of all relevant studies of difficulties students encounter with all categories of words that comprise the non-technical component of the LOLT of science, that

> ... students encounter difficulties with all categories of everyday [non-technical] words common in science classroom language irrespective of whether they learn using their first [home] language or not (linguistic circumstances), or whether they are females or males (their gender). The types of students' difficulties have also been irrespective of individual cultural backgrounds. (Oyoo, 2007, p. 236)

The nature of the first two categories of words in the non-technical component of the LOLT [as already described in this chapter], namely – *logical connectives* and *metarepresentational terms*, can be taken to suggest that any challenges that students have been reported to encounter with these words (see Gardner, 1977; Oyoo, 2007, respectively) can arguably be traced to the relative levels of general proficiency in the instructional language. This supports the assertion that possessing general proficiency or basic competence in the LOLT is a necessary first step for any learning to occur in any language (Oyoo, 2007). The need to possess adequate proficiency in a LOLT as thus defined as a basic requirement, is some support to the campaigns, including by UNESCO (2007), to have all learning in schools to be conducted in the learners' first or home languages. However, an important and relevant question has been posed: "What kind of science can a child learn in the absence, for example, of basic language competence *and* an attendant inability to handle concepts?" (Achebe 1990, p. 162; emphasis added).

We are thus alerted to the fact that learning science in a language calls for more learner attributes than mere possession of general proficiency (i.e. basic language competence) in a LOLT. Yet in situations where the learners' capability *to handle the science concepts* and aptitude for science are identical, it will be an expectation that the only other factor for learners' successful learning is for them to be adequately competent in the LOLT. The discussions that now follow highlight that fact that context of use is yet another important influence on the learners' ease to tell the meanings of every day words when used [in verbal and/or textual interactions] during the teaching and learning of science.

The Impact of Context of Use and Precision in Use on the Difficulty of LOLT Science

The place of context of use in meaning recognition is evidenced in the way every day words mean differently when used in the science context, to their everyday use. How meanings of everyday words change when presented in a science context is now discussed in detail using the words 'reaction', 'diversity' and 'disintegrate'. As in the Macmillan English dictionary (2002, pp. 395–1172),

> ... the meaning of the word *'reaction'* in everyday English refers to the way one feels or behaves as a result of something that happens; *diversity* refers to the fact that very different people or things exist within a group or place, while the everyday meaning of *disintegrate* is to be completely destroyed by breaking into lots of very small pieces.

The word 'reaction' as found in Physics makes it a technical term – a force. In Chemistry, 'reaction' is used to describe what happens when two or more substances are mixed. The word 'diversity', as commonly used in Biology refers to the various types of species such as plants and animals while the word 'disintegrate' as used in Physics is often in reference to the *'decay'* of an *unstable nucleus*. How the word 'disintegrate' is used in physics gives meanings to the words 'decay' and 'unstable nucleus'. As relevant to the science context, 'disintegrate' means a reorganisation of the sub-atomic particles in the nucleus of an atom instead of the 'breaking of the nucleus into lots of small pieces' as is the English meaning. Similarly, the word 'decay' does not refer to 'rotting' or 'decomposition' of the nucleus but to 'birth' of a [daughter] nucleus but whose properties or characteristics are 'very different' from those of the [parent] nucleus.

The way the meanings of words 'diversity', 'reaction', 'disintegrate' and 'decay' change with the context of use suggests that the transformation of meanings of everyday words when used in the science context is the source of difficulties often encountered with everyday words when used in the science context. This is argued on the simple reason that contextual difficulties can be encountered only by those with some proficiency in a language of learning and teaching. Difficulties with the meanings of non-technical words presented in a science context, in the main can therefore be explained on failure to recognize that "every day words cease to be mere English words when used in a science context" (Marshall & Gilmour, 1991, p. 334).

This has now defined the place of context and by implication, the need for precision in use, to enhance the ease with which the meanings of everyday words presented in the science context may be told. Thus while general proficiency i.e. possession of basic language competence is a necessary and first requirement for any learning in *any* language, it can now be fully acknowledged that learning science in *whichever* language will be successful depending also on: level of learner ability/interest in science, being able to detect polysemy and to tell the meanings of everyday words when presented in the science context. Based on this conclusion, a perspective on language adopted in the study reported in this chapter is now discussed.

A Perspective on Language in Learning Science: The Conceptual Framework

The place of proficiency or competence in the LOLT and the role of polysemy in the difficulty of science content have been explained. As well, how word meanings depend on the context of use and therefore why precise use of words/language may be necessary for enhanced learner ability to tell context meanings of the words has also been derived. The picture that now obtains seems to have revealed a link between *everyday words* of the LOLT when used as either technical words (science content knowledge) or as non-technical words (as already broadly discussed in this chapter) and language. The relationship that exists between learning and *words, language, context* and *knowledge* is evident in two complementary assertions by Postman and Weingartner (1971) and Vygotsky (1986).

According to Postman and Weingartner (1971),

> All of what we customary call "knowledge" is language. Which means that the key to understanding a "subject" is to understand its language ... what we call a subject is its language. A "discipline" is a way of knowing, and whatever is known is inseparable from the symbols (mostly words) in which the knowing is codified. (p. 103)

This assertion serves to resolve the place and meanings of both the technical and non-technical words when used in the science context. With regard to when everyday words have been used as technical words or science terminology i.e. science terms, e.g. *force, power, pressure, resistance, work*, etc, it applies to helping learners recognize and resolve polsemy. This is on the fact that whatever science content that is "known cannot be separated from the words in which the knowing of it is codified" (Postman & Weingartner, 1971, p. 103). While recognition of meanings of everyday words in the context of use, i.e. contextual proficiency, is taken care of on the other hand by the fact that the "meaning of each word is its use and function in a specific activity" (Gyllenpalm, Wickman & Holmgren, 2010, p. 1155), that words draw meanings from the context/zone of use has been further revealed in the following words:

> ... the sense [meaning] is ... the sum of all the psychological events aroused in our consciousness by the word. It is a dynamic, fluid, complex whole, which has several zones of unequal stability. *Meaning is only one of the zones of sense, the most stable and precise zone. A word acquires its sense from the context in which it appears; in different contexts, it changes its sense* [*meaning*]. (Vygotsky, 1986, p. 244; emphasis added)

The take away point from these discussions is that guidance by a knowledgeable other is necessary if the new word meanings that are the result of the changed context of use are to be recognized.

In a classroom situation, this guidance need be about shared thinking towards common understandings of the meanings of everyday words [language] used in science context between the teacher and the learners (Oyoo, 2017). Any attempts at shared thinking should go beyond simple focus on general proficiency in the LOLT or only on knowledge of the words (i.e. vocabulary or being able to name and to give dictionary meanings of non-technical words) as used in everyday parlance. The shared thinking will be further enhanced when there is emphasis on precise use of the language and sustained provision of meanings as relevant to the particular contexts of use of the words. It is such an approach that will *count best* i.e. fully serve to help recognition of all meanings of the words used during the learning and teaching of science; science learning will thus have been enhanced.

The link that has been established between *words, language,* the *context of use* and *science content knowledge* in the foregoing discussions was adopted as the conceptual framework and/or working perspective on language in the study reported in this chapter. Since the focus in these discussions is on how words of a language mean differently with changes in the context of use, it is recognizable that a pragmatic perspective on language (Wickman & Ostman, 2002) is the working view adopted here.

Methodology

The research reported in this chapter was conducted in South Africa, a country with 11 official languages but school learning being conducted almost exclusively in either of these two languages: English or Afrikaans. Any learning difficulties observed in South African science learners to whom the LOLT (either English or Afrikaans) is not a first or home language are still generally assumed to stem almost exclusively from such learners' perceived lower levels of proficiency in the LOLT (Oyoo, 2015a; Vorster, Mayet, & Taylor, 2013). The study was to moderate the widespread assumption about the place of general proficiency in a LOLT for all learning. It was an investigation of South African learners' difficulties with the language of learning and teaching via an exploration of Grade 12 physical science learners' difficulties with *everyday words when presented in a science context*. The study also investigated reasons for and whether participant teachers could also be contributors to any learner difficulties with the language typical of the science classroom i.e. everyday words presented in the science context. The following three research questions guided the study:

1. Do South African grade 12 physical science learners also encounter difficulties with everyday words when used in science context?
2. What are the sources of the difficulty of the words?
3. What roles do the teachers possibly play in the difficulties learners encounter with the language of teaching and learning science?

Data Sources

A total of 1107 physical science learners, all Grade 12 of mixed gender (aged between 16 to 18 years) drawn from 35 public secondary schools in Johannesburg area participated in the study. All were English second language learners but were considered highly proficient in English, the LOLT, given that they had used English as the LOLT since Grade 4. A physical science teacher/educator from each school making a total of 35 also participated. All the participant teachers were well qualified to teach physical science at secondary school level and had taught physical science for 5 years to 25 years. Each had to be the physical science teacher to the class that produced learner participants per school. It occurred that all the teachers who participated were male (mainly migrant teachers) though there are also female physical science teachers in South African schools.

Data were obtained from participants through a word test to participant learners followed by group semi-structured interviews but one-on-one unstructured interviews with respective physical science educators. The questionnaire used in the study was the very same questionnaire (word test) which had been used in Oyoo (2004), but adopted with permission. The word test/questionnaire comprised of 30 multiple choice questions each with (the target word underlined) and with four options to choose from: A, B, C or D, as the possible meanings of non-technical words presented in science context. An example of the items with everyday words used in science context as used in the questionnaire is given here of the word *trace*:

The soil contained a *trace* of potassium. This means that it
  A. used to have some potassium
  B. had plants which use potassium
  C. had a very small amount of potassium
  D. had a large amount of potassium

All the non-technical words used in the study (and listed in Table 9.1 in order as they appeared on word test/questionnaire) were relevant to science content in South African schools at grades 10–12, and participant learners were expected to have encountered and had knowledge of the meanings of these non-technical words when used in science context.

TABLE 9.1 Non-technical words presented in science context in the questionnaire

Consecutive	System	Conserve
Displaces	Sensitive	Disintegrate
Limit	Characteristic	Valid
Prepare	Trace	Spontaneous
Dehydrated	Fundamental	Factors
Generate	Constant	Concept
Retard	Contract	Diversity
Effect	Negligible	Linear
Consistent	Evacuate	Convention
Function	Estimate	Random

The participants (learners) were to make their selections by circling the option which they thought had a meaning closest to that of the underlined non-technical word.

Data Analysis Approach

The *questionnaire/word test* responses were first marked then statistically analysed for mean score patterns and trends to arrive at conclusions as answers to the first two main research questions. This was based on a criterion: In South Africa, 30% is the pass mark in any subject in all grades including in the National Senior Certificate Examination, the university entrance examination. In the study however, given that it used Grade 12 learners, if the mean score on an item was 50% or below or on which 50% of the participants showed that they didn't know the contextual meaning of the everyday word as used in word test/questionnaire, the item (word) was considered to be difficult. Relative difficulty between the words was judged on the respective mean scores attained per item such that items on which learner participants scored less than 50% were considered to be very difficult to the participant learners.

The analyses of *the interview* responses on the other hand were done using an interpretive approach to source answers to the second main research question (from the participant learners) and the third main research question (from the participant teachers), but based on the already argued link [attributed to complementary assertions by Postman and Weingartner (1971) and Vygotsky (1986)] between words, language, science content knowledge and context, for telling meanings/sense of words/concepts used in a language.

Content analysis, but as an approach to data analysis, was also used to reveal patterns in the learner and teacher interview responses which in themselves served as answers to specific research questions used in the study.

Results and Discusion

The contents of this section are organised according to the order of the main research questions that guided this study.

Difficulty of the Non-Technical Words to the Participant Learners

As already mentioned, the *questionnaire/word test* responses had to be first marked before being statistically analysed for mean score patterns and trends to emerge as the answers to the first main research question. A scrutiny of the full record of the distribution of the scores on each of the 30 items against the analysis criterion has revealed that five words emerged as 'very difficult'; in a descending order of relative difficulty, the words are: *sensitive* (24%), *spontaneous* (39%), *retard* (47%), *contract* (49%), and *convention* (50%); Table 9.2 shows the respective scores on these five very difficult words in the order as they appeared on the word test/questionnaire.

TABLE 9.2   Respective response selections and percentage scores on the very difficult words test items

No.	Word	Incorrect responses	Correct responses	% Correct
7	Sensitive	774	277	24
12	Contract	561	546	49
14	Spontaneous	675	432	39
19	Retard	582	525	47
24	Convention	555	552	50

Since this study was to detect whether South African Grade 12 physical science learners also encounter difficulties with everyday words when used in a science context but not to compare learners' performance in the word test/questionnaire, the overall pattern in the performance was what was to deliver the message. Thus this study has demonstrated that South African Grade 12 physical science learners who participated in the study also encountered difficulties with everyday words when presented in the science context. This is a finding that has been common in all published studies, so far, in this area. In all other studies however, the word 'spontaneous' has been enduring as the most difficult non-technical word when presented in a science context (Oyoo, 2007).

Why Non-Technical Words Are Difficult

The participant learners' and respective participant teachers' interview responses obtained in the study about *sensitive, retard* and *contract* – three of the five words that emerged as very difficult in the study are used as representative reasons for the difficulty of everyday words when presented in a science context.

Sensitive

The word *sensitive* appeared in the word test/questionnaire as follows:

> The beam balance is a very *sensitive* instrument. This means that it
> A. can be used to weigh very small things
> B. can be used only by sensible people
> C. is hard to understand how it works
> D. gets spoilt very easily

It is evident in the following relative distribution of the learners' selections of the response options (A – 277; B – 78; C – 73; D – 623) that even though the learners mentioned that the word 'sensitive' was familiar to them, only 277 out of 1051 i.e. about 24% of those who responded knew the correct meaning of the word in the context as expected in the questionnaire: that a *sensitive* instrument is one that *'can be used to weigh very small things'* (A). Instead, and as also also evident in Figure 9.1, most of them took a *sensitive* instrument to be one that *'gets spoilt very easily'* (D).

A typical response across the schools that pointed to how the learner participants arrived at their preferred answer D (gets spoilt very easily) is represented in the following excerpt:

Learner 1: When you think of *sensitive* ... you think of ... to spoil.
Learner 2: Something that is fragile ...
Researcher: You think of something that is fragile?
Learners: Y-e-s
Researcher: Okay ... can you elaborate more, if something is fragile what happens?
Learner 3: Breaks easily ...
Researcher: You think of breaking? Laughter
Learners: Y-e-s ... yes
Learner 4: Spoilt easily

The learners further argued that "if you are a *sensitive* person it means you can easily get angry; you are very fragile so other people should handle you with care because your emotions can easily be spoilt". Since they were familiar with the word 'sensitive', the participant learners who missed the correct meaning as suggested by the context of use appeared to have been misled by their

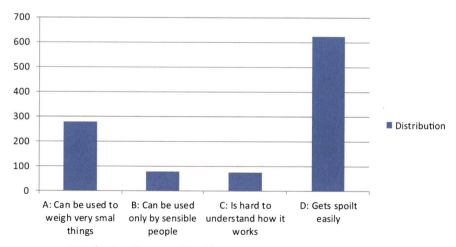

FIGURE 9.1 Distribution of score on 'Sensitive'

common everyday use of the word *sensitive*. The encountered difficulty with this word most evidently stemmed from some lack of prior encounter with the word *sensitive* when presented in the science context or as it did appear on the word test/questionnaire.

Retard

The word *retard* appeared in the questionnaire as reproduced below:

> The pupil was trying to find a chemical that would retard the reaction. This means the chemical would:
> A. speed up the reaction
> B. make the reaction go the other way
> C. slow down the reaction
> D. gives maximum yield from the reaction.

Scores on the word were distributed as follows: A – 279; B – 236; C – **442**; D – 107. Figure 9.2 is a graphical representation of the distribution of option selections. Although *retard* was not an unfamiliar word to the participant learners going by their interview responses, the questionnaire scores revealed that only 47% of all participants who responded to the item knew the correct meaning in the context as in the questionnaire: that to *retard* a reaction is '*to slow down the reaction*' (C). The participant learners who had instead opted for B (*make the reaction go the other way*), while conceding that they used the word *retard* almost daily, did mention that their usage of the word *retard* had instead been

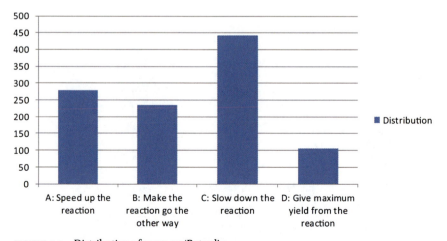

FIGURE 9.2   Distribution of score on 'Retard'

to refer to people who do not think or act in a normal way – people who seem to act opposite of the expected.

Even though this item as was structured applied more to chemistry, even in physics, when references are made to a moving object going through or *undergoing a retardation,* the context meaning is always that the object is moving with a decreasing speed or *slowing down.* Hence, similar to the word 'sensitive' above, the participant learners appeared to have been influenced by how the word has been encountered/used in their daily environment to arrive at their preferred meaning which was wrong as per the context in the questionnaire. The science classroom experiences prior, seemed to have not exposed these participant learners to the word in the context as used on the word test/questionnaire.

Contract

The word *contract* appeared in the questionnaire as follows:

> The experiment was designed to prove that the brass rod would *contract* as the temperature fell. This means the rod would
> A. change colour
> B. become harder
> C. become shorter
> D. become longer

The participant learners selected the response options as follows: A – 237; B – 228; C – 476; D – 92. A total of 561 (51%) of all the learner participants who responded to this item did not know the meaning of the word *'contract'* when used in science context. Instead of selecting the option C (*become shorter*) as what happens to a brass rod when its temperature falls, this huge number was split between the options A (*change colour*), B (*becomes harder*) and D (*become longer*). The distribution of the selected options is also shown in Figure 9.3.

During interviews with participant learners, although they indicated that they had met this word prior, the responses from those who had selected option B (*become harder*) were very interesting. The excerpt below was typical:

Learner: Yes ..., I said so ... I watched the movie Fantastic 4 ... so what happened is that they heated the metal to a very high temperature and they quickly cooled it and it became very hard so you don't expect the metal piece to become smaller but to become harder.

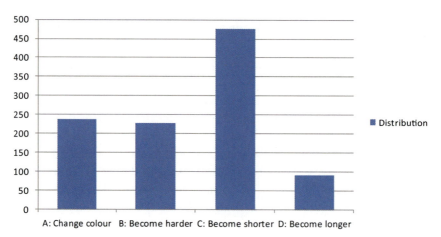

FIGURE 9.3 Distribution of score on 'Contract'

Researcher: Ok-a-y … so that was the reasoning behind that.
Learners: (chorus) … we expected it to become harder.

This excerpt confirms that the learners had once again drawn from their other experiences outside the school/science classroom environment to select 'their correct' meaning of this word. They based their answer on the movie called Fantastic 4 where they had watched a hot metal becoming very hard on being cooled. By using this observation in answering the question as presented in the questionnaire, these participant learners clearly had failed to recognise the context in which the same word was presented in the questionnaire. In the questionnaire, the focus was on the meaning of the word 'contract' not on an observation.

The role of context in the difficulty. In sum, considering the common approaches used in the learners' explanations of how they arrived at their meanings of these three words (wrong against the expectations), it seems clear that outside of school contexts in which they had encountered the words had been particularly strong influences. This is a source of difficulty not directly based on any lack of adequate proficiency in English, the language used in the questionnaire. Since all the words used in the questionnaire (word test) including the three discussed here, were by admission, familiar to the participant leaners, their failure to tell the correct meaning in the context of presentation made it apparent that these words had not been used in their respective science classrooms in ways that could have made them able to tell the science context meanings.

The role of the teacher that could have been, in these learners' ability to tell the contextual meanings of the words which are common (in fact unavoidable) in the discourse/language of any science classroom at the level of these participants and of the science texts was followed up in teacher interviews.

Participant Teacher's Possible Role in the Learners Difficulties Encounter the LOLT Science

To the participant teachers, non-technical words when presented in the science context, including the word 'sensitive' were taken as *simple* English words, incapable of presenting any difficulties to their learners. The participant teachers also saw no difference between non-technical words used in the science context and technical words or everyday words used as science words. They were thus unaware that everyday words when *used in* the science context also do acquire meanings that are special to the science context in the same way as the everyday words *used as* science/technical words e.g. 'work' and 'power'.

Researcher: Do you explain the meanings of everyday words when used in science context to your learners?

Teacher: Yes ... We start from everyday meanings ... when ... looking at *'power',* what *'power'* would mean eeh ... *in the streets and then we get into the scientific or technical meaning of the word* ... There are certain words which we just take for granted ... *we assume* umm ... *that learners understand* and we are communicating ... (emphasis added)

Such revelations indicate that the participant teachers' lacked awareness of the functional value of the non-technical words presented in the science context as well as their potential difficulty. This gap in teachers' knowledge about functional value and nature of the words in the LOLT could have blinded them to the need to give particular attention to the everyday words' meanings as per context of use, and may thus not have been precise in word usage. The participant teachers may thus have been unhelpful to learners' accessing of meanings of everyday words presented in the science context.

Conclusion

This chapter is the outcome of a study that explored whether South African Grade 12 physical science learners also encounter difficulties with the meanings of everyday words when used in science context, reasons for any difficulties encountered and whether teachers could be contributors to the difficulties encountered by learners. The results from the study as presented in this chapter have revealed that participant Grade 12 physical science learners who participated in this study faced difficulties with meanings of everyday words when used in science context in a similar manner as has been reported in all known studies so far in this area (Oyoo, 2012, 2017).

The dominant sources of difficulty with the meanings of everyday words presented in a science context were (1) the influence of how they had encountered these words in outside of school/science classroom experiences and (2) the participant teachers' apparent failure to provide meanings of the words when used during teaching. This failure must have stemmed from their lack of awareness that everyday words when presented in the science context could be misunderstood by the learners (Oyoo, 2006, 2017). The participant teachers' ability to explain meanings of technical words or science words such as 'work' and 'power' however helped learners to resolve any difficulties with the polysemous meanings of everyday words used as science terms. The admission by the participant South African teachers that 'this study was actually an eye opener' (similar to the participant teachers in Oyoo, 2012), can be accepted to indicate that science teachers need be placed to recognise in their daily work, that the context in which a word is used during teaching affects its comprehension. Thus being always precise in use of language during teaching i.e. engaging in "quality talk" during teaching (Murphy et al., 2018, p. 1), will facilitate learner access of correct word meanings in the context of use and resolution of any difficulties with polysemy. Based on discussions at the opening sections of this chapter and these findings, it has now become possible to affirm that: Proficiency in the language of instruction, though a prerequisite for any understanding in any LOLT, may be just one factor of the difficulty of science. Difficulty of the science classroom language, or, for this study, difficulty of non-technical words when presented in the science context are additional factors and attending to these will *count best in science teaching.* In South Africa, as may need be the case in all science learning contexts, this chapter serves as a recommendation that physical science teachers should be encouraged to recognise that if the meanings of non-technical words are shared with the learners during all use, there will be more successful learning of science (Oyoo, 2015b). Since the teachers who participated in this study were appropriately qualified and were of appreciable lengths of service, this detected teacher unawareness will be attended to at initial teacher education stage (Azian, Raof, Ismail, & Hamzah, 2013; Lyon et al., 2018) and (perhaps more aggressively) during continuing professional development of teachers and teacher educators (Korthagen, 2017).

Acknowledgements

This work is based on the research supported by two National Research Foundation of South Africa Grants to the first author: Grant Number 109195 and Grant Number 113631.

References

Achebe, C. (1990). What has literature got to do with it? In C. Achebe (Ed.), *Hopes and impediments: Selected essays* (pp. 154–170). New York, NY & Toronto: First Anchor Books Edition.

Azian, A. A., Raof, A. H., Ismail, F., & Hamsah, M. (2013). Communication strategies of non-native speaker science teachers in second language science classrooms. *System, 41*, 283–297.

Bulman, L. (1988). *Teaching language and study skills in secondary science.* London: Heinemann Educational Books.

Childs, P. E., Markic, S., & Ryan, M. C. (2015). The role of language in the teaching and learning of chemistry. In J. García-Martinez & E. Serrano-Torregrosa (Eds.), *Chemistry education: Best practices, opportunities and trends* (pp. 421–445). Weinheim, Germany: Wiley-VCH Verlag GmbH & Co. KGaA.

Fensham, P. J. (2004). *Defining an identity: The evolution of science education as a field of research.* Dordrecht/London/Boston, MA: Kluwer Academic Publishers.

Gardner, P. L. (1971). *Project SWNG – Scientific words: New Guinea.* Melbourne: Faculty of Education, Monash University.

Gardner, P. L. (1977). Logical connectives in science: A summary of the findings. *Research in Science Education, 7*, 9–24.

Gyllenpalm, J., Wickman, P., & Holmgren, S. (2010). Teachers' language on scientific inquiry: Methods of teaching or methods of inquiry? *International Journal of Science Education, 32*(9), 1151–1172.

Hamid, M. O., Nguyen, H. T. M., & Baldauf Jr., R. B. (2013). Medium of instruction in Asia: Context, processes and outcomes. *Current Issues in Language Planning, 14*(1), 1–15.

Korthagen, F. (2017). Inconvenient truths about teacher learning: Towards professional development 3.0. *Teachers and Teaching: Theory and Practice, 23*(4), 387–405.

Lyon, E. G., Stoddart, T., Bunch, G. C., Tolbert, S., Salinas, I., & Solis, J. (2018). Improving the preparation of novice secondary science teachers for English learners: A proof of concept study. *Science Education,* 1–31. Retrieved from https://doi.org/10.1002/sce.21473

Macmillan English Dictionary for Advanced Learners. (2002). International student edition.

Murphy, P. K., Greene, J. A., Allen, E., Baszcewski, S., Swearingen, A., & Wei, L. (2018). Fostering high school students' conceptual understanding and argumentation performance in science through quality talk discussions. *Science Education*, 1–26. Retrieved from https://doi.org/10.1002/sce.21471

Oyoo, S. O. (2004). *Effective teaching of science: The impact of physics teachers' classroom language* (PhD thesis). Faculty of Education, Monash University, Melbourne, Australia.

Oyoo, S. O. (2006, April). Science teachers' awareness of the impact of their classroom language, In P. L. Jeffery (Ed.), *Collection of papers presented at the International Education Research Conference, University of Western Sydney, Parramatta, Australia*. The Australian Association for Research in Education.

Oyoo, S. O. (2007). Rethinking proficiency in the language of instruction (English) as a factor in the difficulty of school science. *The International Journal of Learning, 14*(4), 231–242.

Oyoo, S. O. (2012). Language in science classrooms: An analysis of physics teachers' use of and beliefs about language. *Research in Science Education, 42*(5), 849–873.

Oyoo, S. O. (2015a). *In South Africa, science should be taught in only one language – How about English?* Retrieved July 9, 2015, from https://theconversation.com/in-south-africa-science-should-be-taught-in-only-one-language-how-about-english-43733

Oyoo, S. O. (2015b). *Helping learners become fluent in the language of science classrooms.* Retrieved June 3, 2015, from https://theconversation.com/helping-learners-become-fluent-in-the-language-of-science-classrooms-41540

Oyoo, S. O. (2017). Learner outcomes in science in South Africa: Role of the nature of learner difficulties with the language for learning and teaching science. *Research in Science Education, 47*(4), 783–804.

Postman, N., & Weingartner, C. (1971). *Teaching as a subversive activity*. Harmondsworth: Penguin Books in Association with Pitman Publishing.

Scott, P. H. (1998). Teacher talk and meaning making in science classrooms: A Vygotskian analysis and review. *Studies in Science Education, 32*, 45–80.

United Nations Educational, Scientific, and Cultural Organization. (2007). *Making a difference: Effective practices in literacy in Africa*. Hamburg: UNESCO Institute for lifelong Learning.

Vorster, C., Mayet, A., & Taylor, S. (2013). The language of teaching and learning in South African Schools. In N. Taylor, S. van der Berg, & T. Mabogoane (Eds.), *Creating effective schools* (pp. 135–156). Cape Town: Pearson.

Vygotsky, L. (1986). *Thought and language*. Cambridge, MA: MIT Press.

Wickman, P.-O., & Ostman, L. (2002). Learning as a discourse change: A sociocultural mechanism. *Science Education, 86*(5), 604–623.

Wilson, J. (1999). Using words about thinking: content analyses of chemistry teachers' classroom talk. *International Journal of Science Education, 21*(10), 1067–1084.

CHAPTER 10

Emancipatory Teaching Practices in the Understandings of Social Sciences Teachers on a Diploma of Education Programme

Stephen Geofroy, Benignus Bitu, Dyann Barras, Samuel Lochan, Lennox McLeod, Lystra Stephens-James and Antoinette Valentine-Lewis

Abstract

Developing a critical-reflective teacher-understanding of teaching practices is an essential element of teacher development on the in-service Diploma of Education programme for secondary-school teachers at the University of the West Indies in Trinidad and Tobago. Teacher development involves engagement with key educational concepts and reflection on practice as teachers facilitate the learning of their charges. Given the post-colonial context characterising the educational system in the West Indies, this research arose out of the need by Social Sciences teacher-educators to find out whether their teachers had developed the kind of critical-reflective understandings that would enhance their classroom practice in an emancipatory fashion. This chapter examines teachers' understandings of their teaching practices to determine whether these understandings can be classified as emancipatory, given the existing post-colonial nature of the educational system. The study assists the Social Sciences teacher-educators to improve their approach to teacher professional development, a key aspect of which involves the process of teacher reflection whereby teachers interrogate theory, practice and context and integrate improved understandings into their profession in an emancipatory manner. In this qualitative case study, data on teacher-understandings were gathered from teacher-participants' written teaching-philosophy statements over the duration of the ten-month programme. Data reduction employed thematic analysis. Choice extracts were then presented and discussed in narrative form including observations and implications. Findings indicate that teacher-participants understand themselves as emancipatory agents, take responsibility for individual growth, however their sense of self as part of a professional community needs to be strengthened. They also possess understandings of their subject-discipline and teaching practice that can be considered as emancipatory.

Keywords

teacher-identity – emancipatory – critical-reflective – teacher understandings

Introduction

In Trinidad and Tobago, the education system is heavily exam-driven and competitive – a characteristic inherited from colonial times. C. L. R. James (1963) captured the way the sociology of colour and class and the narrow nature of the colonial economy shaped a competitive culture of schooling, a concept of success and a teaching practice dominated by performance in examinations:

> The Trinidad government offered yearly free exhibitions ... to either of the two secondary schools: the government's Queen's Royal College and the catholic college, St Mary's ... Through this narrow gate, boys, poor but bright, could get a secondary education. There were at that time few other roads to independence for a black man ... The elementary-school masters all over the island sought bright boys to train for this examination, and to ... win with him was one of the marks of a good teacher. (James, 1963, p. 31)

James also dealt with the subliminal message of control and subjugation underlying colonial education:

> It was only long years after that I understood the limitation on spirit, vision and self-respect which was imposed on us by the fact that our masters, our curriculum, our code of morals, everything began from the basis that Britain was the source of all light and learning .... (James, 1963, p. 39)

Exam-centeredness with its resultant pedagogy based on knowledge transmission has grown in intensity despite all efforts at education reform since the coming of self-government and the declaration of independence in 1962. De Lisle (2012) traces the institutionalisation of high-stakes testing despite the negative effects on classroom pedagogy and the inequality of the high-stakes examination process in selection of candidates for placement and scholarships in secondary schools. He illustrates how the colonial experience gave valorisation and seeming transparency to the examination system and made it difficult to transition away from dependence on such examinations.

Discussing the ideas of Freire (1971), Beckford (1972) and Best (2000), Lavia (2012) explores the limiting nature of colonial education generally and the consequent need for the development of a new epistemic sovereignty through education. Such a progressive outcome requires recognising the rigid system in which schooling is organised (and in which teachers operate) and making concerted efforts toward positive change.

We, the authors of this research, all lecturers at the School of Education, St Augustine campus are deeply interested in promoting substantive change in the classrooms of our nation. We envisage that our immediate reach into the educational system as teacher educators is limited to influencing the teachers who come to us. In this light, positive change can be brought about not so much by targeting the system directly, but by equipping teachers through a professional development programme with relevant understandings and related practices. Critical engagement from within the system thus becomes possible and which eventually may reform the system itself towards greater emphasis on genuine human development.

At the School of Education, St Augustine campus of The University of the West Indies, Trinidad and Tobago, a professional development Diploma in Education programme (Dip Ed) is offered every year over a ten-month period for in-service secondary-school teachers. The Dip Ed (as existed at that time – subsequently changed in 2016) offered to teacher-participants various courses. The *Educational Foundations course* engaged students to develop critical analysis though perspectives gained from Language, Philosophy, Psychology, Sociology, and Health and Family Life Education (HFLE). The *Project in the Theory of Education* was a library-based project in which students were required to critically interrogate a given educational issue. *The Curriculum Process* was a problem-based intervention in the teachers' actual classroom and the *Practice of Education* was a teaching practicum involving critique by tutor and teacher-participant colleagues of actual lessons carried out by the teacher-participant (The University of the West Indies, Faculty of Humanities and Education, 2015).

Teachers' practice can have the effect of either contributing to reproduction of social inequalities (Tzanakis, 2011) or becoming an exercise of emancipatory agency (Freire, 1971). As such the deliberate focus in teacher professional development at the school of education is toward an emancipatory approach. In the disciplinary grouping of the Social Science cohort for example, both *Curriculum Process* and *The Practice of Education,* are geared to direct participants toward an emancipatory praxis.

Objectives of these courses are that teachers: accept responsibility for their self-development as teachers; understand the role of the teacher in the Social

Sciences and Humanities, including catering to students of various socio-economic status; develop skills for teaching and assessing diverse groups of learners; improve (a) critical thinking and (b) personhood development; increase awareness of the nature and purpose of their discipline; apply important concepts linked with teaching and learning; write units of instruction and lesson plans that respond to the nature of the subject; integrate technology in their professional practice (Curriculum Sessions, 2013).

This present study is deliberately delimited in accordance with the intent of focusing solely on teachers' ideas as they reflect on their praxis over the course of the Dip Ed. We do realise that only a long-term follow-up study on teacher-praxis could provide evidence as to whether they have sustained emancipatory learnings acquired over the period of their professional development on the Dip Ed. Determining whether their learning experiences did in fact afford them the required agency to impact upon restrictive educational structures would be a key requirement of such a longitudinal study. The deliberate scope of this present study is thus the initial buddings of emancipatory understandings possessed by teachers by the end of the Dip Ed.

Teacher-educators (researchers) examined the teaching philosophies of teacher-participants (specialists in History, Geography, Social Studies, Caribbean Studies and Business Studies) during the academic year 2015–2016. Social Sciences teacher-educators needed to find out whether teacher-participants had developed critical-reflective understandings related to enhancement of their classroom practice in an emancipatory manner given the post-colonial context of schooling. The aim of the research is therefore: to examine teachers' understandings of their teaching practices to determine whether these can be classified as emancipatory. The written teaching philosophies of Social Sciences teacher-participants, submitted by the end of their professional development programme, is the data set for the present study. Findings would inform adjustments to the Social Sciences teacher-education curriculum.

Theoretical Framework

In a context of a dominant operational paradigm of education for certification, an emancipatory and thus transformative stance as teacher becomes critical. To operationalise such a teaching philosophy, the teacher must be willing to resist dominant discourses from a colonial past concerning class, ethnicity, gender and ability. The very professional development of the emancipatory teacher involves a heightened awareness of the assumptions and hidden inequalities of schooling. In this respect, the promotion of "equity" is a critical goal for justice in educational practice for where education is inequitable "it can disenfranchise whole sections of society" (Haq, 1995, p. 17).

In situations inimical to students' best interests, Lavia (2012) argues for a critical-minded teacher able to subvert the colonial legacy. Professional development of teachers requires a teacher-preparation for the work of decolonisation towards producing graduates as teachers who are emancipatory change-agents and transformative in their understandings of their practice.

In emancipatory pedagogy the teacher develops a competence for reflective action and grows to accept that in problem-solving, decisions made are part of an expanded consciousness of their zone of responsibility. Reflective action toward emancipation is in keeping with the thought of Dewey (1997), Freire (1971) and Schon (1983). Zeichner and Liston (1987) explain that in this approach all the basic assumptions about teaching and learning are held to be problematic and the teacher becomes aware of the moral and ethical implications of the choices made in the classroom. Decision-making is a continuous challenge for teachers and a reflection of the nature of their professional identity. Critical-reflective activity requires understandings about self and accepting responsibility for individual growth (Dewey, 1997).

In an "emancipatory pedagogy", "critical conscientization", the establishment of a "problem-posing education system" (Nouri & Sajjadi, 2014, pp. 78–79), privileging learners' active involvement in knowledge creation and targeting feelings and emotions (Lei, 2007) are key.

Freire (1971) explains that in "liberating education", the dehumanizing "deposit-making", banking-type education (that was a hallmark of the colonial model of teaching and learning) is rejected and replaced by emancipatory, dialogical, pedagogical practice involving "the posing of the problems of men in their relations with the world" (p. 52). Emancipatory pedagogy thus requires a real connection with lived experiences of students and their environment, a relation of "empathy" among knowledge seekers in communication with one another (Freire, 1973, p. 45) and avoids the colonial pitfall of becoming "bookish" (Campbell, 1992, p. 21).

In "problem-posing education" learners "develop their power to perceive critically the way they exist in the world with which and in which they find themselves" (Freire, 1971, p. 56). A pedagogy for liberation involves a heightened awareness (critical consciousness) of the reality in which people are situated and strives to develop a will geared to "critical intervention in reality" (p. 54). Emancipatory pedagogy thus involves "conscientization" or "learning to perceive social, political and economic contradictions and to take action against the oppressive elements of reality" (p. 15). For Freire the goal of this pedagogy is to facilitate for all involved, a process of "becoming more fully human" (Freire, 1971, p. 41). He posits that students actively involved in such an educative process grow in commitment to "the practice of freedom" (p. 54).

Attention to "feelings and emotions" in the context of learning pertains to the affective domain (Krathwohl, Bloom, & Masia, 1964, p. 7) and is linked to positive indicators in relation to cognition, motivation, relation and student esteem (Roger, Weissberg, Wang, & Herbert, 2004). By promoting active involvement of students in the learning process the Trinidad and Tobago National Curriculum Policy is in sync with elements indicative of emancipatory pedagogy. The policy clearly outlines the emotional and value-based aspects to be included in teachers' endeavours. It stipulates that there be "degrees of differentiation exercised" in teaching approaches "sensitive to the levels of student achievement" with "various approaches to teaching, learning and assessment ... to allow all students to participate fully and effectively" (Trinidad & Tobago, Curriculum Planning and Development Division, 2008, p. 7).

Differentiated pedagogy (Tomlinson, 2014) is a method for recognising, incorporating and engaging students tailored to the various types of diversity that can arise in the classroom that include multiple intelligences (Gardner, 2006). In particular the national guiding philosophy for "social studies educators envisages ... the development of a knowledgeable, caring and responsible society" and thus advances a humanistic vision. In this view, students are to grow "socially, physically and emotionally ... interrelate effectively and contribute to peace, harmony and cohesion in the society" (Trinidad & Tobago, Curriculum Planning and Development Division, 2008, p. 21).

Important also, is pedagogical content knowledge where teachers interpret their subject matter to make it meaningful to students (Schulman, 1987). Ball, Thames, and Phelps (2008) state that pedagogical content knowledge is an "amalgam of knowledge of content and pedagogy" (p. 392). The understanding of teachers regarding their subject-discipline is critical since research on teacher education indicates that the degree to which a teacher integrates new ideas and techniques in practice depends largely on the teacher's interpretation of the value of these ideas and techniques (Hughes, 2005). In this regard, fostering student creativity is valuable for envisioning viable alternatives to existing states of affairs, thus offering avenues and opportunities in cases where none appear apparent. Such scope for releasing the imagination is particularly relevant given the current advances in information technologies. Fullam and Langworthy (2014) envisage that in teaching for creativity "the ultimate goal is interdependent learners who ... make the most of the extraordinary world of information, ideas, creativity and connection that digital access opens up" (p. 78).

To challenge the colonial pedagogy, there is need for due vigilance as to the way curricula is framed in subjects such as history, geography, social studies, business studies and indeed all the subject disciplines. The crafting and interpretation of curricula is crucial to help children escape the traps of inferiorisation and marginalisation and to attain a cultural confidence from which to claim a space in the world (Fanon, 1963; Best, 2000). Indeed, curriculum goals target specific outcomes which together seek to equip the students with desirable personal traits: toward the "full ... development of students" ... for "adult life" and with a responsible agency required "for their role as citizens in a democracy" (Ungoed-Thomas, 1997, p. 8).

In the national educational philosophy of Trinidad and Tobago, education is seen as the "means that creates individuals with the intellect and capacity to develop and lead societies, communities, villages, and/or neighbourhoods and families of the future" (Trinidad & Tobago, National Task Force on Education, 1994, p. xviii). The vision statement of the government currently in office, outlines the importance of creativity in learning as it affirms "the importance of developing creativity and innovation to be the key drivers of personal, social and economic development" (Trinidad & Tobago, National Development Strategy 2016–2030, Vision 2030, 2016).

If "the good school is a community of learning" (Ungoed-Thomas, 1997, p. 3) then its cultivation would involve moving away from the isolated "egg-crate" type work of the teacher (Lortie, 1975, p. 14). An understanding of the value of learning in community is necessary if the teacher is to confront individualistic pedagogy (Flinders, 1988; Mirel & Goldin, 2012). In this respect, "teachers who want to transform their practice can greatly benefit from group support" (Shore & Freire, 1987, p. 21). Resisting and confronting an established individualistic paradigm in favour of a more communal learning environment "cannot be carried out in isolation or individualism, but only in fellowship and solidarity" (Freire, 1971, p. 58). To a large extent, it is the school community that is best placed to devise "ways of teaching that respond to individual differences and ... form the basis for a just and non-discriminatory society" (UNESCO, 2009, p. 8).

More specifically, Cochran-Smith and Lyte (1999) suggest the need for professional dialogue and the pooling of collective knowledge in communities of practice. Lieberman and Miller (2011) surveyed various studies of communities of practice and problematic aspects of forming and maintaining them. The power of these communities was highlighted due to the way they privilege theory and practice, encourage members to examine their own practice, try out new ideas, and reflect on what works and what does not. These ideas in teacher education described above and the way they attempt to change teachers' understandings about their practice, can provide an emancipatory avenue for teachers; such can make an impact in winning space for a truly independent and sovereign society given the wider historical and social context in which schooling operates.

Key components of a critical-reflective teacher-education process includes teachers' understandings of: themselves (teacher identity); their subject-discipline; and what they do (their classroom practice). In sum, a critical-reflective understanding employs critique on praxis with emancipation as desired outcome (Critchley, 2001).

Methodology

The methodology employed is that of a qualitative case study (Merriam & Tisdell, 2016) of teachers' understandings of themselves and of their educational practice as expressed in their written statements of their philosophies of teaching. Some guidance from the lecturers was offered as to the structuring of written critical-reflective philosophies and included the following categories: insights from reflections on practice, key concepts, teaching metaphor and applicability to social sciences disciplines.

Key understandings of teacher-identity, the discipline taught and the way the teacher-participants thought about their practice were derived through a thematic analysis approach entailing pre-coding (Boyatzis, 1998), coding and thematising. Pre-coding consisted of highlighting relevant sections of the documents per teacher-participant. Coding was guided by the research questions formulated to investigate teacher identity, social science discipline and practice. The coding process was done manually and collaboratively among the authors (Schreier, 2012) using the constant comparison approach (Fram, 2013). For rigor, coding ensued along with critical discussion and eventual consensus (Kvale & Brinkmann, 2009).

A Microsoft Excel file was used to display the data for data reduction as this was a convenient mode for facilitating discussions among researchers; for group meetings, the excel sheet was projected onto a screen and adjusted as discussions on the data ensued. Part of the process of data reduction involved selecting from among the extracts (that were already coded and placed into themes) those deemed most appropriate for answering the research questions. The extracts selected were the ones that most clearly encapsulated the concept of emancipation.

Of the 53 Social Sciences teachers who pursued the Dip Ed, permission was sought for the use of their philosophies. Of those teacher-participants who agreed, the process of data reduction resulted in an end product involving the incorporation of extracts from 11 teachers whose teaching experience varied between 2–15 years. For confidentiality, teacher-participants were given pseudonyms: Radica, John and Bella teach History; Olivia, Shiva and Emily teach Business Studies; Elsa, Sateesha and Marie teach Geography; and Theresa and Maggie teach Social Studies, while Radica also teaches Caribbean Studies.

Research Questions
1. In what ways do teachers' understandings of themselves reflect their identity as emancipatory?
2. In what ways are teachers' understandings of their subject-disciplines emancipatory?
3. In what ways do teachers understand their teaching practice as emancipatory activity?

Results and Discussion

The findings gained from analysis of the teachers' written statements are discussed under the themes: teacher identity, subject-discipline and teaching practice.

Teacher Identity
Emancipatory Agent

Olivia (of 12 years' experience) expresses the understanding of herself as "reflective practitioner" having "reconstructed" her teaching goals as "not merely cognitive but a complex set of embedded processes and practices that concern the whole person". She grew in her understanding, away from an emphasis on the cognitive domain to holistic development. This critical-mindedness (Lavia, 2012) conveys the concept of herself as subversive of a one-sided cerebral colonial approach toward an agency that is developmental and emancipatory.

Theresa (though a teacher of only 3 years' experience) expressed a similar idea of her role as emancipatory in promoting critical thinking having experienced the Dip Ed. While before she "was adhering to the 'banking concept' [Freire, 1971, p. 46]" she, now "leans towards getting students to create and construct knowledge on their own, rather than pouring knowledge into them like empty vessels".

Sateesha, with just two years teaching experience, did not plan for longevity in the teaching service. Encouraged by her colleagues, however, she made the bold step to pursue the Dip Ed and the following quote is an account of her transformation that fostered a deepening of her understanding of teaching and learning:

> My journey in the Dip Ed programme has been a mind-altering process. I always thought learning occurred when a student determined the correct answer on a test. I have realised that learning is both a product and a process … my concept of teaching has been reworking itself at the different lectures I have attended … Now, I am more confident in my approach and my values, beliefs and aspirations have been brought to the forefront by many days of reflection.

Clearly Sateesha shows movement away from the narrow focus on education for examination (De Lisle, 2012). Sateesha further consolidates her shift in perspective: "Even what I thought education was, has been challenged by starting this programme. It is not about achieving good grades but about ensuring that my students become good individuals who would add value to society". She thus recognises the moral aspect in keeping with a more holistic view of education where developing students' capability "for their role as citizens" (Ungoed-Thomas, 1997, p. 8) is highlighted.

Elsa, who spent a significant portion of her working life in the private sector admits that prior to the Dip Ed her understanding of her role as a teacher was to emulate her own teachers: "I have taught students as I was taught, adopting a 'one size fits all' to a diverse classroom". After teaching for three years she revealed that her exposure to professional development brought significant insights that influenced the way she saw herself as a teacher:

> My experiences in the Diploma in Education Programme revealed to me that I had been a pedagogical caterpillar … I felt as though I had robbed my students for three years … While I had believed that I had embraced the tenets of good teaching, I was still just a larva in the education system … I was enlightened by Gardner's Multiple Intelligences Theory, where instructors need to cater for the differentiated classroom.

With widened understandings of the various ways and preferences by which children learn (Gardner, 2006) Elsa realises that teaching is about responding to the needs of all types of learners in order to provide the requisite support (Tomlinson, 2014).

Taking Responsibility for Individual Growth

Accepting responsibility for individual growth is associated with critical-reflective activity by teachers (Dewey, 1997). Radica testifies that "Having spent the last eight months in the Diploma in Education program I have come to understand that a teacher's practice in the classroom should be grounded in sound theoretical framework".

Also, Maggie who entered the teaching service after 17 years of banking and a short stint in the public service, recalls that the Dip Ed facilitated new learnings for her especially in the affective realm. She illustrates one aspect of her growth experience by referring to what has now become a critical area in the classroom – the use of educational technology in fostering student learning (Fullam & Langworthy, 2014). She confesses that adopting the use of "new and emerging technology ... prior to the Diploma in Education was not something I would have openly embraced, but now I am more receptive and try to become more hands-on with available technology". Having experienced the change in herself, she now has further impetus towards being an empowering educator.

Understanding Oneself in Community

To promote vicarious learning in community, the teaching practice component of the Dip Ed included Field Days whereby teacher-participants could learn from one another and develop a sense of themselves as part of a community of professional practitioners. We had noted that a serious concern raised by critics (Flinders, 1988; Mirel & Goldin, 2012) was the way in which teachers conduct their teaching in isolation from one another. John appreciated this teaching practice grounded in community experience: "The teaching practice sessions were tremendously helpful as I gained insights into different teaching techniques and methods to teach certain topics". John valued the learnings he gained and the potential for enhancement of teacher agency in this community of practice (Cochran-Smith & Lyte, 1999; Lieberman & Miller, 2011).

Likewise, Radica espouses in her philosophy a focus on the importance of relationships in the educational environment:

> Creating a safe environment for students to learn is part of having a positive school culture which is an integral aspect of my school's vision/mission statement to produce grounded [and] holistic students who would eventually form part of the wider society. Students must feel accepted and respected by their teachers and peers so as to set a positive tone and rapport.

Understanding self in community for promoting professional growth is important for reform efforts, especially when working within an established colonial-style education system (Shore & Freire, 1987).

Teachers' Understandings of Their Subject-Discipline as Emancipatory

Interpretation of Subject Matter

According to Hughes (2005) teacher interpretation of the ideas in their discipline is critical for establishing relevance to students. The following extracts attest to teachers who value the import that learning to incorporate the affective domain can afford in the enhancement of their subject matter (Roger, Weissberg, Wang, & Herbert, 2004). Thus, John mentions that:

> I gained an appreciation for using questions that appeal to the affective domain ... I must admit that I didn't know about this prior to doing the Diploma of Education but it's really effective especially in my subject area of Social Studies.

Likewise, on interpreting her subject matter, Sateesha affirms that explicit attention to and incorporation of the affective domain in the learning situation is influential in promoting a beneficial use of pedagogical content knowledge. Such an appropriation of the subject exploits its potential as an empowering tool for promoting awareness, empathy, interest and self-propelled research among students all in sync with national curriculum goals (Trinidad & Tobago, Curriculum Planning and Development Division, 2008). She indicates that:

> By the use of affective objectives, students can become more self-aware, and by extension, empathetic to the world around them. In geography, students now take a greater interest in natural hazards and disasters and are doing their own research when they see disaster events in the media.

For Sateesha, as enthusiasm for the subject is shared, the affective benefits extend to overall personality development. Class activity thus becomes an occasion for growth:

> The students are more interested in coming to classes and are more confident in their own knowledge. Just yesterday when I asked a question, a student who had gotten the answer incorrect was assisted by her classmate who volunteered to explain the concept. This is my new definition of success in the classroom – where students become interested in the work, share their knowledge, and become better people.

Similarly, Radica (a teacher at a school with a strong colonial tradition) hopes, through her subject-discipline of Caribbean Studies, to foster appreciation for the region:

> Given the nature of the Caribbean experience and the way it had framed our contemporary society, understanding our history and assessing our current position as a result is ever more important. This is especially so

with the subject of Caribbean Studies which requires the sixth formers to think critically about the region they inhabit and are native to. The hope here is to bring forth a future Caribbean society that has a wider understanding of and a greater appreciation for their region.

Radica envisions her discipline as having the potential to counter retentions from a colonial-type education that constrains a learner's "spirit, vision and self-respect" (James, 1963, p. 39). Her subject, no longer a tool to consolidate the colonial status quo, is prized for its critical-reflective capacity whereby students can view the world from a Caribbean space.

Subject Matter Context

Both Marie and Bella affirm in their respective disciplines the relevance of grounding their teaching approaches in real life contexts. Their understanding is in keeping with an emancipatory pedagogical approach that engages students with subject content not in the abstract but in familiar life contexts (Freire, 1971; Ball, Thames, & Phelps, 2008). Thus, Marie explicates her general principle in this regard:

> As an educator, I see education as the greatest tool for national development. I think that schools should be given the autonomy to manipulate the curriculum to suit their needs and that every teacher needs to look and understand the area where they work and the areas their students come from and make learning relevant to their everyday lives.

As applied to her subject-discipline, she continues:

> In the field of Geography, fieldwork is very important. I believe in extracurricular activities and field trips. They provide students with an excellent opportunity to learn skills which are not always possible to teach within the classroom. For example, a child living in a rural fishing village studying geography should be made to see the importance of this subject in his life, be it knowing about the tides and ocean currents, reading maps or even the effect that fishing has on coral reefs.

Bella also displays a critical approach to pedagogical content knowledge where content is linked with context for meaningful learning in History. She explains that "as a History teacher ... it is necessary to provide students with a reality outside the traditional classroom, so they can visualise what is being taught and thereby be able to internalise it". In the researchers' view, the meaningful study of Caribbean history is essential for fostering Caribbean identity and a genuinely emancipatory pedagogy; such is a definite change from the "bookish" education that was a hallmark of the colonial enterprise (Campbell, 1992, p. 21).

Teachers' Understandings of Their Teaching Practice as Emancipatory

Promoting Equity

Equity in educational practice (Haq, 1995) is integral to student-centered instruction as it requires inclusion of all learners. Emily (a teacher of 15 years) explains: "I must customise lessons to cater to different learning styles. Visual and performing arts, graphs, case studies, teaching aids ... must be interwoven in the lesson plans to engage all students". Emily's impulse for expanding student choices is therefore emancipatory.

Critical to the emancipatory impulse is a questioning of well-established educational practices as to their usefulness for achieving learning goals (Zeichner & Liston, 1987). This was the case with Elsa who takes issue with the practice of streaming in schools towards greater equity and inclusion:

> Streaming has, since colonial times been practised ... to prevent academically stronger students from being held back by those less proficient in the classroom. I now see the flaw. In a homogenous classroom creativity can be stifled; whereas a heterogeneous group of students add styles, perspectives and shared experiences.

UNESCO (2009) supports her understanding and advocates for a more inclusive educational approach that responds, "to individual differences" geared to the creation of a more "just and non-discriminatory society" (p. 8).

Another way education for equity has emerged is in Shiva's statement in which he recognises the importance of affirming an aspect of local culture as expressed in the language dialect that is the first language of the majority of the population of Trinidad and Tobago. He comments favourably on the value of using the language (creole-dialect) in instruction: "Understanding now that speaking dialect can be encouraged, once students are made aware of the difference between Standard English and dialect". The move away from the traditional colonial view of education that devalued use of the creole language in the classroom is an emancipatory one that promotes a much-needed cultural confidence (Fanon, 1963; Best, 2000). In also recognising the value of Standard English, Shiva expresses an understanding that expanding students' educational capability would also involve competency at Standard English – the official language of schooling.

Information technology, useful in pursuing student-centered approaches, has opened avenues in efforts regarding teaching for creativity (Fullam & Langworthy, 2014). Elsa highlights her awareness of technology's creative possibilities in celebrating her new ability "to create websites and other digital spaces, power point presentations, photo stories and video clips". Employing information technologies creatively in the classroom can promote equity and emancipation especially when operating within an inflexible post-colonial education system with restricted possibilities.

In like manner Marie affirms equity in the classroom by way of catering to learners who prefer kinaesthetic and practical activities in expression of their creativity:

> I have come to the realisation that many kids at my school enjoy working with their hands, they enjoy making things, drawing, painting and colouring and so in my Geography class I try to incorporate some type of hands-on activity as often as I can.

Catering to diversity in the classroom for fostering student creativity and active involvement of students is a mark of an emancipatory educational approach (Trinidad & Tobago, Curriculum Planning and Development Division, 2008; Trinidad & Tobago, National Development Strategy 2016–2030, Vision 2030, 2016).

Humanistic Development

Emancipatory practice is geared to achieve the full humanisation of persons (Freire, 1971). Consistent with this humanistic understanding, Bella values the positive effects that human interaction makes to her practice as a teacher. In her understanding, the benefits of the humanising process are not confined to classroom boundaries. She mentions that "when relationships are formed in the classroom, it impacts and guides students outside of the classroom".

In Emily's understanding, the learner and the learner's human development is the goal of teaching. She indicates quite clearly her journey from the "banking" or "transmission" practice to a transactional practice where all in the learning environment engage in interaction and eventual transformation. She expresses her own journey of engagement with knowledge in the learning encounter:

> My approach to teaching has been one of transmission of knowledge to my students through "chalk and talk". This was the way I received instruction from my teachers, and I was of the belief that this is what

was necessary for successful learning. However, I learnt about other techniques, namely transaction and transformation ... I become more transactional in my teaching where I will create more situations and allow my students to develop their own knowledge in navigation of their learning. It is my hope that their understanding and conceptualisation will be transformed and that they develop into good human beings, as the end result.

Emily's vignette connects with an important concept that Freire is at pains to point out pertaining to the use of knowledge in a pedagogy for liberation. Knowledge developed in dialogical relationship requires that the parties involved in the learning process experience themselves in a relationship of empathy essential to his view of education as humanisation (Freire, 1971, 1973).

Observations

Given the length of experience that Olivia (12 years) had in teaching within the post-colonial education system, it is noteworthy that she valued the learnings provided on the Dip Ed and expressed understandings that highlighted quality of relationships in the classroom and new strategies for enhancing learning. Also heartening are the expressed understandings of Theresa, Sateesha and Elsa who all declared an enhanced and emancipatory teacher identity. This augurs well for them as teachers at the early stage of their careers.

Radica and Maggie demonstrate some movement in disposition born of their critical reflection. Radica recognises that familiarity with relevant pedagogical literature is a moral imperative that should drive the teacher to good practice. Maggie's openness to learn new features of her craft, her valuing new input and her will to persevere, attests to her personal changes in disposition. Their attitudes thus entail acceptance of responsibility for professional growth as teachers.

Though John understood the value of self in community and appreciated learning along with his colleagues on teaching practice field days, overall, such understandings were limited among other teacher-participants in the research sample. The lack of expressed understandings by other teacher-participants could be due to the isolationist-type image of the teacher as professional inherited from the colonial era.

Regardless of their subject discipline some teachers affirmed the importance of the affective domain in interpreting their subject matter and the value of life context for the empowerment of their students. In particular, Radica, working at a well-established school from the colonial era, sees the importance of her subject-discipline as a medium for creating a Caribbean identity, subverting the idea of inferiorisation and generating momentum towards building epistemological sovereignty for her Caribbean students.

Teacher-participants, with both long and short experience in the established educational system, have understood their teaching practice as one promoting equity and humanistic development. While exclusivity was a mark of colonial education, the Dip Ed may have influenced teachers' views as to the importance of catering to student diversity. In a culture of education which fosters examination for certification and a pedagogy based on transmission, teacher-participants' understandings of education as humanisation are signs that they view their overall practice in an emancipatory manner. The fact that some teachers developed a renewed commitment to the wider goals of education such as good citizenship suggests a deepening of their sense of what education is for.

Implications

Given the valuable emancipatory understandings displayed among teacher-participants, the current Social Sciences teacher-education curriculum approach can be continued and consolidated both at the university and at the school. At the School of Education these findings should serve to reinforce the need to promote community and relevance to school context. At the schools it is necessary that school leaders promote the idea of collaboration and support the new ideas the graduates gain from their diploma in education programme.

Recognising the existing challenge involved in fostering an awareness of the value of belonging to a professional community of practice, elements for building such awareness need strengthening during the programme. This process of building a learning community could involve its incorporation in course objectives for the social sciences and by actual activities to promote its sustainability.

Actualizing and sustaining emancipatory self-understandings require institutional mechanisms such as continuous teacher development initiatives and administrative procedures at the level of the school system to provide support for teachers to guard against reversion to post-colonial teaching practices.

Conclusion

The findings do indicate that emancipatory understandings are apparent in teachers' views. Understandings of teacher identity, subject-discipline and teaching practice show this clearly. A cause for further exploration consists in professional community of practice and sustaining emancipatory understandings.

References

Avalos, B. (2010). *Teacher identity construction in reform driven contexts: A Chilean study*. Retrieved from http://aiaer.net/ejournal/vol22210/3

Ball, D. L., Thames, M. H., & Phelps, G. (2008). Content knowledge for teaching: What makes it special? *Journal of Teacher Education, 59*, 389–407.

Beckford, G. (1972). *Persistent poverty: Underdevelopment in plantation economies of the Third World*. Kingston, Jamaica: The University of the West Indies Press.

Best, L. (2000). Independent thought, policy process. In K. Hall & D. Benn (Eds.), *Contending with destiny: The Caribbean in the 21st century*. Kingston, Jamaica: Ian Randle.

Boyatzis, R. E. (1998). *Transforming qualitative information: Thematic analysis and code development*. Thousand Oaks, CA: Sage Publications.

Campbell, C. (1992). Colony and nation. *A short history of education in Trinidad and Tobago 1834–1986*. Kingston: Ian Randle.

Cochran-Smith, M., & Lyte, S. (1999). Relationships of knowledge and practice: Teacher learning in communities. In A. Iran Najad & C. Pearson (Eds.), *Review of research in education* (Vol. 24, pp. 249–305). Washington, DC: American Educational Research Association.

Critchley, S. (2001). *Philosophy – A very short introduction*. New York, NY: Oxford University Press.

Curriculum Sessions. (2013). *Social sciences: Programme of work for 22nd July–23rd August, 2013* [In-house document]. St. Augustine: School of Education, UWI.

De Lisle, J. (2012). Secondary school entrance examinations in the Caribbean: Legacy, policy, and evidence within an era of seamless education. *Caribbean Curriculum, 19, 109–143*.

Dewey, J. (1997). *Experience and education*. New York, NY: Touchstone.

Fanon, F. (1963). *The wretched of the earth* (C. Farrington, Trans.). New York, NY: Grove Weidenfeld.

Flinders, D. J. (1988). Teacher isolation and the new reform. *Journal of Curriculum and Supervision, 4*(1), 17–29.

Fram, S. M. (2013). The constant comparative analysis method outside of grounded theory. *The Qualitative Report, 18*(1), 1–25. Retrieved from http://nsuworks.nova.edu/tqr/vol18/iss1/1

Freire, P. (1971). *Pedagogy of the oppressed*. New York, NY: Seabury.

Freire, P. (1973). *Education for critical consciousness*. New York, NY: Seabury.

Fullam, M., & Langworthy, M. (2014). *A rich seam: How new pedagogies find deep learning.* London: Pearson.

Gardner, H. (2006). *Multiple intelligences: New horizons.* Cambridge, MA: Perseus Books.

Haq, M. (1995). *Reflections on human development.* New Delhi: Oxford University Press.

Hughes, J. (2005). The role of teacher knowledge and learning experiences in forming technology integrated pedagogy. *Journal of Technology and Teacher Education, 13*, 277–302.

James, C. L. R. (1963). *Beyond a boundary.* Kingston: Sangster's Book Stores Limited.

Krathwohl, D. R., Bloom, B. S., & Masia, B. B. (1964). *Taxonomy of educational objectives: Handbook II: Affective domain.* New York, NY: David McKay.

Kvale, S., & Brinkmann, S. (2009). *Interviews: Learning the craft of qualitative research interviewing* (2nd ed.). Thousand Oaks, CA: Sage Publications.

Lei, Q. (2007). EFL teachers "factors and students" affect. *US-China Education Review, 4*(3), 60–67. doi:10.2307/1170741

Lavia, J. (2012). Resisting the inner plantation: Decolonisation and the practice of education in the work of Eric Williams. *Postcolonial Directions in Education, 1*(1), 9–30.

Lieberman, A., & Miller, L. (2011). Learning communities: The starting point for professional learning is in schools and classrooms. *Journal of Staff Development, 32*(4), 16–20.

Lortie, D. C. (1975). *School-teacher: A sociological study.* Chicago, IL: University of Chicago.

Merriam, S., & Tisdell, E. (2016). *Qualitative research: A guide to design and implementation.* San Francisco, CA: Jossey-Bass.

Mirel, J., & Goldin, S. (2012). Alone in the classroom: Why teachers are too isolated. *The Atlantic.* Retrieved from https://www.theatlantic.com/national/archive/2012/04/alone-in-the-classroom-why-teachers-are-too-isolated/255976/

Nouri, A., & Sajjadi, S. M. (2014). Emancipatory pedagogy in practice: Aims, principles and curriculum orientation. *International Journal of Critical Pedagogy, 5*(2), 76–87.

Roger, P., Weissberg, M., Wang, C., & Herbert, J. W. (2004). *Building academic success on social and emotional learning: What does the research say?* New York, NY: Teacher College Press.

Schon, D. (1983). *The reflective practitioner: How professionals think in action.* Cambridge, MA: Basic Books.

Schreier, M. (2012). *Qualitative content analysis in practice.* London: Sage Publications.

Schulman, L. S. (1987). Knowledge and teaching: Foundations of the new reform. *Harvard Educational Review, 57*(1), 1–21.

Shore, I., & Freire, P. (1987). *A pedagogy for liberation: Dialogues on transforming education.* New York, NY: Bergin & Garvey.

The University of the West Indies (UWI), St. Augustine Campus, Faculty of Humanities and Education. (2015–2016). *Post graduate regulations and syllabuses.* St. Augustine: Author.

Tomlinson, C. (2014). *The differentiated classroom: Responding to the needs of all learners.* Alexandria, VA: ASCD.

Trinidad and Tobago National Task Force on Education. (1994). *Education policy paper (1993–2003)* (White Paper). Port of Spain: Author.

Trinidad & Tobago, Curriculum Planning and Development Division. (2008). *SEMP – Secondary education modernisation programme, forms 1–3 social studies curriculum.* Port of Spain: Ministry of Education.

Trinidad & Tobago. Ministry of Social Development and Family Services. National Development Strategy 2016–2030, Vision 2030. (2016). *Many hearts, many voices, one vision.* Retrieved from: http://www.social.gov.tt/wp-content/uploads/2017/01/V2030-as-at-August-29th-2016.pdf

Tzanakis, M. (2011). Bourdieu's social reproduction thesis and the role of cultural capital in educational attainment: A critical review of key empirical studies. *Educate – The Journal of Doctoral Research in Education, 11*(1), 76–90.

Ungoed-Thomas, J. (1997). *Vision of a school: The good school in the good society.* London: Cassel.

United Nations Educational, Scientific and Cultural Organization. (2009). *Policy guidelines on inclusion in education.* Paris: UNESCO.

Zeichner, K. M., & Liston, D. P. (1987). Teaching student teachers to reflect. *Harvard Educational Review, 56*(1), 23–48.

CHAPTER 11

Pedagogical Confrontations as a Lens for Reflective Practice in Teacher Education

Wendy Moran, Robyn Brandenburg and Sharon M. McDonough

Abstract

Being a teacher educator is a complex endeavour and it is through systematic, and evidence-based reflection in and on practice that teaching pedagogy is more deeply understood. Extant literature reveals that reflective practice plays an integral role in understanding teacher educators' work. This chapter focuses on pedagogical confrontations as a lens for reflective practice to reveal the complexity of teacher educators' work. The term 'pedagogical confrontations' (PCs) signifies incidents, interactions or events in teaching which cause us to pause and critically examine our practice. In this chapter we examine the context, descriptions and responses of participant-identified pedagogical confrontations. Through independent and collaborative analysis of the confrontations we identify three key themes: (1) professional roles; (2) the importance of relationships; and (3) the changing nature of universities and teacher education. Using PCs as a lens for reflective practice reveals the relationship between one's values and pedagogical practices and we contend that recognition and deeper knowledge of this relationship leads to richer understandings of teacher educators' work.

Keywords

reflective practice – pedagogical confrontations – teacher educators

Introduction

Teacher educators engage in multi-dimensional work as they prepare pre-service teachers (PSTs) for the transition to the teaching profession. Teacher educator work is underpinned by both personal and professional values that interplay with contextual factors and demands, leading teacher educators to experience 'pedagogical confrontations' (PCs). In our previous work, we have defined 'pedagogical confrontations' (PC) as "incidents, interactions or events in learning and teaching which cause us to pause and critically examine our practice" (Brandenburg, McDonough, & Moran, 2016, p. 270). In this chapter, we highlight that in using PCs as a lens for reflective practice, the values held by teacher educators are revealed; relationships between pedagogical practices and values are identified; and more deliberate and intentional decision-making is made possible.

Background

As teacher educators we research our practice as a means to discover more about our own work, the influences of values and beliefs on teacher educator practice, and about the field of teacher education more broadly. This study builds on two specific areas in our recent research. First, our research focusing on the importance of critical incident identification and analysis in our practice as teacher educators (Brandenburg, 2012; McDonough, 2014); and second, our research (Brandenburg, McDonough, & Moran, 2016) through which we identified pedagogical confrontations (PCs) within our own experiences and subsequently used them to identify and examine the assumptions held underlying our PCs. These two bodies of research led to the genesis of this current study which seeks to uncover the way teacher educators, from a range of international contexts, experience PCs and the implications of these for practice. This research is important given the increasingly intensified and complex work undertaken by teacher educators. Deeper understanding of the beliefs and values underpinning teacher educators' practices through the use of PCs will lead to more clearly identifying the pedagogical choices available when navigating the complexities of teacher educator practice.

Conceptual Framework

The notion that teacher educators' work is sophisticated and complex has been highlighted by MacKinnon and Bullock (2016) who argue that it requires "engaging with practice beyond the technical" and bringing to the "surface the sophisticated thinking, decision making and pedagogical reasoning that underpins pedagogical expertise" (p. 292). This is further supported by Nyamu-pangedengu and Lelliott (2016) who contend that teacher education comprises three aspects, including the "content to be taught, how it is taught and the thinking and pedagogical reasoning behind the teaching that is employed"

(p. 86). Revealing the complexity of teaching requires teacher educators to use "the cauldron of practice to expose pedagogy (especially one's own) to scrutiny" (MacKinnon & Bullock, 2016, p. 292). This scrutiny requires an examination of the personal and professional values, that, according to Brandenburg and McDonough (2017), "are manifested in our professional actions, pedagogy and practice" (p. 234). Dinkleman (2011) asserts that more research is needed regarding the nature of teacher educator beliefs and commitments at the heart of pedagogical choices as this research will enable discernment of professional identities and facilitate a genuine focus on identity development. We contend that using PCs as a lens for reflective practice may be useful in achieving this goal.

Pedagogical Confrontations

PCs are found within the teaching context and represent incidents, interactions or events which cause educators to pause and critically examine their practice (Brandenburg, McDonough, & Moran, 2016). PCs may be philosophical, political, ethical, emotional and/or organisational in nature, and while they are typically grounded in everyday practice, they are unanticipated (Brandenburg, McDonough, & Moran, 2016). PCs derive from the body of work that identifies and scrutinizes "critical incidents" (Brandenburg, 2008; Brookfield, 1995; Tripp, 2012). While the term 'critical incident' has multiple interpretations, it is widely accepted that critical incidents describe events to which there is no immediate resolution. PCs are distinctively different to critical incidents however, in that their focus is grounded in pedagogical practice. A PC challenges teachers' beliefs, ethics, emotions, and/or philosophies about the approaches they employ and when reflected upon can be confirmation of what is already known or a catalyst for change. In drawing on PCs as a lens for reflection we identify the interconnections between personal and professional values and the pedagogy and practices of teacher educators as demonstrated in Figure 11.1.

The Aim of the Research
The aim of this research is to understand more about the sophisticated and complex nature of teaching and learning in teacher education. We examine the nature and type of PC teacher educators experience as they seek to design and implement meaningful learning opportunities. Through learning more about these confrontations and the way teacher educators respond to them, we generate an understanding of the challenges facing teacher educators, and the implications for the field. In undertaking this study, we examine the following questions:

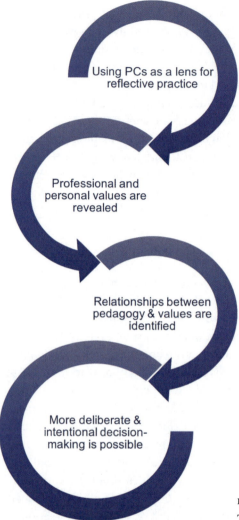

FIGURE 11.1
The role of PCs in teacher educators' work

- What pedagogical confrontations do we experience in our work as teacher educators?
- How do teacher educators respond and how does this influence pedagogical practice?
- How might pedagogical confrontations inform and impact our practice?

Research Design and Methodology

This chapter draws on a qualitative study using data provided by 15 educators from six countries in answer to questions related to a self-identified PC. Given that the views of the educators are self-reported it was logical to also include the authors' PCs collected earlier and combine them with those gathered from around the world. The authors of this chapter form a subset of three within the group of 15 educators.

Data Collection and Organisation

The process of inquiry into the confrontations was adapted from Kosnik's (2001) 'Critical Incident Analysis' and aimed to provide the researchers with the opportunity to examine the nature of the PCs and the values underpinning both the confrontation and the response to it. Ethics approval for this study was granted in 2015 (Human Research Ethics Committee, Project No. B15-154) prior to commencement of the study. An online survey consisting of open-ended questions was considered to be the most accessible for international data collection and least compromising of the depth of responses, while also ensuring participants would not have to contribute excessive time to participate.

The survey introductory page explained the term 'pedagogical confrontations' and assured participants of anonymity and confidentiality before asking demographic questions regarding the country of residence, number of years in teacher education, and the types of courses/programs taught at university. The remaining eight questions required answers to the following:

1. Please state the month of your confrontation (select from the last 12-month period)
2. Please give your pedagogical confrontation a title
3. Describe briefly the context of your pedagogical confrontation
4. Please provide a detailed description of the event or incident as it occurred and your response
5. What does your response to the event or incident say about you?
6. What values are inherent in the situation and your response?
7. Did your 'enactment of practice' change as a result of the confrontation? Please explain
8. Based on your reflection of this pedagogical confrontation, what do you believe are the implications or outcomes for teacher educators and/or teacher education?

Participants

The three researchers completed the survey initially before drawing on a purposive sampling approach to distribute it to other higher education colleagues known to them. They also invited participants from the 2014 10th International Conference on Self-Study of Teacher Education Practices as the individuals in this group were most likely to be currently in teacher education positions and were not unfamiliar with self-reporting reflections on their work. As stated earlier, this expanded the dataset by a further 12 educators creating a total group of 15 participants who represent the following countries: Australia, Iceland, New Zealand, South Africa, UK and USA.

Data Analysis Process

Data analysis were conducted adhering to the basic phases of thematic analysis (Braun & Clarke, 2006) and involved first an overall familiarisation of the data, then highlighting key concepts, words and phrases to generate initial categories (Lankshear & Knobel, 2004). Within each confrontation, points of tension, self-realisations, and explicitly stated reasons for actions and responses were all noted and considered. Then across the set of PCs similarities and differences were examined to enable reviewing, defining and naming of themes before finally selecting appropriate exemplars. All phases of analysis were conducted individually before discussing collaboratively to expose and confront prejudices or perspectives of individual researchers that might influence the selection and defining of themes (Bogdan & Biklen, 2007). Points of convergence and dissonance were identified and resolved through discussion to enhance trustworthiness in the analysis process (LaBoskey, 2004). The collaborative process resulted in the identification of three key themes that characterised the nature of the pedagogical confrontations experienced by participants. The themes will be explained in more detail in the analysis and discussion of results but are named here:
– Professional roles (PR)
– The importance of relationships (R)
– The changing nature of universities and teacher education (CN)

Details of the participants' PCs and the connection to the three themes can be found in Table 11.1.

Each participant's confrontation could be easily classified under at least one of these three themes confirming the appropriateness of the themes across the data set. While the majority of the confrontations aligned exclusively with one theme, two participants' confrontations were classified into two themes (Ray and Harry) and Ruth's confrontation, links with all three themes.

Analysis and Discussion of Results

In this section, we describe the themes and present selected examples that illustrate the nature of the PCs and the participant responses.

Professional Role

> I am a teacher educator – this is not my 'job', it is a part of me, yesterday, today and tomorrow. (Ray)

In analysing the participants' PCs we identified that eight of the 15 focused on how they, or others, understood and/or enacted their professional role as a teacher. The PCs demonstrated the multiple and complex dimensions of the professional role of teacher educators, while also showing the emotional impact of the PCs on the teacher educator and their views of their work. Ray's PC demonstrated his perception of his role and responsibilities of a teacher educator, when he defends continuing his broader subject focus despite the Academic Director's (AD) demands to narrow it. Ray opposes this directive believing the breadth to be "valid, worthy and useful". In doing so we can see that Ray has a professional commitment that indicates his role is more than just a job. In refusing to acquiesce to the AD's insistence, Ray sees himself as working to his own personal values. He identifies his PC as having implications for teacher education as he argues that the "integrity of subject co-ordinators regarding decision making" is important and he contends that there should be both "professional and personal support for academics" due to the "emotional impact of supporting preservice teachers".

Analysis of the PCs highlights that a key element of the professional role is being able to support students through teaching that demonstrates an "awareness of pedagogical modelling for preservice teachers" (Jennie). Kerry's confrontation *This course is a waste of time* describes her dilemma in approaching teacher education colleagues believing them to be unprofessional in their work and attitude, while both Jennie and Robyn perceived they had not practised what they preached. Pedagogical modelling as a teacher educator is a role they believe to be important (Loughran & Berry, 2005), with this importance reflected in Kerry's identification that an implication of her PC is that "we need a pedagogy of teacher education". She argued that the professional role of teacher educators requires an understanding and appreciation of PSTs "as adults ... who should be taught using a dialogical/ respectful/ appropriate pedagogy".

In the PCs described by Sasha, Wendy and Sharon we identified 'professional role' as being connected with the responsibility of the teacher educator to support PSTs' knowledge and skills, particularly in situations when they might not be meeting the demands of the profession. Both Wendy and Sharon questioned their professionalism perceiving they 'failed' to enact their role in facilitating PST understanding of the learning process and reflective skills, and

TABLE 11.1 Brief descriptions of the pedagogical confrontations

Name	Years of experience	Title	Theme	Description of pedagogical confrontation
Robyn	17	Closing the Gap	PR	In conducting a 3-hour class with professionals from a range of disciplines, Robyn introduced a vast selection of critical reflection approaches at a quick pace conscious that time was short. Before concluding the class, one participant requested the need to 'close the loop' on at least one area covered alerting Robyn to the fact that she had left too much content implicit.
Wendy	20	Developing genuine pedagogical decision-making	PR	In supervising a preservice teacher (PST) on a lengthy professional experience, it became apparent the PST was unable to deeply reflect. Wendy felt inadequate when, after providing countless opportunities and strategies for growth, the PST had still not developed the skills to make deliberately sound pedagogical decisions.
Sharon	6	Walking the tightrope	PR	Sharon's confrontation was situated in a three-week professional experience. School placements were in short supply and Sharon's dilemma focused on her desire to challenge the mentor teacher's views (who she had not met previously) while ensuring continuance of the school-university relationship.
Sam	25	Clouded futures	CN	Teacher education hierarchy accused Sam of being divisive, resistant to change and negative when she objected to the dismissal of her working party's program development ideas.

(cont.)

PEDAGOGICAL CONFRONTATIONS AND REFLECTIVE PRACTICE 207

TABLE 11.1 Brief descriptions of the pedagogical confrontations (cont.)

Name	Years of experience	Title	Theme	Description of pedagogical confrontation
Mark	35	Cognitive dissonance	CN	A teacher in Mark's class questioned his choice of learning techniques and methods claiming that Marks' pedagogical approach wasn't supported or endorsed in their schools.
Tori	10	Deepening pedagogical relationships	R	Tori endeavoured to build relationships with all her students, however circumstances often created opportunities where deeper connections were forged with only some students.
Sasha	15	The value of professional behaviour in PSTs	PR	Poor attendance, punctuality, participation and a lack of courtesy from one student in a teacher education course led Sasha to question his responsibilities in ensuring professional values and quality teachers.
Kerry	20	This course is a waste of time	PR	A PST objected to Kerry's methods in literacy teaching claiming that she was not learning anything and the course was a waste of time, yet later discussion revealed that her outburst was really about the teaching approaches of other professors. Should Kerry approach her colleagues and discuss the feedback received?
Jennie	10	Do as I say, not as I do	PR	Jennie, burdened by a heavy workload, was unable to return assessments in the timely manner she had always demonstrated. Jennie felt she had not modelled good practice and in light of this reconsidered the fairness of her students' workload.
Clara	5	Digital conformity: a form of pedagogy	CN	A university declaration required a blended learning course to change to mostly on-line and left Clara concerned about how her strengths as a teacher would translate into this new model.

(cont.)

TABLE 11.1 Brief descriptions of the pedagogical confrontations (*cont.*)

Name	Years of experience	Title	Theme	Description of pedagogical confrontation
Nick	8	Please just tell me what to do	R	Supervision of a masters' student and the value of developing research autonomy was made difficult when the student pleaded for a more directed approach.
Jack	16	A question of sensitivity	R	Objections were raised by some students in Jack's class that his illustrative story, relating to an experienced Physics teacher who requested help from elementary teachers, was offensive. Jack considered how to deal with the potential sensitivities in every class.
Harry	6	When rhetoric doesn't match reality	R/CN	Harry felt frustrated and angry by the university's favouring of 'economics' over their own rhetoric concerning relationships with schools and with regard to quality teacher education courses.
Ruth	23	Online does not mean whatever	PR/R/CN	A doctoral student repeatedly failed to complete online assignments on time, or correctly, and didn't respond to offers of assistance. Ruth felt that a face-to-face course would have enabled earlier and more effective intervention.
Ray	22	Academic Director or Arrogant Dictator	PR/CN	Due to student feedback, the university required Ray to refocus his effective course on wellbeing and resilience to instead cover behaviour and classroom management only.

in gatekeeping for the profession (Koster, Korthagen, Wubbels, & Hoornweg, 1996). This perceived failure of carrying out the professional role can be seen to impact on teacher educator emotions, something identified by Ray's comments noted earlier. It is also reflected by Jennie when she states, "Did it disturb me that I was failing to fully support my students' development as teachers? Absolutely". This same concept of having a responsibility to support student development as part of the professional role is highlighted in Ruth's persistence with an uncommitted doctoral student in a 'make-up' online subject. She does this even though she would prefer to avoid conflict and "hates" online teaching. The PCs associated with the concept of professional role indicate that teacher educators have a set of values and understandings about what they see as their role and they use those as a means of considering their pedagogy and practice.

> *The Importance of Relationships*
> I often say to my students that teaching is all about communication and relationships, but I have only come to see this as key to my teaching over recent years. (Tori)

Five of the participants described PCs characterised by the importance of building and maintaining meaningful and authentic pedagogical relationships that contribute to student learning. Participants regard respect as central to these relationships, as well as understanding the needs of individual students, reflecting Rodgers and Raider-Roth's (2006) notion of teaching as engaging in an authentic relationship with students. Tori in *Deepening pedagogical relationships* demonstrates her awareness of the Australian Professional Standards for Teachers (AITSL, 2011) requiring teachers to know their students and how they learn, questioning "how do I apply this to my own teaching?". She notes that earlier in her career, she didn't focus on getting to know students as she was more concerned with the curriculum. However, four consecutive years of working with students on an international practicum has shown her the importance of relationships in being a teacher educator. Tori seeks to recognise the nature of the relationships she has with adult learners, are the relationships "personal, professional and pedagogical? – what do these terms mean in relation to my work with PSTs?". She notes too that her PC reflection identified an important implication for teacher education: that as universities change and face-to-face teaching becomes less the norm, it is "imperative that we maintain pedagogical relationships with our students".

In a similar way, Nick's confrontation entitled *Please just tell me what to do* identifies the discomfort when supervising a research student in which he 'pulled away' from direct instruction and encouraged the student to make her own decisions toward the end of her thesis. He recalls the time when his own supervisor did something similar and how hard it was for him. He writes of trying to find the "right thing" for students while acknowledging that "the 'right thing' may in fact be a different approach from one student to another". He concludes that as educators exercising sympathy with regard to the emotional component of our students' lives will enable us to recognise the importance of not only explaining our pedagogical choices to our students but also reassuring them when our approaches leave them feeling uncertain. Nick echoes similarly expressed views of Kitchen (2005, 2009) who values empathy and respect as critical aspects of relational teacher development and affirms the centrality of relationship in professional development and renewal. This desire to recognise students as individuals and respect their needs is also demonstrated by Ruth, in *Online does not mean whatever,* who shows an awareness of her online students' lives and describes how she "can't say 'no' when my doc [doctoral] students need something that is within my ability to deliver". She notes that meeting her online student face-to-face complicated what would have been ordinarily a straight-forward fail grade. In doing so, Ruth privileges the relationship with the students and their learning over her own personal preferences.

Privileging relationships is also present in Jack and Harry's confrontations: Jack seeks to be sensitive to the relationships he has with students by being careful with his words and "not pretend[ing] to understand how some information may come across to others"; while Harry works to maintain hard won relationships with schools and students. Harry also questions how the university might demonstrate the meaningful, authentic approach to relationship building that he strives to achieve asking, "How do you get the best out of people?". He shared that the confrontation he described caused him deep hurt, further emphasising that for him, teacher educators' work is personal and relational.

While Jennie's and Ray's PCs are largely concerned with the professional role, concluding comments from both respondents spoke of the need to recognise the affective domain in teacher educators' work with PSTs. Ray asserted that an implication for teacher education institutions is the need for personal and emotional support while Tori, Ruth and Harry considered how these meaningful relationships might be developed as the nature of teacher education changes.

Changing Nature of University and Teacher Education
The pedagogical work I do as a teacher educator is not the way future teacher education is going to be practiced. (Sam)

Governmental, university and policy stakeholders continue to scrutinise teacher education and teacher educators, the result being an increasing move towards standards and standardisation of the profession (Australian Institute of Teaching and School Leadership (AITSL), 2011, 2014; General Teaching Council of Scotland, 2012; National Board for Professional Teaching Standards, USA, 2016; National Institute of Education, Singapore, 2009). Teacher educators have acknowledged the increasing standardization and regulation of the profession and, as Mark suggests, teacher educators "need to have an even greater awareness of how far teaching in our public schools – especially in an era of high-stakes testing – has become mechanized and standardized". A key outcome of increasing, and often externally mandated standardisation of the profession is, as Ray states, "[the] risk of changes where changes and amendments are made without due process". Six of the pedagogical confrontations reveal the impact on teacher educators of the changing nature of universities and teacher education. In particular, Sam, Mark, Harry and Ray highlight the ways in which organisational and operational arrangements and changes directly affected their perceptions and experiences of their university as a workplace.

The question of professional integrity within the context of economically rationalist approaches applied by both internal and external agencies when enforcing changes to programs is the focus of Sam's, Mark's, Harry's and Ray's PCs in particular. Harry states that the university is "a business and it's not about quality ... [it] is a hierarchy [that] is full of rhetoric about quality but in reality will always favour economics. They have lost sight of their true mission. They have the ability to rationalise any situation to suit their needs". Sam also suggests that "the university doesn't walk its talk", and Mark notes that one must "confront political realities ... and assert [one]self as [a] thinker ... [and as] humanists". All four participants mentioned experiencing personal hurt; that they felt "totally devalued by the hierarchy of the university" (Harry) and experienced a "reduced passion for ... teaching" (Sam).

A prominent theme identified in association with changes in the university reflected some comment about the almost universal move away from face-to-face teaching to blended and fully online modes of teaching, demanding changes to "the organisation and form of teaching and evaluation of teaching and learning" (Clara in *Digital conformity: a form of pedagogy*). Ruth and Clara identified the core impact of the demand for online teaching and described the ways in which these changes were deeply influencing how they were both required to modify their pedagogical approaches. Each of the respondents revealed the impact of these demands on their professional identities as teacher educators (Erickson, Young, and Pinnegar, 2011; Rice, Newberry, Whiting, Cutri and Pinnegar, 2015), an ever-evolving education research focus.

The Role of Assumptions in Pedagogical Confrontations

In our analysis we identified a range of PCs and how they collectively illustrate the themes of professional role, the importance of relationships and the changing nature of universities and teacher education. We also noticed the role of assumptions underpinning these PC reflections. Referring to the work of Brookfield (1995, 2012) and our earlier work (Brandenburg, McDonough, & Moran, 2016) we then engaged in another level of analysis where we examined each confrontation by identifying and classifying the assumptions as causal, prescriptive or paradigmatic. Brookfield (2012) argues that paradigmatic assumptions are firmly and deeply held beliefs that are challenging to shift. The analysis of the PCs revealed the identification of firmly held paradigmatic assumptions in many of the PCs, for example, collaboration and democratic decision-making (Sam); teaching as political activism, whereby learning to teach is underpinned by critical reflection (Mark); face-to-face teaching is critical in the learning process (Ruth and Clara); developing meaningful and genuine relationships is crucial to developing a teaching pedagogy (Harry and Tori); and understanding wellbeing and relationships are vital to quality teaching and learning (Ray). Interestingly, the only theme in which *all* confrontations were underpinned by paradigmatic assumptions was the third: the changing nature of universities and teacher education. The analysis of data relating to this theme indicated to us how embedded the assumptions are that structure and "frame the whole way that we look at the world" (Brookfield, 2012, p. 3) and ultimately, the ways in which these deeply held, and often not immediately apparent paradigmatic assumptions impact our daily work as teachers and teacher educators. Paradigmatic assumptions are the most difficult to uncover, and they are only "examined critically ... after a great deal of resistance to doing this, and it takes a considerable amount of contrary evidence and disconfirming experiences to change them" (Brookfield, 2012, p. 11). To examine this further we isolated the examples associated with the third theme to explore the participants' responses to the changing nature of universities and teacher education, and the factors that may have mediated their responses.

Confrontations, Assumptions and Responses

In the confrontation, *Clouded futures*, Sam, a teacher educator for 25 years, details his reaction to the appointment of a chair to lead the 'last minute feedback' for university approval for a new degree. Sam disagreed with the process as it clearly challenged the democratic, social and critical human orientation that directed his pedagogy. His deputy dean subsequently contacted him and inferred he was trying to be "divisive and negative about the new development". Sam was then provided with a "list of all [his] shortcomings and feedback" and told "people had stopped taking [him] seriously". His reaction was to reflect on his nature: "I am passionate about what I do", and "not very tolerant to other perspectives" and to realise that he needed to be a "better operator at the political level ... and work with the key levers in any situation". Likewise, Mark, a teacher educator for 35 years, in his PC *Cognitive dissonance*, describes his response to a student's question relating to learning and teaching tasks that demand individual constructions and perceptions of teaching, when schools are mandating high-stakes testing and standards-based teaching. His paradigmatic assumption reflects the belief that "teaching should be a journey towards self-discovery and not a march towards conformity and standardization". His response was to re-examine his assumptions and in doing so, he re-committed even more firmly to his "life's mission to help others and myself and keep the passion alive, and help restore the political systems and mechanisms that will allow teachers to reclaim their right as the curriculum-decision makers of their professional lives". Harry (six years' in the tertiary sector), despite feeling undervalued when refused extra resourcing to expand a successful university-school partnership, decides "to be resilient and continue to develop the program". He states that his motivation for this decision "is for the sake of the PSTs and schools". Sam, Mark and Harry responded to the changing nature of universities and teacher education by holding firm to their assumptions and not allowing them to be loosened.

In contrast, Clara, a teacher educator of five years, in response to a requirement to change a blended learning course to mostly online wrote, "the new organization has thus pulled some of the ground we build our pedagogy on from underneath us and places challenges we have not fully responded to as constructively as we wish". The mandate for online teaching was directly opposed to her paradigmatic assumption that face-to-face teaching is imperative, yet while she fears that her "versatile teaching methods in action will be lost ... the connections with students will be looser ... and a part of the education ... will be poorer", she and her colleagues are prepared to "grapple with the change that comes from above" and continue to "look for ways to be the teachers we want to be". Clara's response demonstrates that she is prepared to risk and challenge her paradigmatic assumption to experiment with new approaches to teaching and learning and claims "it is a work in progress". Ruth too, challenges her own assumptions about teaching online and engages in this form of work in order to support her students despite feeling frustrated that online delivery weakened aspects of her course that had been strengths. In doing so, we see that the responsibility she feels to carry out her professional role is greater than her own personal preferences in teaching.

Examining these responses relating to changes imposed by universities and teacher education institutions, there is variation in the responses. We note that some participants were willing to modify or re-imagine their current practice to address the demands of the institution, yet others held firm to their beliefs. We wonder if the notion of 'deviance credits' applies here. Brookfield describes deviance credits as "the institutional brownie points that teachers accrue by taking on tasks ... that earn them a reputation as organisation loyalists" (Brookfield, 1995, p. 41) and he contends that we "can take an oppositional stand and still have our voice heard" (p. 41). From the participants' descriptions of their roles at the university, is it possible that Sam, Mark and Harry were able to maintain their paradigmatic assumptions in the face of organisational and structural pressure due to the accumulation of 'deviance credits'?

Implications for Teacher Educator Researchers

When we initiated this research we were seeking to identify the pedagogical confrontations we experience, how they might connect with others' PCs, and their impact on teaching practice. Analysis of the data highlighted the role assumptions play, in particular paradigmatic assumptions, in both the PCs and our responses to them. This was an unexpected outcome of our research and although we have previously used 'assumption hunting' as a lens to examine our practice (McDonough & Brandenburg, 2012), we were surprised by the power of paradigmatic assumptions in the work and lives of teacher educators. In returning to our own PCs, each of us considers the role of assumptions and 'deviance credits' in our responses and within our context, reminding ourselves that "assumptions are rarely right or wrong [sic.], they are best thought of as more or less contextually appropriate" (Brookfield, 2012, p. 15).

In reflecting on her PC, Sharon identified that she holds a paradigmatic assumption about the value of critical reflection in the teaching and learning process. Sharon's decision to refrain from challenging the mentor teacher about her professional role in developing critical reflection skills in the PST could now be validated as appropriate given the high-stakes of school placement shortages (i.e. the context), and her lack of deviance credits with the school. Engaging in the self-study process has enabled Sharon to make explicit the factors that had influenced her PC and her response. Robyn has reflected on the ways in which her own paradigmatic assumption related to teaching academics from multi-disciplines about critical reflective practice has been challenged and questions now whether indeed, this skill can be taught.

Wendy, by using a PC to reflect on her supervisory role with a final year PST on a professional experience placement, came to understand that she was motivated by a strongly held assumption, that is, that all PSTs are capable of learning how to critically reflect – it is simply a matter finding the right method to teach them. This assumption led Wendy to invest substantial time and effort both emotionally and professionally over a 10-week period rather than accept that the PST may not have been capable of developing the reflection skills at that point in time, or may not have been able to develop them at all. Wendy resisted accepting that her efforts did not get the PST "over the line", yet she did not want to risk her relationship with the mentor teachers by giving the PST further time to develop. We are reminded at this point by Dinkleman (2011) that "the clinical features of teacher education programmes often create demands on teacher educators that are not experienced by professors in other parts of the university. As activity predicated on relationships, all responsible teaching requires emotional and psychological investment of some sort" (p. 315). The emotional and psychological investment can make assumption-challenging all the more difficult.

Using PCs as a lens for reflective practice has revealed and confirmed the complexity of teacher educators' work. In particular, it has highlighted the ways in which personal values may conflict with the perceived role of teacher educators, the emphasis on relationships, and institutional expectations. As Elliott-Johns (2015) suggests, "turning the lens on ourselves, as teacher educators, is a constructive starting point in gaining clarity and greater understanding about what we mean by ... reflection ... and why we think 'reflection' is an important element of teacher education" (p. 34). We contend that using PCs as a lens for reflective practice enables us to analyse the values and beliefs that underpin our pedagogical decisions and practices offering an opportunity for critique and reconsideration in light of new and changing contexts.

Conclusion

This study reveals the nature and type of pedagogical confrontations that teacher educators experience in their work. The three themes: professional roles; the importance of relationships; and the changing nature of universities and teacher education; highlight the range and the variety of both experiences and responses, confirming that PCs can lead to insight and growth for self, others and the profession. Our responses to confrontations are informed by the assumptions we hold and may be mediated by one's professional standing within an institution and/or by the context in which we operate. The impact on pedagogical practice manifests differently among teacher educators with some willing to trial new approaches that are at odds with their paradigmatic assumptions, and others who hold a renewed determination to enact their firmly embedded beliefs. Through the use of PCs as a lens to examine practice we have identified that despite personal loss or risk, participants remain committed to the field in which they work.

Through engaging in this research we have identified the role and value of PCs as a means to further understand the sophisticated and complex nature of teaching. We sought to generate a collective understanding of pedagogical confrontations and the responses of teacher educators to these experiences. Through deep analysis of the 15 narratives we were able to confirm the importance of using PC reflective practice in identifying the values that underlie our pedagogical choices thereby creating opportunities for us to more objectively determine our future actions. Furthermore, this research has revealed that PCs enable us to refine our identities as teachers when we are in the business of teaching fledgling teachers. Dinkleman notes "As more research becomes available about the ideas, commitments and beliefs that animate the pedagogical choices teacher educators make in the context of their programmes, more opportunities present themselves for teacher educators to craft their identities as teachers of teachers in a profession that previously left identity development unseen and inaccessible to others" (2011, p. 319). We conclude by inviting our readers to add their voice to building the body of research concerned with teacher educator values, identities, assumptions and practices, further extending and developing a shared understanding of our work in this highly valuable profession.

Acknowledgements

The authors would like to sincerely thank the participants who contributed their narrations and events for analysis in this chapter. We are fully cognisant that to contribute took time and effort and we are very grateful. We hope that we respectfully and accurately represented your confrontation and in doing so have provided you with further thoughts about your work.

References

Australian Institute for Teaching and School Leadership (AITSL). (2011). *Australian professional standards for teachers*. Retrieved from http://www.aitsl.edu.au/australian-professional-standards-for-teachers

Australian Institute for Teaching and School Leadership (AITSL). (2014). *Australian professional standard for principals*. Retrieved from https://www.aitsl.edu.au/tools-resources/resource/australian-professional-standard-for-principals

Bogdan, R. C., & Biklen, S. (2007). *Qualitative research for education: An introduction to theories and methods* (5th ed.). Boston, MA: Pearson Education Inc.

Brandenburg, R. (2008). *Powerful pedagogy: Self-study of a teacher educator's practice*. Dordrecht: Springer.

Brandenburg, R., & Gervasoni, A. (2012). Rattling the Cage: Moving beyond ethical standards to ethical praxis in self-study research. *Studying Teacher Education, 8*(2), 183–191.

Brandenburg, R., & McDonough, S. (2017). Using critical incidents to reflect on teacher educator practice. In R. Brandenburg, K. Glasswell, M. Jones, & J. Ryan (Eds.), *Reflective theories and practices in teacher education* (pp. 223–236). Singapore: Springer.

Brandenburg, R., McDonough, S., & Moran, W. (2016, July 31 – August 4). *From pedagogical confrontations to pedagogical invitations: A self-study of teacher educators' work*. Paper presented at the 11th International Conference on Self-Study of Teacher Education Practices, Herstmonceux Castle, East Sussex, England.

Brookfield, S. (1995). *Becoming a critically reflective teacher*. San Francisco, CA: Jossey-Bass.

Brookfield, S. (2012). *Teaching for critical thinking: Tools and techniques to help students question their assumptions*. San Francisco, CA: Jossey-Bass.

Braun, V., & Clarke, V. (2006). Using thematic analysis in psychology. *Qualitative Research in Psychology, 3*(2), 77–101.

Dinkleman, T. (2011). Forming a teacher educator identity: Uncertain standards, practice and relationships. *Journal of Education for Teaching, 37*(3), 309–323.

Elliot-Johns, S. (2015). Towards meaningful reflection in teacher education as professional learning. In D. Garbett & A. Ovens (Eds.), *Teaching for tomorrow today* (pp. 33–41). Auckland: Edify.

Erickson, L. B., Young, J. R., & Pinnegar, S. (2011). Teacher educator identity: Emerging understandings of person, positioning, roles, and collaborations. *Studying Teacher Education, 7*(2), 105–107. doi:10.1080/17425964.2011.591123

General Teaching Council for Scotland [GTC]. (2012). *The standards for registration: Mandatory requirements for registration with the General Teaching Council for Scotland*. Retrieved from http://www.gtcs.org.uk

Kitchen, J. (2005). Looking backward, moving forward: Understanding my narrative as a teacher educator. *Studying Teacher Education, 1*(1), 17–30.

Kitchen, J. (2009). Relational teacher development: Growing collaboratively in a hoping relationship. *Teacher Education Quarterly, 36*(2), 45–62.

Kosnik, C. (2001). The effects of an inquiry-oriented teacher education program on a faculty member: Some critical incidents and my journey. *Journal of Reflective Teaching, 21*(1), 65–80.

Koster, B., Korthagen, F. A., Wubbels, T. H., & Hoornweg, J. (1996). Roles, competencies and training of teacher educators: A new challenge. In E. Befring (Ed.), *Teacher education for quality* (pp. 397–411), Oslo: Lobo Grafisk.

LaBoskey, V. (2004). The methodology of self-study and theoretical underpinnings. In J. J. Loughran, M. L. Hamilton, V. K. LaBoskey, & T. Russell (Eds.), *International handbook of self-study of teaching and teacher education practices* (pp. 817–869). Dordrecht: Springer.

Lankshear, C., & Knobel, M. (2004). *A handbook for teacher research: From design to implementation.* London: Open University Press.

Loughran, J., & Berry, M. (2005). Modelling by teacher educators. *Teaching and Teacher Education, 21*(2), 193–203. doi:10.1016/j.tate.2004.12.005

Mackinnon, A., & Bullock, S. (2016). Playing in tune: Reflection, resonance and the dossier. In D. Garbett & A. Ovens (Eds.), *Enacting self-study as a methodology for professional inquiry* (pp. 291–296). Herstmonceux: S-STEP.

McDonough, S. (2014). Rewriting the script of mentoring pre-service teachers in third space: Exploring tensions of loyalty, obligation and advocacy. *Studying Teacher Education, 10*(3), 210–221.

McDonough, S., & Brandenburg, R. (2012). Examining assumptions about teacher educator identities through self-study of mentoring roles. *Studying Teacher Education: A Journal of Self-Study Practices, 8*(3), 169–182.

National Board for Professional Teaching Standards [NBPTS]. (2016). *Five core propositions for teaching.* Retrieved from http://boardcertifiedteachers.org/about-certification/five-core-porpositions

National Institute of Education [NIE], Singapore. (2009). *A teacher education model for the 21st Century: A report by the National Institute of Education.* Retrieved from https://www.nie.edu.sg/docs/default-source/te21_docs/te21-online-version---updated.pdf?sfvrsn=2

Nyamupangedengu, E., & Lelliot, A. (2016). Using modelling as a method of teaching a content course to pre-service teachers: Lessons learnt. In D. Garbett & A. Ovens (Eds.), *Enacting self-study as a methodology for professional inquiry* (pp. 85–92). Herstmonceux: S-STEP.

Rice, M., Newberry, M., Whiting, E., Cutri, R., & Pinnegar, S. (2015). Learning from experiences of non-personhood: A self-study of teacher educator identities. *Studying Teacher Education, 11*(1), 16–31. doi:10.1080/17425964.2015.1013024

Rodgers, C. R., & Raider-Roth, M. B. (2006). Presence in teaching. *Teachers and Teaching: Theory and Practice, 12*(3), 265–287.

Tripp, D. (2012). *Critical incidents in teaching developing professional judgment.* London: Routledge.

CHAPTER 12

Beyond the Observed in Cross-Cultural Mentoring Conversations

Lily Orland-Barak and Ella Mazor

Abstract

This chapter explores mentoring and mentored learning in pre-service education at the encounter between two cultures (Arab-Druze student teachers and Jewish mentor teachers). Drawing on an illustrative case study from a larger data set of mentoring conversations and open-ended interviews in a study of intercultural mentoring, we propose an analytical framework for examining complexities within mentoring relationships that considers the social and cultural values, forms of communication, and reasoning and behavior of mentors and student teachers that may remain latent and unacknowledged. The discussion invites teacher educators, curriculum developers, and policy makers to consider how to support the development of mentors as culturally sensitive and responsive professionals.

Keywords

mentoring and mentored teacher learning – cross-cultural teacher education – socio-cultural perspectives on student teacher learning in practice

Introduction

The diverse socio-cultural contexts within which mentors work call for an orientation to teacher mentoring that is culturally responsive (Cochran-Smith, 2004; Villegas & Lucas, 2002). This requires of mentors to understand how ideologies, rituals, values, belief systems, and behaviors play out in mentoring interactions when student teachers and teachers come from different cultural, ethnic religious backgrounds and educational orientations (Orland-Barak, 2010). These differences turn our attention to possible misunderstandings that might emerge when minority student teachers are inducted into teacher education programs that follow different ideological, cultural and pedagogical orientations, such as the case presented in this chapter of Druze student teachers studying to become teachers in a Jewish teacher education program.

Culturally responsive mentors (both in pre-service and in-service education) are, then, seen as socio-culturally conscious professionals who understand how their mentees' ways of thinking, behaving and being are deeply influenced by factors such as ethnicity, social class, and language (Orland-Barak, 2010; Sleeter, 2011). As such, they are expected to develop affirming attitudes towards mentees who differ from the dominant culture, and a commitment to act as agents of change with an understanding of the cultural and political forces that shape the school contexts within which they function. Mentors are also expected to be sensitive to their mentees' histories, past experiences and how these might shape their visions of teaching and learning (Becher & Orland-Barak, 2017; Villegas & Lucas, 2002). To this end, culturally responsive mentoring practices should include opportunities for interrogating and surfacing dilemmas and discrepancies between participants' ingrained assumptions and beliefs about teaching and pedagogy and those promoted by a particular educational or institutional policy (Villegas & Lucas, 2002). Creating such opportunities is still a major challenge in the preparation of mentors, given the fact that, traditionally, mentoring practices have mostly privileged certain cultural values over others, often resulting in emergent conflicts between competing cultures in mentoring settings (Orland-Barak, Kheir-Farraj, & Becher, 2013). These conflicts cause the mentor to face a harsh moral reality, especially in cases of overt political friction and explicit or hidden cultural differences.

Reminding ourselves that that any kind of practice must be understood in the cultural, social and political context within which it occurs (Berger & Luckmann, 1966), this chapter focuses on the complex forms and meanings that culturally responsive mentoring takes when examined in contexts of cultural diversity. True, the past three decades of educational research have contributed important insights as to how ideological, moral and political agendas play out to shape the realities of teacher education (Cochran-Smith, 2004; Craig, 2016; Liston & Zeichner, 1991; Tirri, 1999; Tom, 1984; Valli, 1990). What we miss, though, are more studies on how these aspects eventually direct strategic reasoning and deliberation in mentors' practice (Athanases & Achinstein, 2003; Rodgers, 2006). This chapter attends to this lens by focusing on a re-examination of mentoring reasoning and deliberation through questions that consider moral, political and ideological implications. Through an illustrative mentoring case,[1] we propose new interpretative readings of a mentoring interaction by conducting 'different readings' into the same mentoring conversation. These readings underscore the multifaceted and often controversial character of a particular espoused mentoring approach when deliberated in the 'here and now' complex setting of practice.

Specifically, we discuss the gaps and discrepancies in mentoring conversations between student teachers and mentors in an intercultural setting, where the mentor belongs to one culture and the student teacher to another. The illustrative case is taken from of large data set of narratives and mentoring conversations with participants from different cultural and ethnic backgrounds (Mazor, 2003). Earlier study on mentoring conversations surfaced the centrality of student teachers' professional relationships with their mentor teachers for sustaining their process of learning to teach. It also surfaced the latent tensions and struggles that student teachers from a minority Arab-Druze background experienced while trying to implement progressive methodologies of teaching English in their respective Druze villages.

The significance of these early findings for cross-cultural teacher education and mentoring and mentored learning as a culturally responsive practice in teacher education, prompted us to re-examine the initial data corpus, this time, focusing on the connection between the mentoring conversations and the open-ended interviews that revolved around those conversations. Specifically, we explore how, at the encounter between two cultures (Arab-Druze student teachers and Jewish mentor teachers), mentoring conversations unfold to mediate the mentee's understanding of her situation.

Mentoring Conversations as Contexts for Learning to Teach

In this chapter we further explore the complexities inherent in mentoring conversations as contexts for learning to teach, particularly in situations where the mentor and the student teacher come from different cultural, ethnic and religious backgrounds. Mentoring conversations between student teachers and mentors constitute the core of mentoring practices and their investigation has gained prominence in the study of mentored learning. Studies reveal that conversations generally revolve around curricular and pedagogical concerns, issues related to pupils' evaluation and progress, classroom management issues and innovative methods (Achinstein & Athanases, 2006; Rachamim & Orland-Barak, 2018; Timperley, 2001; Wang, 2001). A recurrent finding in this area points to the learning value of the mentoring conversation for internalizing specific behaviors and strategies for effective teaching, often underrating exploration of assumptions and rationale behind student teachers' actions (Timperley, 2001). A number of early studies have also explored the conditions that sustain learning conversations as opportunities for the development of interpersonal reasoning (Noddings, 1991), for 'pushing' participants to develop new ideas (Pfeiffer, Featherstone, & Smith, 1993), for articulating, analyzing, and framing dilemmas; and for solving pedagogical problems (Clark, 2001; Florio-Ruane, 1991). Previous study in the context of teacher education in Israel (Orland-Barak & Klein, 2005) explored connections between participants' beliefs about mentoring conversations and what is actually realized in practice. The inquiry surfaced fundamental gaps between mentors' expressed beliefs and their realized actions during mentoring conversations: Whereas mentors' attributions conveyed a more collaborative, democratic view of a mentoring conversation, closer to reflective, dialogical approaches, the actual conversations were more prescriptive and controlling, reflecting a more instructional/ apprenticeship orientation to a mentoring conversation.

Referring to the mentoring conversation as a text, we offer 'different readings of the same mentoring text', illustrating how each of these readings uncovers a unique layer of interpretation of the text. Specifically, each of these readings surfaces complexities inherent in the kind of voices and issues in the conversation and in the strategic use of particular intervention modes and roles.

Interpretative Framework: Mentoring as a Discursive Practice

In order to analyze mentoring conversations in an inter-cultural setting of mentored learning to teach, we draw on views of professional learning which emphasize a discursive view of mentored learning that incorporates the acquisition of praxical domains of professional competence and performance, which attend to the ideological, cultural and pedagogical agendas that guide mentors' moves and forms of assistance (Orland-Barak, 2010). These domains go beyond observed mentoring strategies and include interrelated competencies such as appreciation of the uniqueness of a mentoring interaction as grounded in the particular discourses, power relations and dominant educational agendas of the various participants in the interaction; participation modes to identify potential tensions and possible co-operative breakdowns during mentoring interactions, including the dynamic and social/political character of particular mentoring interactions and relationships with teachers, colleagues, school principals and project leaders; and improvisation skills which respond to 'here and now' situations while creating meaningful connections between theory and practice and to the framing and reframing of problems, connecting experience, beliefs and knowledge in action (Orland-Barak, 2010, pp. 9–11).

A discursive view of mentor professional learning, thus, considers how mentors appreciate the way in which complex or ambiguous situations they encounter are framed by participants' personal and cultural views and practices in a given context. It also engages the mentor in an introspective and retrospective process of reflection, recording how personal theories, beliefs and actions play out and might often contradict each other in actual mentoring situations. In the process, the mentor builds repertoires of unique cases as well as judicious replications of experiences across contexts both on the level of 'what does it represent in one's mentoring context' as well as on 'how this case might differ from other similar cases encountered. A discursive approach to mentoring also entails articulating dispositions to act through questions such as: 'What am I learning about my developing concept of mentoring? What teaching /learning conditions typify my particular mentoring context and the teaching situation and how might these alter in new contexts? How might different interactions influence decision making? A discursive view also positions mentors as social agents, who are sensitive to how participants' resources are privileged, appropriated, rejected and/or deployed in mentoring activity (Fairclough, 1989; Linell, 1998). Specifically, it focuses on what and who determines the starting point in a mentoring conversation, what are the mentor's purposes in a conversation, what does the mentor attended to (and what not), what develops as the focus of the conversation, and how are participants' different cultural backgrounds and organizational represented and attended to in the conversation. Conducting different readings into the same mentoring conversation allowed for attending to these questions. They enabled us to surface both the mentor and the mentee's educational, pedagogical and ideological reasoning and actions, as grounded in the social-cultural contexts and backgrounds within which they function.

Mode of Inquiry

Our inquiry explored the way in which mentoring conversations unfold to mediate learning in an inter-cultural setting of mentored learning to teach. With this focus in mind, we conducted new cycles of hermeneutic readings to the initial broad data set. We juxtaposed (1) the transcribed mentoring conversations with (2) the transcribed open interviews conducted with the mentors and the student teachers after each mentoring encounter and with (3) the interviews with each mentor geared to surface their espoused approaches to mentoring and mentored learning. Altogether, we triangulated three types of data sources collected from the larger study. The data was organized into 'sets of events' each of which included the transcribed mentoring conversation and the open interviews that followed with both the mentor and the student teacher. This yielded a pool of twelve 'sets' per case (three per semester over a period of four semesters). The analysis included both content and language analysis according to the following stages: The first stage entailed content analysis of the issues that were raised both in the mentoring conversation and in the open ended interviews to identify commonalities and differences that surfaced within and across sets (Moustakas, 1994). The teaching scenarios that they discussed were similar to recurrent themes in the literature of learning to teach, especially with those related to novices' hardships, concerns and aspirations in learning to teach and being exposed to new methods of teaching that are unfamiliar to them (Kagan, 1992; Rust, 1994; Wideen et al., 1998). Specifically we identified talk about maximizing time and participation, classroom control and issues of discipline, lesson planning, organization of content, techniques for classroom organization, relationships with parents, teachers and the school administration. We then turned to a language analysis of the interviews to identify the expressions, phrases and language moves to substantiate findings from the content analysis. The language analysis revealed that although the content of talk (i.e. the classroom incidents raised by both students and mentors in the interviews) revolved around common foci of concerns, their respective interpretations of how the same incident had unfolded in the lesson were different. For example, in one set of events both mentor and student teacher mentioned incidents around class participation as a focus of concern. Yet, whereas the mentor contended that she had tried to advance the mentee's understanding of the need to maximize participation by constructing the activity gradually so as to cater for a variety of learning styles and levels, the student teacher was more concerned with the pupils' preference to use Arabic rather than English which had impeded, in her view, participation in the foreign language lesson. Our synthesis of the language analysis across the entire data corpus examine revealed that in many cases whereas the mentor had thought that she had advanced the mentee's thinking in a particular issue raised during the mentoring conversation, the mentee felt that the issue had not been addressed as expected.

We found that these differences were not unique to the intercultural setting but could be attributed to familiar discrepancies of perceptions in the literature regarding what constitutes meaningful learning between student teachers and their mentors (Hawkey, 2000; Miller-Marsh, 2002; Zanting et al., 1998). We should also note that neither the analysis of the conversations nor the open-ended interviews explicitly uncovered cultural codes as core issues that concern the mentor or the student teacher. The absence of this theme is particularly interesting for the findings in the cross-cultural cases (i.e. Jewish mentors with Arab-Druze students) of earlier study (Mazor, 2003). However, the language analysis did draw our attention to recurrent expressions of Druze student teachers such as "I *know* our schools" (emphasis in original); "I know the pupils and what they are used to", "They [the pupils] have never done it before", "it is just not like what they are used to", or "I don't know how they will react, it is so different". At the outset, such statements might not carry a cultural load, yet when examined against the particular setting of mentored learning, we wondered whether the student teachers had unique insights into the pupils' experiences because they shared the same cultural background.

Our analysis of the data sets yielded two kinds of typical gaps, both of which highlight interesting differences between participants' attributions to mentoring and mentored learning: (1) Discrepancies between the mentors' and the student teachers' envisioned roles (as evidenced in the interviews prior to the mentoring conversation) and their realization in action (as evidenced in the mentoring conversation and in the interviews following the mentoring conversation); (2) Gaps between what the mentor saw as the right pedagogy and teaching and the student teacher's views about successful teaching. In the selected case, we take the reader through our stages of interpretation of the above identified gaps as they play out in *one set of events*.

The Case

This illustrative case of the selected mentoring conversation took place towards the end of the first year of the research (end of the second year of practice teaching). The excerpt was selected with several considerations in mind: From the perspective of the participants, the mentor and mentee had already been working together for almost a year and had established mutual trust and a stable working relationship. From a research perspective, the selected 'set of events' portrays the typicality of our findings across data sets (Shulman, 1992).

Prior to engaging in the various 'deconstructions' of the text, let us familiarize with the background of the student teacher, of her school and of the mentor. The selected mentoring conversation between the mentor and Einat, the student teacher/mentee was conducted around a teaching incident. Following the background for the conversation, the context and the participants involved, we will engage in a first 'surface' reading of selected excerpts from the illustrative case (the mentoring conversation and the open interviews). The first reading is followed by additional interpretative 'discursive readings' grounded in the above discussed theoretical-analytical framework. These discursive readings surface the cultural grounding of emergent gaps identified between the mentor and the mentee's understanding of mentoring and of mentored learning.

Different Systems – Different Orientations

The Druze-Arab background of the student teacher and the Israeli-Druze school system necessitate a short introduction into some of the differences between the two cultures of teaching and learning. The Druze people constitute a separate sector within the Arab population, distinguishing themselves both religiously and nationally (Ben Dor, 1973, 1976; Dana, 1998). Israeli policy towards the Druze respects their aspired need for a separate religious as well as political status (Al-Haj, 1988). The Israeli Ministry of Education was the first to follow the government's decision to grant the Druze a separate status and since 1976, Druze school system has been independent in terms of pedagogical content, tools and materials (Fallach, 1982). The Druze school system operates separately from the Jewish and Arab school systems and reflects the national, religious and cultural beliefs of the Druze population they serve. The various subgroups and educational systems in Israel (religious or secular Jewish and Arab schools; Christian, Druze or mixed Arab schools) differ in their programs and school cultures (Harrison, 1995). The independence of the Druze educational system is reflected in their textbooks and in the syllabuses and curricular content of specific subject matter, which are written especially for this sector. The differences are not only in the prime language of teaching (Hebrew or Arabic) but also in their stated goals, requirements and expectations from teachers and students. Amongst many others, Druze schools differ from Jewish schools in the ideologies they advance related to the respective cultures that define them: Jewish schools stress the development of students' self-potential whereas Druze schools emphasize Druze humanitarian values such as mutual help and reciprocity and valuing formal knowledge. Methods of teaching and perceptions of teachers' roles differ too. Many secular Jewish schools promote inductive and discovery modes of teaching, forwarding alternative methodologies through group work and individual tutoring. Teachers are also perceived to be less controlling than in Druze schools, where most of the teaching is still teacher led, deductive and the teacher's authority is highly valued (Harrison, 1995; Nasseraldin, 2018).

The Student-Teacher

Einat is a Druze student teacher in her last year of studies towards a B.Ed. and an English language teaching certificate. She is in her twenties and has had a successful record as a student. Although coming from an observant Druze family, Einat was allowed to pursue high education because her father believed it to be an important value even for the young women in the family. Nevertheless,

Einat was permitted to study only at the college (not at the university) since the population at the college is mostly female.

For primary and high school education, Einat attended Druze schools in her village. As she contends, the studies in the college provided her not only with an opportunity to acquire higher education but also, allowed her to experience studying in an educational system quite different from the one she was used to, and to work with people from backgrounds different than hers. In various conversations with Einat, she expressed her criticism of the traditional teaching methodologies used in the Druze school, and her desire to learn and practice innovative teaching methodologies that could help bring about change in the Druze educational system (Mazor, 2003).

The Mentor and the Teacher Education Institution

The mentor referred to in this chapter is an experienced mentor in the English department of a teachers' college. An EFL teacher herself, she is involved in both in-service and pre-service mentoring programs in Jewish and non-Jewish schools. Specifically, her area of interest is multicultural education which she teaches at the college and in other professional forums. Her students at the college describe her as open, attentive and very supportive in her interpersonal interactions and highly sensitive to issues of minorities, equality and discrimination. The Druze student that she mentored, Einat, was part of a group of students of mixed cultural background, all in their last year of practice teaching in the English teacher education program at the college.

The undergraduate mentoring program at the college spans over a period of three years (out of four years of study) twice a week, throughout the entire academic year. Each year students are assigned to different schools in diverse educational settings, to encourage maximum exposure to a variety of teaching approaches. Despite the stated commitment to diversification of teaching placements, the approach to mentoring student teachers in these settings follows a uniform approach to the professional learning of prospective teachers, with fixed criteria of observation and assessment, as established by the college mentors themselves.

The Mentoring Conversation

Consider the following excerpt from a student teacher's account of an English lesson taught in a sixth grade in a primary school in a Druze village in Israel

(Mazor, 2003). The account constituted the starting point for the mentoring conversation between the mentor and the student teacher (the mentee).

1. Mentee: I was going to teach them this story about a blind girl, Shirley. So, in preparation for the reading I thought it was important not only for them to know the key vocabulary but also to have the context, the atmosphere of it ... so, I planned to ask them to stand up, close their eyes and perform some activities with their eyes closed. This would have also allowed them to use English to express their experience, feelings and thoughts. But I did not expect the chaos it created in class. They were following my instructions but it all turned into a joke – they were laughing and joking about doing these things with their eyes closed and I did not know what to do about it, I was afraid I was going to lose control of the class so I stopped the activity. I did not expect such a reaction. Kids here [the Druze school] are usually more obedient and respectful of the teacher ...
2. Mentor: I understand that you felt you were going to lose control ...
3. Mentee: Yes, there was a lot of noise in the class, they were all laughing and joking.
4. Mentor: So you stopped the activity ...
5. Mentee: Yes, that's not what I wanted but I was not prepared to lose control with all that laughing and joking anymore.
6. Mentor: You wanted ....
7. Mentee: I wanted them to feel and experience what it is like to be blind.
8. Mentor: What would indicate for you that the pupils actually experienced what it means to be blind?
9. Mentee: I wanted them to talk about it, how they feel, what it was like for them.
10. Mentor: And the laughter and joking signaled ...?
11. Mentee: That they were having fun and they did not pay attention to the point I was trying to make ...
12. Mentor: A lot of noise means to you that the class is not paying attention to the point?
13. Mentee: Of course, how can they learn if there is noise in the class ...
14. Mentor: So the noise bothered you ...
15. Mentee: I got angry!! They were showing lack of respect ... laughing ...
16. Mentor: Lack of respect? Towards what?
17. Mentee: Towards me ...
18. Mentor: I understand from what you say that you feel they were showing disrespect towards you and that bothers you.

19. Mentee: Yes, they are usually very respectful towards me. Besides, Druze children, especially in this class, are well behaved.
20. Mentor: I see ... so their behavior caught you by surprise. But let us think of other explanations for the children behaving this way at this point of the lesson ...
21. Mentee: I don't really know ...
22. Mentor: How about looking for sources outside your own experience ... are there any people you would want to ask for advice?
23. Mentee: Maybe hear from you ...
24. Mentor: We could talk about that if that is what you think would help you most at this point ... for example, one possible way of looking at it is interpreting the children's misbehavior as reflective of their age level and of the specific situation they were put into ... any thoughts on this?
25. Mentee: Why? Can't they relate to the limitations that blind people experience at this age? After all, they are already in the sixth grade. Besides, the story is in the textbook written for their age level!
26. Mentor: True, but I was thinking more in terms of their feeling of embarrassment and the unexpected task of being put in a situation where they have to walk around the class with their eyes closed. Did you listen to what they were saying when laughing and talking?
27. Mentee: I think they were joking. They were using the opportunity to talk to each other about other things besides English. I felt they thought I was giving them a break.
28. Mentor: I suggest you reconsider what I said before about kids feeling embarrassed ... giving us the wrong impression that their behavior is a sign of disrespect towards us.
29. Mentee: I don't really know. I didn't hear what they were saying but they usually do not behave like this!
30. Mentor: Look, I have had many similar experiences in my own classes which have taught me that my understanding of what I think is happening is not always the full picture. I still think there is something to be said about the children's sense of surprise with being put in a situation of experiencing blindness-maybe that's what they were talking about. So my suggestion is that in the future you pay attention not only to what they do but also to what they say to each other and talk about during the interaction. It might be the case that what caused the noise had to do with a certain aspect of your classroom management during the activity and we can talk about that, but it could also be the case that the noise had little to do with you and more with their emotional response towards the situation.

Same Conversation – Different Interpretations

A Strategic 'Surface' Reading

Let us now return to our case to examine what the mentor and the student teacher claimed about the learning value of the above mentoring conversation. The mentor commented the following:

> I think she understood that noise is not necessarily a discipline problem but can derive from other sources. I also tried to make her see that noise does not necessarily mean lack of respect towards her, that it might be possible that there are other reasons for the children laughing. I suggested that it might be due to the fact that the experience of acting like blind people might have caused embarrassment or that it might be a matter of age, but Einat was really worried about losing control of the class.

With regard to the way in which she thought she had assisted the student teacher, she asserted:

> I asked Einat to tell her story first and then used that as a starting point for thinking about her fear to lose control of the class so that she would arrive at her own personal understanding of the situation. Although I said several times that I understand how she feels, I tried to avoid giving her recipes because I think that telling her what to do will not eventually help her in the long run. She needs to find the answers by herself.

We asked the mentor to elaborate on how she helped the student find her own answers and she replied:

> I reassured her that I understood how she felt and also asked questions to try and push her to think in other directions that would lead her to other explanations. But she could not think of any other possibilities for the noise that was going on in class so I felt at that point that I had to offer some suggestions. She is so preoccupied with discipline at this stage of her learning that she cannot see beyond that. I encounter that all the time with new teachers and it is understandable. Like most new teachers, Einat is always talking about noise, pupils' paying attention or not ... it feels like control is really her main issue right now. But I think that in the end I made her realize that the noise could have been more a question of embarrassment of the pupils.

Adopting notions from mentoring, we could rephrase the mentor's position as follows: By using supportive strategies such as mirroring (#2), paraphrasing (#18), and open ended comments and questions (#4, #10) the mentor claims that she manages to lead the student teacher to consider other possible interpretations of the situation. Informed by her pedagogical expertise, the mentor knows that, as characteristic of a novice (Rust, 1994; Feiman-Nemser, 2001). Einat is reacting to her hardships primarily as a case of discipline problems and class control. Thus, the mentor's interpretation of the situation is that Einat's focus on the issue of classroom control, prevents her from examining other possible reasons for the pupils' misbehavior, such as their age level and emotional response to the situation (pretending they are blind). This was apparent in her efforts to suggest other explanations: 'one possible way of looking at it is interpreting the children's misbehavior as reflective of their age level and of the specific situation they were put into' (#24).

The student teacher's experience of learning revealed, however, a somewhat different perspective of what she claims to have gained from the mentor's assistance during conversation:

> I am not sure. I felt it was a discipline problem but Lora (the mentor) kept pushing me to think of other possibilities. She is very experienced and I feel there is a lot to learn from her. I guess she can be right in what she said about the pupil's embarrassment and that's why they laughed. I know the pupils in this school. They are used to frontal teaching and I need to give them time to get used to other ways of teaching, but the noise was a problem.

In her comments on how the mentor had assisted her, she contended:

> She gave me ideas and she suggested looking at my pupils' reaction in another way because of their age and embarrassment with the situation. I had not thought about that before. But I still don't know how I should behave if I get this kind of noise again in my class. I am still worried about how to handle the discipline and that they will not respect me as their teacher and what will the principal say?

In her narrative, Einat makes it a point to stress her still very strong sense of distress and anxiety about the issue of discipline and respect, which were her main concerns at the beginning of the conversation and which she feels had not been fully addressed.

Thus, while the mentor claims to have advanced the student teacher towards new understandings of the event, the student's response conveys a more ambiguous picture: Despite the options and reasons provided by the mentor to assist her in reinterpreting her problem with classroom control, the mentee still doesn't know how she should behave should she get this kind of noise again in her class. She is still worried about how to handle classroom management and that they will not respect her as their teacher. Although Einat's experience and sense of distress has been acknowledged at the beginning of the conversation through questions which encouraged her to articulate her own feelings, her final feeling is that she doesn't know how she should behave should she be confronted with the same situation again.

The emergent discrepancies between both accounts of learning from the experience intrigued us. Whereas the mentor wants to advance Einat's understanding of the pupils' possible state of discomfort and embarrassment from the activity, Einat is still, first and foremost, deeply concerned with issues of lack of respect and authority and with her frustration and distress in being unable to implement her expected ideals (to become an agent of change in her traditional village) through the integration of more communicative activities in the classroom. How can we interpret these emergent discrepancies in both accounts? Let us turn to our interpretative framework for conducting 'different readings into the same text'.

First Discursive Reading: Experiences, Beliefs and Knowledge Connected through Improvisation

We begin by focusing on how mentors improvise through questions and responses that connect and attend to the student teacher's remarks. On the surface, communication is sustained by interventions such as echoing and picking up on feeling cues (Heron, 1990) which are geared to access Einat's thoughts and feelings of distress as she engages in sense making of her teaching. At times, even, and as part of the mirroring strategies, at times the mentor paraphrases Einat's feelings and experiences. We question, however, what the mentor is really listening to and for what purpose. Could the cathartic intervention strategies assumed by the mentor (allowing Einat to discharge her professional frustration) have been used as a strategic bridge to arrive at what the mentor-as-expert had initially identified to be the core professional issues at stake? Thus, 'what is listened for' questions the mentor's 'authentic listening' to the student's sense of distress. Such behavior seems particularly discrepant from the mentor's stated ideas during the initial interview about connecting to the mentee and about what she regards as successful communication in mentoring: 'It is always important to be sensitive to the student's feelings and about what she says she is trying to say that she really needs from me ... I should help the student teacher find her own answers ... the student is always the starting point ... giving tips and answers is not my style ...'.

Such incompatibility between the stated and the realized, underscores tensions between encouraging the student teacher to voice her feelings and understandings of the situation and 'threading in' a prioritized text of the mentor-as expert. Thus, a critical reading of the conversation challenges us to re-examine the use of certain interventions that characterize personalistic approaches to mentoring.

Second Discursive Reading: Whose Texts Are Acknowledged in Participation?

Let us now examine the question of whose text is being represented and acknowledged while participating in the conversation. Whereas we might interpret the mentor's questions as being meant to address Einat's sense of distress in her perception of the situation as a classroom management problem, we have learned from the student teacher's interpretation of the mentor's intervention that her need was not fully acknowledged. Rather, it seems that the mentor-as-expert provides a more elaborate interpretation of the situation which goes *beyond* the student teacher's expressed hardships. This interpretation prioritizes what the mentor understands to be the core issues at stake, not necessarily voiced by the student teacher. In this sense, critical reading calls for examining possible tensions that might emerge between espousing an approach that claims to attend to the student teacher's concerns and the actual development of the conversation, which develops more around the mentor's own ideas about the situation discussed.

Attending to the question 'What is the focus of the conversation?' we learn that the mentor chooses to emphasize the connection between pupils' emotional responses (focusing on psychological explanations) and the suitability of the activity for their age level as the leading focus. This choice is guided by the mentor's text-as-expert who identifies problems of classroom management as a result of Einat's lack of awareness of the incompatibility between her choice of activity and her pupils' developmental stage. Thus, the mentor does not confine to Einat's expressed perception of the situation 'all the way' but shifts the direction of the conversation by voicing her own avenues of interpretation: 'Let us think of other explanations for the children behaving this way at this point of the lesson' (#16), alluding to her expertise as teacher and mentor: 'Look, I have had many similar experiences in my own classes which have taught me that my understanding of what I think is happening is not always the full picture. I still think there is something to be said about the children's sense of surprise with being put in a situation of experiencing blindness-maybe that's what they were talking about ... it could also be the case that the noise had little to do with you and more with their emotional response towards the situation' (#30).

A critical reading of 'whose text is it 'and 'what is the focus of the text' raises, then, questions of what is foregrounded and what kind of knowledge is being validated throughout the mentoring interaction. The mentor contends that by employing a combination of strategies she is gradually scaffolding the student teacher's understanding of the issue of pupil behavior. Whereas the mentor seems to be focusing on the 'why' behind the action, the student teacher-as-novice is primarily concerned with the 'what to do' of her actions. Metaphorically, the mentor is being 'blind' to what the student teacher claims to be her major problem i.e. dealing with classroom control and gaining the respect of her pupils. These two issues of control and respect, which lie at the core of her discourse, can be traced both to her novice state as well as to her Druze cultural background and educational upbringing. With this dual focus in mind we wonder, then, whether the mentor has brought to her awareness the implications of her mode of intervention which prioritizes her own text-as-expert over the student teacher's voiced text of distress. The question of 'whose text is it' intertwines, then, with the cultural codes that are attended (or not) throughout the conversation. These are elaborated in the following reading.

Third Discursive Reading: Appreciating Cultural Codes

Appreciating the cultural and interests that are represented in the mentoring relationship would entail asking how and whether the mentoring interaction leads both, the mentor and student teacher to examine their respective texts as reflective (or not) of the 'authoritative discourses' to which they might feel accountable in their work. In Bakhtin's words (1981), this would imply attending to how authoritative discourses (i.e. the acknowledged discourses or external agendas dictated by project leaders and/or inspectors to which mentors see themselves accountable) operate to promote a particular direction or agenda during the conversation. Considering the strong cross-cultural features of the interaction, what are the implications of attending to such considerations for the form and character of the mentoring interaction?

To address this question, let us return to the cultural and educational ideologies that can be appreciated in the mentor-student teacher interaction. For example, one might wonder why the mentor did not grant the student teacher an opportunity for making connections between her cultural codes and values and her actual behavior in practice. Specifically, when Einat maintained that there was a lot of noise and laughter in the class and that pupils could not learn with such noise (#11), the mentor could challenge Einat's ingrained assumptions about what constitutes an effective learning environment, with a focus on how the mentee's views about classroom management and teachers' roles reflect the way in which she herself was educated. Furthermore, when suggesting that there might be other reasons for the pupils' disruptive behavior, the mentor could encourage reflection on how the frontal, deductive teaching and learning traditions of the Druze school culture might bear an influence on the pupils' resistance to the more progressive methodologies advanced in Einat's class. In doing so, space could be opened for Einat to scrutinize her teaching as entrenched between her concern to lose control as typical of novices, the traditional background of her school culture, her own traditional background as a Druze pupil, and her expressed aspirations to promote change in her village through the dissemination of innovative teaching methodologies that she had been exposed to in the college. Put differently, focusing on questions that lead the students to explore their own ingrained beliefs can constitute an important opportunity for uncovering their taken for granted patterns of teacher behavior.

Examining cultural and educational codes in our reading of 'what the text is about' challenges us to explore, for example, whether the mentor, of a mainstream background, is really aware of the uniqueness of the Druze educational school system. As mentioned earlier, such a system follows an ideology of advancing Druze tradition and formal knowledge transmitted through frontal, deductive teaching and learning modes, and through a view of the role of the teacher as in full control of the classroom. In this vein, we may ask whether the mentor has appreciated the tensions that might emerge from inherent gaps between dominant traditional orientations of the Druze educational school system and, likewise, her own dominant discovery, inductive, learner centered methods as advocated by mainstream teacher education colleges. Identifying and appreciating gaps between these two 'dominant narratives', would allow for further framing of local considerations of 'what to say' and 'how to intervene' within the socio-cultural agendas and orientations that constitute a given mentoring context. For example, one might conjecture that, being less familiar with inductive, experiential modes of learning, Druze pupils might experience difficulties in participating in activities that call for learning outcomes generated from what they might perceive as 'informal' and less structured experiences (moving around the class with their eyes closed and reporting on the experience to the class). Appreciating such difficulties, both at the levels of pupil response [their source of laughter] and student teacher's response [anger at their laughter], could allow the mentor to foreground impediments, limitations and strategies to overcome them when a desired innovative pedagogy is being implemented in a particular socio-cultural context.

When the mentor scrutinized her own practice, she could explore how her assumptions about effective teaching and learning played out in the direction that she chose to undertake with the student teacher: By focusing on connections between noise, pupils' attention and learning to pedagogical issues solely, she was less responsive to possible exploration of the cultural and social codes that might influence the student teacher's educational reasoning and actions. Alternately, the mentor could defy her own enacted orientation to personalistic approaches to mentoring. She could, for example, examine how the roles she undertook throughout the conversation were actually directed by the college guidelines for student observation and evaluation (characterized, as mentioned in earlier section, by a uniform approach to mentoring student teachers, structured by rigid predetermined criteria of observation and assessment).

The above issues illuminate the controversial interplay between adopting facilitative roles in mentoring and more directive roles meant to guide, protect and often rescue the novice teacher in her first years of professional socialization (Hall et al., 2008; Mazor, 2003). They also call for appreciating and foregrounding similarities and differences between the cultural codes and values of the mentee, of the school context, and of the mentor, to inform the latter on the strategic and pedagogical course of action undertaken in her supportive role to promote the mentee's professional growth.

The additional deep readings, framed by questions of text prioritization, forms of access and communication and values, thus, somehow problematize premature conjectures uncovered in initial surface readings as to the personal growth approach espoused by the mentor. These new readings encourage us to move beyond the individual voices of the participants to attend to the collective discourses that shape their reasoning and actions.

Beyond the Observed in Mentoring Conversations

A consideration of the multiple agendas that might direct the orientation of a particular mentoring interaction constitutes what we regard as the broadest reading of a mentoring text. Such a reading moves us beyond a focus on the kind of strategies employed in a mentoring interaction to questions that confront mentors and mentees with how their ingrained assumptions, values and cultural backgrounds might affect their professional thinking and deliberation. Such a reading challenges both mentor and mentee to jointly question how their practices reflect, for example, the interests of a particular school system or institutional orientation. Examining these aspects can allow for surfacing complexities that might emerge between mentors' strategic reasoning, actions and the agendas that direct a particular orientation to mentoring. In doing so, mentors are invited to scrutinize familiar orientations to mentoring in terms of how they can either marginalize or empower certain voices or views during interaction. By exposing different readings of the same mentoring conversation, we hope to have raised awareness of how such readings can take us 'beyond the observed' in mentoring conversations.

Preparing Culturally Sensitive Mentors

We invite teacher educators, curriculum developers and policy makers to consider ways to educate culturally sensitive mentors who question their assumed roles. To this end, we call for preparing mentors to 'wear multiple reading lenses' to access a mentoring text, as a way of scaffolding a kind of learning that endorses the complexities and intricacies of values, ideologies and local considerations. Specifically, we suggest preparing mentors for the culturally sensitive character of their work, appreciating how their choices and pedagogical reasoning may reflect their idiosyncratic ideologies and cultural codes. This calls for surfacing how cultural codes and values might direct particular forms of strategic and pedagogical reasoning in a particular mentoring interaction.

Extending the Conversation to the Critical Context of Mentoring Practices

Believing that social agency is inherent in any kind of educational endeavor, this chapter suggests attending to the culturally-sensitive character of mentors' work, whereby the mentors perceive themselves as socio-culturally conscious professionals. This entails recognizing that perception is influenced by one's location in the social order, one who views cultural and political differences as resources for learning rather than problems to be overcome; and who realizes that critical dialogue constitutes a professional means towards a culturally critical responsive mentoring agenda (Orland-Barak, Kheir-Farraj, & Becher, 2013).

Note

1   The case was selected from a pool of mentoring cases collected as data for previous study. The data for the case included observations of mentoring conversations, written accounts of critical incidents and semi-structured interviews with mentors and novice teachers of the Druze sector.

References

Achinstein, B., & Athanases, S. Z. (Eds.). (2006). *Mentors in the making: Developing new leaders for new teachers*. New York, NY: Teachers College Press.
Al-Haj, M. (1988). The socio-political structure of Arabs in Israel: External vs. internal orientation. In J. E. Hofman (Ed.), *Arab-Jewish relations in Israel: A quest in human understanding* (pp. 249–270). Bristol, IN: Wyndham Hall Press.
Athanases, S. Z., & Achinstein, B. (2003). Focusing new teachers on individual and low performing students: The centrality of formative assessment in the mentor's repertoire of practice. *Teachers College Record, 105*(8), 1486–1520.
Bakhtin, M. (1981). *The dialogic imagination: Four essays by M. M. Bakhtin* (M. Holquist, Ed., C. Emerson & M. Holquist, Trans.). Austin, TX: University of Texas Press.
Becher, A., & Orland-Barak, L. (2017). Context matters: Contextual factors informing mentoring in art initial teacher education. *Journal of Teacher Education, 69*(5), 477–492.
Ben Dor, G. (1973). The military in the politics of integration and innovation: The case of the Druze minority in Israel. *Asian and African Studies, 9*(3), 339–369.
Ben Dor, G. (1976). Intellectuals in Israeli Druze society. *Middle Eastern Studies, 12*(2).
Berger, P. L., & Luckmann, T. (1966). *The social construction of reality*. London: Penguin Books.
Cochran-Smith, M. (2004). The problem of teacher education. *Journal of Teacher Education, 55*(4), 295–299.
Clark, C. M. (2001). Good conversation. In C. M. Clark (Ed.), *Talking shop: Authentic conversation and teacher learning* (pp. 172–182). New York, NY: Teachers College Press.
Craig, C. (2016). The structure of teacher education. In J. Loughran & M. L. Hamilton (Eds.), *International handbook of teacher education* (pp. 69–135). Dordrecht: Springer.

Dana, N. (1998). *The Druze*. Tel Aviv: Bar Ilan University. [in Hebrew]

Fairclough, N. (1989). *Language and power*. New York, NY: Longman.

Fallach, S. (1982). *Druze education in Israel*. Jerusalem: Prime Minister's Office. [in Hebrew]

Feiman-Nemser, S. (2001). From preparation to practice: Designing a continuum to strengthen and sustain teaching. *Teachers College Record, 103*(6), 1013–1055.

Florio-Ruane, S. (1991). Conversation and narrative in collaborative research: An ethnography of the Written Literacy Forum. In C. Witherell & N. Noddings (Eds.), *Stories lives tell: Narrative and dialogue in education* (pp. 234–256). New York, NY: Teachers College Press.

Harrison, G. (1995). *Unity and pluralism in school cultures and curricula in the Israeli educational system*. Jerusalem: The Institute for Research on Educational Systems. [in Hebrew]

Hawkey, K. (2000). Mentor pedagogy and student teacher professional development. *Teaching and Teacher Education, 14*(6), 657–670.

Heron, J. (1990). *Helping the Client*. London: Sage Publications.

Kagan, D. M. (1992). Professional growth among pre service and beginning teachers. *Review of Educational Research, 62*(2), 129–169.

Linell, P. (1998). *Approaching dialogue: Talk, interaction and contexts in dialogical perspectives*. Amsterdam: John Benjamins.

Liston, D. P., & Zeichner, K. M. (1991). *Teacher education and the social conditions of schooling*. New York, NY: Routledge.

Mazor, E. (2003). *Druze student teachers in Jewish schools: Strangers in practice teaching placements-learning to teach English* (Unpublished doctoral dissertation). The Hebrew University, Jerusalem, Israel. [in Hebrew]

Miller-Marsh, M. (2002). The influence of discourses on the precarious nature of mentoring. *Reflective Practice, 3*, 103–115.

Moustakas, C. (1994). *Phenomenological research methods*. Thousand Oaks, CA: Sage Publications.

Nasseraldin, H. (2018, September). *Minority and majority teachers' learning at the workplace: The case of Arab novices in Israel*. Paper presented at the BERA Annual Conference, Newcastle, UK.

Noddings, N. (1991). Stories in dialogue: Caring and interpersonal reasoning. In C. Witherell & N. Noddings (Eds.), *Stories lives tell: Narrative and dialogue in education* (pp. 157–170). New York, NY: Teachers College Press.

Orland-Barak, L. (2010). Introduction: Learning to mentor-as-praxis foundations for a curriculum in teacher education. In *Learning to mentor-as-praxis* (pp. 1–13). New York, NY: Springer.

Orland-Barak, L., Kheir-Farraj, R., & Becher, A. (2013). Mentoring in contexts of cultural and political friction: Moral dilemmas of mentors and their management in practice. *Mentoring & Tutoring: Partnership in Learning, 21*(1), 76–95.

Orland-Barak, L., & Klein, S. (2005). The expressed and the realized: Mentors' representations of a mentoring conversation and its realization in practice. *Teaching and Teacher Education, 21*(4), 379–402.

Pfeiffer, L. Featherstone, H., & Smith, S. P. (1993). *"Do you really mean all when you say all?" A close look at the ecology of pushing in talk about mathematics teaching.* National Centre for Research on Teacher Learning: Michigan State University.

Rachamim, M., & Orland-Barak, L. (2018). When style meets pattern in mentoring talk: Implications for student teacher community learning environments in practice teaching. *Cambridge Journal of Education, 48*(2)1–19.

Rodgers, C. (2006). "The turning of one's soul" – Learning to teach for social justice: The Putney Graduate School of Teacher Education (1950–1964). *Teachers College Record, 108*(7), 1266–1295.

Rust, F. O. (1994). The first year of teaching: It's not what I expected. *Teaching and Teacher Education, 10*(2), 205–217.

Shulman, L. (1992). Toward a pedagogy of cases. In J. Shulman (Ed.), *Case methods in teacher education* (pp. 1–29). New York, NY: Teachers College Press.

Sleeter, C. E. (Ed.). (2011). *Professional development for culturally responsive and relationship-based pedagogy.* New York, NY: Peter Lang.

Tirri, K. (1999). Teachers' perceptions of moral dilemmas at school. *Journal of Moral Education, 28*(1), 31–47.

Timperley, H. (2001). Mentoring conversations designed to promote student teacher learning. *Asia-Pacific Journal of Teacher Education, 29*(2), 111–123.

Tom, A. R. (1984). *Teaching as a moral craft.* New York, NY: Longman.

Valli, L. (1990). Moral approaches to reflective practice. In R. T. Clift & M. G. Pugach (Eds.), *Encouraging reflective practice in education: An analysis of issues and programs* (pp. 39–56). New York, NY: Teachers College Press.

Villegas, A. M., & Lucas, T. (2002). *Educating culturally responsive teachers: A coherent approach.* Albany, NY: State University of New York Press.

Wang, J. (2001). Contexts of mentoring and opportunities for learning to teach: A comparative study of mentoring practice. *Teaching and Teacher Education, 17*, 51–73.

Wideen, M., Mayer-Smith, J., & Moon, B. (1998). A critical analysis of the research on learning to teach: Making the case for an ecological perspective on inquiry. *Review of Educational Research, 68*(2), 130–178.

Zanting, A., Verloop, J. D., Vermunt, J. D., & Van Driel, J. H. (1998). Explicating practical knowledge: An extension of mentor teachers' roles. *European Journal of Teacher Education, 21*(1), 11–28.

PART 3

Innovative Teaching Procedures

CHAPTER 13

Responsive Teachers in Inclusive Practices

Hafdís Guðjónsdóttir, Edda Óskarsdóttir and Jóhanna Karlsdóttir

Abstract

This research is a narrative inquiry, conducted in collaboration between three researchers and six school teachers who were purposefully chosen to participate. Data was collected through reiterated cycles of note taking, photographing, videotaping, reflective discussions, and four focus group discussions. The purpose of the study was to collect examples of innovative teaching in order to promote the construction of inclusive pedagogy and education for all in inclusive environments. The aim was to learn how teachers organize their subject teaching in diverse and inclusive classrooms. The findings indicate that teachers' beliefs and openness towards diverse pupils are important for supporting learning for all pupils. Further, the findings give an insight into an inclusive pedagogy that teachers have created.

Keywords

inclusive pedagogy – responsive teachers – inclusive practice

Introduction

Inclusive education builds on a vision and hope for a better school for all and the dimensions are human rights, justice, and respect for differences, democracy and active participation of all learners in the school system (European Agency, 2015). Ideas of inclusion assume that every pupil has equitable access to education and that schools organize learning spaces that accommodate everyone. For teachers, it is a continuous search for pedagogy and approaches to meet diversity in inclusive schools. The teachers are the key to developing inclusive practices and pedagogies in dealing with heterogeneous classes, because they are the ones who decide and develop the learning environment where pupils are meant to learn and work within the structures of the school system (Fullan & Hargreaves, 2016).

Inclusive education is an on-going act directed towards quality education for all. Issues around the terminology are challenging, but the main objective is to respect pupil differences and to eliminate all forms of discrimination (UNESCO, 2008, 2017). As such, inclusive education is a movement against exclusion of any kind and a reaction to political segregation and social inequality (Petrou, Angelides, & Leigh, 2009). The goal of inclusion is to work against inequality and nurture people's sense of belonging in school and society. Inclusive schools aim to find ways to educate all their pupils successfully, work against discrimination, and ultimately lead to an inclusive, just society where everyone is a valid participant (Booth, 2010; Slee, 2011; UNESCO, 1994, 2001, 2017). Inclusion is aimed at accommodating to diverse groups of pupils in order to work against their segregation (Loreman, 2017). Understanding of the term 'diversity' is expanded beyond disability or ethnic difference to focus on the value of differences in gender, socio-economic status, cultural group, abilities, learning styles and interests (Ainscow, Booth, & Dyson, 2004; Loreman, 2017). Embedded in this understanding of inclusion, there is a shift from emphasizing the source of learning difficulties or difficulties in school as coming from within the pupil or stemming from his/her social circumstances, to viewing the influence of the system of education or the environment as problematic (UNESCO, 2009, 2017). According to this perspective, schools must be active in identifying hindrances to participation and use available resources to remove them (Loreman, 2017; UNESCO, 2001).

Following the educational legislation in 2008, a new national curriculum for early childhood, compulsory and upper secondary education came into effect in Iceland in 2011. This legislation and curriculum aims to embed inclusive education across the system (European Agency, 2017). The curriculum guide presents a move from detailed objectives towards a focus on learning outcomes and basic educational ideas. The educational policy evident in the national curriculum is based on six fundamental pillars of literacy in the widest sense, education for sustainability, democracy and citizenship, education for equality, creativity and health (Ministry of Education Science and Culture, 2011).

This emphasis in legislation and curriculum means that teachers in Iceland are continuously searching for pedagogy and approaches to meet both the demands of the curriculum and increased pupil diversity in inclusive schools. Teachers are the key to developing inclusive practices and pedagogies in dealing with heterogeneous classes, because they are the ones who, based on their beliefs and knowledge, decide and develop the learning environment where pupils are meant to learn and work within the structures of the school system (Ainscow, 2008; European Agency, 2003).

The purpose of the study was to collect examples of innovative teaching in order to promote the construction of inclusive pedagogy and education for all in inclusive environments. The aim was to learn how teachers organize their subject teaching in diverse and inclusive classrooms.

The question that led the research was: How are teachers responding to diverse pupils in their subject teaching?

Inclusive Education, Practice and Pedagogy K

Because of the defined right and the encompassing mandate laid out by UN Conventions, such as the Convention of the Rights of the Child and Convention on the Rights of Persons with Disabilities, all schools and education systems worldwide face the challenge to develop an inclusive culture, inclusive structures, and inclusive practices (Ainscow, 2008). The fundamental theoretical foundation in the Icelandic education policies involves inclusion, accessibility and the participation of all pupils in the school environment. Diversity and different needs, pupils' abilities and other characteristics are respected and every kind of discrimination and exclusion in schools should be eliminated (Ministry of Education, Science and Culture, 2011). This has called for a creation of inclusive practices and inclusive pedagogy in schools.

Florian and Black-Hawkins (2011) have distinguished among inclusive education, inclusive practice and inclusive pedagogy to explain the term 'inclusive' which is a broad term with many meanings. As discussed in the section above, inclusive education stands for the process of increasing participation and decreasing exclusion in the policy context. Inclusive practice stands for how administrators, teachers and staff organize and lead schooling to give the concept of inclusion meaning in their practices. Inclusive pedagogy, then, focuses on how teachers understand the concept of inclusion and apply that understanding in the way they teach and organize learning in inclusive schools.

Inspiring teaching practices promote inclusion, honor diversity, cultures and ethnic experiences, and build the learning environment on the different contributions and identities of each pupil. Teachers in these practices endeavor to understand the experiences and perspectives their pupils bring to the educational settings. They employ pedagogy that responds to the diversity in the group through the curriculum design, learning activities, classroom climate, instructional materials, teaching techniques and assessment procedures (Gay & Kirkland, 2003; Loreman, 2017).

Pedagogy is composed of the act of teaching and the ideas, values and beliefs informing, sustaining and justifying that act (Alexander, 2013). The term pedagogy appears in the educational literature to explain the disparate and complex issues of the teaching profession. Three consistent uses of the term 'pedagogy' can be found in the literature; (a) to cover teaching methods, instructional programs and curricula; (b) as an all-embracing term for education in poststructuralist thought; and (c) to express and address moral education and discourse about teaching and learning (Bruner, 1996; Freire, 2005; Van Manen, 1991, 1999).

A fundamental premise in the inclusive pedagogy approach is based on rejecting ability labelling as a deterministic notion of fixed ability that has historically underpinned the structure of education (Florian & Spratt, 2013). Thus, inclusive pedagogy is particularly aimed at contesting practices that represent provision for most with additional or different experiences for some (ibid.), because the very act of focusing on difference intensifies the isolation and marginalization of children and adds to the social construction of disability (Grenier, 2010).

Ideas of inclusion assume that every pupil has equitable access to education and that schools organize learning spaces that accommodate everyone in the spirit of universal design. The practice of teaching diverse groups of pupils is then grounded in pedagogy that includes more than a skill in using prescribed instructional practices. Rather, this practice integrates professional knowledge about teaching, learning and child development, and involves an ethical and social commitment to children (Guðjónsdóttir, 2000).

Pedagogical qualities of the responsive professional teacher are witnessed in teachers who understand child development and individual differences, are committed to the education of all pupils, and who have a knowledge base which enables them to differentiate between pupils as they develop a curriculum for all (Guðjónsdóttir, 2000). Thus, inclusive education calls for changes and development in teachers' work and classroom practices as they attend to diverse groups of pupils and build the teaching on the individual as well as the whole group (Day & Gu, 2010; Guðjónsdóttir, 2000). The main emphasis is on carefully planned teaching, conducted in a way that supports pupils in improving their learning (Arthur-Kelly, Gordon, & Butterfield, 2003; Idol, 2006). Therefore, it is in the hands of teachers to change and develop pedagogy, curriculum and assessment to benefits all pupils.

For developing inclusive practices three fundamental pedagogical principles are important (Óskarsdóttir, 2017). The first principle is that the classroom and the subject teachers are responsible for and committed to the education of *all* their pupils. The second principle addresses co-agency, with the pupils as active agents in their learning. The third principle focuses on the learning environment, and the necessary materials or activities for learning to occur.

It is the responsibility of the teachers to create inclusive environments with learning spaces for all pupils, but pupils are responsible for their own learning. The teachers should focus on the strengths, abilities and the interest each pupil brings to the classroom and avoid focusing on ability labelling (Hart, Drummond, & McIntyre, 2007).

By incorporating pedagogical knowledge, understanding and skills into practice, an opportunity to differentiate among pupils, contexts, methods, materials, resources and outcomes is created in designing a curriculum for all pupils. Teachers, in planning their teaching and providing scaffolding for pupils, can create a space to include everyone in the general classroom by drawing on pupils' resources. However, it is not only the classroom teacher who needs to be aware of the diversity in the pupil group, subject teachers need to be aware of that also. As they plan their subject teaching, they must consider that pupils learn in different ways.

It is important for teachers to belong to a collaborative community of professionals committed to improving practice. Several factors are important for successful collaboration. It is critical to establish time to collaborate, trust in each other's professionalism, to create openness to diversity, and to use personal resources in an active and positive way. Furthermore, it is important that the collaboration is meaningful and controlled by the teachers. It can be detrimental to collaboration in schools if it is mainly based on consulting with experts, or if it is based on existing hierarchical and political status differences (Óskarsdóttir, 2017).

Inclusive practices arise not only from teachers' education and experience, but also from cultures of teaching, beliefs, values and community expectation. To establish inclusive practices, schools could focus on constructing a climate of creativity, trust and tolerance that enables teachers to continually question their actions and evaluate and renew their practice. Most often teachers find it more successful to plan relevant and interesting learning activities in collaboration with other educators and professionals. Then they learn from each other as they share and evaluate their professional knowledge and experience (Óskarsdóttir, 2017). This kind of shared professionalism can empower teachers to work towards their beliefs and values of inclusive pedagogy and practices.

Methodology: Narrative Inquiry

This research is a narrative inquiry, conducted in collaboration between the researchers and the participants. Because of the focus on experience and the qualities of life and education, narrative inquiry is situated in qualitative methodology (Clandinin & Connelly, 2000). The purpose of this study was to collect examples of inclusive practices in order to promote the construction of inclusive pedagogy and education for all in inclusive environments. The aim was to learn how teachers organize their subject teaching in diverse and inclusive classrooms.

Narrative inquiry seeks to understand experience by making people's stories the central focus of research, the stories are lived and told (Clandinin, 2007; Clandinin & Connelly, 2000). Thus, the narrative inquiry was appropriative in our study as the aim was to understand and learn how teachers organize their subject teaching in diverse and inclusive classrooms. Narrative inquiry is first and foremost a way of thinking and learning about experience (Connelly & Clandinin, 2006).

The research questions that led this narrative inquiry were as follows:
- How are teachers responding to diverse pupils in their subject teaching?
- How do teachers organize and plan their teaching?

Three researchers (the authors) from the University of Iceland (UI), and six school teachers from four compulsory schools participated in this research. The three researchers from the UI are all former teachers at grade schools (teaching grades 1–10). Part of the role of researchers doing narrative inquiry is their credibility towards the participants (Connelly & Clandinin, 2006). The teacher community recognizes our experience as school teachers of 19–30 years and welcomes us to collaborate with them in researching their teaching practices. The school teachers were chosen purposefully and invited to participate as practitioner researchers. The teachers teach at four different schools that are organized for grade 1-10, and all known for their inclusive practices. The teachers teach at different grade levels, in different subjects, and some are also classroom teachers that teach their group most subjects; all are experienced teachers who have taught for 10–30 years.

Data was collected through reiterated cycles of participant observation, reflective discussions and focus group discussions for three years. In the field, the researcher-participant relationships underpin much of what narrative inquirers do as they live and work alongside participants in their stories. A narrative inquiry with teachers is constructed or co-constructed, to re-present their professional experiences (Clandinin & Connelly, 2000). In this narrative inquiry the researchers and the teacher researchers collaborated as they collected the data.

The researchers visited each school two times for a whole school day and collected data through field observations by note taking, photographing and videotaping the practice. As well as gathering data through an open view, the focus was on the way the teachers organized their classroom practices, what they taught and how.

The teacher researchers wrote cases from their practices, took photos and videos and gave them to the researchers to narrate. Four focus group meetings with all the six teachers were held and the discussions recorded. In the meetings, reflective discussions were chosen to elicit the views of the teachers' practices as clearly and accurately as possible. The group also discussed the teachers' pedagogy, the way they taught and their thought behind it. All the data was transcribed into written text by the researchers.

Narrative analysis is used within narrative inquiry and stories are constructed from the data (Clandinin, 2016). In this study the phenomena under study was inclusive practices so we looked for stories, threads and connections that exemplified that. The analytical process took place concurrently through the research period (Wolcott, 2005) as we looked for thematic elements and the "narrative threads" or "story lines" that were interwoven and interconnected like a braid throughout the data sets (Clandinin & Connelly, 2000). The challenging part was to reconstruct the stories from the transcribed text and show how we discovered and constructed meaning through the narrative inquiry along with the teacher researchers. At this stage of analysis, we focused on (a) broadening the data, or writing narrative descriptions of the inclusive learning spaces, (b) burrowing as we went deeper into the data by listening closely to how each individual was making personal and professional sense of the data, and in the end (c) re-storying or finding out how to tell the story of these inclusive practices as a shared interaction (Garvis, 2015).

To enhance the credibility of the data, multiple sources (four different schools and six teachers), data collection methods (reflective discussions, field observations and focus group discussion), time (reiterated cycles of data collection) and modes of analysis were used. The trustworthiness (Lincoln & Guba, 1985) of these findings, the narratives, will be found as the readers of this narrative inquiry feel that the evidence and the argument of the study has convinced them of the claim (Polkinghorne, 2007). Validity of the account therefore relates to personal meaning drawn from the narrative stories, not to a measurable truth. Reading these accounts can give others an opportunity to develop insights into, or come to understand, the ways in which these teachers create inclusive learning environments and learning spaces and how they themselves can develop their practice (Dunn, 2003; Kelchtermans, 1993). In the next chapter we will introduce the narratives from these teachers in their own words, with their own names.

We were interested in the storied experiences of teachers and learners that happens in inclusive classrooms. Through our narrative inquiry into the curriculum making of teachers and the analysis, we report here narratives on four themes related to creating inclusive pedagogy. The themes are understanding inclusive education, organizing teaching, teaching moments, and collaboration.

Creating Inclusive Pedagogy

The findings reveal four main themes emerging from the participant observation, reflective discussions and focus group discussions. The first theme illustrates how the teachers understand inclusive education and how that affects their teaching. The second theme informs the way teachers organize and prepare their teaching in different subjects for diverse pupils. The third theme focuses narratives of teaching moments in inclusive environments. The fourth theme discusses the collaboration the teachers found important to be able to respond to diverse group of pupils.

Understanding Inclusive Education

All of the teachers showed that they have a conceptual understanding of inclusion. Hrafnhildur's attitude can be found in her words: "I think that pupil's well-being is most important in inclusive schools. And that everyone can achieve their goals", while Ásta finds that "it is most important that we have equal rights. We should all have equal rights to employ our strengths whoever we are. We are all different and the bottom line is that we should enjoy our strengths." All of the teachers emphasize the importance of attending to the differences between pupils, not to focus on sameness. As Fanney explains:

> Inclusive education demands that the teacher has diverse ways of teaching. I cannot have the same material for all, I have to plan it carefully and that is more fun and more interesting for pupils. We are not all the same and that is important for everyone to understand.

According to these teachers attending to diverse pupils means having multiple ways of teaching organization and methods to meet the different ways pupils learn. The teachers place emphasis on a respect for the pupils' different resources they bring into the classroom, their different abilities, interest, experiences and culture. They also find it important that all pupils learn to respect and value each other's differences and strengths.

Organizing Teaching

The teachers emphasize that when they organize their teaching, they think of the whole group and then they adjust their planning to each group, as each group is different. Special art classes are organized to be once a week for two class periods and taught by an art teacher. Most often the art teacher teaches many different groups through the week. Eyrún, an art teacher in a rural school, shares her views on teaching diverse groups as she organizes her teaching:

> To be able to meet pupils' needs in a diverse group, it is important to be flexible and meet them where they are at. When I organize my teaching, I have to consider how long my pupils can stay on task or be engaged in one lesson, for example to teach class lessons twice a week instead of a longer lesson once a week. Sometimes I can arrange it so that I have two lessons with the lunch break in the middle and that helps those that need to have a break. I also have to think about the size of the groups.

For some pupils working on the same thing for 80 minutes can be too long and the teacher has to think of different ways to adjust to that, sometimes by breaking up the lesson, and other times to group the class into smaller groups.

> I have learnt from experience that it doesn't suit pupils to have high demands for the finishing of the art projects and such, not to be stuck on details that are not important. Last but not least, it is important to keep the joy of working at the center – to get pupils to enjoy what they are doing. I always emphasize that art is an experiment and that we are always experimenting. That is why we do not always expect a masterpiece each time we create something.

In this discussion Eyrún explains a critical factor to organizing teaching in diverse classrooms, that is to know your pupils and their resources. To Eyrún, knowing pupils' resources means recognizing their strengths, needs, interests and background and using this knowledge to create classroom environments and tasks that give all the learners opportunities. In a similar sense, Fanney, who teaches English in 9th grade, explains her preparations:

I have [...] really a diverse group. This means I have to think about the composition of the group for each lesson. I teach two groups English in 9th grade. But this doesn't mean I can teach the same way in each group. For example, today I was teaching English poetry, and, in this group, I have a pupil that is dyslexic, so I think about how I can help him to work with the poetry. [...] So it often helps me in preparing lessons to begin to think about the pupils that need a lot of support and then I find some solutions that work for everyone ...

Fanney builds on her knowledge of the resources in the group when she organizes her teaching and begins by figuring out what everyone can do and then she adds tasks of different levels, for different ways to work and allowing for different ways of presenting the work. Hrafnhildur, who teaches swimming in a compulsory school, has a similar rule when she prepares her teaching and she focuses on the goals of the lesson:

When I'm planning teaching for a diverse group of pupils, I mainly keep in mind that the learning goals are appropriate for each pupil, no matter if these goals are the same or not. I plan the lesson for everyone, there are some that are afraid of water, others that can't do this or that, and then there are some newly immigrated to Iceland who haven't had swimming lessons before.

In Iceland swimming lessons are mandatory and most often organized once a week for all pupils through grades 1–10. Swimming pools are spread all through the country and to go swimming with family or friends is a popular pastime. Therefore, it is considered to be critical that all children learn how to swim. Visiting Hrafnhildur as she met her pupils for the first time:

This is the first lesson of the term, and Hrafnhildur begins by talking to the group. She tells them that she hopes that someone has a problem with swimming because then she will have a challenge and that is what she wants. She tells the pupils that they are at different levels in swimming and that is how it should be. She continues and says: We will not all be doing the same things, not swimming the same way or the same number of laps around the pool. Some of you need to repeat things more often while others are adding on their skills and this is all normal. It is my job to be on top of this and I will do my best to teach you all how to swim.

Addressing the way pupils (and humans in general) are different and need different supports or tasks to succeed is important for promoting equitable practice in schools like Hrafnhildur explains to her pupils.

In a lesson with Ásta, a support teacher at primary level, she similarly addresses differentiation in tasks as a way to accommodate to pupil differences in her preparations. She had a group of third grade pupils come to her small classroom. There are three boys and three girls and they are all learners of Icelandic as a second language. Ásta asks them to sit on the floor with her in the corner and she shows them pictures of farm animals in Iceland, they discuss the animal names in Icelandic, what they eat and other identifications. After a bit of a discussion she asks them to work in pairs and places each pair at a different station in the room. Each pair is working on a task related to the theme of farm animal but at different levels of difficulty.

> [...] In this way I try to adapt the assignments to the pupils' abilities. So that everyone can do the assignment in some way with different levels of support ... I always have to keep the individuals in mind each time when I'm planning my work.

All the pupils are learning Icelandic but at a different level. Ásta is well aware of the differences in their language abilities and she reacts by giving them differentiated tasks that build on their word knowledge and reading ability.

Eyrún integrates art and mathematics and that can offer great possibilities for pupils.

> Creative representations can help pupils to understand concepts and methods better, especially in relation to tessellations, patterns and such. In my experience the pupils who had difficulties with understanding the methods and concepts in the text books, showed good understanding when they had dealt with same concepts creatively in the art lessons.

By integrating subjects, Eyrún uses creativity to reach pupils who are at the concrete or representational level in mathematics, enabling them to understand abstract mathematical concepts and methods.

The narratives show that in organizing and preparing teaching the teachers build on the knowledge they have of pupils, by considering pupils' resources and what would get them interested in wanting to do the assignments. They have found that group work, playing games and having fun has positive effects on pupils' success in school. It can give teachers insight into pupils' abilities and also cast a light on their social dynamics.

Teaching Diverse Groups of Pupils

There is a common thread running through the teachers' narratives about their teaching practices. The thread weaves through themes of being sensitive to their groups, knowing the pupils and responding to their needs. Also, the themes of enjoying work, having fun and working collectively on assignments are strong descriptors of how the teachers describe their teaching.

Eyrún's narrative of teaching a complicated group of third graders, casts a light on her sensitivity to her group:

> Eyrún was teaching third grade art last year, and that was a rather demanding group. The group had 12 pupils and one of them had difficult behavior. Because of the group the school administration and Eyrún decided to have one lesson (40 minutes) two times a week, not two lessons in row once a week as was the most common practice. This change made her to think about the projects based on a short lesson length. She kept in mind that:
>
> – The projects were exciting and interesting for all
> – The instructions were clear and easy to follow
> – The projects could be finished in one lesson or it would be easy to divide the projects between more lessons without losing the momentum or enjoyment of working on them (which could be demanding for some pupils)
> – The projects were flexible which gave pupils the freedom to create and implement in their own way.

Visiting Eyrún during the first lesson of the autumn we experienced her sensitivity towards her pupils and how she gives them a space to get their head together.

> Eyrún had pupils mix food-coloring in water. One pupil, Jón, ran outside to the playground because he didn't want to take part in the lesson. He was sitting on the swings and we could see him out of the classroom window. Eyrún continues her work with the pupils but we could see that she also had an eye one Jón. When the pupils had been mixing and playing

with different mixtures of water and food-coloring for a while, one pupil ran to the window and yelled: 'Hey Jón, you don't know what you are missing! This is so much fun!' That was all that was needed. Jón came back inside and took part for the rest of the lesson.

We can both sense the trust and sensitivity Eyrún, the teacher, shows towards her pupils. Instead of running after the pupil she gives him the space he needs to rebalance and come back when he is ready and urged by his classmate. Later, Eyrún told us that she never had any problems with him running out or not willing to participate after that lesson.

Hrafnhildur decided to make the swimming lessons the most fun lessons in school. Of course, she has rules that everyone has to obey, such as listening to her when she is speaking.

> But what do I do in the lessons? I have games, yoga, synchronized swimming, rescue swimming, relaxing, kayaking, reading lessons, lessons with toys, candlelight swimming, preparing for endurance swimming and watching videos. I use all kinds of things and toys in the pool and try to have the lessons as diverse as I can. This is so that every pupil can find something that interests him or her. Of course, pupils sometimes have to do things that they do not consider to be fun, but then I just put some music on and set the volume high.

As mentioned before, in Iceland swimming lessons are compulsory. Going to the swimming pool all year round is a popular activity among families, therefore it is thought to be important that children learn how to swim. However, it is not easy for all children and some pupils are even afraid of going into the swimming pool, therefore it is important that the teacher uses different and effective ways to get the pupils to participate.

Hildur teaches exercise-lessons in first through tenth grade in her school Grundarskóli where the older pupils have a role in teaching and working with the younger ones.

> I take material from books and create diverse activities where I emphasize mixed age grouping, co-teaching and subject integration with diverse groups of pupils. I also stress that pupils collaborate across age groups. One example of a subject for these lessons is traffic education where the older pupils assist the younger ones with finding the safest way to walk between home and school, connecting the assignments with art education, information technology and creative writing. Together they make

videos of activities, like how to cross a street. The pupils also write short stories and make cartoons after having gone on field trips with the older pupils.

In this narrative we learn about how pupils at different age levels collaborate, how they assist each other, work together and create different projects together.

In Fanney's and Ingunn's school, workshops are scheduled regularly in the timetable. The teachers plan the workshops together around the principles of integrating the subjects, randomly assigning pupils to mixed age groups of 5 to 7 pupils in each group and designing assignments that call for creative solutions. An example of such an assignment is a workshop where each group chooses a feeling to explore further. This can be for example about the feelings of love, sorrow, anger, fear, or joy.

The first task for each group is then to act out the feeling that they chose and take at least 5 photos of what it looks like. The second task is to explain the feeling and write a text based on sources that the pupils find online or in books, or the group creates their own explanation. The third task is to write a poem that is connected to the feeling. The group then chooses one of their own to read the poem out loud to everyone in the large group. The fourth assignment is to make a short video with a sketch that interprets the feeling in some way. The fifth and last task is to write a song about the feeling and sing it for the large group.

> With this way of working we aim to reach all pupils, build on their strengths and connect to their interests. The workshops support everyone's participation and we discuss with the large group that within each small group they are all responsible for the outcomes of the work, they know what is expected and we give them clear instructions on what they need to do to get an A for the assignments. The teenagers and older children in each group know that they are role models for the younger ones in showing them how to get everyone to participate and give everyone a role in working on the tasks.

The way workshops are organized in Fanney's and Ingunn's school, everyone has a role in group work and there is collective responsibility for the outcome of their tasks.

As can been seen in all the teachers' narratives, the teachers focus on their pupils, their interest, knowledge and abilities. By building on pupils' resources, they plan their teaching, they create a strong frame around their pupils and their learning but at the same time they are flexible. In the sense of democracy, the teachers give their pupils a voice and the chance to influence the choice of activities and where, how or with whom learning takes place. Thus, pupils are given responsibility for their learning.

Collaboration

Working with and through others in preparing teaching and inside the classroom was emphasized as important for reaching all pupils. With the support of special educators, teacher assistants or social educators, the teachers were able to create a learning space that could include all of their pupils, providing differentiation and meeting pupils' needs. As Fanney explains:

> When I work with the special needs' teachers, I first decide on an assignment and then I get the special needs teacher to review it for me and find ways to adapt it for some pupils. This collaboration has been very successful. It makes my life and work a little easier.

In some cases, the teachers thought that the presence of assistants inside their classrooms distracted pupils. Hrafnhildur, who works with the support personnel, states that although "many pupils in the school have support, I don't want the support personnel to come into the swimming pool because I feel that it distracts the pupil. The pupils work well with me and while that works, they come here unsupported".

Ásta has many years of teaching experience and is building a new role for herself as a support teacher in her school.

> In my work, I now increasingly am taking pupils out of their classroom to work with me. These pupils might need more practice, for example with learning to read. Even though I try to plan their work so that they enjoy coming here and enjoy the work, I am still in my heart not pleased with this arrangement. I feel that the learning should take place in their classrooms, as much as possible.

In her words a dilemma can be detected in that she would like pupils to be in their classrooms with their classroom teacher and peers, but in her role as a special needs teacher, the standard practice in her school is to take pupils out to work with them in small groups. She, however, collaborates with the classroom teachers to assess if the pupils can take part in what is happening in the classroom or if they should work in small groups with her.

Discussion

The purpose of the study was to collect examples of innovative teaching in order to promote the construction of inclusive pedagogy and education for all in inclusive environments. The aim was to learn how teachers organize their subject teaching in diverse and inclusive classrooms. We chose narrative inquiry for the study because we wanted to make the teachers' stories the central focus of the research. In our chapter on findings we focus on the four main themes that emerge from the data; understanding inclusive education, organizing and preparing teaching, teaching moments in inclusive environments and collaboration.

Bringing together how the teachers understand inclusive education they all emphasized the importance of attending to pupils' differences, strengths, wellbeing, and equal rights. They also discussed the importance of respecting and valuing the different abilities pupils bring into the classroom. This understanding and these values are in line with how inclusive practice is explained by people in the forefront of inclusive education (e.g. Ainscow, Booth, & Dyson, 2004; Booth, 2010; Slee, 2011; UNESCO, 2017), that inclusive education is an on-going act directed towards quality education for all and should lead to an inclusive, just society where everyone is a valid participant.

The pedagogy that the teachers in this research employ falls under the three fundamental pedagogical principles Hart, Drummond, and McIntyre (2007) identified as necessary for the development of inclusive practices. One of the principles addresses co-agency, where the pupil is seen as an active agent in his/her education and there is the interplay between the teacher and the pupil. The teacher creates learning spaces for the pupils, but the pupils are responsible for their learning with the support from the teacher. Pupils are diverse, and all the teachers emphasized that school and learning should be interesting in a way that all the pupils wanted to participate. Therefore, as they plan their teaching, the teachers have in mind pupils' resources, their interest, strength, and experiences. The teachers understand that it is critical to have pupils' experiences and perspectives in mind as they decide what and how to teach and how to create learning spaces for their pupils. Their pedagogy is to respond to the diversity in the group, to the whole group but also each individual, through the curriculum design, learning activities, classroom climate, learning spaces, instructional materials, teaching techniques and assessment procedures (Gay & Kirkland, 2003; Loreman, 2017; Spratt & Florian, 2015).

Another principle is that of trust, in that the teacher trusts that pupils want to learn and does not blame them when they do not learn. The teacher asks what needs to be different for pupils who are unsuccessful in their learning, what needs to be changed in the learning environment, materials or activities, rather than asking what is wrong with the pupil (Hart et al., 2007). We can sense the trust Eyrún, the teacher, shows towards her pupils when she, instead of running after the pupil, gives him the space he needs. Fanney and Ingunn make sure that everyone has a role in their group they are responsible for, and Hildur encourages her pupils to work together, assist each other, and create different projects together. Pupils working together, and collaborating was a common practice in all the classrooms.

Hart, Drummond, and McIntyre (2007) point out the principle of everybody that relates to the responsibility the teacher has towards her pupils, in the sense that the teacher is responsible for and committed to the education of all the pupils in the classroom, not just some of them. This responsibility can however be shared with other staff, such as special education or assistant teachers who collaborate with the teacher in supporting the pupils. In this research findings the teachers emphasized that collaboration is very important and that the cooperation from support personnel helped them to create learning spaces for all their pupils to become successful learners. They wanted to focus on collaboration rather than support and found it important that there are teams with individuals that work together planning and teaching rather than support persons. However, to create a collaborative community of professionals committed to improving practice it is critical to establish time to collaborate, create openness to diversity, and that the collaboration is meaningful and controlled by the teachers (Óskarsdóttir, 2017).

The narrative inquiry gave us the opportunity to make the teachers' stories the central focus of our research. These are their stories as they lived and told them and how we understood them (Clandinin, 2007; Clandinin & Connelly, 2000). Referring to Alexander (2013) pedagogy is the act of teaching together with the ideas, values and beliefs that inform, sustain and justify that act (Alexander, 2013). The narratives from this research indicate that when teachers build on inclusive pedagogy, they use the diversity in the group to design the curriculum, learning activities, classroom climate, instructional materials, and teaching techniques (Florian & Black-Hawkins, 2011; Gay & Kirkland, 2003; Loreman, 2017).

Conclusions

The findings indicate that to promote inclusive education that supports learning for all pupils, teacher beliefs about inclusion are important as well as their openness towards diverse pupils. Further, the findings give an insight into the inclusive pedagogy that the teachers have generated. The important features of the inclusive pedagogy are that teaching is planned for all pupils and it builds on the goals to be reached, on the use of innovative strategies in teaching, and on using group work where pupils get the opportunity to set their goals and work towards them. The inclusive pedagogy is also based on a cooperation between the teacher and others in the school, such as special needs teachers, support teachers and teacher assistants, to strengthen the ability to reach the diverse group of pupils.

Across all school phases in Icelandic schools, examples of innovative teaching practice are evident. A resent audit of the education system shows that, overall, the educational personnel are qualified, experienced, motivated and committed, and open to innovative approaches to curriculum and teaching (European Agency, 2017). The narratives presented in this research will be useful for supporting the ongoing development of inclusive schools in Iceland and also elsewhere, and for advancing a strong sense and practice of inclusive pedagogy. This can be achieved by utilizing the stories of inclusive practice and pedagogy from teachers in our roles as teacher educators in preparing new teachers to work in diverse classrooms. The narratives of practice will then serve the purpose of giving preservice teachers and others an insight into how teachers in the field are constructing inclusive pedagogy and how their values and professional knowledge supports their efforts.

References

Ainscow, M. (2008). Teaching for diversity: The next big challenge. *The Sage handbook of curriculum and instruction* (pp. 240–258). Thousand Oaks, CA: Sage Publications.

Ainscow, M., Booth, T., & Dyson, A. (2004). Understanding and developing inclusive practices in schools: A collaborative action research network. *International Journal of Inclusive Education, 8*(2), 125–139.

Alexander, R. (2013). *Essays on pedagogy.* London: Routledge.

Arthur-Kelly, M., Gordon, C., & Butterfield, N. (2003). *Classroom management: Creating positive learning environments.* Thomson.

Booth, T. (2010, June 11). *How should we live together? Inclusion as a framework of values for educational development.* Paper presented at the Kinderwelten Conference, Berlin.

Booth, T., Nes, K., & Strømstad, M. (2003). *Developing inclusive teacher education.* London: Routledge.

Bruner, J. S. (1996). *The culture of education.* Cambridge, MA: Harvard University Press.

Clandinin, D. J. (Ed.). (2007). *Handbook of narrative inquiry.* London, UK: Sage Publications.

Clandinin, D. J. (2016). *Engaging in narrative inquiry: Developing qualitative inquiry* (Vol. 9). New York, NY: Routledge.

Clandinin, D. J., & Connelly, F. M. (2000). *Narrative inquiry*. San Francisco, CA: Jossey-Bass.

Connelly, F. M., & Clandinin, D. J. (2006). *Narrative inquiry*. In J. L. Green, G. Camilli, & P. B. Elmore (Eds.), *Handbook of complementary methods in education research* (3rd ed., pp. 477–487). Mahwah, NJ: Lawrence Erlbaum.

Day, C., & Gu, Q. (2010). *The new lives of teachers*. London: Routledge.

Dunn, D. S. (2003). Teach me about your life: Narrative approaches to lives, meaning, and transitions. *Journal of Social and Clinical Psychology, 22*(5), 604–606.

European Agency. (2003). *Inclusive education and classroom practices*. Odnese: Europen Agency for Development in Special Needs Education.

European Agency. (2015). *Agency position on inclusive education systems*. Odnese: Europen Agency for Special Needs and Inclusive Education.

European Agency. (2017). *Education for all in Iceland – External audit for the Icelandic system for inclusive education*. Odnese: Europen Agency for Special Needs and Inclusive Education.

Florian, L., & Black-Hawkins, K. (2011). Exploring inclusive pedagogy. *British Educational Research Journal, 37*(5), 813–828. doi:10.1080/01411926.2010.501096

Florian, L., & Spratt, J. (2013). Enacting inclusion: A framework for interrogating inclusive practice. *European Journal of Special Needs Education, 28*(2), 119–135. doi:10.1080/08856257.2013.778111

Freire, P. (2005). *Education for critical consciousness*. New York, NY: Continuum.

Fullan, M., & Hargreaves, A. (2016). *Bringing the profession back in: Call to action*. Oxford, OH: Learning Forward.

Garvis, S. (2015). *Narrative constellations: Exploring lived experience in education*. Rotterdam, The Netherlands: Sense Publishers. doi:10.1007/978-94-6300-151-9_2

Gay, G., & Kirkland, K. (2003). Developing cultural critical consciousness and self-reflection in preservice teacher education. *Theory into Practice, 42*(3), 181–187.

Grenier, M. (2010). Moving to inclusion: A socio-cultural analysis of practice. *International Journal of Inclusive Education, 14*(4), 387–400. doi:10.1080/13603110802504598

Guðjónsdóttir, H. (2000). *Responsive professional practice: Teachers analyze the theoretical and ethical dimensions of their work in diverse classrooms* (Unpublished dissertation). University of Oregon, Eugene.

Hart, S., Drummond, M. J., & McIntyre, D. (2007). Learning without limits: Constructing a pedagogy free from determinist beliefs about ability. In L. Florian (Ed.), *The Sage handbook of special education* (pp. 499–514). London: Sage Publications.

Idol, L. (2006). Toward inclusion of special education etudents in general education: A program evaluation of eight schools. *Remedial and Special Education, 27*(2), 77–94. doi:10.1177/07419325060270020601

Kelchtermans, G. (1993). Teachers and their career story: A biographical perspective on professional development. In C. Day, J. Calderhead, & P. Denicolo (Eds.), *Research on teacher thinking: Towards understanding professional development* (pp. 198–220). London: Falmer Press.

Lincoln, Y. S., & Guba, E. G. (1985). *Naturalistic inquiry.* Beverly Hills, CA: Sage Publications.

Ministry of Education Science and Culture. (2011). *The Icelandic national curriculum guide for compulsory school: General section.* Retrieved from http://www.menntamalaraduneyti.is/utgefid-efni/namskrar/adalnamskra-grunnskola/

Loreman, T. (2017). Pedagogy for inclusive education. Oxford Research Encyclopaedia of Education. doi:10.1093/acrefore/9780190264093.013.148

Óskarsdóttir, E. (2017). *Constructing support as inclusive practice: A self-study* (Unpublished dissertation). University of Iceland, Reykjavík.

Petrou, A., Angelides, P., & Leigh, J. (2009). Beyond the difference: From the margins to inclusion. *International Journal of Inclusive Education, 13*(5), 439–448.

Polkinghorne, D. (2007). Validity issues in narrative research. *Qualitative Inquiry, 13*(4), 471–486.

Slee, R. (2011). *The irregular school: Exclusion, schooling and inclusive education.* London: Routledge.

Spratt, J., & Florian, L. (2015). Inclusive pedagogy: From learning to action. Supporting each individual in the context of "everybody". *Teaching and Teacher Education, 49*(2015), 89–96. Retrieved from https://doi.org/10.1016/j.tate.2015.03.006

UNESCO. (1994). *The Salamanca statement and framework for action on special needs education.* Salamanca: UNESCO. Retrieved from http://unesdoc.unesco.org/images/0009/000984/098427eo.pdf

UNESCO. (2001). *Open file on inclusive education.* Paris: UNESCO. Retrieved from http://unesdoc.unesco.org/images/0012/001252/125237eo.pdf

UNESCO. (2008, November 25–28). *Inclusive education: The way of the future.* Conclusions and Recommendations of the 48th Session of the International Conference on Education (ICE), Geneva, Switzerland.

UNESCO. (2009). *Policy guideline on inclusion in education* (UNESCO Ed.). Paris: UNESCO.

UNESCO. (2017). *A guide for ensuring inclusion and equity in education.* Paris: UNESCO.

Van Manen, M. (1991). *The tact of teaching: The meaning of pedagogical thoughtfulness.* Albany, NY: State University of New York Press.

Van Manen, M. (1999). The language of pedagogy and the primacy of student experience. In J. J. Loughran (Ed.), *Researching teaching: Methodologies and practices for understanding pedagogy* (pp. 13–27). London: Falmer Press.

Wolcott, H. F. (2005). *The art of fieldwork.* Walnut Creek: AltaMira Press.

CHAPTER 14

The Use of Video during Professional Experience for Initial Teacher Education

Michael Cavanagh

Abstract

This chapter reports an investigation of pre-service teachers' use of video during professional experience as a tool for self-reflection and for the provision of feedback by their supervising teachers. Nine triads, comprising a pre-service teacher (PST), supervising teacher and university advisor participated in the study. Each week during a four-week professional experience placement, PSTs identified a 'puzzle of practice' and used smartphones to video a five-minute excerpt from one of their lessons. They annotated their video excerpt with time-stamped comments and uploaded it to a secure website. There, the supervising teacher and university advisor could view the video, read the annotations, and add their responses. Annotations were coded to identify the depth of the reflections using four categories: Descriptive; Evaluative; Reflective; Imaginative. Participants also provided feedback on their experiences through a survey. Results indicate that the process helped PSTs to reflect on classroom practice and provided opportunities for professional dialogue among triad members.

Keywords

video – reflection – professional experience – teacher education

Introduction

An important goal for initial teacher education programs is to provide experiences for pre-service teachers that allow them to integrate theoretical and practical knowledge for teaching (Hennissen, Beckers, & Moerkerke, 2017). One important means by which this integration can be achieved is through in-school professional experience placements. In particular, the learning of beginning teachers can be advanced through programs which promote pre-service teachers' reflective practice and provide targeted feedback which can assist pre-service teachers to make sense of classroom events (Loughran, 2002). Studies of pre-service teachers' practice during professional experience afford an opportunity to investigate how they enact their reflective practice and the factors which might support its development (Stenberg, Rajala, & Hilppo, 2016). This chapter presents the results from a small-scale pilot study on the use of video as a tool for self-reflection and the provision of feedback for pre-service teachers. In the study, pre-service teachers video-recorded short episodes of significance from their lessons each week during a four-week placement. They then made time-stamped comments and shared the annotated videos with their supervising teacher and university advisor. The supervisors could provide feedback by responding to the pre-service teachers' reflections and adding further comments of their own to the videos. The annotations were analysed for the depth of reflection they exhibited and participants' views about the video reflection process were also investigated.

Reflective Practice

Dewey (1933) noted that reflective thinking arises from a quandary or dilemma which calls for a response and brings to mind a range of alternatives. Reflective thinking necessitates a deliberate act of searching or inquiry which aims to resolve the ambiguities and direct future actions. Dewey refers to five phases of reflective thinking which, though they may occur in any particular order, combine together in the process of reflective thinking. The phases include suggestions which impel the mind towards a possible resolution of the dilemma; transforming the puzzling experience into a problem for which a solution may be found; making hypotheses and forming suggestions which can initiate and guide observations; the conceptualisation of an idea or plan; and testing the hypothesis by direct or imaginative action.

Dewey's ideas have been further analysed by Rodgers (2002), who suggested that reflection is primarily about making sense of experience so as to propel the learner forward with a deeper understanding from one occurrence to the next. Reflective thinking requires a disciplined and methodical approach that is fundamentally different from how we respond to random thoughts or ideas. Reflection also occurs primarily through interactions with others because expressing our thoughts to others exposes the strengths and weaknesses of our ideas. Finally, reflective thinking requires an attitude that values one's own and others' personal and intellectual growth.

Reflection was theorised by Schön (1983) as activated by an unexpected event or interruption to the anticipated flow of a lesson which provokes a response. Through reflection, the teacher can analyse why the event took place in order to identify possible future actions should the incident occur again. Schön (1983) describes 'reflection-in-action' which is characterised by tacit knowledge and is an unconscious reaction to an event based on prior experience (Meierdirk, 2017). The practitioner's growing awareness and ability to notice these unforeseen episodes in the moment can assist in the process of 'reflection-on-action' after the conclusion of the lesson (Benade, 2015). Hence 'reflection-on-action' is retrospective in nature and supports a process of reviewing and interpreting the event so that one can develop a plan for future action (Crichton & Valdera-Gil, 2015).

Reflective practice is an engagement in ongoing and focused reflection in which questions are constantly framed and re-framed in response to classroom observations and experiences as they arise (Cavanagh & Prescott, 2010). Hence reflective practice is characterised by actions which occur in response to noticing some event during a lesson, attempting to interpret the incident and considering alternative perspectives. Reflective practice draws on our personal experience to make a judgement and determine future actions in responding to what has been noticed (Coffey, 2014). The intention of reflective practice is therefore to increase the teacher's understanding of the event, challenge currently held beliefs and expand their individual practice (Sellars, 2012).

The development of pre-service teachers' reflective practice is considered a crucial part of teacher education programs (Alger, 2006). Reflection allows pre-service teachers to shift from a preoccupation with self to consider student learning (Davis, 2006). However, before pre-service teachers can begin to reflect on their classroom practice, they must first learn to take note of what is occurring as they teach so they can separate events of relatively minor importance from more salient elements of a lesson. As Sherin, Russ, and Colestock (2011, p. 79) note, "A crucial part of teaching, then, involves observing the classroom and choosing to make sense of those aspects of the class that are pedagogically relevant". In doing so, pre-service teachers can advance from general descriptions of lesson activities to begin analysing causes and reimagining future actions (Levin, Hammer, & Coffey, 2009).

Studies have also shown that, despite the challenges associated with shifting from their own actions to consider student learning outcomes, pre-service teachers can learn to become more reflective practitioners (Spitzer, Phelps, Beyers, Johnson, & Sieminski, 2011). Pre-service teachers who develop a capacity for reflective thinking become more aware of the assumptions on which their teaching decisions and actions are based (Yost, Sentner, & Forlenza-Bailey, 2000) and are better able to make connections between theory and practice (Ward & McCotter, 2004).

The Use of Video
One means of becoming more reflective is through the use of video. Video has been used successfully to support reflection in initial teacher education (Kong, Shroff, & Hung, 2009) and by more experienced teachers (van Es, Tunney, Goldsmith, & Seago, 2014). Video allows pre-service teachers to analyse their practice by creating a space between the classroom actions and their reflections on them (van Es & Sherin, 2002). Video affords the opportunity to view the lesson multiple times so patterns of practice can emerge (Yerrick, Ross, & Molebash, 2005). Chung and van Es (2014) found that video supported pre-service teachers in analysing their teaching practice and helped them develop skills in making sense of learning and teaching. Danielowich (2014) reported that sharing videos with peers exposed pre-service teachers to a range of different interpretations of their classroom practice, broadening their ideas about teaching.

Video may also help in the assessment of pre-service teachers and to provide feedback (Masats & Dooly, 2011). Video allows supervisors to notice aspects of the class which they might not have remembered after observing the lesson 'live' (Rich & Hannafin, 2009). Kleinknecht and Gröschner (2016) used a video reflection system somewhat similar to the one used in the present study. They developed a 'video feedback cycle' of self-reflection, peer feedback, expert feedback from teacher educators and further self-reflection "aimed at a feedback balance including to what extent comments as alternatives were regarded as helpful" (p. 48). The authors provided prompts to encourage structured forms of self-reflection and compared the reflections of pre-service teachers engaged in the video process with a control group who used journal writing and found that video feedback from peers and academics helped expand pre-service teachers' ability for self-reflection.

In a study by Gelfuso and Dennis (2014), pre-service teachers engaged in what the authors referred to as a 'teaching cycle'. The participants videotaped their lessons and used the recordings for self-reflection and analysis. Later, the pre-service teachers met with an experienced Literacy Content Coach for a reflective conversation about their teaching and the student learning evident in their lessons. During these conversations, the coach drew attention to ideas that were deemed relevant to the pre-service teacher's practice and its impact on student learning while pre-service teachers shared their video self-reflections and evidence. The authors concluded that the combination of video and interaction with knowledgeable others could provide support for key aspects of reflection by pre-service teachers; however, they noted that "much remains ambiguous about the combination of these two support structures and their effects on reflective practices" (p. 3). The present study was designed to investigate how the combination of self-reflection and interaction with more experienced teachers via video commentary could be used to support pre-service teachers' reflective practice.

The aim of the present study was to investigate how the use of time-stamped video annotations might support pre-service teachers' reflection and enhance the provision of feedback from supervising teachers and university advisors. The research questions that guided the study are: What are the differences in levels of reflection for pre-service teachers, supervising teachers and university advisors? How do pre-service teachers, supervising teachers and university advisors regard the video process as a tool for self-reflection and the provision of feedback?

Theoretical Framework

Van Es and Sherin (2002) developed a 'Learning to Notice Framework' incorporating three key elements: first, teachers identify important aspects of a teaching situation (describing); second, they apply knowledge of the context to analyse it (evaluating); and third, they link the specific experience and their thinking about it to general principles about learning and teaching (interpreting). Noticing and reflecting on classroom events have been shown to be enhanced when they are accompanied by a willingness to imagine alternatives that can lead to changes in future actions (Jacobs, Lamb, & Philipp, 2010). Lane, McMaster, Adnum, and Cavanagh (2014) drew on these ideas to develop a four-level framework to describe the depth of reflection in pre-service teachers' reflective writing: D_1–Descriptive, D_2–Evaluative, R_1–Reflective and R_2–Imaginative. Descriptive responses simply retell or describe events which have been noticed in the classroom. Evaluative responses take an additional step to make some kind of value judgement about what has been observed. Reflective responses contain an analysis of what is noteworthy about a particular lesson event and include some analysis of why things turned out as they did. Imaginative responses are those in which pre-service teachers can interpret classroom scenarios and make suggestions about how lessons could be taught differently and improved. The levels are described with examples from the present study in Table 14.1.

Methodology

Context and Participants
In Australia, initial teacher education programs are required to include a minimum of 80 days of supervised professional experience in schools, usually

TABLE 14.1 Four levels of reflection and examples

Level	Example
D1–Descriptive: Purely descriptive responses	"The students were all paying attention at the start of the lesson and no one was calling out"
D2–Evaluative: Descriptive responses containing an evaluative element	"I was very impressed in the way you motivated the students during the lesson. They were all engaged and participating"
R1–Reflective: Responses which make a judgement and justify it	"You could slow down your task explanation as some students respond to visual rather than auditory cues – that is, they need to see something rather than, or as well as, hear it"
R2–Imaginative: Responses that explain possible causes and/or imagine future actions	"After listening to my supervisor's comments, one improvement I definitely could have implemented would be to set firmer time scales on the different parts of the lesson"

completed as a combination of block teaching for perhaps three or four weeks at a time plus additional days. During the professional experience placement, the supervising teacher observes the pre-service teacher's lessons each day and provides feedback. Sometimes this is done using an observation sheet provided by the university where brief comments about the lesson can be added; at other times, feedback may be given verbally in a short discussion following the class. University advisors typically visit the school once, around the middle of the placement, to meet with the pre-service teacher, observe a lesson and discuss the pre-service teacher's progress with the supervising teacher. Importantly, the task of formally assessing the pre-service teacher's practice is for the supervising teacher and the university advisor's role is to liaise between the university and the school by supporting the pre-service and supervising teachers.

Pre-service teachers who were undertaking professional experience and university advisors from the university were invited to participate in the study via an email. Once the pre-service teacher participants were identified and placed at a school, their supervising teachers were invited to participate via email. In total, nine triads participated in the study. Each triad comprised a pre-service teacher (five primary and four secondary; eight female and one male), the supervising teacher (n=9) and a university advisor (n=5; some advisors were allocated to more than one triad). Five pre-service teachers were undertaking their first professional experience placement and four were undertaking their final placement. A half-day Information Session was held prior to the start of the placement to explain the process of recording, annotating, uploading and sharing video excerpts and to outline the requirements for the project. All of the pre-service teachers and university advisors attended the Information Session; however, as it was held during a school vacation period only two of the supervising teachers attended.

Following Danielowich (2014), no suggestions were given to participants about how they should reflect or provide feedback. This protocol was followed in order to investigate how the participants would reflect using the video platform without being given any prior indication of how they should do so. The aim of the hypothesis for the study was that such an approach would could result in reflective video annotations. If the results did not support this hypothesis then it would indicate that prompts or scaffolds would need to be developed for similar studies in the future.

For the present study, pre-service teachers identified a 'puzzle of practice' or area of their classroom practice on which they wanted to focus, either to improve in that aspect of their teaching or because they wanted to explore it further through self-analysis and obtaining feedback on from their supervisors. In doing so, it was hoped that pre-service teachers might develop their ability to identify significant episodes from their lessons (Sherin, Russ, & Colestock, 2011). The pre-service teachers then video-recorded from a lesson of their choice a short (five to eight minute) excerpt that was related to their puzzle of practice. They then uploaded the excerpt to a secure website where they added time-stamped comments onto the video. An email alert was automatically sent to supervisors and advisors so they could view the annotated video and add their feedback for the pre-service teacher, who could make further annotations. This process was undertaken each week during the teaching block so that pre-service teachers produced four annotated video excerpts. Figure 14.1 shows a screenshot of an annotated video.

Data Collection and Analysis

Upon completion of the placement, 47 video clips (some pre-service teachers chose to create more than the required four videos) incorporating 777 annotations were available for analysis. The author and a research assistant independently coded 67 annotations from four randomly selected videos using the four levels of reflection developed by Lane et al. (2014) (see Table 14.1) and agreed in 42 instances (63%). After discussing the discrepancies, 32 annotations from four different videos were independently coded, with agreement in 29 instances (91%). Discrepancies were discussed and the remaining coding was then completed by the research assistant.

FIGURE 14.1   Screenshot showing an annotated video

Gelfuso and Dennis (2014) reported that most studies of pre-service teacher reflection tend to focus on artefacts "left behind after the process of reflection has occurred" and "As a result, it seems little is understood about the facilitation of the process of reflection" (p. 10). Hence, the present study also sought to understand the participants' views about the video reflection process and whether it had assisted the development of pre-service teachers' reflective practice. This occurred through a written questionnaire at the end of the four-week placement. Although the questions varied slightly for pre-service teachers, supervising teachers and university advisors, the aim was to gather information from all participants about how they had used the video reflection process and whether they felt it had been useful as a means of providing feedback and reflecting on practice. All 23 participants (nine pre-service teachers, nine supervising teachers and five university advisors) completed the questionnaire.

Qualitative survey data were analysed by the author through a process of reflexive iteration (Srivasta, 2009), an inductive approach which involves revisiting the data multiple times to identify emerging themes. Questionnaire responses were analysed according to two of the phases outlined by Elo and Kyngas (2008): preparation and organising. In the preparation phase, the researcher becomes familiar with the data by reading through the questionnaires multiple times. This phase led to general comprehension of participant responses and the creation of tentative codes for later categorisation. Next, in organising the data, codes were applied to each participant response which included significant information or meaning. Sometimes the code was a direct response from the questionnaire, such as "the student, university advisor and school supervisor could all comment, contribute and make suggestions was incredibly useful and created a feeling of collaboration" which was coded as "collaboration". At other times, the code was derived from the questionnaire response, such as "my supervising teacher provided in depth responses, that you would not necessarily receive in person" was coded as "feedback". Another important aspect of the organising phase is collapsing similar codes into categories. For example, the codes "shared dialogue" and "interaction" were categorised as "triad sharing". As a further synthesis of the codes, where similar categories were identified, these were combined into one. For example, "time-stamped comments" and "focused comments" were merged into a category called "targeted feedback".

Results and Discussion

Video Annotations

Table 14.2 shows the number and percentage of annotations for the four levels of reflection for pre-service teachers, supervising teachers and university advisors. Overall, D–2 Evaluative comments occurred about twice as often as the other three categories. This was particularly so for supervising teachers and university advisors, highlighting how they are accustomed to assessing pre-service teachers' classroom practice and encouraging pre-service teachers by positively evaluating their efforts. University advisors made more annotations than pre-service teachers or supervising teachers, perhaps because the university advisors were all retired and had more time to devote to the task.

Pre-service teachers' annotations were most often at the D1–Descriptive level which is consistent with previous research findings (e.g., Chung & van Es, 2014) about their propensity to describe lesson events rather than analyse them. This relatively high proportion of D1 annotations might also indicate that the lack of guidance for pre-service teachers on how to reflect on classroom practice suggested by Danielowich (2014) was unsuccessful. Supervisors'

TABLE 14.2 Participants' annotations coded according to the four levels of reflection

Role	D1	D2	R1	R2	Total
Pre-service Teacher	82 (40%)	38 (18%)	50 (24%)	36 (17%)	206
Supervising Teacher	15 (9%)	62 (39%)	41 (26%)	40 (25%)	158
University advisor	77 (19%)	192 (46%)	69 (17%)	75 (18%)	413
Total	174 (22%)	292 (38%)	160 (21%)	151 (19%)	777

annotations were predominantly at the D2–Evaluative level (39% for supervising teachers and 46% for university advisors) which probably reflects how supervisors see their role as assessing pre-service teachers' classroom practice. The rate of responses at the R1–Reflective and R2–Imaginative levels for all three participant groups is relatively low which suggests that it might have been better to provide participants with examples of descriptive and reflective comments to highlight the differences between them. Even so, just under half of the pre-service teachers' annotations were at the higher R1–Reflective and R2–Imaginative levels which compares favourably with their supervisors.

Kleinknecht and Gröschner (2016) used a similar video reflection system. They analysed video comments using four categories (perceive, evaluate, reflect on consequences, reflect on alternatives), equivalent to the four levels used here; however, unlike the present study, they provided prompts to pre-service teachers to guide their self-reflections. Posttest results for their video group showed that when dealing with positive events pre-service teachers' comments were categorised at 12%, 22%, 33% and 33% respectively. It is likely that the higher proportions for reflective comments obtained by Kleinknecht and Gröschner (2016) are a consequence of the prompts they provided.

Questionnaire Data
Video Affordances

The video affordance reported in the project were largely consistent with results from previous studies (e.g., van Es & Sherin, 2002; Yerrick, Ross, & Molebash, 2000). Although initially anxious about 'performing', pre-service teachers felt that the use of video allowed them to notice a great deal more about their classroom practice since "you are so engrossed in what you are doing in the lesson that at times you aren't able take not of everything that is going on around you" whereas "with the video you watch the lesson again and see what you need to work on". The pre-service teachers in the present study generally found the video to be seen as an objective record of the specific episode which enabled them "to see my positives and negatives in the classroom and being able to improve on this every single lesson". As another pre-service teacher commented:

> It also gave me confidence in situations where I thought I had explained something poorly only to watch the video and actually feel like it wasn't as bad as I had thought.

Video allowed pre-service teachers to reflect on their teaching styles since it enabled them to scrutinise the language they used when addressing students, examine the amount of student participation, consider the effectiveness of their questioning techniques, examine student interaction in peripheral areas of the room, and acknowledge their professional strengths and weaknesses. In addition, the cycle of recording, reflecting, annotating and enacting became a rhythm that emerged as the professional experience placement continued:

> Once I saw what I needed to work on, I could practice this in my next lesson and then watch it and see if worked. It almost felt like I was able to re-live the moment and then improve on it.

The video reflection process also helped pre-service teachers shift their focus from their own actions and start to notice the impact of their teaching on student learning. As one pre-service teacher explained, "Through critiquing my own practice, I have been able to re-watch my lessons through the students' point of view". Viewing the video prompted pre-service teachers to consider "when my students' were most engaged and least engaged" which prompted further reflections about why this might be the case. For example,

> It was particularly useful in getting to see my lessons from the perspective of the children. It meant I was able to adapt my stance, where children were seated so that they could best see the board, ensure that I stopped talking when I had to write something on the board, etc.

There were affordances of the video process for supervising teachers also. The videos provided "a true picture" of the pre-service teacher's practice and the routine of providing video feedback "helps me as a teacher and develops my skill set to help support teachers in the future". For another supervising teacher, the video reflection process "challenged some assumptions about how video could be used to refine teaching practice". Another supervising teacher who was also a lead teacher at the school commented on the wider impact of the project in his school:

> Each year, teachers at the school set goals aligned to the Standards and provide evidence of their attempt to achieve the goals. The project modelled for supervisors how video analysis works and they may now choose to use video as a source of evidence.

Targeted Feedback

Pre-service teachers who were undertaking their final professional experience placement often compared the kind of feedback they had received on previous placements with the video feedback. They often commented that previous feedback tended to be "general" and "did not address concerns based on actual information" and "it isn't clear what they are talking about when you get feedback at the very end [of the lesson]". Pre-service teachers also contrasted the supervisor's verbal feedback given at the end of the lesson with their video feedback. Verbal feedback was usually given in between lessons but the "[school] day does not always allow an in depth conversation on the lesson". In contrast, the video feedback was more focussed because it related to "specific moments" that could be easily identified from the time-stamped comments.

> Having the comments time stamped was particularly useful so that I could see the specific moments that he was referring to which isn't always as clear when you get feedback at the very end.

Video comments were regarded by pre-service teachers as more thoughtfully considered and honest feedback because the supervisor had time to quietly reflect on the video excerpt away from the demands of the school environment.

By allowing the teacher to go home and look over the lesson allowed for a more thorough analysis and response.

> I believe that being behind a computer screen allows for a more honest response and therefore I received motivating corrections and encouragement throughout the four weeks.

Feedback was most useful when it was given promptly. Some pre-service teachers reported that there were times when feedback from the university advisor was delayed by two or three days. In those instances, the feedback was received after the pre-service teacher had taught again and the focus of their reflections may have shifted somewhat so that the feedback was not as useful as it might have been if received earlier.

Two of the university advisors felt that their video feedback was "clinical" and "less personal" in nature because it was not discussed at the school. Another critique of the university advisors' feedback related to the fact that they did not attend the school in person and, as one pre-service teacher wrote, "... did not know the students, their abilities, likes/dislikes etc.". As a result, some pre-service teachers regarded the university advisor feedback as "not particularly relevant" as it was given out of the context of the entire lesson. A supervising teacher made a similar comment:

> As the university advisor was not privy to the whole lesson, they could not always observe the context of the lesson, the transition of the lesson activities or the way in which lessons were concluded. They were also not always privy to any behavior issues, lesson problems that could either be edited out or not captured in the filming.

Supervisors believed the video process gave pre-service teachers time to ponder their feedback and allowed pre-service teachers to then upload additional questions or comments after they had been fully considered. Some supervising teachers reported that pre-service teachers would often request additional advice in person the following day to clarify how they could implement the feedback suggestions into their next lesson "thus enabling deeper understanding of the points of discussion". Overall, supervisors reported that they felt the video process enhanced their feedback to pre-service teachers.

> Being able to see the student reflections meant that I was able to not only comment on the positives and areas for further development but also respond to her thoughts and feelings. I think this made the feedback more worthwhile and thought out.

There were also advantages for the supervisors as they began to consider how their feedback could support the pre-service teachers' development. The opportunity to give considered feedback in targeted and concise video annotations was seen by some supervising teachers as a stimulus to reconsider how they could not only look back on the lesson just taught but also feed-forward with suggestions for future lessons as well.

> The opportunity to make short but pertinent comments as the lesson was being played out was mutually beneficial as both the student takes note of feedback, but equally, supervising teacher is encouraged to consider just-in-time feedback but also observations that can impact on future lessons too.

Consistent with the findings of Rich and Hannafin (2009), supervising and advisors did not need to rely on or report only what they remembered from the lesson. They could re-watch and analyse the segments multiple and did not need to make detailed notes during the lesson for fear of potentially missing important lesson moments.

> I feel it is more effective than a post class feedback session as this allows further viewing and critique by both the education student and the supervising teacher. This also allows for both the education student and superior to view multiple elements of the lesson to provide additional feedback in regards to classroom practice.

Reflective Practice

The majority of participants commented favourably on the role of the video reflection process in supporting the development of pre-service teachers' reflective practice. One pre-service teacher commented that "annotating the video meant that I could reflect on my practice and improve" while another mentioned that "the annotations required me to really critique my lesson and undertake a proper reflection, which I am not sure if I would have done otherwise". A common response from pre-service teachers was that they were able to reflect on and address issues based on actual information, rather than "feelings" they had about the lesson in a more objective manner.

> It allowed me to go back and analyse how I'd taught my lessons and how the students were responding. In a calmer environment at home I could stop and pause on parts of the lessons and reflect.

One pre-service teacher described how she was able to see exactly what was needed in terms of classroom management, where lines of questioning did/did not work and to address these issues intelligently rather than emotionally. Another pre-service teacher wrote that reflecting on her videos gave her confidence in situations where she previously thought she had explained something poorly; watching the video helped her realise that her classroom practice was better than she had originally thought. Hence the present study supports the finding of Kleinknecht and Gröschner (2016) that video can enable pre-service teachers to adopt a more balanced view of their practice.

Viewing the videos allowed more focussed reflections from pre-service teachers because "it is much harder to reflect on your own practice from memory or your supervisor's notes than watching recordings". As reported by van Es and Sherin (2002), taking the time to watch the video provided a space for review and reflection before planning the next lesson so it "enables me to go back and reflect on my lesson rather than just moving on". Reflection was also seen not only as identifying aspects of practice where improvements could be made, but also that it "taught me the process of undertaking the analysis and then putting it into action". The process of annotating the video excerpts was seen as an essential element of the reflection process because, as one pre-service teacher noted, it "required me to really critique my lesson and undertake a proper reflection, which I am not sure if I would have done otherwise". Another pre-service teacher described annotating the videos as "undertaking proper reflective practice" and another observed that "annotating the video meant that I could reflect on my practice and improve".

Supervising teachers generally regarded the video footage as a "great reflection tool" for pre-service teachers because it allowed the pre-service teachers to "more accurately reflect on and deconstruct the lesson". One of the university advisors noted that the short video excerpts afforded an opportunity for a "micro-analysis" of a portion of the lesson which could serve as the basis for specific reflections and then be used to make "generalisations about the overall teaching practice". Supervising teachers also commented on how they felt the video reflection process assisted their pre-service teacher to advance, as the following example illustrates.

> My student was able to very accurately identify her relative strengths and weaknesses, notice things that she had not noticed during the lesson, and make very good summations on what she needed to change in the next lesson.

It is not possible to say for certain that these changes were a direct result of the video reflection process but it is encouraging to note that comments like the one above were expressed by all but two of the supervising teachers involved in the study.

Triad Communication

Participants generally found that communication among the triad members via the videos was useful and, as a supervising teacher documented "a genuine conversation amongst the three voices could be conducted". A university advisor commented that "different points of view could be canvassed" while another noted how "some things observed by one were not necessarily picked up by another" so the combined feedback from both supervisors was more comprehensive. A classroom teacher also commented on the collaborative nature of the triad communication:

> The collaborative element of the video was extremely meaningful. The fact that the student, university advisor and school supervisor could all comment, contribute and make suggestions was incredibly useful and created a feeling of "collaboration" rather than "assessment".

These comments suggest that a 'teaching cycle' similar to the kind reported by Gelfuso and Dennis (2014) can occur remotely via video with some success.

A key feature of the video reflection process was the role taken by the university advisor. Instead of the usual practice of visiting the school once to observe a lesson and meet in person with the supervising teacher and the pre-service teacher, in this project the university advisor commented on the four video excerpts via the online platform. Advantages of the new approach were that it "took less time than visiting the school" (university advisor) and "allows for multiple lessons to be viewed and a variety of outcomes to be assessed" (supervising teacher). The ability to view multiple lessons also allowed the university advisor to observe and comment on the development of the pre-service teacher's practice over time, which they could not do after watching a single lesson. However, many participants felt that the lack of personal contact from the university advisor was detrimental because "in five minutes you cannot properly assess the progress" (supervising teacher) and "you will say more verbally – once it is written down there is a more formal approach" (supervising teacher). Also, being remote from the school made it more difficult for the university advisor as "you don't really understand the whole context unless the student adds an explanation". Also, as noted by a university advisor, the view of the classroom through the camera does not allow for a full appreciation of what is occurring in the lesson:

> Because the camera is fixed and independent, it tends to show only the teacher and in most (but not all) situations is centred on his or her teaching. It does not allow for observation of students in response to the teacher or give the viewer a sense of the overall activity.

The triads operated with varying degrees of success. In some, the communication channels were less effective; there were infrequent postings and sometimes annotations received no response. Some supervising teachers felt that they had little say in their involvement in the project or preferred not to change their usual practice of providing written and oral feedback. At times, there were technological problems which resulted in some pre-service teachers feeling disengaged, stressed, and overwhelmed by the process. These pre-service teachers and their supervising teachers felt that they were dedicating too much time to videoing rather than lesson planning or classroom teaching. The success of the triad was often dependent on the willingness of the team members to do the work. As one supervising teacher commented, "While it was a slight extra burden on my time, the value of the reflection was more than worth it".

Conclusion

The study has shown some benefits in the video process for self-reflection and feedback during professional experience. The process encouraged professional dialogue within triads and was seen as largely beneficial to pre-service teachers' professional growth. These benefits were maximised if all participants understood the aims and requirements of the project and the technology functioned properly.

The results need to be interpreted in light of some limitations of the study. Since an experimental design was not used and there was no control group it is not possible to say for certain that the gains reported in pre-service teachers' reflective practice might not have occurred without the video process. Also, the pre-service teachers who participated in the study were all volunteers so it is not possible to determine whether similar results might be obtained if the process was scaled up and made mandatory across a teacher education program. The relatively short duration of the study over four weeks might not have allowed sufficient time for participants to adjust to the video process. Also, the lack of direction about how to undertake self-reflection and provide feedback to encourage deeper levels of reflection proved problematic. Participants needed more guidance on how to reflect and provide feedback and there needed to be protocols in place to ensure all participants were fully aware of the project aims and the importance of timely feedback.

Despite these limitations, the study identified some important affordances of the video reflection process, particularly the use of brief excerpts with time-stamped comments that can target specific aspects of teaching through a cycle of reflecting, annotating and receiving feedback as a source to guide future teaching practice.

References

Alger, C. (2006). 'What went well, what didn't go so well': Growth of reflection in pre-service teachers. *Reflective Practice, 7*(3), 287–301.

Cavanagh, M., & Prescott, A. (2010). The growth of reflective practice among three beginning secondary mathematics teachers. *Asia-Pacific Journal of Teacher Education, 38*(2), 147–159.

Chung, H. Q., & van Es, E. A. (2014). Pre-service teachers' use of tools to systematically analyze teaching and learning, *Teachers and Teaching, 20*(2), 113–135.

Coffey, A. M. (2014). Using video to develop skills in reflection in teacher education students. *Australian Journal of Teacher Education, 39*(9), 86–97.

Crichton, H., & Valdera-Gil, F. (2015). Student teachers' perceptions of feedback as an aid to reflection for developing classroom practice. *European Journal of Teacher Education, 38*(4), 512–524.

Davis, E. A. (2006). Characterizing productive reflection among preservice elementary teachers: Seeing what matters. *Teaching and Teacher Education, 22*(3), 281–301.

Danielowich, R. M. (2014). Shifting the reflective focus: Encouraging student teacher learning in video-framed and peer-sharing contexts. *Teachers and Teaching, 20*(3), 264–288.

Dewey, J. (1933). *How we think.* Buffalo, NY: Free Press.

Elo, S., & Kyngas, H. (2008). The qualitative content analysis. *Journal of Advanced Nursing Research Methodology, 62*(1), 107–115.

Gelfuso, A., & Dennis, D. V. (2014). Getting reflection off the page: The challenges of developing support structures for pre-service teacher reflection. *Teaching and Teacher Education, 38*, 1–11.

Hennissen, P., Beckers, H., & Moerkerke, G. (2017). Linking practice to theory in teacher education: A growth in cognitive structures. *Teaching and Teacher Education, 63*, 314–325.

Jacobs, V. R., Lamb, L. C., & Philipp, R. A. (2010). Professional noticing of children's mathematical thinking. *Journal for Research in Mathematics Education, 41*(2), 169–202.

Kleinknecht, M., & Gröschner, A. (2016). Fostering preservice teachers' noticing with structured video feedback: Results of an online- and video-based intervention study. *Teaching and Teacher Education, 59*, 45–56.

Kong, S., Shroff, R. H., & Hung, H. (2009). A web enabled video system for self-reflection by student teachers using a guiding framework. *Australasian Journal of Educational Technology, 25*(4), 544–558.

Lane, R., McMaster, H., Adnum, J., & Cavanagh, M. (2014). Quality reflective practice in teacher education: A journey towards shared understanding. *Reflective Practice, 15*(4), 481–494.

Levin, D. M., Hammer, D., & Coffey, J. E. (2009). Novice teachers' attention to student thinking. *Journal of Teacher Education, 60*(2), 142–154.

Loughran, J. J. (2002). Effective reflective practice: In search of meaning in learning about teaching. *Journal of Teacher Education, 53*(1), 33–43.

Masats, D., & Dooly, M. (2011). Rethinking the use of video in teacher education: A holistic approach. *Teaching and Teacher Education, 27*, 1151–1162.

Meierdirk, C. (2017). Reflections of the student teacher. *Reflective Practice, 18*(1), 23–41.

Rich, P., & Hannafin, M. J. (2009). Video annotation tools: Technologies to scaffold, structure, and transform teacher reflection. *Journal of Teacher Education, 60*(1), 52–67.

Rodgers, C. R. (2002). Defining reflection: Another look at John Dewey and reflective thinking. *Teachers College Record, 104*(4), 842–866.

Schön, D. A. (1983). *The reflective practitioner: How professionals think in action.* London: Temple-Smith.

Sellars, M. (2012). Teachers and change: The role of reflective practice. *Procedia – Social and Behavioral Sciences, 55*(5), 461–469.

Sherin, M. G., Russ, R. S., & Colestock, A. A. (2011). Accessing mathematics teachers' in-the-moment noticing. In M. G. Sherin, V. R. Jacobs, & R. A. Philipp (Eds.), *Mathematics teacher noticing* (pp. 79–94). New York, NY: Routledge.

Spitzer, S. M., Phelps, C. M., Beyers, J. E., Johnson, D. Y., & Sieminski, E. M. (2011). Developing prospective elementary teachers' abilities to identify evidence of student mathematical achievement. *Journal of Mathematics Teacher Education, 14*(1), 67–87.

Srivasta, P. (2009). A practical iterative framework for qualitative analysis. *International Journal of Qualitative Methods, 8*(1), 76–84.

Stenberg, K., Rajala, A., & Hilppo, R. (2016). Fostering theory–practice reflection in teaching practicums. *Asia-Pacific Journal of Teacher Education, 44*(5), 470–485.

van Es, E. A., & Sherin, M. G. (2002). Learning to notice: Scaffolding new teachers' interpretations of classroom interactions. *Journal of Technology and Teacher Education, 10*(4), 571–596.

van Es, E. A., Tunney, J., Goldsmith, L. T., & Seago, N. (2014). A framework for the facilitation of teachers' analysis of video. *Journal of Teacher Education, 65*(4), 340–356.

Ward, J. R., & McCotter, S. S. (2004). Reflection as a visible outcome for pre-service teachers. *Teaching and Teacher Education, 20,* 243–257.

Yerrick, R., Ross, D., & Molebash, P. (2005). Too close for comfort: Real-time science teaching reflections via digital video editing. *Journal of Science Teacher Education, 16*(4), 351–375.

Yost, D. S., Sentner, S. M., & Forlenza-Bailey, A. (2000). An examination of the construct of critical reflection: Implications for teacher education programming in the 21st century. *Journal of Teacher Education, 51*(1), 39–49.

CHAPTER 15

Storytelling and Living Praxis in the Pre-Service Teacher Classroom

Brian Mundy

Abstract

At Victoria University in Melbourne many years have been spent developing a praxis model of education. Under this model praxis has been defined as ethical action for the public good. For the author praxis is focused around building theory from practice, to improve outcomes for both teachers and students. The author's personal educational theory on praxis has evolved into a living praxis pedagogy and model. In this model, the educator and pre-service teacher (PST) build upon initial understandings, evaluate progress, reflect and act in an ongoing reflexive process. In the Tertiary classroom this often manifests itself through the action of storytelling. This chapter will explore the relationship between stories and living praxis and suggest a process of narrative inquiry that can be used in the Tertiary classroom. Stories from placement/practicum have long been used in teacher education classes. Diagrams will be used to present this process and how it can be understood. This chapter will describe how these stories can evolve into understandings and personal theories of practice. It will explore the narrative inquiry process of live-tell-retell-relive and unpack how this can be used in the classroom to help scaffold PST theorising. It will outline the collaborative processes that occur in the classroom, the roles of the teacher educator, the individual PST and of other PSTs. The chapter will use data from PSTs, teacher evaluations and teacher observations to provide evidence of the success of the approach undertaken.

Keywords

praxis – storytelling – narrative inquiry – pre-service teacher theorizing – living theories

Introduction

In 2014 I was awarded a citation by the Australian Office of Learning and Teaching for making an outstanding contribution to student learning. Since then I have spent time reflecting on my practice as a teacher educator to identify why PSTs respond positively to my teaching. This chapter continues to explore the key factors I identified in Figure 15.1 in *Connecting theory and practice in the pre-service teacher classroom in Teaching for Tomorrow Today* (edited by Garbett & Ovens, 2015) that built this positive response from PSTs (Mundy, 2015). In particular it focuses on the role stories have played in the classroom to engage students, connect practice to theory and provide authenticity.

During this reflective process I have also drawn upon my 30 years of secondary and tertiary teaching and the living educational theories published in my doctorate (Mundy, 2013) to better connect theory and practice.

A common challenge for teacher educators is to be able to effectively connect theory and practice and in particular to link the experiences of the PST in

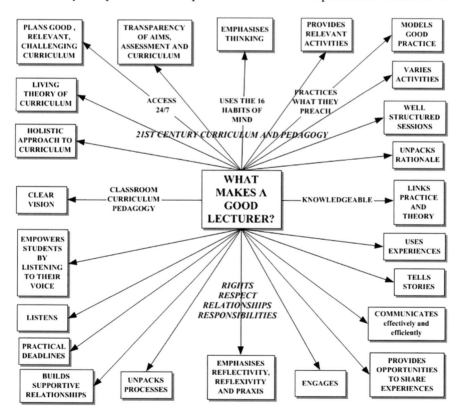

FIGURE 15.1   What makes a good lecturer (from Mundy, 2014)?

placement with those of the university setting. This chapter explores how this connection can be enhanced through the use of stories from placement and the teaching experiences of the lecturer. As a mentor for PSTs in school and indeed at the university, I frequently heard my PSTs state, that many of their university studies were disconnected from the real classroom. In 2010 I became a tertiary educator in order to develop and implement a curriculum and pedagogy that more closely links actual practice with the appropriate theory and that expresses an holistic, complex and constantly evolving approach, that can be more closely connected to the classrooms of 21st century PSTs. My teaching is predominantly in the second year program of the Bachelor of Education P-12 degree at Victoria University. In this program I teach core subjects called Engaging students, High Expectations and Teaching Primary Science. Both of these subjects either are or have been praxis inquiry subjects and as such are expected to be linked to placement experiences when possible and also to support PSTs as they prepare for or are experiencing a school placement. Within these subjects I use what I have termed a Living Praxis approach that will be detailed in this chapter.

Theoretical Framework

Aristotle initially conceived the concept of Praxis as thoughtful and practical doing. Whilst in 1970 Paulo Freire in his work Pedagogy of the Oppressed (1970, p. 176) defined praxis as 'reflection and action directed at the structures to be transformed".

These 2 shorter definitions have since been expanded by Carr and Kemmis (1986) as the concept has been further considered with action, truth, and respect being key concepts.

> We can now see the full quality of praxis. It is not simply action based on reflection. It is action which embodies ... commitment to human wellbeing and the search for truth, and respect for others. (Carr & Kemmis, 1986, p. 190)

At Victoria University in Melbourne many years have been spent developing our praxis model of education. Under this model Praxis has been defined as ethical action for the public good. Figure 15.2 summarises the key elements of the praxis model under the headings of research, pedagogy, underpinning values, assessment and curriculum. It shows how the praxis model has been embedded across our practices and behaviours at Victoria University.

STORYTELLING AND LIVING PRAXIS

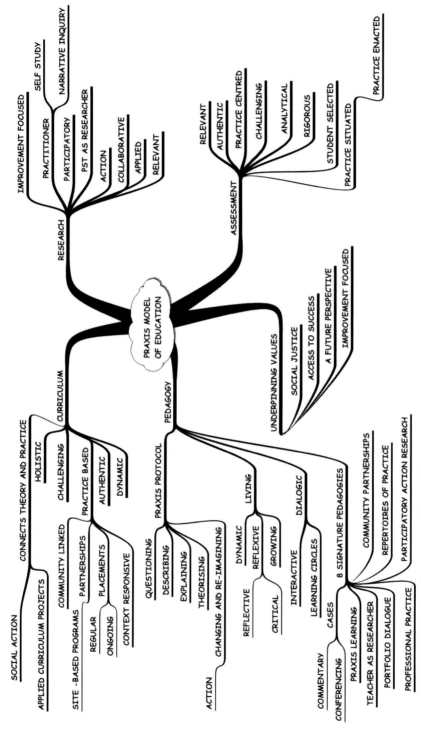

FIGURE 15.2 A praxis model of education at Victoria University

For the author praxis is focused around building theory from practice and then taking action to improve outcomes for teachers and students.

The author's personal educational theory on praxis has evolved into a living praxis pedagogy and model. In this model, the educator and PST build upon initial understandings, evaluate progress, reflect and then act in an on-going co-constructive, reflexive process to improve outcomes.

A Living Praxis Approach

This process and the reaction to student inputs and student voice can lead to what I have termed a 'living praxis' experience. My use of this term has developed from reading of the work on praxis and of Whitehead and McNiff (2006) on living theories of educational practice.

> These theories are living in the sense that they are theories of practice, generated from within our living practices, our current best thinking that incorporates yesterday into today and which holds tomorrow already within itself. (Whitehead & McNiff, 2006, p. 2)

In first year subjects, students have written praxis based case studies and in second year their first written assessment has been to complete a praxis inquiry. Each of these tasks are completed using the 5 stage praxis inquiry protocol developed at Victoria University. In the first stage (practice questioned) PSTs are asked to choose a topic or dilemma for their case or inquiry and then to identify between 3 and 6 questions covering at least one each of ontological, epistemological and technical types. In stage two (practice described) they describe the situation relevant to these questions using observations from their placements. They are identifying what they see. Stage three, (practice explained) is a summary explanation from the student, based on discussions with the mentor and the literature, regarding these observations. PSTs are answering the question why using other people's theory. The fourth stage (practice theorised) is personal theorising by the PST identifying and stating what they think is occurring and why. The fifth and final stage (practice changed) is when the PSTs re-imagine the classroom as they would like to see it. This is the action phase of praxis where PSTs are looking at change in the context, how to resolve the dilemma or how to improve outcomes for the students in the class and/or the teacher.

Praxis inquiry (learning) is one of the 8 signature pedagogies used throughout the education courses at Victoria University (Arnold et al., 2014). The full 8 signature pedagogies were listed on Figure 15.2 and include community partnerships, participatory action research, repertoires of practice, portfolio dialogue, praxis learning, cases and commentary, professional practice and teacher as researcher.

Initially an assessment tool, the praxis inquiry protocol is now used by the author, throughout the discussions that are held each week in learning circles. It is used in an informal and a flexible manner. In my classroom the learning circles are whole of class discussions, whereas in other classes the learning circles are frequently smaller simultaneously occurring groups. My whole group learning circles exist to support the co-construction of theory by PSTs and lecturer. This is what I term a living praxis approach. The discussion within the circle follows the 5 stages of praxis inquiry with contributions from both PSTs and the lecturer leading to changed perspectives, understanding or new personal living educational theory.

> PSTs are continuously questioning and up-dating their personal understandings and theories for classroom management, assessment or catering for individual differences etc. In this way they are continuously linking theory and practice, and developing their own personal living theories of educational practice. (Mundy, 2015, p. 401)

Methodology

This chapter is the outcome of an ongoing narrative inquiry (Clandinin, 2013) and self study (Samaras, 2011; Webster & Mertova, 2007) by the author. Reflections have developed and been recorded in written and visual journals that represent field data and then discussed with colleagues in praxis inquiry meetings and at college and conference presentations. These reflections and visuals are written as and when ideas are initiated by readings, discussions presentations or reflections.

Critical events have included these presentations and a narrative workshop attended by the author that was led by Jean Clandinin in September 2016. The theory and conclusions presented here developed through analysis of these events, discussions with colleagues and students. The author has been conducting self study and producing written and visual narratives of his thinking over many years. This was an important component of his PhD studies where journals were kept between 2003 and 2008. This has continued irregularly throughout his employment as an academic at Victoria University (Since 2010). In more recent years the narrative data has predominantly takes the form of

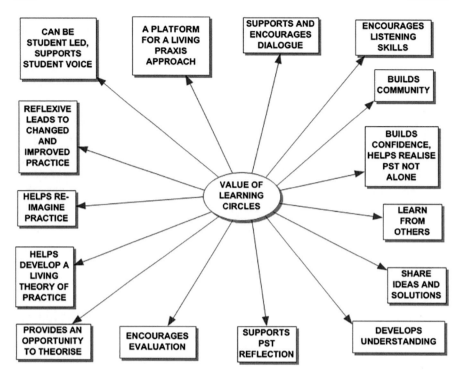

FIGURE 15.3 The value of learning circles

visuals such as those included in this chapter. Over the last 5 years more than 100 hundred figures have been produced representing thinking on aspects of teaching at Victoria University.

Validity of these processes and conclusions has been supported by teacher observations, PMIS (Positives, Minuses, Improvements/Interesting) and SET (anonymous Student Evaluation of Teacher) results. These provide evidence of success and constructive ideas for improvement. These reflections, updates to diagrams, SET surveys and PMIs are regularly collected. SET data for examples is released at the end of each semester and provides feedback on the success of the discussion process used in the classroom.

Learning Circles

As mentioned above the author makes use of learning circles to support the process of living praxis and the growth of living educational theories. The value of these learning circles is summarised in Figure 15.3.

The process enables PSTs to learn from each other, develop reflexivity and build confidence. It is frequently PST initiated and hence supports student voice. It is based around dialogue, each student has the opportunity to speak

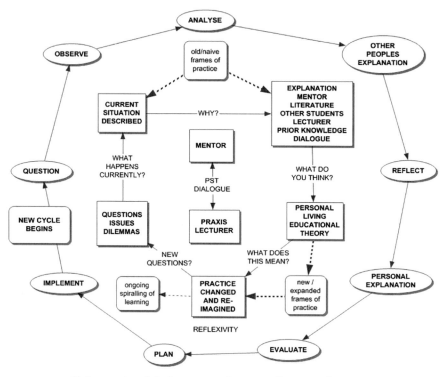

FIGURE 15.4   Living praxis and the learning circle process (from Mundy, 2015)

and raise issues, share observations, ask questions, provide an input and also very importantly encourages PSTs to listen to each other. The circles provide a platform for the living praxis approach. Student confidence is built up as they realise that other students have the same questions, doubts and concerns. As they listen to each other they also hear ideas, theories, strategies and solutions that they can draw upon and apply in their own placement contexts. Their own understandings of teaching, students and schools grows in this environment. During this process, as they voice their own ideas and listen to those of other students they are engaging in a reflective process that may eventually lead to action. Improving their skills at reflection develops over time into an increasingly reflexive approach as they start to re-imagine and improve classroom practice. This on-going interactive process helps develop each students' individual living theory of practice.

Figure 15.4 diagrammatically summarises the relationship between Living Praxis and Learning Circles.

At the centre of Figure 15.4 is dialogue. Dialogue occurs between PSTs, between individual PSTs and their mentor and between PSTs and the university lecturer. This dialogue takes place both in the university classroom and on placements before, during and after classes observed or conducted by the PST. They are usually separate from each other but on rare occasions such as when on-site programs occur there may be 3-way dialogues incuding the PST, mentor and university lecturer at the same time. The dialogue occurring between the university lecturer and the PST is critical to this process. This is why the author chooses to use whole group discussions rather than smaller ones for this process. This allows them to learn from each other as PST peers may also contribute to the process of dialogue providing ideas, comments and solutions as issues are discussed.

Surrounding this dialogue process is the living praxis cycle based on the praxis inquiry protocol. This protocol has 5 distinct stages that will be unpacked in even more detail later in the chapter. In essence the 5 stages include questioning practice, describing practice, explaining practice, theorising practice and re-imagining or changing practice. Key questions for each stage have also been identified in the diagram. I describe the protocol as a cycle as after stage 5 there is always the potential for new questions and thus an on-going spiralling of learning may occur. Around the outside of the praxis cycle are the key elements recognisable within an action research process. I believe this approach fits well alongside a teacher (in this case the PST) as researcher model (one of the signature pedagogies) as the processes being utilised by the PST align well with the action research process. During the course of the process PST frames of reference develop and expand, with increased understanding, and they move from a naïve frame to an ever more complicated and complex one.

Living praxis is a process that leads to the continuing refinement of personal theory. It is an ongoing, cyclical, action learning process. It is also a lifelong learning process as the PST/teacher up-dates their understanding, theory and practice in this reflexive manner.

> Your theory is created from within your work and represents your present best thinking. It is always developing because you are always in the process of development. Your theory is not static; it is living, part of your life. It is your own living theory. (Whitehead, 1989, 1993)

Figure 15.5 shows the process during a class when living theory is developing. It illustrates the roles played by the classroom lecturer and other students in helping to develop the living theory for an individual. It shows the distinctive stages of discussion that occur as the praxis protocol is being used to support the development of PST individual/personal theory and to assist the PST to re-imagine and change practice to improve outcomes for school students and the teacher in their classroom. It suggests stages of the process that are

STORYTELLING AND LIVING PRAXIS 291

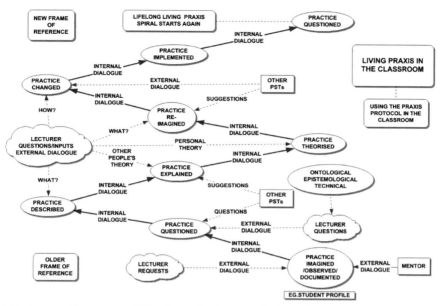

FIGURE 15.5   The process of living theory development during a class

metacognitive, when internal dialogue is occurring (when the PST is reflecting, developing, considering, evaluating ideas) and also when external dialogue between individuals, peers and the lecturer are occurring. In this way Figure 15.5 is attempting to unpack the intersubjective dialogue that is occurring within the classroom. The figure also shows how the PST moves from an old position of understanding to a newer one which can change the frame of reference of the PST. This process is also seen as one that should occur throughout the career of a teacher as they continuously develop and refine their own living educational theories of practice as they move from being a PST to a practicing teacher in their own classrooms. This is thus identified as a lifelong living praxis spiral reflecting connections back to action research cycles.

This process best occurs when students are in the midst of placement. At Victoria University we have usually had students complete 12 Tuesdays across the year and around their 3 weeks of block placements. These Tuesdays have as their major focus an Applied Curriculum Project however PSTs also have time to undertake classroom observations, collect data for discussions or complete some small group or whole class teaching. These activities provide a rich source of data for our discussions and allow students to reflect on their observations and start the process of developing their living theory. Ideally, they can use this theorizing to re-imagine their practices in the following blocks or semesters. This process clearly reflects my definition of praxis whereby students are building their personal living theories from practice and in particular placement observations and developing understandings that lead to improved outcomes for the PSTs themselves and the students in their classrooms.

An important element of my classroom practice is that of listening to student voice (Mitra, 2003) and the empowering of PSTs. My two praxis classes begin with the opportunity for the PSTs to share their preparations for placement or their recent placement experiences including their questions, concerns, challenges, issues, and successes. (Mundy, 2015, p. 401) This is very important part of the class as it is a time to connect theory and practice and discuss what concerns our PSTs. The Bachelor of Education degree involves a high degree of placement experience. In second year, PSTs attend their primary school placement sites for up to 14 Tuesdays alongside 3 weeks of block placement. These Tuesday placement days involve the PSTs in completing a variety of tasks. A priority on the Tuesday is the collaborative Applied Curriculum Project (A.C.P). The ACP is typically a school decided project addressing a curriculum need or shortfall. Alongside this, PSTs also have the opportunity to conduct focused observations of mentors and their pedagogy, attend a variety of meetings (staff, team, planning, curriculum etc.), get to know the grade they are teaching and eventually participate in some 1:1, small group and whole class teaching. Hence the first phase of our praxis inquiry classes begins with an opportunity to de-brief on placement, share questions, identify and raise issues and celebrate successes. Listening to students is an important skill for young teachers to develop and that needs to be modelled in our university classes. This phase may last up to 30 minutes.

The second opportunity for student input is the sharing of experiences, observations and reflections on a weekly topic or theme. PSTs will bring along their observations, data sheets, student profiles, artefacts they have collected and their questions. This phase of the class can be quite extensive and consequently formal lecture components of the class may slide later into the session. Indeed this may become part of a flipped curriculum process wherein the lectures are viewed after the class, with the whole class or learning circle discussion based on the student observations and data, taking up the majority of class time.

Results

As a result of these processes a number of outcomes have been observed. These include:

- Development and refining of PST personal living educational theory. Students often speak of their increased understanding of theory and their own personal theory is stated within formal praxis inquiries based assessments.
- Increased engagement and participation in class leading to positive evaluations. The SET and PMI data provides much rich evidence of increased engagement through student comments and responses to the questions. The expectation of participation is very high and reinforced at the start of a unit and each week.
- Development of a community of learners. Learning circle processes support the development of this community as responses to questions and issues are developed and shared by peers and the lecturer.
- Improved connections occurring between lived experience and theory. The stories told come direct from placement. The discussions of these stories allow and support the development of theory from the lived experiences of the PSTs and the lecturer.
- PSTs leaving the class with strategies and ideas to improve future practice. PSTs have the opportunity to share a story each week and the lecturer and peers provide strategies to trial in their future classrooms. Again this supports the development of theory from practice.
- PSTs developing reflexive practice. An emphasis in the classroom is placed on students reflecting on practice to improve outcomes hence they take action moving from reflectivity to reflexivity.
- PSTs feeling more empowered. PSTs in the classroom have a clear voice. This is an opportunity to ask questions, raise issues and address concerns.
- Increased authenticity of discussion and experience. The discussion within the classroom addresses authentic concerns as the students are going into placement classrooms and observing/living situations and then getting the opportunity to address them very quickly. They often go on to trial a strategy the very next week and then report back on its effectiveness or not.
- Positive interactions and relationships between PSTs and lecturers. The supportive quality of the discussions has led to positive relationships between the lecturer and PSTs. This reflects in the enjoyable nature of the classes and the positive outcomes shown by the SETs and PMIs.

Formal Student feedback about the processes in the classroom has also been consistently positive. The SETs (Student Evaluation of Teachers surveys) are completed at the end of each unit and provide quantitative and qualitative feedback. Examples of the feedback from students are shown in Table 15.1 and comments below.

TABLE 15.1 Student evaluation results

% Agree for survey questions	VU	Conditions SA 4/20	Conditions F 19/50
Overall teaching quality satisfaction	82.2	100	100
Good at explaining things	82.0	100	100
Effort to understand student difficulties	79.1	100	100
Helpful feedback	76.9	100	100
Makes the subject interesting	78.0	100	100
Motivated the student to do their best	74.2	100	95

SET Semester 2 2015, SA = St Albans campus VU, F = Footscray campus VU

SET Comments (Semester 2, 2015)

- "Fantastic modelling of teaching. I like how you not only encouraged us to speak within the class, but also gave time for each person's answer".
- "He allowed us to have a say in the class, with plenty of opportunity to share our ideas and feelings regarding placement or the topic being discussed in class".
- "I loved that the classes were discussion based and he made them interesting and inclusive. Every idea was built upon and the environment was comfortable and you felt like you could share your opinion".

Another method of identifying the validity of my work was through the observations of a visiting lecturer. This showed the increased engagement developed through the process being used, the sense of community being fostered and also the high participation rate due to the expectations that had been created. This came about after presenting at the ATEA conference in 2016 when a member of the audience asked if they could attend and observe the processes I had described within the class. This provided me with additional feedback on the quality of interactions occurring. See quote below.

> Thank you again for having me in your tutorial. I found the experience to be very valuable. What I liked the most about the tutorial was the framework of expectations that you have set up – this clarified the input of each student in the class and maintained everyone's engagement ... I

liked the way you brought every student in and the sense that I got overall was that students were each valuing and respecting each other and themselves, and were invested in learning, in large part through sharing their experiences. That was wonderful to see, so inspiring. (Visiting lecturer, October 2016)

Implications/Discussion

Narratives, Narrative Inquiry and Living Praxis

My classroom is full of stories. Stories of practicum are told by PSTs, stories of past experiences are told by myself. As a narrative researcher I often tell stories of my experiences in school, completing my studies or indeed re-tell stories from other PSTs in previous classes. Stories from the recent experiences are shared followed by observations and stories related to the weekly theme such as assessment, classroom management or differentiation. It is particularly around and through these stories that the living praxis process described above is threaded. These stories are often told at the beginning of classes. Each student is asked to reflect on the theme such as differentiation. In this example they are asked to construct short profiles of students in their classes with different needs. After sharing the profile the PST is asked to describe how the student's needs are catered for by the classroom teacher. We then share other possibilities across the group. I am challenging the PSTs to identify how they can improve outcomes for the student. They or I share pieces of theory and other authors ideas before I return to the original presenting PST and ask them to consider what they have done and what they would change after our classroom dialogue. It is always a rich discussion that provides all students with the possibility to share ideas and better understand similar situations in their own or future classes. This process is repeated with a number of different examples of different types of individual differences, special needs or behavioral issues. It is after this part of the session that I turn back to my tutorial presentation and present some of the key theory and literature on differentiation that has not already arisen. Students leave the session with an increased understanding of why, how and what to differentiate. There is a strong element of authenticity to these discussions as we are starting our discussions with real students cases with aspects that are challenging for the PSTs and their mentors. They leave the discussion with practical ideas to trial and implement.

The next couple of diagrams illustrate how stories and narrative inquiry fit into this living praxis approach. The diagrams show the complexity of the process as action learning, praxis inquiry and narrative inquiry processes are

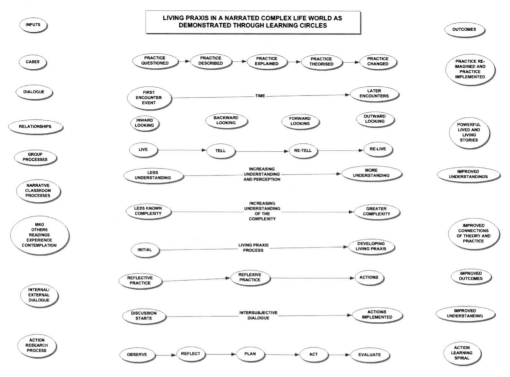

FIGURE 15.6   Living praxis in a narrated complex classroom

blended together within learning circles in the development of living educational theory and living praxis. Figure 15.6 uses a simplified systems approach and identifies the range of inputs, processes and activities that occur within the learning circle. This reflects the complex nature of the dialogue.

There are a range of potential inputs into these narratives as listed in Figure 15.6. Students may have writeen a formal case student of an incident or situation. Alternatively they may have made notes or observations for a student profile. They also sometimes describe cases that have not been written up. All of these situations provide data for desciption and analysis. The PSt may also have had previous discussions with the mentor and wish to further unpack the ideas that had been discussed. The relationships within the university tutorial group, between the students, with the lecturer and indeed with the mentor may also provide an input into the environment of trust, empathy and constructivist learning that needs to be developed. The protocols and processes employed by the university lecturer are also important here in constructing an environment that is comfortable for students to share their successes, issues, failures, concerns and questions. Significant inputs into this classroom process are the more knowledgeable others existing in the room. The lecturer, other students, authors of key readings represent important voices to learn from and with in a constructivist learning environment. The internal and external dialogue also represent key inputs into the discussion. Students also have a right to be able to pass or contribute to the discussion however, the right to pass must not be abused and I would normally expect the PST to contribute to the next round of discussion after utilising this right to pass once. It is critical to set up an environment where students feel safe and able to make suggestions and take risks without being censored or feeling unsafe. In estanblishing this type of learning environment I am also attempting to model processes that PSTs can also utilise as they set up their own discussion based classrooms in the future.

The processes occurring in this environment are complicated and many. As the 5 stages of the praxis inquiry process are completed and indeed frequently being repeated with each individual case or example many other processes are taking place. There is the live, tell, re-tell and re-live process that Clandinin (2013) describes and which will be expanded upon in the next diagram. There is a process of increasing understanding of the individual case as perceptions and dialogue occurs. Frequently this growth of understanding is accompanied by an awareness of the increasing complexity of classroom situations. Classrooms with 25 students are incredibly complex dynamic systems as these students interact with each other. Another key process is the action learning cycle that is occurring throughout the discussions. Students are returning to classes where they will observing, reflecting, planning, acting and then evaluating what they hear in their university classrooms and the initial stages of this will be occurring during the in-class discussions.

The outputs as described in Figure 15.6 include ideas for new practices that can be implemented and classrooms that may be re-imagined. I constantly stress the importance of imagining the type of classroom you would like to have. A second outcome is the story itself hopefully one that leads to an empowered student and one that can be told again. Increased understandings and improved connections between theory and practice are also key outcomes of the actual process of story telling. Reflexivity and the accompanying actions are also important outcomes as the PST emerges from the classroom as a reflexive practitioner having absorbed the living praxis ethos of seeking to improve outcomes for their students and themselves through better connections between theory and practice as well as practical ideas to trial and implement.

Figure 15.7 presents the links between the praxis inquiry and the phases of storytelling that Clandinin (2013) describes. This figure is more of a flow chart suggesting the various processes that occur from the lived, to the tell, the retell and finally the relive stage.

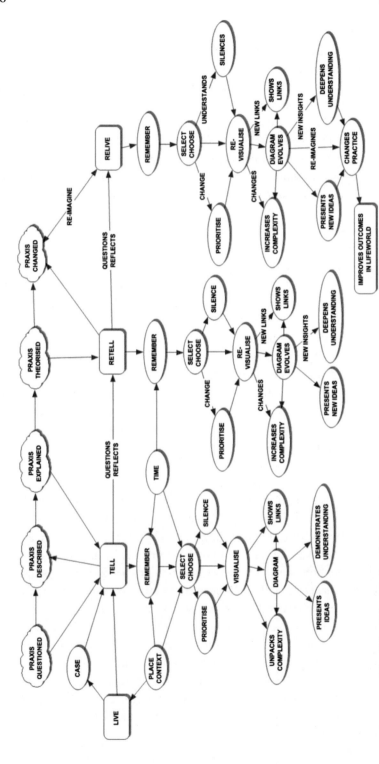

FIGURE 15.7 Visualising living praxis and the narrative

> The stories lived and told in a narrative inquiry relationship are always a co-composition, an intentional co-composition. The stories are co-composed in the spaces between us as inquirers and participants. (Clandinin, 2013, p. 24)

The stories told by PSTs and the teacher academic in the classroom have been lived by an individual in a particular context, they are then told to the group and as this occurs understandings develop for all participants in the learning circle.

All stories of practice start with the actual lived experience. What is shared by the storyteller, represents one understanding of the events from one particular perspective, and in that specific context. This represents the describe phase of praxis inquiry. As the story is related in the classroom its storyline depends on the memory of the storyteller, their personal observations and their current understandings. As we tell stories we choose what to relate and in so doing select priorities and leave some elements out. These elements are silenced by lack of observation, understandings or choice. We tend to visualise the story, with our current understandings of the complexity incorporated. Time passing and further re-telling may add to our understanding, increase the complexity of our understanding and add further dimensions.

Questions are a key element of the living praxis process that can occur during storytelling and may be asked at any time. Questions may be asked to launch the discussion, during the storytelling or once it has finished. Questions may be asked to initiate discussion, clarify an element in the story or to add depth to the description and analysis. Questions are asked by the teacher educator, by the individual, or other PSTs leading to discussions of explanations (praxis explained). New understandings and personal theories may develop as these questions are considered and answers explored (praxis theorized). These may be shared further within the group or with the mentor back at the school when a re-telling process occurs.

Finally, after further discussion, changes may be identified and implemented (praxis changed) and the re-living process may occur. During this process students are again choosing to remember key elements with their new understandings, they are re-visualising their practice, developing new diagrams of their understandings. Most importantly they are taking action and living in their newly re-imagined classrooms with their own theories being implemented and changes to improve practice enacted. Improved outcomes hopefully emerging in their individual lifeworld.

For the teacher academic they too will follow this process. The re-telling process is very important for the teacher academic in particular. For them the lived stage may have occurred many years ago and it is often in the re-tell and re-live stages that new understandings may still develop. Indeed stories may be told and relived many times and understandings refined as a result. New insights having been gained due to inputs from students and the individual's own reading, growth and internal dialogue over time.

Finally, Table 15.2 provides a detailed re-visiting of the praxis inquiry protocol that we have been using at Victoria University for many years. For some time I used this protocol essentially as an assessment instrument however, in recent years as more and more stories have been told, and I have better understood the complexities of the classroom dialogue occurring, I have realized that the protocol is also very much a teaching tool. It is a tool that can be used to unpack and de-construct PST narratives leading to the personal theorizing of students. The table lists the 5 important stages of the protocol from questioning through to re-imagining practice and against each of these stages it suggests some activities or key questions to be considered. These questions may be posed by the lecturer who understands the process or indeed by other students. They can be used to guide the discussion and indeed they can also support the new lecturer in understanding the processes occurring and support discussion. Relevant concepts and ideas are also included within the table to increase the depth of discussion. The first column of the table also summarises some of the important concepts that are inherent in this process.

Findings and Conclusions

For the students in his classes and the author himself there have been many positive outcomes from conducting this research and the process of writing this chapter. Student outcomes were summarized in the results section. For the author there has been

- an expanded understanding of his personal theory of living praxis
- an increased understanding of the role of storytelling in the PST classroom. Story telling in each of its phases contributes to understanding for both the student and the lecturer. Personal theories develop and eventually are implemented to improve outcomes.
- an improvement in teaching and learning practices as reflected in continuing positive results in formative assessments, PMIs and SETs conducted
- further development of my own personal living theories
- increased opportunities to share new learning and understanding
- excellent feedback and evaluations from PSTs as demonstrated by the evidence presented
- further opportunities to develop the thinking around narrative inquiry and praxis.

TABLE 15.2   The Praxis Inquiry Protocol and questions for its use as a teaching instrument (adapted from Mundy, 2018, p. 46)

	Practice	Activities – components – possibilities
eaching process – Rationale Dialogue and Collaboration Integrating and connecting theory and practice Linking praxis – and practice Living praxis process Teaching and learning moments Teaching for the possibility of being taught	Changing/ re-imagining	What is a good vision? How are you improving life? How is the new vision emancipatory? What values and virtues underpin this new vision? How are you developing a vision What would you change? What could you do differently in your own classroom? Imagine this situation in your classroom in 3 years, what would you do? What does it look, sound and feel like?
	Theorising	Understanding – learning from – being taught by – second knowing – who we are – how we are – is that what I desire? Personal theory – I believe, I think, I value What do YOU think? Inter-subjectivity – intra-subjectivity – developing your ideas – refining and exploring possibilities
	Explaining	Consciousness – complexity – sophisticated business – dialogue – uncertainty –truth/reality – responsibility – co-producers Why – Rationale – what do you think? – What do your peers think? Other people's ideas and theories – peers, mentors Introduction/Use of the relevant literature/theory
	Describing	Situated context – judgements in concrete situations – challenges – pragmatic reality – subjectivity What do you see? Authentic cases – Sharing and Discussion of artefacts from different classrooms Un-packing the situation/case – What? – When? – Where? – Who? – How?

(cont.)

TABLE 15.2 The Praxis Inquiry Protocol and questions for its use as a teaching instrument (adapted from Mundy, 2018, p. 46) (*cont.*)

Practice	Activities – components – possibilities
Questioning	How can we find space? – Teacher/school priorities – Interruptions – Challenges – Purpose Questions:- Ontological (experience, understanding and commitment) – Epistemological (knowledge and its application) – Technical (effective strategies and techniques) What do I wonder about? What are your current issues and questions from your classroom, the school, the system? What do I do well? What can I do better? How can I do better?

For teacher educators and other PSTs this chapter has described processes that can be used across teacher education classrooms that discuss placement experiences. It has outlined a way in which a community of learners can be established that respect the ideas of others and builds on them to improve outcomes for students, PSTs and teacher educators. It suggests a living praxis approach that could be used for both assessment and improving classroom dialogue. It provides guiding questions to support that process. The chapter has also started to unpack the specific processes involved in classroom dialogue.

This will now extend into investigating how successful processes, such as those described, can be maintained and improved, in blended and on-line classrooms and under a new 4 week intensive block model that is now being implemented at Victoria University. These present major challenges as we go forward with the changes in structure and increased use of technology expected in our tertiary classrooms.

References

Arnold, J., Burridge, P., Caccattolo, M., Cara, C., Edwards, T., Hooley, N., & Neal, G. (2014). *Researching the signature pedagogies of praxis teacher education*. Brisbane: AARE – NZARE.

Carr, W., & Kemmis, S. (1986). *Becoming critical: Education, knowledge and action research.* London: Falmer Press.

Clandinin, D. J. (2013). *Engaging in narrative inquiry.* Walnut, CA: Left Coast Press.

Freire, P. (1970). *Pedagogy of the oppressed.* Bloomsbury Academy.

Mitra, D. (2003). Student voice in school reform: Reframing student-teacher relationships. *McGill Journal of Education, 38*(2), 289–304.

Mundy, B. (2013). *The millennial school: A theoretical basis for curriculum design in a time of educational transgression* (Doctoral thesis). Melbourne University, Australia.

Mundy, B. (2015). *Connecting theory and practice in the pre-service teacher classroom in Teaching for tomorrow today* (D. Garbett & A. Ovens, Eds.). Auckland: ISATT Conference.

Mundy, B. (2018). Praxis learning – Living praxis – Living practice. *The Journal of Teaching, Learning and Society (JTLS), 1,* 40–49.

Samaras A. P. (2011). *Self-study teacher research improving your practice through collaborative inquiry.* Thousand Oaks, CA: Sage Publications.

Webster, L., & Mertova, P. (2007). *Using narrative inquiry as a research method.* New York, NY: Routledge.

Whitehead, J. (1989). Creating a living educational theory from questions of the kind, "How do I improve my practice?" *Cambridge Journal of Education, 19*(1), 42–52.

Whitehead, J. (1993). *The growth of educational knowledge: Creating your own living educational theories.* Bournemouth: Hyde.

Whitehead, J., & McNiff, J. (2006). *Action research and living theory.* Thousand Oaks, CA: Sage Publications.

CHAPTER 16

Pedagogy Students' Attitudes towards Collaborative Learning with Video Games: Considering Demographic Information and the Variety of Digital Resources

Marta Martín-del-Pozo, Verónica Basilotta Gómez-Pablos and Ana García-Valcárcel

Abstract

In modern society, people are surrounded by technology, which they use to communicate, inform, study, work and entertain. However, digital technologies can also be used to implement innovative educational practices. Video games are being increasingly incorporated into different educational levels and educational settings. However, the use of video games in educational settings is heavily dependent on educators' attitudes towards them. Therefore, in this chapter, we want to search for and research about the attitudes from a specific type of educators to discover their predisposition towards video games. In this regard, we analyse the attitudes of higher education students in the undergraduate Degree in Pedagogy at the University of Salamanca (Spain) towards one of the approaches to implementing video games in education: collaborative learning with video games. As the future graduates of this course will be working in various educational contexts, it is important to know their current attitudes towards the use of video games in education and, specifically, towards collaborative learning with video games. This study is an ex post facto study that uses a specially created attitude scale. The questionnaire contains questions about the students' demographics, the variety of digital resources they use and their frequency of playing video games. The results show that higher education students in pedagogy have positive attitudes towards collaborative learning with video games, suggesting that they are likely to implement innovative practices using video games in collaborative learning activities in the future. Furthermore, male students and students who play video games more frequently have better attitudes towards using video games in collaborative learning activities. In addition, those with smartphones at home have more positive attitudes than those without. Finally, students' ages and the variety of digital resources they use to play video games at home impact their attitudes towards collaborative learning with video games.

Keywords

higher education – pedagogy – video games – collaborative learning

Introduction

In modern society, people use technology every day and in all aspects of their lives, including education. Digital technologies are being increasingly incorporated into education because they allow educators to implement innovative practices in the classroom. One such digital technology is video games, which are being used as educational resources at different educational levels. There is increasing interest in the possibility of using video games to achieve educational objectives not only in formal contexts, but also in non-formal and informal contexts.

Video games can be used effectively for educational purposes and can promote learning outcomes (Martín & Martín, 2015). However, the successful implementation of technologies in educational settings depends on educators' attitudes, as well as technological infrastructure, support from other teachers and administration and sufficient teacher training. For this reason, it is important to examine educators', teachers' and future teachers' attitudes towards incorporating video games in the classroom.

In this chapter, we want to search for and research about the attitudes of a specific type of educators to discover their predisposition towards video games in education. In this regard, we analyse the attitudes of first-year higher education students studying for an undergraduate degree in pedagogy at the University of Salamanca (Spain). We seek to determine their current attitudes towards one methodology for using video games in education: the incorporation of collaborative learning using video games into their learning and future teaching. We also analyse the relationship between their attitudes and other variables: gender, age, variety of digital resources at home, variety of digital resources used to play games at home, presence of specific digital resources at home, use of specific digital resources to play games at home and frequency of playing video games for entertainment.

In that sense, the importance of the study is justified in several aspects. Firstly, taking into account that video games are useful resources for the classroom and a growing trend in the educational field, it is important to search and research the attitudes of educators towards them and, in this case, towards collaborative learning using video games. Having positive attitudes is the basis for building an appropriate training and promoting an efficient educational use of these digital resources in the future. Secondly, as we said previously, in this study we focus on the attitudes towards a specific methodology related to the use of video games in education, that is collaborative learning with video games. Thirdly, we are going to analyse educators' attitudes considering the variety of digital resources at home and the variety of digital resources used to play games. Then, if having a great variety of resources at home or using a great variety of resources favours a better attitude, governments and other institutions will have to provide these resources in the training of these professionals to help those who do not have. Finally, it is important to highlight that in this work we focus on the professional of pedagogy (specifically in their initial training), professionals who are rarely taken into account in educational research, above all about their opinions and attitudes towards new resources and methodologies, whether in their initial training or in-service.

Theoretical Framework

Video Games in Education
Video games are increasingly used for entertainment among not only children and young people, but also adults. In 2016, there were an estimated 2,515 million video game players in the world (ICO Partners & Newzoo, 2016). However, video games are also powerful educational tools. The possibility of using video games as educational resources has gained increasing attention in the field of educational technology and across the full spectrum of educational agents (teachers, students, educators and parents). Several authors (e.g. AEVI & GfK, 2011, 2012; Revuelta & Guerra, 2012; Simkova, 2014) have shown that video games can support conceptual learning, skill development, positive attitude improvement, competency learning, motivation, self-esteem, self-confidence and improved relationships among classmates and friends.

In the realm of video games, there are two main types of video games: games for entertainment (Meyer & Sørensen, 2009) and serious games. Games for entertainment are commonly known as video games: that is, they are called 'commercial games' or commercial-off-the-shelf (COTS) games, and their purpose is to entertain the player. By contrast, serious games are video games whose main purpose is not entertainment or enjoyment, but to send a message, provide an experience or teach content (Michael & Chen, 2006). The possible range of purposes for serious games is very wide, including educational, military, health, journalistic and conscientious objectives. In that sense, in this text we are going to focus on the general concept of video games as a digital media, that is to say, taking into account both serious games and games for entertainment.

According to Martín, Basilotta, and García-Valcárcel (2017), the existing literature on video games and education can be organised into different groups (we add some examples of literature about each group): (1) students create video games and learn something through the process of creation (e.g. Akcaoglu & Koehler, 2014; Chiazzese, Fulantelli, Pipitone, & Taibi, 2018; Li, 2010); (2) teachers, researchers and developers create serious games (e.g. educational games) to teach students through their use in education (Homer, Plass, Raffaele, Ober & Ali, 2018; Parong et al., 2017; Rooney, 2011); (3) games designed for entertainment are used in classroom settings (e.g. Barr, 2017; Jiménez-Porta & Diez-Martinez, 2018; Ye, Hsiao, & Sun, 2018); and (4) researchers analyse the educational possibilities of specific video games and educational proposals (e.g. Marín & Sampedro, 2015; Martín & Martín, 2015; Montero, Ruiz, & Diaz, 2010). Further, to systematise the knowledge and findings of different studies, the topic has attracted a growing body of systematic literature reviews (e.g. Ritzhaupt, Poling, Frey, & Johnson, 2014; Vlachopoulos & Makri, 2017), illustrating the relevance of video game use in modern educational research.

Video games can be used in education in different ways. In this text, we focus specifically on collaborative learning with video games: an educational approach described and exemplified in the work of Martín (2015). Martín et al. (2017) defined collaborative learning with video games as:

> ... the implementation of educational activities in which students work together in pairs or groups, sharing responsibilities, negotiating, discussing and contributing their ideas to achieve an objective (e.g. a project, a task, or to solve a problem) and the main resource of the activity is a video game. In other words, 'collaborative learning with video games' refers to the use of video games in collaborative learning activities, in which the collaboration between peers can occur inside the game, outside the game or both, depending on the activity or the methodological strategy used by the teacher. (p. 4)

Thus, the methodological approach of collaborative learning with video games combines the benefits of collaborative learning (e.g. the development of different skills, such as explaining ideas to others, listening carefully to others, helping others, taking part in dialogs constructively, making decisions in groups, etc.) with the educational benefits of using video games (any type of video game, whether they are games for entertainment or serious games) in education.

Professionals in Pedagogy

Professionals in pedagogy, or people who have a degree in pedagogy, are professionals related to the educational field. However, since the term 'pedagogue' (in Spanish, 'pedagogo') does not exist in all languages (Bellerate, 2009), it is important to explain the term and the profession more deeply.

According to Millan (1988), professionals in pedagogy are professionals who design, manage and apply educational interventions in different contexts from an applied science perspective to achieve maximum efficiency and effectiveness. Bellerate (2009) notes that this term is commonly used to refer to professionals engaged in theoretical–critical reflections on the nature of the pedagogical science of education (or 'pedagogy') and the factors and people that take part. The field of this profession is education, and professionals in pedagogy consider all aspects of the educational process. In fact, according to ANECA (2004), such educators conduct their work in two main areas: institutional education and education in other contexts. In terms of institutional education, these educators (1) teach, advise or guide students in personal, professional or scholarly issues; (2) design, develop and coordinate educational programmes; (3) design, develop and produce educational resources; (4) manage, coordinate and advise in educational centres; (5) research educational issues; (6) participate as educational experts in educational services; and (7) advise on educational programmes. On the other hand, ANECA (2004) has claimed that the most meaningful fields involving education in other contexts are the following: business, publishing, mass media and information and communication technologies (ICT), health, the environment, social services, public services management and sociocultural and socio-community fields. This wide range of fields enables professionals in pedagogy to hold various roles, including those of teachers, educators, coaches, eLearning development consultants or human resource managers.

As we can see, professionals in pedagogy can contribute work in different contexts to improve them from an educational perspective. However, to accomplish this, people interested in this area must receive appropriate training at the university level. We focus specifically on the Degree in Pedagogy (in Spanish, 'Grado en Pedagogía'): a higher education undergraduate degree offered by 22 Spanish universities.

One of these universities is the University of Salamanca, where our study is conducted, and it is stated that the degree is intended to train professionals in educational systems, institutions, contexts, resources and processes, as well as in the processes of personal, professional, social and cultural development that come together in an integrated way in individuals and groups over their lifetimes. Thus, the degree seeks to qualify professionals to take part in various educational plans, programmes and actions, considering their design, analysis, management, development, assessment and counselling. The professional fields covered by students of the Degree in Pedagogy are very wide, meaning that, after their studies, these students can work in variety of jobs.

Digital technology is a useful resource for all fields involving pedagogical educators because it can be used to manage syllabi for different subjects, enhance learning, improve workers' qualifications, promote skills, improve communication and assess skills. As previously discussed, video games are one type of technology that can be used in the educational field. For this reason, the specific competencies ANECA (2004) established for the undergraduate Degree in Pedagogy include some related to ICT:

– 'To assess educational resources, materials and training programmes aimed at different groups, levels and curricular areas" (including different types of educational resources such as visual, auditory, audiovisual and computer resources) (ANECA, 2004, p. 175).
– 'To coordinate the design, application and assessment of educational and training programmes through ICT (e-learning)" (ANECA, 2004, p. 177).
– 'To act as a consultant in the pedagogical use and curricular implementation of educational resources" (including different educational resources such as visual, auditory, audiovisual and computer resources) (ANECA, 2004, p. 179).

For students to develop these competencies in the Degree in Pedagogy, this content must be taught in different subjects, and, for example, the syllabus for this degree at the University of Salamanca includes the subjects 'Information and Communication Technologies in Education' (6 ECTS – European Credit Transfer and Accumulation System) and 'Teaching Materials Design and Assessment' (6 ECTS).

Thus, learning about ICT is important for students in the Degree in Pedagogy, and one ICT resource with potential for use in educational settings is video games. Students' attitudes towards ICT, including attitudes towards video games as an educational resource, can influence their training in this topic. For this reason, it is important to explore educators' attitudes towards the use of video games, as these attitudes can influence their support or lack thereof towards incorporating video games into their teaching.

Attitudes towards Video Games in Education

The notion of attitude can be understood as a predisposition to respond in a generally favourable or unfavourable way to an object, institution, person, event, situation or symbol, following the point of view of Messana (2009). In this regard, according to Tejedor and García-Valcárcel (2006), teachers' attitudes towards pedagogical innovations and ICT in the classroom are one of the main factors influencing their adoption and integration. In that sense, this fact can be applied to any type of teacher (e.g. secondary or higher education) or educator (people working in either pedagogy or social education).

With regard to our topic of video games in education, there is an increasing interest in educators' and teachers' attitudes towards video games in educational settings. That is to say, there is an increasing interest in their unfavourable or favourable predisposition towards the situation of applying video games in educational settings. For example, AEVI and GfK (2012) found that 79.2% of the teachers in their study sample had positive attitudes towards video games as an educational resource in primary education. Similarly, Noraddin and Kian (2014) researched university teachers' perceptions of video game use in educational practices at Malaysian universities, and the results showed that most teachers had positive attitudes towards video game use in their classroom. The interest in attitudes towards video games in education extends from in-service teachers and educators to pre-service teachers and educators: that is, higher education students in a university degree related to education. For instance, in a sample of pre-service teachers from different university programmes (early childhood, middle school, secondary education, special education and other programmes), Bensiger (2011) showed that pre-service teachers thought that video games enhanced learning and would be interested in implementing video games in their educational practices if they received the opportunity. Martín et al. (2017) found that pre-service primary school teachers showed positive attitudes towards the specific methodology of collaborative learning with video games.

However, educators' attitudes may be affected by different variables, such as gender, age, the variety of digital resources they have at home or use to play video games and the frequency of play. For example, with respect to gender, a considerable body of literature examines women's use of video games, women's preferences, images of women in video games (both inside games and on covers) and female characters and their roles in video games (e.g. García & Bueno, 2016; Guerra & Revuelta, 2015). These issues might influence women's attitudes towards not only video games, but also video games in education. Several studies have also reported that male students and teachers have better attitudes towards video games in general and video games in education than female students and teachers (Bonanno & Kommers, 2008; Hainey et al., 2013; Martín et al., 2017). Concerning age, AEVI and GfK (2012) showed that the youngest teachers are the most likely to use video games as an educational resource. In terms of frequency of playing video games, previous studies have shown that students, teachers, parents and other people who play more frequently and have more experience with video games have better attitudes towards or higher acceptance of video games in general and video games in education in particular (Bonanno & Kommers, 2008; Bourgonjon, Valcke, Soetaert, De Wever, & Schellens, 2011; Martín, García-Valcárcel, & Basilotta, 2016). Finally, if teachers and educators have a greater variety of resources at home and play video games with a greater variety of resources in their free time, they may be more likely to have a more positive attitude towards video games as an educational resource.

In this chapter, we focus on first-year pedagogy students at the University of Salamanca to examine their attitudes towards the use of video games in collaborative learning. Since the early stages of pedagogy students' training can influence their attitudes towards preferred resources, it is important to ensure that they develop positive attitudes towards effective methods of teaching.

We aim to determine future educators' general attitudes towards collaborative learning with video games and identify any differences in attitudes according to gender, age, the variety of digital resources at home, the variety of digital resources used to play at home, the presence of specific digital resources at home (computer, home console, hand-held console, tablet, smartphone and smart TV), the use of specific digital resources to play games at home (computer, home console, hand-held console, tablet, smartphone and smart TV) and the frequency of playing video games as entertainment.

Methodology

The objective of this chapter is to search and research whether first-year higher education pedagogy students have generally positive or negative attitudes towards collaborative learning with video games (as we said previously, considering the general notion of video games, including games for entertainment and serious games). We also examine whether certain independent variables regarding demographic issues and the variety of digital resources generate statistically significant differences among students' attitudes. As the studied phenomenon has already happened, this study is an ex post facto study.

Our initial hypotheses are as follows:
- First-year higher education pedagogy students have positive attitudes towards collaborative learning with video games.
- Male first-year higher education pedagogy students have more positive attitudes towards collaborative learning with video games than female students.
- There are differences in first-year higher education pedagogy students' attitudes according to age.
- There are differences in first-year higher education pedagogy students' attitudes according to their variety of digital resources at home.
- There are differences in first-year higher education pedagogy students' attitudes according to the variety of digital resources used to play video games at home.
- There are differences in first-year higher education pedagogy students' attitudes according to whether they have specific resources at home (computer, home console, hand-held console, tablet, smartphone and smart TV).
- There are differences in first-year higher education pedagogy students' attitudes according to whether they play video games using specific resources at home (computer, home console, hand-held console, tablet, smartphone and smart TV).
- First-year higher education pedagogy students who play more frequently have more positive attitudes towards collaborative learning with video games.

Thus, the variables to consider are:
- Dependent variable: attitude towards collaborative learning with video games
- Independent variables: gender, age, variety of digital resources at home, variety of digital resources used to play at home, presence of specific digital resources at home (computer, home console, hand-held console, tablet, smartphone and smart TV), use of specific digital resources to play video games at home (computer, home console, hand-held console, tablet, smartphone and smart TV) and frequency of playing video games for entertainment.

Using a quantitative approach to attain the research objectives, we used a questionnaire comprising 33 items using 5-point Likert attitude scales ranging from 1 (strongly disagree) to 5 (strongly agree). The Cronbach's alpha coefficient for the scale was 0.908, indicating a high internal consistency. The complete attitude scale and all its items can be found in the work of Martín et al. (2017). The questionnaire also included demographic questions and questions related to students' experiences with video games.

The questionnaire was administered during the class time of the Information and Communication Technologies in Education course from the first year of the undergraduate degree in pedagogy in University of Salamanca. We used Google Forms to collect data and we performed descriptive and inferential analyses using SPSS 22 software.

Results

Firstly, we present the results concerning the sample characteristics. The total sample comprised 61 first-year higher education pedagogy students: that is, students from the first year of the undergraduate Degree in Pedagogy from the University of Salamanca (Spain). Of the participants, 47 were women (77%) and 14 were men (23%). The students were 18 to 24 years old: 28 were 18 years old (45.9%), 13 were 19 years old (21.3%), 8 were 20 years old (13.1%), 3 were 21 years old (4.9%), 5 were 22 years old (8.2%), 2 were 23 years old (3.3%) and 2 were 24 years old (3.3%).

Overall, the first-year higher education pedagogy students showed positive attitudes towards collaborative learning with video games. The students obtained a mean ($\bar{X}$) of 3.88 (out of 5), which is above the midpoint of the scale and close to option 4 (agree; standard deviation = 0.40). Furthermore, the minimum value was 2.94, and the maximum value was 4.82 (Table 16.1).

TABLE 16.1 Descriptive statistics for 'Attitude towards collaborative learning with video games'

	N	Minimum value	Maximum value	$\bar{X}$	Standard deviation
Attitude towards collaborative learning with video games	61	2.94	4.82	3.88	0.40

Before analysing the other variables, we tested the normality of the distribution of the data to determine the need for a parametric or non-parametric test. We tested the normality of the distribution using the Kolmogorov-Smirnov test and obtained a result of 0.055 (K-S test > .05). This result indicates a normal distribution, meaning that we were able to conduct inferential analysis using a parametric test. We conducted an inferential analysis to determine whether any statistically significant differences existed among the variables.

Demographic Variables

In this section, we focus on demographic variables: student participants' gender and age. Regarding gender, we performed an independent samples t-test with a significance level of $\alpha = .05$. The results showed a statistically significant difference between the groups ($p = .016$), indicating more positive attitudes from the male students than from the female students (Table 16.2).

TABLE 16.2 Analysis of statistical differences in attitude towards collaborative learning with video games according to gender

Gender				Statistics		
Men n = 14		Women n = 47		T	p	Effect size d Cohen
M	SD	M	SD			
4.10	0.30	3.81	0.40	2.480	.016	0.38

Concerning age, we performed a paired samples t-test with a significance level of $\alpha = .05$. The results showed a statistically significant difference ($p = .000$), indicating differences in the first-year higher education pedagogy students' attitudes towards collaborative learning with video games according to age (see Table 16.3).

TABLE 16.3 Analysis of statistical differences in attitude towards collaborative learning with video games according to students' age

	Statistics	
	T	p
Age: Attitude towards collaborative learning with video games	70.632	0.000

Variables Related to Digital Resources and the Use of Video Games

In this second section, we focus on variables related to the digital resources first-year higher education pedagogy students have at home and the digital resources they use to play games.

Firstly, the variable for the variety of digital resources at home measures the number of different devices students have at home. In the questionnaire, we used a yes or no question to ask the students if they had different specific resources at home (computer, home console, hand-held console, tablet, smartphone and smart TV). With this information, we created a new variable measuring the number of different digital resources students had (ranging from 0 to 6). For instance, if a student said they had computer and home console, they were marked as having two different resources. It did not matter how many home consoles they had. We performed a paired samples t-test with a significance level of α = .05 for the variety of digital resources at home and the attitude towards collaborative learning with video games (see Table 16.4). The results did not show a statistically significant difference (p = .159), indicating no differences in the first-year higher education pedagogy students' attitudes towards collaborative learning with video games according to the variety of digital resources at home.

TABLE 16.4   Analysis of statistical differences in attitude towards collaborative learning with video games according to the variety of digital resources students have at home

	Statistics	
	T	p
Variety of digital resources at home	1.427	0.159

However, although we did not find differences in general, we wanted to know whether there could be statistical differences according to the presence of different types of specific digital resources at home, including computer, home console, hand-held console, tablet, smartphone and smart TV. As before, we considered only the presence of each resource and not the number students had at home. We performed an independent samples t-test with a significance level of α = .05 for each digital resource, considering the students who had the specific resource and students who did not. The results showed a statistically significant difference according to the presence of a smartphone at home (p = .022), showing more positive attitudes from those students who had smartphones at home ($\bar{X}$ = 3.91) than those who did not ($\bar{X}$ = 3.48) (see Table 16.5). Regarding the other digital resources, there were no statistical

TABLE 16.5 Attitudes towards collaborative learning through videogames according to the availability (yes/no) and use of digital resources at home

Resources at home	Yes n	Yes M	Yes SD	No n	No M	No SD	Statistics t	Statistics p	Effect size d Cohen
Computer	61	3.88	0.40	–	–	–	–	–	–
Home consoles	33	3.92	0.41	28	3.83	0.40	0.876	0.385	0.225
Hand-held consoles	30	3.83	0.37	31	3.87	0.44	0.162	0.872	0.041
Tablet	43	3.86	0.42	18	3.91	0.38	-0.445	0.658	-0.125
Smartphone	56	3.91	0.39	5	3.48	0.32	2.357	0.022	1.100
Smart TV	27	3.88	0.50	34	3.88	0.31	0.66	0.948	0.170

differences. Further, it is important to note that all members of the sample had a computer at home.

The variable concerning the variety of digital resources used to play at home refers to the number of different devices students used to play video games at home. In the questionnaire, we asked the students whether they used different specific digital resources to play games at home (computer, home console, hand-held console, tablet, smartphone and smart TV) with a yes or no question. With this information, we created a new variable about the number of different digital resources the students used to play games (ranging from 0 to 6 digital resources). For instance, if a student said he or she played video games with hand-held and home consoles, the student was marked as using two different resources to play video games. It did not matter whether the students used two different types of hand-held consoles. We performed a paired samples t-test with a significance level of $\alpha = .05$, considering the variety of digital resources used to play at home and the attitude towards collaborative learning with video games. The results showed a statistically significant difference ($p = .000$), indicating differences in the first-year higher education pedagogy students' attitudes towards collaborative learning with video games according to the variety of digital resources used to play at home (see Table 16.6).

Given the identified differences, we wanted to deepen our knowledge and determine whether there were statistical differences according to the use of

TABLE 16.6 Analysis of statistical differences in attitudes towards collaborative learning with video games according to the variety of digital resources used to play video games at home

	Statistics	
	T	p
Variety of digital resources used to play video games at home	−7.992	0.000

a specific type of resource to play games at home (computer, home console, hand-held console, tablet, smartphone and smart TV). As before, we did not consider whether students played video games at home with more than one element of each resource, only whether they used or did not use this resource to play at home. We performed an independent samples t-test with a significance level of α = .05 for each digital resource, considering students who played with the resource and students who did not. The results did not show any statistically significant differences in terms of the use of specific resources to play games at home (see Table 16.7).

TABLE 16.7 Attitudes towards collaborative learning through videogames according to the availability (yes/no) of digital resources at home

Resources used at home to play video games	Yes			No			Statistics		
	n	M	SD	n	M	SD	t	p	Effect size d Cohen
Computer	40	3.85	0.41	21	3.94	0.40	−0.874	0.386	−0.236
Home consoles	26	3.99	0.34	35	3.80	0.43	1.892	0.063	0.490
Hand-held consoles	20	3.89	0.36	41	3.87	0.43	0.169	0.866	0.046
Tablet	24	3.86	0.44	37	3.89	0.38	−0.324	0.747	−0.085
Smartphone	36	3.84	0.40	25	3.93	0.42	−0.845	0.401	−0.220
Smart TV	3	4.00	0.34	58	3.87	0.41	0.532	0.597	0.315

Finally, in terms of the students' frequency of playing video games, a one-way ANOVA test was performed with a significance level of α = .05. The findings confirmed a statistically significant difference among students' attitudes based on their frequency of playing video games (*p* = .013; Table 16.8). Additionally, as Table 16.9 shows, statistically significance differences (α = .05 significance level) were found in post-hoc comparisons between groups A (never play) and D (play every day; Scheffe: *p* = .020; Bonferroni: *p* = .011) and between B (play occasionally) and D (play every day; Scheffe: *p* = .032; Bonferroni: *p* = .020). These results indicate that students' attitudes become increasingly positive as time spent playing video games increases.

TABLE 16.8   Attitude towards collaborative learning with video games according to the frequency of playing video games as entertainment

	Frequency of playing video games as entertainment								Statistics		
	A Never n = 11		B Occasionally (1–3 days a month) n = 36		C Frequently (1–3 days a week) n = 11		D Every day n = 3				
	M	SD	M	SD	M	SD	M	SD	F	*p*	Effect size η^2
Total sample n = 61	3.73	0.41	3.83	0.39	3.97	0.30	4.53	0.14	3.93	.013	0.172

TABLE 16.9   Post-hoc comparisons among groups generated by the frequency of play

Significant differences among groups	Scheffe *p*	Bonferroni *P*
A–D	.020	.011
B–D	.032	.020

Discussion and Conclusions

While video games can be used in a variety of settings involving educators, the effective implementation of video games (whether games for entertainment or serious games) can heavily depend on educators' attitudes towards its effectiveness. In this chapter, we searched and researched about the attitudes towards video games of a specific type of educators and we focused on establishing the first-year higher education pedagogy students' attitudes towards video games before they began working in their chosen field. Our findings showed that, in general, the students had positive attitudes towards collaborative learning with video games. These results are in line with other studies that show positive opinions of pre-service educators towards ICT (Flores-Lueg, 2017; Marín & Reche, 2012; Roig-Vila, Mengual-Andrés, Sterrantino, & Quinto, 2015) and towards video games in educational settings (Bensiger, 2011; Martín, 2018; Ray, Powell, & Jacobsen, 2014).

In terms of specific variables, both demographic variables and variables related to digital resources or the use of video games, the male students and those who typically played video games more frequently have better attitudes towards using video games in collaborative learning. These findings support the findings of previous studies (Bonanno & Kommers, 2008; Bourgonjon et al., 2011; Hainey et al., 2013; Martín et al., 2017; Martín et al., 2016), despite the differences between these samples (college students, parents, higher education students, in-service primary teachers, pre-service primary teachers) and our sample (higher education students of pedagogy) and the various focuses of the other studies (attitudes towards gaming, acceptance of digital game-based learning, perceptions and thoughts on the use of games in education) and the specific topic of our research (collaborative learning with video games, which was also examined by the two latest references, Martín et al., 2017; Martín et al., 2016, but with different types of samples). In addition, those who had smartphones at home had more positive attitudes than those who did not. The students' age and the variety of digital resources used to play games at home also impacted attitudes towards collaborative learning with video games, in particular, and towards video games as an educational resource in general.

We believe our work contributes to the search and research on the attitudes of educators or future educators towards the use of video games in education, and these findings add to the growing body of literature on the understanding of educational agents' attitudes towards this resource. Furthermore, with regard to the educational implications, our study helps to point out the importance of providing future educators with all the necessary resources in their training, and the importance of allowing them to use and experiment with different digital resources frequently since their attitudes can be influenced by this situation. In this way, it would help to reduce differences in attitudes and knowledge due to the lack of economic or material resources.

However, given the small sample size, caution must be taken when generalising our findings. To further our research, we intend to obtain a broader sample from our university, including not only students from the first year of the degree in pedagogy, but also from different years (second, third and fourth). We also seek to collect data in a longitudinal way over different academic years. In addition, we intend to obtain a broader sample from other universities and compare their opinions with people working as this kind of educator in different fields. We also worked from only a quantitative perspective, using an attitude scale. In the future, it would be relevant to also use a qualitative approach to achieve complementary data.

In conclusion, while video games can be useful in all educational fields, the effective use of video games in collaborative learning depends heavily on educators' attitudes towards them as a resource. Universities should, therefore, search and research how to give future educators the opportunity to use video games and learn about their effective educational use to encourage the formation of positive attitudes towards them, considering, among the aspects to take into account, to provide a great variety of digital resources to the educators in their training.

Acknowledgements

This research was made possible through the funding of a FPU predoctoral grant from the Ministry of Education, Culture and Sport of Spain. Also, it was made possible through the funding of a predoctoral grant from the Junta de Castilla y León, cofinanced by the European Social Fund.

References

AEVI y GfK. (2011). *Estudio Videojuegos, educación y desarrollo infantil. Fase cualitativa* [document]. Retrieved from http://www.aevi.org.es/web/wpcontent/uploads/2015/12/Informe-de-resultados-Fase-Cualitativa-ADESE.ppt

AEVI y GfK. (2012). *Estudio Videojuegos, educación y desarrollo infantil. Fase cuantitativa* [document]. Retrieved from http://www.aevi.org.es/web/wpcontent/uploads/2015/12/10376-Informe-Adese-Fase-Cuantitativa-200120121.pptx

Akcaoglu, M., & Koehler, M. J. (2014). Cognitive outcomes from the Game-Design and Learning (GDL) after-school program. *Computers & Education, 75*, 72–81. doi:10.1016/j.compedu.2014.02.003

ANECA. (2004). *Libro Blanco del Título de Grado en Pedagogía y Educación Social, 1*.

Barr, M. (2017). Video games can develop graduate skills in higher education students: A randomised trial. *Computers & Education, 113*, 86–97. doi:10.1016/j.compedu.2017.05.016

Bellerate, B. A. (2009). Pedagogo. In J. M. Prellezo (Ed.), *Diccionario de Ciencias de la Educación* (pp. 890–891). Madrid: CCS.

Bensiger, J. (2011). *Perceptions of pre-service teachers of using video games as teaching tools* (Doctoral dissertation). University of Cincinnati, Cincinnati, Ohio.

Bonanno, P., & Kommers, P. A. M. (2008). Exploring the influence of gender and gaming competence on attitudes towards using instructional games. *British Journal of Educational Technology, 39*(1), 97–109. doi:10.1111/j.1467-8535.2007.00732.x

Bourgonjon, J., Valcke, M., Soetaert, R., De Wever, B., & Schellens, T. (2011). Parental acceptance of digital game-based learning. *Computers & Education, 57*(1), 1434–1444. doi:10.1016/j.compedu.2010.12.012.

Chiazzese, G., Fulantelli, G., Pipitone, V., & Taibi, D. (2018). Engaging primary school children in computational thinking: Designing and developing videogames. *Education in the Knowledge Society, 19*(2), 63–81. doi:10.14201/eks20181926381

Flores-Lueg, C. (2017). Actitud de futuros maestros frente al uso de TIC en educación: Un análisis descriptivo. *Notandum, 44*, 53–68. doi:10.4025/notandum.44.6

García, N., & Bueno, T. (2016). Women's image on video game covers: A comparative analysis of the Spanish market (2011–2015). *Revista Prisma Social, 1*, 120–155.

Guerra, J., & Revuelta, F. I. (2015). Visión y tratamiento educativo de los roles masculino y femenino desde el punto de vista de los videojugadores: Tecnologías emergentes favorecedoras de la igualdad de género. *Revista Qurriculum, 28*, 142–160.

Hainey, T., Westera, W., Connolly, T. M., Boyle, L., Baxter, G., Beeby, R. B., & Soflano, M. (2013). Students' attitudes toward playing games and using games in education: Comparing Scotland and the Netherlands. *Computers & Education, 69*, 474–484. doi:10.1016/j.compedu.2013.07.023

Homer, B. D., Plass, J. L., Raffaele, C., Ober, T. M., & Ali, A. (2018). Improving high school students' executive functions through digital game play. *Computers & Education, 117*, 50–58. doi:10.1016/j.compedu.2017.09.011

ICO Partners & Newzoo. (2016). *The European mobile game market* [document]. Retrieved from https://www.slideshare.net/ICOPartners/european-mobile-gamemarket

Jiménez-Porta, A. M., & Diez-Martinez, E. (2018). Impacto de videojuegos en la fluidez lectora en niños con y sin dislexia. El caso de Minecraft. *RELATEC – Revista Latinoamericana de Tecnología Educativa, 17*(1), 77–90. doi:10.17398/1695-288X.17.1.77

Li, Q. (2010). Digital game building: Learning in a participatory culture. *Educational Research, 52*(4), 427–443. doi:10.1080/00131881.2010.524752

Marín, V., & Reche, E. (2012). Universidad 2.0: Actitudes y aptitudes ante las TIC del alumnado de nuevo ingreso de la Escuela Universitaria de Magisterio de la UCO. *Píxel-Bit, 40,* 197–211.

Marín, V., & Sampedro, B. E. (2015). Cómo trabajar las matemáticas en educación primaria a través de los videojuegos. *Revista Educação, Cultura e Sociedade, 5*(2), 15–27.

Martín, M. (2015). Videojuegos y aprendizaje colaborativo. Experiencias en torno a la etapa de Educación Primaria. *Education in the Knowledge Society (EKS), 16*(2), 69–89. doi:10.14201/eks20151626989

Martín, M. (2018). *Los videojuegos en la formación docente: Diseño, aplicación y evaluación de una propuesta formativa* (Doctoral dissertation). University of Salamanca, Salamanca.

Martín, M., Basilotta, V., & García-Valcárcel, A. (2017). A quantitative approach to pre-service primary school teachers' attitudes towards collaborative learning with video games: Previous experience with video games can make the difference. *International Journal of Educational Technology in Higher Education, 14,* 11. doi:10.1186/s41239-017-0050-5

Martín, M., García-Valcárcel, A., & Basilotta, V. (2016). Actitudes de docentes de Educación Primaria hacia el aprendizaje colaborativo con videojuegos. Uso previo de videojuegos como elemento diferenciador. In C. González & M. Castro (Eds.), *Libro de Actas del XVI Congreso Nacional y VII Congreso Iberoamericano de Pedagogía: Democracia y Educación en el siglo XXI. La obra de John Dewey 100 años después* (pp. 981–982). Madrid: XVI Congreso Nacional y VII Congreso Iberoamericano de Pedagogía.

Martín, M., & Martín, J. L. (2015). Propuesta didáctica en torno a Habilidades para la Vida y videojuegos: Los Sims 2, Comunicación Efectiva y aprendizaje colaborativo. *Press Button, 1*(1), 90–126.

Messana, C. (2009). Actitud. In J. M. Prellezo (Ed.), *Diccionario de Ciencias de la Educación* (pp. 33–35). Madrid: CCS.

Meyer, B., & Sørensen, B. H. (2009). Designing serious games for computer assisted language learning – A framework for development and analysis. In M. Kankaanranta & P. Neittaanmäki (Eds.), *Design and use of serious games: Intelligent systems, control, and automation: Science and engineering* (Vol. 37, pp. 69–82). Dordrecht, Netherlands: Springer. doi:10.1007/978-1-4020-9496-5_5

Michael, D., & Chen, S. (2006). *Serious games: Games that educate, train and inform.* Boston, MA: Thomson Course Technology.

Millan, M. (1988). Pedagogo. In *Diccionario de las Ciencias de la Educación* (p. 1087). Madrid: Santillana.

Montero, E., Ruiz, M., & Díaz, B. (Eds.). (2010). *Aprendiendo con videojuegos. Jugar es pensar dos veces*. Madrid: Ministerio de Educación & Narcea S.A. de Ediciones.

Noraddin, E. M., & Kian, N. T. (2014). Academics' attitudes toward using digital games for learning & teaching in Malaysia. *Malaysian Online Journal of Educational Technology, 2*(4), 1–21.

Parong, J., Mayer, R. E., Fiorella, L., MacNamara, A., Homer, B. D., & Plass, J. L. (2017). Learning executive function skills by playing focused video games. *Contemporary Educational Psychology, 51*, 141–151. doi:10.1016/j.cedpsych.2017.07.002

Ray, B. B., Powell, A., & Jacobsen, B. (2014). Exploring preservice teacher perspectives on video games as learning tools. *Journal of Digital Learning in Teacher Education, 31*(1), 28–34. doi:10.1080/21532974.2015.979641.

Revuelta, F. I., & Guerra, J. (2012). ¿Qué aprendo con videojuegos? Una perspectiva de meta-aprendizaje del videojugador. *RED. Revista de Educación a Distancia, 33*.

Ritzhaupt, A., Poling, N., Frey, C., & Johnson, M. (2014). A synthesis on digital games in education: What the research literature says from 2000 to 2010. *Journal of Interactive Learning Research, 25*(2), 261–280.

Roig-Vila, R., Mengual-Andrés, S., Sterrantino, C., & Quinto, P. (2015). Actitudes hacia los recursos tecnológicos en el aula de los futuros docentes. *Revista d'innovació educativa, 15*, 12–19. doi:10.7203/attic.15.7220

Rooney, P. (2011). *Harnessing serious games in higher education: A case study* (Doctoral dissertation). University of Sheffield, Sheffield, UK.

Simkova, M. (2014). Using of computer games in supporting education. *Procedia: Social and Behavioral Sciences, 141*, 1224–1227. doi:10.1016/j.sbspro.2014.05.210

Tejedor, F. J., & García-Valcárcel, A. (2006). Competencias de los profesores para el uso de las TIC en la enseñanza. Análisis de sus conocimientos y actitudes. *Revista española de pedagogía, 64*(233), 21–43.

Universidad de Salamanca. (2018). *Grado en Pedagogía* [web]. Retrieved from http://www.usal.es/grado-en-pedagogia

Vlachopoulos, D., & Makri, A. (2017). The effect of games and simulations on higher education: A systematic literature review. *International Journal of Educational Technology in Higher Education, 14*, 22. doi:10.1186/s41239-017-0062-1

Ye, S. H., Hsiao, T. Y., & Sun, C. T. (2018). Using commercial video games in flipped classrooms to support physical concept construction. *Journal of Computer Assisted Learning, 34*(5), 602–614. doi:10.1111/jcal.12267

Index

being a teacher   42, 44, 47, 55, 57, 134, 199, 209

case study   xxii, 23, 29, 63, 69, 70, 125, 128–133, 135, 137, 138, 179, 186, 192, 219, 286, 296
content and language integration   140, 141
contextual of use   160
critical-reflective   179, 180, 182, 183, 186, 191, 214
cross-cultural teacher education   219, 221

didactic mediation   63–65, 68, 79

emancipatory   xxiii, 179–185, 187, 189–196, 301
English as a Foreign Language (EFL)   xxii, 23, 25, 27, 38, 140, 142–144, 153, 155
English as Medium of Instruction (EMI)   140–143, 152, 154–157
English as Second Language (ESL)   xxii, 131, 138, 140, 142–146, 151–157, 167

Iberian perspectives   42, 44–46
inclusive pedagogy   xxiii, 243, 245–248, 250, 258–260
inclusive practice   124, 243–249, 258, 260
in-service teacher   15, 105, 107–121, 310

language proficiency   136, 137, 145, 160
living theory   282, 286, 287, 289–291, 300

mentored teacher learning   219, 221–223, 225, 227
mentoring   xxiii, 23, 27, 28, 30, 32, 33, 35, 38, 39, 84, 85, 87–90, 94–99, 219–225, 227–231, 233–238
mentoring teacher learning   85, 219–223, 225, 227–229
metacognition   89, 93, 105–121
metacognitive support   105
mixed method   69, 88, 105, 109

narrative inquiry   xxi, xxiv, 243, 247–250, 258, 259, 282, 287, 295, 296, 299, 300

pedagogical confrontation   xxii, 199, 200, 202–209, 211–216

Pedagogical Content Knowledge (PCK)   26, 33, 63, 65–68, 79, 184, 190, 191
places of learning   3, 12, 16
polysemy   160, 161, 163, 165, 176
positioning theory   125–130
practical knowledge   34, 38, 69, 84–87, 90, 93, 94, 96–99, 263
practicum   xxi, xxii, xxiv, 13, 23–30, 33–37, 50–52, 84–86, 88, 89, 92, 93, 97, 98, 109, 181, 209, 282, 295
praxis   xxiv, 181, 182, 186, 282, 284–283, 295–302
pre-service teacher theorizing   282
pre-service teacher   xxi–xxiv, 13, 28, 33, 38, 84–99, 105, 109, 111, 115–121, 125–138, 199, 205–207, 214, 215, 260, 263–279, 282, 283, 286, 288, 290, 291, 293, 295–297, 300, 310
primary education   53, 84, 88, 310
professional experience   85, 206, 215, 248, 263, 264, 267, 268, 273, 279
professional learning community   23, 25–30, 35, 37
professionalism   42, 43, 46–49, 55, 56, 205, 247

reflection   xxi, xxiii, xxiv, 6, 28, 34, 36, 43, 54, 56, 57, 67, 84–86, 88–99, 113, 118, 127, 128, 131, 138, 144, 153, 156, 179, 183, 186, 188, 194, 199, 201, 203, 204, 206, 209, 212, 214, 215, 223, 235, 263–279, 284, 287–289, 292, 308
reflective practice   86, 199–201, 214–216, 264–265, 267, 270, 276, 277, 279
responsive teacher   243–260

scholarship of disruption   xxi, 3, 5–8, 12, 14–17
scholarship of integration   3, 5, 7, 8, 12, 17
science classroom   160–165, 167, 173–176
second language learner   121, 126–128, 136, 167
semiotic   63, 67, 69
socio-cultural perspective   37, 219
South Africa   xxi, xxii, 160, 167–170, 175, 176, 204
storytelling   xxiv, 282–302

student satisfaction   xxii, 140, 142–146, 151–157
student teacher learning in practice   24, 219
student teaching   23–25, 33, 34, 38, 125, 128, 129

Task-Based Interactive Approach   140, 141, 144–157
teacher education   xxi–xxiv, 3–10, 12–17, 23–26, 28, 33, 38, 39, 42–46, 49–58, 85, 106–110, 120, 121, 125–127, 130, 137, 176, 182, 184–186, 195, 199–216, 219–221, 227, 235, 263–279, 282, 302
teacher educator   xxi, xxiii, 3–17, 23–25, 27, 33, 35, 36, 42, 43, 54, 57, 58, 86, 126–128, 167, 176, 179, 181, 182, 199–203, 205, 209–216, 219, 237, 260, 266, 282, 283, 299, 302
teacher educator learning   3–17
teacher identity   128, 186, 187, 194, 195
teacher understanding   179, 180
teacher/student relationship   125, 130
teaching practice   xxi, xxiii, 23, 25, 26, 28, 30–32, 34, 36, 37, 52, 53, 84, 86, 89, 97, 98, 105, 106, 109, 112, 115–117, 119, 135–137, 179, 180, 182, 187, 192, 194–196, 214, 245, 248, 254, 260, 266, 273, 277, 279

video   xxi, xxiii, xxiv, 63, 72, 88, 193, 243, 248, 249, 255, 256, 263, 264, 266, 267, 269, 271–279, 304–320

Printed in the United States
By Bookmasters